Societies and Military Power

A volume in the series

CORNELL STUDIES IN SECURITY AFFAIRS

edited by Robert J. Art, Robert Jervis,
and Stephen M. Walt

A full list of titles in the series appears at the end of the book.

Societies and Military Power

INDIA AND ITS ARMIES

STEPHEN PETER ROSEN

Cornell University Press

ITHACA AND LONDON

First published 1996 by Cornell University Press.

Printed in the United States of America

♾ The paper in this book meets the minimum requirements
of the American National Standard for Information Sciences—
Permanence of Paper for Printed Library Materials, ANSI Z39.48-1984.

Library of Congress Cataloging-in-Publication Data

Rosen, Stephen Peter, 1952–
    Societies and military power : India and its armies / Stephen Peter Rosen.
       p.   cm.—(Cornell studies in security affairs)
    Includes bibliographical references and index.
    ISBN 0-8014-3210-3 (alk. paper)
    1. Sociology, Military—India—History.   2. India—Social conditions.   3. India—
History, Military.   I. Title.   II. Series.
UA840.R67   1996   96-11014
306.2'7'0954—dc20

Contents

Preface

This book is about the impact of social structures on the military power of nations from different cultures. Because social structures can vary across cultural boundaries, this approach can help explain why countries from different cultures that otherwise appear similar have different military capabilities. Because social structures can be replicated across cultural boundaries, it can also help explain why countries from different cultures can have similar capabilities, despite their cultural differences. The book investigates, for example, why the Ottoman and Mughal Empires, both ruled by Turkish-speaking, Persian-reading military elites with similar literary cultures, generated such different amounts of military power. Why did the armies of eighteenth-century England and eighteenth-century India have such different military strengths, despite similar levels of technological development in both countries? But it also examines why historians of Hapsburg Austria in the nineteenth and early twentieth centuries observed that Austria had some of the same problems generating military power that troubled postindependence India.[1]

The thesis of this book is not, however, a determinist argument from social structures to military power. The book is also about politics, specifically about civil-military politics. The political and military leaders in a society can exercise some measure of political choice in deciding how to structure their military organizations. Those decisions can affect the way the ambient structures in the general society carry over into the

[1] On the similarities in social origins and composition of the Austrian and postindependence Indian Army officer corps, see Istvan Deak, *Beyond Nationalism: A Social and Political History of the Hapsburg Officer Corps* (New York: Oxford University Press, 1990), pp. 5-8.

military. Political decisions to separate militaries from their societies can affect and enhance the power of the military *organization*, but they can also create civil-military tensions that reduce the effective military power available to the *state*.

The approach is somewhat different from the perspectives on culture and strategy now dominant in the academic and policy worlds. Explanations of international relations that emphasize the structure of the international system and the international distribution of power downplay the role of social structures in creating military power. According to realist theories of international relations, different societies in the same international system will, over time, tend to generate the same *amount* of military power from a given level of resources. Nations that interact with one another will come to have similar military organizations and similar military doctrines, despite internal social differences, because they will be forced to generate as much military power from a given amount of resources as the most militarily efficient member of that system. On the other hand, explanations of strategic behavior have been developed that emphasize the importance of differences in culture. The strategic culture perspective argues that the *uses* of military power will differ because the subjective ideas in the minds of strategic elites will lead them to view the same facts of international politics differently, with different consequences for their strategies. Even this very simple contrast between realism and strategic culture makes obvious not only that there are important intellectual differences about the significance of society but also that it is important to be clear about what different theories are trying to explain, as well as how.

The argument in this book is that the *amount* of offensive and defensive military power that can be generated by a military organization from a given level of material resources is affected by the social structures that are dominant in its society, and that efforts to divorce a military organization from the influences of the dominant social structures have consequences for the amount of usable military power available to the state. Offensive military power is defined as the surplus of military power, beyond what is needed to maintain domestic order, that can be projected beyond the boundaries of a country. Defensive military power is the ability to resist foreign military invasion.

Social structures can affect the generation of military power in two ways. First, people in a political unit can identify themselves with social structures in ways that can create divisive loyalties within the political unit. This can create fissures in the unit that reduce the effective military power of the unit as a whole. In terms of offensive power, internal social divisions can increase the amount of military power needed to maintain internal domestic order, reducing the surplus of military power that can be projected abroad. Defensively, the fissures in the unit can create internal vulnerabilities that can be exploited by invaders. Second, the social structures that create fissures in the unit at large can be carried over into the military organizations of that unit, resulting in divisions that reduce their military power. Military organizations may try to insulate and divorce themselves from the problems created by the social structures in the political unit. But this separation from society may create distrust of the military when it rejects the social structures accepted by the society as a whole.

The book emphasizes the importance of two independent variables: the dominant social structures of a country and the social divisions they create, and the degree to which the military organizations divorce themselves from their society. The dependent variable is the amount of offensive and defensive national military power that can be generated from a given quantity of material resources. Although the amount of power that can be generated will affect national strategy, so will many other factors, most notably the strategy of the enemy. As a result, it is too much to ask of a perspective that looks inside units that it explain external strategies entirely. The ability or inability of a political unit to defend successfully against foreign invasion and the ability of a unit to project various amounts of power abroad are obviously affected by many other factors beyond the two emphasized by this theory: population size, size of the military budget, type of government, levels of technology, and so on. It is my claim that there are noteworthy cases in which military power has differed in ways that cannot be explained by the standard factors. The challenge I face is to find comparative cases that make it more or less possible to isolate the importance of social structures and levels of military separation from society.

To be specific, this challenge is addressed by means of an examination of the social and military history of India in comparative perspective. I chose India because the broad span of its history allows for considerable variation in the two independent variables of social structures and separation of the military from society. Because India as a geopolitical unit has had something close to its present boundaries for many centuries and because the nature of the military threat to India remained relatively constant for many centuries (the threat of hostile cavalry coming from the northwest), a long historical look at India made it possible to estimate Indian defensive military power relative to a roughly constant threat. When Indian history did not display sufficient variation in the independent variables or displayed these variations together with too many others, the differences between Indian and non-Indian societies facilitated comparisons with cases from elsewhere in Europe and Asia that could highlight the impact of variations in one variable while others remained constant.

Although the essential argument of the book is straightforward, its development requires the presentation of a considerable amount of historical data over a series of chapters. The argument also requires one chapter, Chapter 2, that is not about military power but about how one should understand Indian society and social structures. For this reason, it may be useful for the reader to have, early on, an intellectual map of the book that provides an overview of the argument as a whole, as well as a guide to the chapters, which will be more or less relevant to the concerns of different readers.

In Chapter 1, I look at some of the intellectual problems that exist with previous efforts to understand whether and how "strategy," broadly defined, might vary across cultural boundaries, somehow defined. I then argue that efforts to understand military power without taking into account variations in the internal societies of political units are inadequate. Then I develop a perspective that can be applied to individual cases to generate insights into the issues created by specific social structures and military-society relations. This chapter will be of most interest to political scientists, who will want to know how clearly the theory is laid out, how it differs from other theories, and how the theory can be translated into questions that can be empirically researched and tested. For example, the question of how "culture" is different from "social structure," and just what is meant by that rather broad term, is explored in this chapter.

Then comes Chapter 2. Indian society is at least as complicated as any other large and ancient society. If someone wants to theorize about Indian society and Indian military power, the understanding of Indian society that drives the theory must be set forth and justified. From the perspective of the central theory of this book, the dominant social structure for a set of cases has to be specified and justified at the outset to preclude subsequent tinkering with the definition of the independent variable so as to make the theory come out right. Determining just what the dominant social structures are may also be an intellectually and empirically difficult task, and it is far from trivial. The social structures of India on which this book focuses are those related to caste. The significance, or lack of it, of caste has been subject to enormous discussion. Because the existence and character of caste relations in India are central to the operationalization of my argument, in Chapter 2 I review the scholarly discussion of that subject, defending the use of caste as an objective factor against those who argue that caste is merely an intellectual construction contrived by those who wished to subjugate India politically. Very briefly, I adopt the view of caste held by every Indian

[x]

nationalist leader, including Nehru, as well as by the vast majority of Indian and non-Indian scholars. Of course, social divisions other than caste exist in India—those of linguistic, regional, or religious origin, for example. By emphasizing caste, I do not mean to deny their existence. For the purposes of this book, I argue that it is adequate to subsume those other differences into caste differences. Religious and linguistic divisions in India, as has been noted by many scholars, tend to become caste-ified—that is, differences in human behavior across and within these other divisions tend to become structured by caste law and practices. Religious and linguistic differences generally do not reduce the levels of social divisions in India that are the product of caste law and practices. India specialists will be most interested in Chapter 2. I hope they read both that chapter and the specific historical chapters in which the sweeping characterizations of Indian society are modified by observations on the specific conditions of various times and places in Indian history. They should rest assured that this book does not operate on the basis of a timeless, eternal, and geographically homogenous picture of Indian society.

The case studies then follow. I present them chronologically because the independent variables of social structure and separation of the military from society vary chronologically in the case of India. Ancient India (Chapter 3) had a highly developed religious and literary culture that was quite different from that found in Europe of the same period. Although ancient India was internally fragmented by caste and subcaste, there is general agreement that the caste system in earlier periods was not as rigid as it would later become. The armies of ancient India were not distinct from society, but that was the case in many other non-Indian ancient societies as well. So ancient India, while very different from European society in its literary and religious culture, differed less from parts of Europe with regard to the independent variables than it would in the future. If literary and religious "culture" is important, therefore, the strategic behavior of ancient India should be very different from that of ancient Europe. To make matters analytically more interesting, a few European military organizations *were* divorced from their original host societies. If fragmented social structures and the separation of the military from society are important, the strategic behavior of ancient India should more closely resemble that of the European countries in which the armies were not distinct from society, even though the Indian and European "cultures" are very different, and should differ from the European societies that display low levels of social fragmentation or high degrees of military separation from society.

Moving to medieval times, we can observe Mughal India (Chapter 4) in which a Turkish-speaking military elite governed a fragmented Indian society but was dependent on that society for military resources in ways that led to low levels of separation between the society and the Mughal military. At roughly the same time, we can consider the Ottoman Empire, governed by a Turkish military elite as well, ruling a society that was also fragmented by ethnicity and religion; but this empire created a highly professional army which was composed of Christian slaves raised from their youth within the confines of the military and which was, as a result, clearly separated from the society. Even though the elites in the two empires shared some Persian literary and religious influences, they differed starkly on the second dependent variable. Also in medieval times, Europe was experiencing what historians have come to call a military revolution, the main effect of which was to increase sharply the professionalization of the military that separated it from civil society, thus, according to this argument, changing its military power.

Moving closer to modern times, the British Empire in India (Chapter 5) both ruled over and affected the nature of Indian society in a variety of ways that are still debated by historians and sociologists. What the British Empire did that is beyond debate was very quickly to professionalize the Indian armies and separate them from Indian society. By comparing the Mughal and British Indian empires, we come as close as is possible in the real world to an experiment through which we can view the impact of the separation of the military from society while holding social structures more or less constant. If military power varied, the importance of the variable of separation of the military from society will be highlighted. At the same time, British and Indian literary and religious cultures remained poles apart. If there were changes in Indian military power toward European patterns, this would again tend to suggest that "culture," in the sense of religious or literary culture, was not decisive.

Finally, modern India retained, on the whole, the military organizational practices it inherited from the British. The period from 1947 to about 1980, discussed in Chapter 6, was too short to produce any fundamental transformation of Indian society. The main change in India was an increase in the tension between civilian society and the Indian military as Indian nationalists replaced British rulers in the civilian government while the army officer corps remained separate from society and largely a product of British influences. If Indian strategic behavior was marked by severe problems related to the increased separation of the army from society, that would tend to support the argument in this book.

The historical chapters makes references to each other and to the central argument elaborated in Chapter 1 when appropriate. However, they have been written with the objective of making them individually accessible to those who have read this guide and now wish to move directly to substantive empirical discussions.

Early in the work on this book, I got sick, again. This time, Dr. Ezekial Emanuel made me well. Such a fine doctor is Dr. Emanuel.

Without Stephen Cohen, the scholarly study of Indian military affairs might not exist in the United States. He provided me with generous assistance at several critical points, and this book would certainly not have been written were it not for him.

Robert Jervis read an essay in which I first tried to think through the ways in which Indian society and the behavior of the Indian military might be linked. An exquisitely polite man, he told me he thought it was not well organized. I threw the essay out and started work on this book from scratch.

Aaron Friedberg, Samuel Huntington, Peter Katzenstein, Robert Keohane, and Randall Schweller provided valuable comments on the first chapter. Also for that chapter, the editors of the journal *International Security* gave me permission to use portions of an article they published entitled "Military Effectiveness: Why Societies Matter," vol. 19, no. 4 (Spring 1995): 5-31.

I acknowledge the love my wife, Mandana Sassanfar, and my sons, Guive and Kamran, gave and continue to give me, without which I would not be writing much of anything.

STEPHEN PETER ROSEN

Cambridge, Massachusetts

[1]

The Problem of Societies and Military Power

The question of the possible differences in military behavior and thought across cultural boundaries has occurred to American academics and policymakers from time to time when events in the real world have brought them into strategic contact with states whose domestic societies were clearly different from American society. Those states—sometimes, but not always, non-European—were different with regard to their dominant religious or literary cultures and seemed to display military behavior that was equally foreign. But because the issue of cultural differences came up in the context of wars or encounters that threatened war, the importance of cultural differences in explaining differences in strategic behavior was particularly difficult to untangle from the many other factors affecting the perception and reality of hostile behavior. The urgent drama of war or conflict tended to estrange the engaged parties even when they were closely related by history or religion, to magnify the apparent significance of even small differences in culture and behavior where they did exist, and to make difficult the careful empirical study of the opponent so as to sift out the causes of the differences in military behavior. The practical and psychological difficulties of doing comparative analyses of the military behavior of different cultures were increased by the fact that the scholars who were familiar with the cultures of non-Western societies tended to be anthropologists who were usually not also professional students of Western military history. This limited their ability to make sound comparative military evaluations. The combined effect of these analytical problems can be seen in Ruth Benedict's classic study, *The Chrysanthemum and the Sword*, first published in 1946.[1] In that book,

---

[1] Ruth Benedict, *The Chrysanthemum and the Sword: Patterns of Japanese Culture* (New York: Meridian, 1974).

the ferocious, suicidal defenses of the Japanese in World War II were linked to the Japanese concepts of honor and shame. Written during the war, the book could not be based on Benedict's own firsthand observations of the Japanese military but on early reports of Japanese military behavior and on such observations of Japanese popular culture as were available in wartime America. Further, the comparisons of Japanese and American cultural patterns, while often insightful and plausible, were not based on a review of American culture and military behavior as systematic as Benedict's study of the Japanese.

The validity of Benedict's insights was easier to test after the war. On the basis of Benedict's work, for example, one could suggest that American and Japanese strategic leaders had different strategic outlooks that would lead them, if they considered the same strategic circumstances, to different conclusions about the appropriate military response. But long after the war, careful examinations of the analysis underlying the war plans of the United States and the Japanese in 1945 clearly showed that Japanese leaders, despite being cut off from good information about American thinking, were able to think through and anticipate the American plans accurately, while the American planners were able to do the same for the Japanese.[2] This is by no means to deny that there were real cultural differences between the American and Japanese leaders in World War II or that there were observable differences in the behavior of their military organizations. But Japanese and American leaders could, when they needed and chose to, think like their counterparts, despite those differences.

The cold war defeats of French and American armies in Asia again led Westerners to wonder if they were not encountering a different and culturally distinct form of war, this time deriving from Chinese culture. "Human wave" military tactics practiced by the Chinese troops in the Korean War and guerrilla war tactics in Indochina seemed alien to Western armies.[3] Perhaps they were the result of a different Chinese culture that was embodied in the classics of Chinese military literature. However, one of the few explicit, side-by-side comparisons of Chinese and European military classics, Sun Tzu's *Art of War* and Carl von Clausewitz's *On War*, found as many substantive similarities as differences and

---

[2] "So, as American planners . . . decided in the first half of 1945 what to do in the second half, Japanese planners also were deciding what the Americans would do. Moreover, the Japanese estimated U.S. intentions merely by simulating the Americans' decision-making process. . . . The Japanese shadow process reached conclusions broadly similar to those of the American planners." Thomas Huber, *Pastel: Deception in the Invasion of Japan* (Fort Leavenworth, Kans.: Combat Studies Institute, 1988), pp. 35, 41.

[3] See Samuel Griffith's introduction to Mao Tse Tung's *On Guerrilla Warfare* (New York: Praeger, 1961), p. 8.

[2]

conjectured that the observed differences were due not to differences in culture but to the fact that Clausewitz focused on fighting battles and military campaigns, whereas Sun Tzu was more concerned with the strategic problems of national leadership.[4] If one then looked more closely at areas of obvious disagreement between Sun Tzu and Clausewitz, the role of cultural explanations became murky. For example, Sun Tzu baldly stated that "all warfare is based on deception," whereas Clausewitz asserted that "an accurate and penetrating understanding is a more useful and essential asset for the commander than any gift for cunning," "cunning" being Clausewitz's term for deception.[5] This is a clear difference. But the examples of deception given by Sun Tzu reveal interaction between military commanders who had been educated together and who had often fought alongside one another as allies before becoming battlefield adversaries.[6] It may be that Sun Tzu's writings did not reflect a uniquely Chinese way of war, but the analysis of the wars with which he was familiar. Those occurred in the time of the warring states, during which war was practiced by generals who in many cases knew each other well from peacetime and war and who were able to use that personal knowledge for purposes of deception in ways that generals more foreign to each other could not. If Sun Tzu's observations were artifacts of the limited sample of wars he was able to observe, then inspection of similar, non-Chinese wars might reveal "Chinese" military behavior. That is, in fact, the case. The accounts of the interactions of generals equally familiar with each other in European or American history provide examples of Western generals behaving as if they had read Sun Tzu. For example, Ulysses S. Grant in his early western campaigns in the American Civil War conducted military actions against Confederate commanders at Fort Henry and Fort Donelson, commanders whose habits of mind he knew because he had fought alongside them in the Mexican War. Grant described how he was able to deceive them on the basis of his prior personal knowledge. Grant also engaged in an elaborate deception campaign at Vicksburg, all in the context of the American Civil War, the

[4] Michael I. Handel, *Masters of War: Sun Tzu, Clausewitz, and Jomini* (London: Frank Cass, 1992), pp. 155–156.

[5] Sun Tzu, *The Art of War*, trans. Samuel B. Griffith (New York: Oxford University Press, 1971), VII-12, p. 106. Carl von Clausewitz, *On War*, ed. and trans. by Michael Howard and Peter Paret (Princeton: Princeton University Press, 1976), pp. 202–203.

[6] Sun Tzu, *The Art of War*, "The Author," p. 9: the ambush at Ma Ling in 341 B.C. was sprung by General Sun Pin on his "his erstwhile friend P'ang Chuan." In "The Biography of Sun Tzu," pp. 59–62, Sun Pin and P'ang Chuan are said to "have studied military theory together," and at Ma Ling, Sun Pin, knowing that P'ang Chuan believed Sun Pin's troops to be cowardly, deceived P'ang Chuan into believing Sun Pin's troops were fleeing by gradually reducing the number of campfires visible to P'ang Chuan on three successive nights.

[3]

war in which the American "cultural" tendencies toward wars of attrition and mass production were allegedly born.[7]

Military experience in wartime also led to questions about whether different cultures had different tolerances for casualties in war. This issue arose in World War II with regard to the Japanese and then again in 1950 with the "human wave" attacks conducted by the Chinese in the Korean War. But the so-called Asian contempt for life in battle that was displayed in World War II and Korea was not unknown in recent European and American military history. It was routine for military units in the American Civil War and European armies in World War I to take losses of over 50 percent in single battles in what might easily be called "human wave" attacks.[8] Did this mean that American or western European culture was "Asian" less than one hundred years ago, or simply that repeated experience with costly wars led democracies to become averse to heavy casualties?

In short, the first efforts to understand the relevance of cultural differences, somehow defined, for strategy began with the observation of "obvious" differences in culture and "obvious" differences in military behavior, jumping to the conclusion that the first was the source of the second. On examination, however, many seemingly obvious differences in military behavior and outlook that initially appeared to be clearly related to cultural differences turn out to be either nonexistent or just as plausibly explained by noncultural factors. Although isolated parallels between Eastern and Western military writings and practices do not prove that culture does not affect the conduct and theory of war, they certainly suggest that the subject requires a different kind of analysis than can be provided simply by setting the differences in the military behavior displayed by different societies alongside their cultural differences.

---

[7] Ulysses S. Grant, *Personal Memoirs of U. S. Grant* (New York: Charles Webster, 1894), pp. 173, 184–185, discusses his personal knowledge of the Confederate commander General Pillow, at Fort Henry, and of Brigadier Buckner, at Fort Donelson, and how he exploited his knowledge to plan his attacks. For his elaborate deception plan that fed false information to the enemy at Vicksburg, see p. 299.

[8] John Terraine found that 115 American army regiments on both sides in the Civil War suffered losses of over 50 percent in single battles, and several had losses of over 80 percent. British forces suffered *daily* casualty rates ranging from 2,121 to 5,848 in five major battles in World War I. See his *The Smoke and the Fire: Myths and Anti-Myths of War, 1861–1945* (London: Sidgwick and Jackson, 1980), Tables A–D, pp. 38–41. Joseph Rothschild notes that Westerners who see a culturally distinct Shiite aspect to the human wave attacks conducted in the war between Iran and Iraq must come to terms with the massive losses suffered by the British forces in 1916 in the Battle of the Somme; see his "Culture and War," in *The Lessons of Recent Wars in the Third World, vol. 2*, ed. Stephanie G. Neuman and Robert E. Harkavy (Lexington, Mass.: Lexington Books, 1985), p. 53.

SOCIETIES AND MILITARY EFFECTIVENESS:
REALISM AND THE PROFESSIONAL SOLDIER

Given the problems with the common ideas concerning strategy and cultural differences, why should we not accept the realist perspective that the pressures of international competition lead military organizations to look and act the same in order to extract the maximum amount of military power from a given level of resources? The sophisticated neorealist students of international relations, who focus on the distribution of power into sovereign states under conditions of anarchy as the basis of strategic behavior, can pose a reasonable question. The beliefs and military practices of different cultures, they would acknowledge, might well vary initially. But, over time, the action of the international system will demonstrate what forms of behavior succeed and fail and by that means either socialize all national leaders into a common set of military practices or eliminate those who do not, reducing the importance of internal differences across cultural boundaries. Since this process of socialization could not be instantaneous, realist theorists should, to be rigorous, specify for how long and to what extent culturally idiosyncratic military practices could persist, or else the realists would have to allow for indefinitely long "lags" during which idiosyncratic practices survived. Realists would also have to allow that isolated international subsystems might develop shared practices that differed from the dominant modes of military behavior in other subsystems.[9] But, allowing for those exceptions, realists would insist that to the extent that states from one cultural area came into contact with states from a different culture, the means used to generate military power by those states would tend to converge to the most effective example, regardless of cultural differences.

Realists aside, there are powerful reasons to think that military organizations might *not* reflect local internal social conditions so much as the functional requirements of their profession. What is the special character of the relationship of military organizations to their host societies? Some organizations by their nature are more likely than others to reflect the larger patterns of social organization of their societies, whereas others will be shaped more by the special nature of their tasks. It is plausible to argue that, for example, businesses, labor unions, or civil services

---

[9] For the best neorealist discussion of the relationship between international structure and the military doctrines of individual countries, see Barry Posen, *The Sources of Military Doctrine: France, Britain, and Germany between the World Wars* (Ithaca: Cornell University Press, 1984), p. 75 in particular. Kenneth Waltz takes a more extreme view of the impact of the international system on national military doctrines in his *Theory of International Relations* (New York: Random House, 1979) pp. 124–128.

which serve the citizens of the host society on a day-to-day basis and which employ a broad spectrum of citizens who go home every day to live in civil society when they leave work will be more likely to reflect the general characteristics of their host societies. The workers in those institutions would, in their workplace activities, continue to display the loyalties to the social structures in the society at large. But not all institutions are like businesses and civil services. In his essay on national character, David Hume argued that different societies would display different characteristic forms of behavior. But Hume also took into account the way that the professional character of certain organizations might isolate them from the influences of their societies. Closed, highly ordered organizations within a society might not resemble their host society as much as they did other such organizations in other countries: "A soldier and a priest are different characters in all nations, and all ages," Hume asserted, and cited as a not altogether false maxim that "priests of all religions are the same," because, like soldiers, they live in highly structured, closed societies divorced from their host society.[10] A society might have its own distinctive character, but whether that character was reflected in its military organization would depend on the relationship of the organization to society: whether it was closed to and unrepresentative of that society or the reverse.

Max Weber in "The Meaning of Discipline" asserted that rational discipline, of which military discipline is the archetype, would and should override loyalties to general social structures, in particular, identification with and loyalties to the social orders of traditional Europe. Rational, functional discipline would eradicate the habits of behavior that civilians brought with them as the army turned them into soldiers.[11] Armies, to the extent that they were rationally disciplined, would function in ways dictated solely by the need to reach their organizational goal and would be uninfluenced by anything else, including the structures of the societies from which they emerged. Samuel P. Huntington's book *The Soldier and the State* continued in the Weberian tradition. In it, Huntington persuasively chronicled the problems that European military organizations had experienced when elements in a society insisted on exporting aspects of civilian society into the military. French aristocrats serving in the military, for example, insisted on receiving the deference that they commanded in society because of their rank in the upper classes, not their

---

[10] David Hume, "Essay XXI: Of National Characters," in Hume, *Essays: Moral, Political, and Literary,* ed. Eugene Miller (Indianapolis: Liberty, 1985), pp. 197–198.

[11] Max Weber, "The Meaning of Discipline," in *From Max Weber: Essays in Sociology,* trans. and ed. H. H. Gerth and C. Wright Mills (New York: Oxford University Press, 1958), pp. 253, 256–257.

military rank, contrary to the requirements of military discipline. Middle-class English Parliamentarians in the seventeenth century insisted that the organization of the English military reflect the changes underway in English society in the relations among the social orders. The lesson that Huntington drew from these examples was that such efforts to make the military mirror society were bad for the military and for civilians. Objective civilian control, as well as military effectiveness, was maximized when the military did not reflect any of the competing elements of society, when it was "isolated" from politics, and when it concentrated on its profession: the "management of violence." When military organizations were not so isolated, they reflected the divisions and conflicts of society, reducing their power and the ability of the civilian government to control them.

There is, however, an interesting paradox in Huntington's account. Alongside his injunction to military organizations to reject the pressures to mirror their societies, he chronicled how many premodern and modern societies *resisted* this professional separation of their military organizations from their societies. Jacksonian Americans in the nineteenth century wanted a democratic officer corps, and in the 1920s the officer corps of the American army wanted to reject its status as "a separate caste" and end "the 'splendid isolation' of the Regular Army" from American society. The French officer corps never stopped reflecting and being penetrated by French social and political divisions, up to and including the time of Charles de Gaulle. Even the most professional European officer corps—in Huntington's view, that of Prussia and then Germany—had difficulty sustaining its isolation from society.[12]

At the theoretical level, Huntington's argument for objective civilian control of the military, achieved by emphasizing the Weberian functional rationality of the internal structures of the military and by excluding influences from civilian society, was and is compelling. Empirically, we know that such isolation and professionalization can be achieved, even under difficult circumstances. In one extreme case, the influence of Chinese social forces on their military units was reduced by physically removing those Chinese units from their society and giving them foreign professional military training and leadership. In World War II, the United States Army took two divisions' worth of Chinese Nationalist troops out of China into Ramgarh, India, trained them by standard American army training methods, gave them American officers, and commanded them successfully in battle against the Japanese, giving the

---

[12] Samuel P. Huntington, *The Soldier and the State: The Theory and Politics of Civil-Military Relations* (New York: Vintage, 1957), pp. 26–29, 34–37, 106, 119–120, 123.

lie to the then current stereotype of culturally cowardly Chinese soldiers.[13]

But it is just as clear from Huntington's work and the work of others that societies are uncomfortable with military organizations whose structures do not reflect the dominant characteristics of their societies. The fact that there will be arguments about which social characteristics should be dominant in society has never stopped societies from trying to build some of those characteristics into their military organizations, and as a result, the divisions within the larger societies have tended to be reflected, to a greater or lesser extent, in the military organizations that defended those societies. When those military organizations have remained isolated from their host societies, that too has been a source of tension between them and their host societies.

SOCIAL STRUCTURES AND MILITARY ORGANIZATIONS: GERMANS AND ITALIANS

To develop this observation, it is useful to examine what happens when military organizations *do* reflect the divisions of the societies from which they come, divisions created by identification with and loyalties to social structures within the political unit that encompasses the society. One crude and preliminary way of putting this question is to ask if certain societies have consistently produced more or less militarily effective armies than other societies having different social structures. If differences in military effectiveness can be found, it may be possible, even if difficult, to examine the impact on those armies of the structures of their host societies or, alternatively, whether and to what extent those armies were able to reduce the influence of such social structures. The military effectiveness of armies from different cultures is always difficult to evaluate, let alone the sources of that effectiveness, because so many factors affect the outcome of battles, which is the ultimate measure of military effectiveness. Levels of weapons technology vary, as do the numerical strength of the armies engaged in battle, the individual competence of commanders, and many other things, none of which are the necessary product of social structures, though they may be affected by them. Military history does, however, provide some imperfect natural experiments

---

[13]Charles F. Romanus and Riley Sunderland, *China-Burma-India Theater: Stilwell's Mission to China* (Washington, D.C.: GPO, 1953), pp. 97, 153, 156–157, 175–176, 179, 353. So complete was Stilwell's control of the Chinese officers that he exulted in his diary: "I'm in command, and this time I can shoot them up to the grade of major. I don't think I'll have to." See Joseph Stilwell, *The Stilwell Papers*, ed. Theodore White (London: Macdonald, 1949), p. 139.

that help suggest what role social structures may have played in affecting military effectiveness.

In European feudal societies, the dominant social structures were the different orders of society. Within the militaries of those societies, the divisions among the social orders were reflected in the sharp military division between the aristocratic, mounted knights and the common foot soldiers. Yet differences existed in the extent to which the relations among the social orders in Europe were reflected in military formations. The Battle of Crécy in 1346 was waged between a French army and the victorious English army which was perhaps greatly outnumbered and which was certainly no more than equal in strength to the French army. This battle is often portrayed as an example of how superior technology, in the form of the longbow, helped numerically inferior English forces defeat French armored, mounted knights. The most detailed accounts, however, indicate that different relations among the social orders present in the armies on the battlefield affected battlefield organization and tactics in ways that gave victory to the English. The English had archers, but so did the French forces, in the form of hired Genoese crossbowmen. But the French mounted knights would not support or cooperate with their archers on the battlefield. The French knights declined to advance with or behind the advancing line of crossbowmen toward the English. When the Genoese crossbowmen, outranged by the English longbowmen, were forced to pull back, the French knights assumed the archers were retreating out of cowardice: "Instead of opening intervals in their line to let the routed infantry pass to the rear, they came pricking hastily down the slope crying 'Away with these faint-hearted rabble! They do but block our advance,' and crashed into the panic stricken mob . . . and began to slash right and left among the miserable Genoese to force their way to the front. This mad attempt to ride down their own infantry was fatal to the front line of the French cavalry," who entangled themselves with their own men within range of English archers.[14] The English knights, in contrast, were willing to get off their horses and fight on foot alongside their archers. The effects of the English and French social structures, imported in differing degrees into their respective armies, clearly played some role in determining their effectiveness on the battlefield. Other factors, such as the technical superiority of the English longbow in rates of fire and range and the use of foreign mercenaries by the French, were also important in explaining the French defeat. Nonethe-

---

[14]Charles Oman, *A History of the Art of War in the Middle Ages*, vol. 2, *1278–1485* (Novato, Calif.: Presidio, 1991), pp. 141–142. See also Hans Delbrück, *History of the Art of War*, vol. 3, *Medieval Warfare*, trans. Walter Renfroe (Lincoln: University of Nebraska Press, 1990), pp. 455–456, 458, 466–469.

less, it remains the case that the English knights were willing to sacrifice the symbols and roles that belonged to their social class and to fight on foot next to the common soldiers for the sake of the army as a whole, whereas the French knights were not so disposed. Social structures, the loyalties they generated, and the degree to which their influences could be excluded from the military seem to have been relevant to military effectiveness in battles in which the opposing sides possessed approximately equal technology and numbers.

Are there other examples from preindustrialized societies of how the social divisions created by dominant social structures carried over into the military organizations with consequences for the military power of those organizations? The collapse of the Egyptian army in the 1967 war against Israel led to some inquiries into the cause of Egyptian military failure. One Israeli analyst who was the chief of military intelligence and then a social scientist noticed that captured Egyptian officers, when asked, could not give the names of any of the men in their units and appeared surprised that they should be expected to do so. This, together with the willingness of Egyptian officers to abandon their men in battle, led the analyst to conclude that the "anomic" character of Egyptian society revealed and mirrored the low levels of trust across the boundaries of social class or beyond the primary groups in Egyptian society, which in turn led to an army that could easily disintegrate under stressful circumstances.[15] Clearly, the leadership abilities of the Egyptian officers were deficient, but the study was flawed because no attempt was made to see if factors other than the general character of Egyptian society were responsible for the poor performance of the officers. In addition, the emphasis on the allegedly "anomic" character of Egyptian society would not easily explain the improved Egyptian military performance in 1973.

What of armies from more industrialized nations in which the old social structure of hierarchical orders had been replaced by rational forms of organization? Is there any evidence that social structures affected military effectiveness in the armies of these societies? In casual discourse, many people would acknowledge without reflecting that Germans are better soldiers than Italians, implying that something about the societies of both countries had something to do with the performance of these two national groups in battle. Did the social structures of twentieth-century Italy affect the performance of its armies? Three systematic efforts to understand all factors contributing to Italian military incom-

---

[15] Y. Harkabi, "Basic Factors in the Arab Collapse during the Six-Day War," *Orbis* 11 (Fall 1967): 677–691. Other observers have provided anecdotal evidence that the officers in the Egyptian army were still drawn from the non-Egyptian families brought into Egypt by the Ottoman Empire and were ethnically distinct from the ordinary soldiers, thus creating barriers to communication and cooperation within the army.

petence in this century have led to similar assessments. Italian army units were less effective than German or Allied units in World War I, the interwar period, and World War II in such basic military skills as the coordination of artillery and infantry. Why?

Writing dispassionately long after the fact, one historian of the Italian army in World War I, John Gooch, noted that factors *not* obviously specific to Italy—high levels of illiteracy in the Italian peasants conscripted into the army, Italian senior officers who rejected any new military concepts, and bad staff organization in the army—could account for much of the Italian incompetence in World War I. But Gooch noted that broader patterns of social distrust that derived from the structural divisions in Italian society *did* have consequences for the Italian army: "The mass of manpower which made up the Italian armies could not rest on any quiet sense of legitimacy of the military as a governmental activity crucial to the welfare of society. Quite the opposite was true. From the moment that compulsory military service was first introduced in 1854, a system of lotteries and exemptions encouraged Italians to think of it . . . as a duel between the individual and the state." For its part, the officer corps tended to be autocratic and high-handed toward the common soldiers. They neglected troop training and believed in and inflicted harsh physical punishment on their troops. The conclusion reached by Gooch was that "the nature of Italian political culture and the structure of Italian society produced an army whose potential effectiveness was drastically restricted, so much so that it has caused one leading Italian military historian to conclude recently that even if [the Italian army commander] had greater elasticity of ideas, the instrument at his disposal would not have produced very different results."[16] These findings are suggestive, but it remains possible to argue that poorly trained, suspicious Italian soldiers and incompetent Italian officers were the result of poorly drafted conscription laws, lack of money for training, and other factors that might or might not have had their roots in the structure of Italian society.

Italian military performance was also poor in its colonial and limited wars of the 1930s, and a study of this period helps resolve some of the issues concerning Italian culture and military performance. Italian military spending between 1926 and 1940 was equal to that of France. The army's tacit support for Mussolini in 1922 was repaid by his support for the army. Efforts were made to develop doctrines appropriate for the

---

[16]John Gooch, "The Italian Armed Forces in World War I," in *Military Effectiveness*, ed. Allan R. Millett and Williamson Murray, vol. 1, *The First World War* (Boston: Allen Unwin, 1989), pp. 172, 174, 181–183. The Italian historian referred to is Lucio Ceva; his book is *Le forza armata*. Gooch also cites H. Stuart Hughes's judgment of the Risorgimento: "If the solutions they [the Italian political leaders] devised were mostly rather mediocre, so was the physical and political material with which they had to work."

colonial wars in Africa, the primary site of army fighting. But the performance of the army in Ethiopia and Spain remained poor. Why? The judgment of the historian Brian Sullivan also pointed to the reflection of Italian social structures in the army.

> Despite the Fascist regime's totalitarian pretensions, its efforts to create a new social hierarchy and political system based on merit, popular consensus and charismatic leadership had little influence on the largely monarchist officer corps. The rigid distinctions among conscripts, NCOs [noncommissioned officers], and junior and senior officers . . . remained firm in the interwar period. Far more than material shortcomings, these attitudes weakened the army by preventing the growth of trust, communication, and mutual comprehension necessary for mental and tactical flexibility on the battlefield. The military leadership's lack of concern for the morale and well-being of the enlisted men stood in blatant contrast to the care lavished on the officer corps. Most troops lived in decayed, filthy quarters, dressed in ill-fitting uniforms, and subsisted on wretched rations. . . . Officers had little contact with their men and usually dealt with them through the ignorant, brutal NCO Corps.[17]

Finally, in a study of the tendency for Italian units to become encircled and imprisoned by smaller forces in North Africa in World War II, the historian MacGregor Knox went out of his way to deny charges that Italian soldiers were cowards because they were Italians, noting how under German leadership they could inflict defeats on the British. But even Knox, who was predisposed not to believe in the cultural inferiority of Italian soldiers, acknowledged the impact of Italian society on the army. To be sure, some failures at the level of military doctrine were not clearly due to culture. But "its approach to morale, unit cohesion, and relations between officers, NCOs and enlisted men was inconsistent with any tactical system aimed at defeating the enemy. Nationwide recruitment, in a nation as divided by dialects and particularisms as Italy, made unit cohesion difficult to achieve at the best of times. . . . The caste mentality of the officer corps precluded, and was designed to preclude, a relationship of trust with the lower orders."[18]

If the influence of divisive social structures of the host society can help explain the bad performance of some armies, does the influence of co-

[17]Brian Sullivan, "The Italian Armed Forces, 1918–1940," in Millett and Murray, *Military Effectiveness*, vol. 2, *The Interwar Period*, p. 200. See also pp. 169, 171, 186, 200–201.

[18]MacGregor Knox, "The Italian Armed Forces, 1940–1943," in Millett and Murray, *Military Effectiveness*, vol. 3, *The Second World War*, pp. 141, 162, 164–166, 171.

hesive social structures explain the performance of good armies, or are good armies the result of Weberian and Huntingtonian separation of the army from society that leads to the creation of a disciplined, rational military society? More simply, was the German army good because it was a rational, disciplined organization, or was it good because it was full of German soldiers who had been molded by German society? The available evidence does not allow a clear answer to this question. Studies conducted by the United States Army after World War II showed that in that war, German army forces, when performing a given mission, whether on the offense or defense, would consistently inflict higher American casualties per German soldier than the American soldiers would inflict on Germans when performing the same mission, despite the fact that American forces had more and better military supplies.[19] The accepted explanation for superior German performance was supplied in the famous study published by Morris Janowitz and Edward Shils on the basis of interviews with German POWs. Superior German officers trained and led their troops so well that high levels of unit cohesion were achieved, which in turn produced high levels of military effectiveness.[20] But more recent studies by Omer Bartov showed very clearly that on the eastern front, at least, German army units took so many casualties so quickly that there was no time for military training in German units, while officers were likely to die long before they were able to have any impact on the cohesion of their unit. This extremely rapid loss of men and officers led to what has been called "the destruction of the primary group"[21] that was supposed to be the cause of superior German military performance.

One inference that may be drawn from Bartov's study was that if the Germans fought well, it was because of something they brought with them from their own society to the army, rather than the ability of the army to transform civilians into radically different social beings. What it was that they brought with them is harder to determine. Bartov himself argued, without clear evidence, that what German civilians brought with them into the army was a strong belief in the Nazi ideology, not attitudes derived from the structure of German society. How Bartov would account for the superior German military performance of units from anti-

[19] See Martin Van Creveld, *Fighting Power: German and U.S. Army Performance, 1939–1945* (Westport, Conn.: Greenwood, 1982), chap. 2.

[20] Morris Janowitz and Edward Shils, "Cohesion and Disintegration in the Wehrmacht," in *Center and Periphery*, ed. Edward Shils (Chicago: University of Chicago Press, 1975), pp. 345–383.

[21] Omer Bartov, *Hitler's Army: Soldiers, Nazis, and War in the Third Reich* (New York: Oxford University Press, 1991), pp. 34, 36–42, 44–47.

Nazi areas of Germany or the superior performance of the army in pre-Nazi days is not clear.[22]

Wider-ranging comparisons of the impact of social structures on military effectiveness across large cultural divides are intriguing but even more difficult because so many variables appear to be changing at once. Small European armies defeated much larger South Asian armies in the seventeenth and eighteenth centuries. Clearly, the European armies were much better at generating military power from a given number of soldiers. But might this not be due to gross disparities in the levels of technology in the opposing armies, which tended to overwhelm any possible differences in effectiveness due purely to the influence of society? The cross-cultural disparities in military effectiveness that seem to be easily explained by differences in levels of technology turn out to be, on closer examination, more puzzling. During the first wave of British imperialism, groups of several thousand European soldiers repeatedly defeated Indian armies many times their size. Technologically, the British were in the first phases of the industrial revolution that gave the British textile industry, for example, an advantage over Indian textile crafts, an edge that contributed to the destruction of the latter. But it is incorrect to generalize from textile technologies to militarily relevant technologies. Good comparative surveys of technological levels in Europe and India that have been published more recently show that in the technologies pertinent to military capabilities, India was the equal if not the better of Europe. Quantitatively, for example, India produced two hundred thousand tons of iron in 1750, about the same as in all of Europe the same year, excluding Russia. On a per capita basis, that gave Europe perhaps a 50 percent advantage, which was hardly crushing considering that there were other strategic demands on European iron not related to India, whereas Indian iron production was largely created to supply shipbuilders and gun makers. Qualitatively, Indian steel was better than British steel, in part because the surface iron ore available in India was better than that available in Europe, in part because Indian steelmaking techniques were superior. Indian steel was exported to Syria, where it was made into "Damascus" swords, and to Sheffield, England, where it was studied as late as 1820 to help English steelmakers close the technological gap with India. Indian bronze was worse than English bronze, but Indian brass was better than European brass and made better artillery barrels. No less a judge of weaponry than Arthur Wellesley, the

[22] See James S. Corum, *The Roots of Blitzkrieg: Hans von Seeckt and German Military Reform* (Lawrence: University of Kansas Press, 1992), pp. 1–50, for a detailed account of an astoundingly professional and politically blind army in World War I and the early interwar period before Nazi ideology existed.

future duke of Wellington, wrote that seventy Indian artillery pieces he captured in battle were "the finest brass ordnance I have ever seen," and he equipped his own troops with them. Indian musket barrels were as good as or better than British barrels because they were made with spiral rather than longitudinal welds. They were stronger and less likely to burst and so could take a larger gunpowder charge and shoot twice as far as European muskets.[23] The number of muskets produced in India ran well into the tens of thousands. In the mid-1600s, for example, there were twenty thousand musket-armed Rajputs in a standing force in the service of the Mughal emperor in Delhi.[24] Yet the military subjection of India was accomplished by British forces that were a fraction of the size of Indian armies, let alone of the Indian population. Why?

CULTURE, STRATEGIC CULTURE, AND OPERATIONAL CODES

I began this chapter by discussing some of the less successful efforts to relate culture to strategy and then tried to see if one could simply ignore those internal differences in political units across cultural boundaries that might be relevant to variations in military behavior. A number of historical examples suggested that differences in societies might lead to significant, persistent differences in military performance. If one accepts the possibility that differences in society might have military implications, what kind of explanations are available? The search for explanations related to social differences would lead first to the theories of strategic culture that have been developed to explain possible differences in the military behavior of peoples from European and non-European cultures. This concept, however, turns out to be difficult to apply and to be more concerned with how military power is used than with how much can be generated from a given amount of material resources.

Intellectually, strategic culture is related to the specific idea of a Bolshevik "operational code," as advanced by Nathan Leites[25] and the concept of "political culture" advanced by Lucian Pye, Sidney Verba, and others. Leites' concept of the operational code was subsequently elaborated during the cold war to explain different approaches by the Soviet leadership toward nuclear weapons. This code was a consistent, system-

---

[23] Arnold Pacey, *Technology in World Civilization* (Cambridge: MIT Press, 1990), pp. 66, 78, 80–81, 115, 128, 131. See also Philip Mason, *A Matter of Honour* (New York: Holt, Rinehart, and Winston, 1974), pp. 40, 98–99.

[24] Niccolao Mannucci, *Storia do Mogor, or Mogul India, 1653–1708*, trans. William Irvine (London: John Murray, 1907), 2:422.

[25] See Nathan C. Leites, *Operational Code of the Politburo* (New York: McGraw Hill, 1951).

[15]

atic set of policy preferences and modes of analysis that was alleged to dominate the thought of Soviet leaders. Because their ideas were different from those dominant in the minds of American leaders, Soviet leaders could respond in ways not expected by Americans on the basis of the observation of material factors alone. An operational code is not the same thing as "culture," but it shares with culture the idea that the dominant texts—religious, literary, or political—of a society give some insight into the habits of thought of those who read them. It is important to notice that however significant the operational code of the Bolsheviks might have been for understanding Soviet elite behavior, it would be unwarranted, on the basis of the Soviet case, to assume that other societies had their own operational codes that were revealed in their political texts. Membership in Soviet elites was well defined, and the behavior of the Soviet elite during the period relevant to Leites' work was highly constrained in both its behavior and its interpretation of political texts. Institutional mechanisms existed to insure that interpretations of the original textual sources of Communist thought were politically correct, and mechanisms enforced politically correct behavior. Other societies might well have far more loosely defined and controlled elites that make the concept of an operational code irrelevant. It is one thing to say that the Bolshevik elite had an operational code that could be understood by reading Marx and Lenin and quite another to claim, for example, that there is an Islamic operational code that could be understood by reading the Koran.

The other source of the concept of strategic culture is the more general concept of "political culture" advanced in the 1960s by students of political development to suggest why non-European nations might not replicate European political history as they developed political institutions in response to industrialization. According to this argument, the historical development of a given society produced different systems of "nonpolitical beliefs—such as feelings of basic trust in human relations, orientation towards time and the possibility of progress, and the like—[which] can be of overriding importance" in shaping political institutions.[26] These sets of beliefs constituted, in each country, that nation's political culture. Political culture could not be assumed to be uniform across cultural boundaries, even if countries adopted common forms of economic organization, industrialization in particular, because common economic modes of organization would be overlaid on older systems of beliefs and would not simply replace them. The result would be varying products of

[26]Lucian W. Pye, "Introduction: Political Culture and Political Development," in *Political Culture and Political Development*, ed. Lucian W. Pye and Sidney Verba (Princeton: Princeton University Press, 1965), pp. 8–11.

the interaction between the old beliefs and the new forms of economic organization.[27] Particularly as Western colonial patterns of government receded in time and prestige, local "subjective attitudes, beliefs, and values prevalent among the dominant groups in the society" would increasingly shape the political development of non-European governments.[28] Lucian Pye argued that Asian political culture, for example, had produced a startlingly different definition of political power as an established status hierarchy, rather than the ability to change the behavior of others. In the Asian definition, in this view, power was that which enabled a ruler *not* to have to make decisions and wield his or her authority.[29]

Subsequent efforts to refine and apply the concept of political culture referred to political culture as "a short-hand expression for a 'mind set' which has the effect of limiting attention to less than the full range of alternative behaviors, problems, and solutions which are logically possible," or as an "ideational code" that is the "property of a collectivity." This mind-set or code would be composed of different sets of assumptions about the nature of the universe and the appropriate political activities of the community.[30] Culture or local, generationally transmitted knowledge could also influence how members of a collectivity process information in ways that can affect the economic interaction within and the development of different societies.[31] These variants on the concept of political culture have clear links back to the concept of the operational code and forward to the discussion of strategic culture.

The use of political culture in political development theory was and is characterized by an emphasis on the persistent patterns of subjective beliefs developed over time that shaped and framed choices about domestic politics. "Strategic culture" is in many ways an analogous concept applied not to the entire political class of a nation but to the subset of political-military decision makers. Their beliefs and assumptions, it is argued, framed their choices about international military behavior, in particular, the choices concerning decisions to go to war; preferences for offensive, expansionist, or defensive modes of warfare; and levels of wartime casualties that would be acceptable. Jack Snyder first used this term to help ex-

---

[27] See, for example, S. N. Eisenstadt, "Post-Traditional Societies and the Continuity and Reconstruction of Tradition," *Daedalus* 102 (Winter 1973): 1–28.

[28] Samuel P. Huntington, "The Goals of Development," in *Understanding Political Development*, ed. Myron Weiner and Samuel P. Huntington (Boston: Little, Brown, 1987), pp. 22, 26.

[29] Lucian W. Pye, *Asian Power and Politics: The Cultural Dimension of Authority* (Cambridge: Harvard University Press, 1985), pp. 20–22.

[30] David J. Elkins and Richard E. B. Simenon, "A Cause in Search of Its Effect, or What Does Political Culture Explain?" *Comparative Politics* 11 (January 1979): 127–146.

[31] Douglass C. North, "Transaction Costs, Institutions, and Economic Performance," ms., no date, pp. 21–23.

plain differences that were gradually becoming apparent in the attitude of the Soviet military toward nuclear war when compared with the dominant views in the United States.[32] Kenneth Booth, also concerned primarily with the Soviet Union, plausibly suggested that "cultural heredity," defined as the "set of patterns which present observable and sharp discontinuities among groups of peoples," can focus the attention of national leaders toward certain options and away from others. Soviet strategic culture would affect the way in which war was viewed, the perceived utility of the use of force, and the relative importance associated with the concepts of deterrence and defense. Specifically, the Soviet experience in World War II would be interpreted and remembered for some time afterward by Soviet leaders and would shape Soviet views on strategy in ways that might not be the same as other countries with different experiences.[33] Azar Gat turned the concept of strategic culture back on Western Europe and used it to argue that Clausewitz's *On War*, a work that might otherwise be considered an imperfect attempt to arrive at objective general strategic truths, was in fact a "culture-bound . . . military theory" that was the product of the Napoleonic Wars and the intellectual milieu of the German Counter Enlightenment.[34] Yitzhak Klein summarized this entire school of thought when he defined strategic culture as "the habits of thought and action . . . of particular national military establishments," or "the set of attitudes and beliefs held within a military establishment concerning the political objective of war and the most effective strategy and operational method of achieving it." Klein, like earlier writers, emphasized the importance of capturing the subjective attitudes and assumptions in the minds of the leaders who made policy in war that defined for them which facts would be perceived as important.[35]

More recently, a new generation of scholars has thoughtfully elaborated and employed the concept of strategic culture outside the context of the Soviet Union. This definition is utilized, developed, and evaluated in the context of China by Alastair Iain Johnston, who also refers to the assumptions, symbols, myths, and beliefs held by national leaders that affect their perception of available acceptable strategic options, "a nebulous ideational milieu which limits behavioral choices" and "which acts to establish long-lasting strategic preferences by formulating concepts of the role

---

[32] Jack Snyder, *The Soviet Strategic Culture: Implications for Nuclear Options* (Santa Monica, Calif.: Rand R-2154-AF, 1977).

[33] Kenneth Booth, *Strategy and Ethnocentrism* (New York: Holmes and Meier, 1979), pp. 64–66, 73–77, 82–83.

[34] Azar Gat, *The Origins of Military Thought: From the Enlightenment to Clausewitz* (Oxford: Oxford University Press, 1991), pp. ix, 171–175, 181–187.

[35] Yitzhak Klein, "A Theory of Strategic Culture," *Comparative Strategy* 10 (January–March 1991): 3–23.

and efficacy of military force in interstate political affairs."[36] Thomas Berger has used analogous concepts to explore the changing set of beliefs, derived from interpreted historical experience, that affected the willingness of post–World War II Japan and Germany to go to war.[37] Elizabeth Kier, while emphasizing the importance of subjective factors that affect the perceptions of military elites, has criticized the utility of the concept of political culture as being too broad. Instead, she stressed the role of domestic politics in shaping the attitudes of a society toward its military and the political views of the military with regard to its host society, all while acknowledging the importance of the internal culture of the professional officer corps, a culture that was not determined by the distribution of domestic political power. Kier's definition of culture is intelligent if still quite complex and broad. By focusing on the habits of thought of the officer corps of an army, however, she obtains the same benefits as Leites' original use of the idea of an operational code—that is, she focuses on the ideas of a group of men whose education and behavior are tightly constrained. Her approach is compatible with that taken by the advocates of strategic culture because, in Kier's view, culture also operates by affecting the subjective perspectives inside military heads.[38]

Only the most dogmatic materialist would deny the importance of the dominant ideas in the minds of those who act politically or strategically. The problems with strategic culture tend to lie in its application. Those scholars who employ the concept of strategic culture must tell us how they can gain access to the subjective perspectives of the leaders whom they are studying. In his review of the problems of doing cross-national survey research, Sidney Verba catalogues the host of problems scholars have in obtaining reliable, genuinely comparable data about the beliefs of the members of different cultures, even when scholars can question the people they are studying.[39] Verba correctly notes that the same question may mean different things when posed to people in different coun-

[36] Alastair Iain Johnston, "An Inquiry into Strategic Culture: Chinese Strategic Thought, the Parabellum Paradigm, and Grand Strategic Choice in Ming China" (Ph.D. diss., University of Michigan, 1993), pp. 1–22, 45.

[37] Thomas Berger, "America's Reluctant Allies: The Genesis of the Political-Military Cultures of Japan and West Germany" (Ph.D. diss., MIT, 1992), pp. 11, 20, 25. Berger defined political culture as "the constellation of attitudes, perceptions, and patterns of behavior regarding national defense, the armed forces, and the use of force in a particular political system," referring to political-military culture as a form of "negotiated reality." In so doing, he accepted the importance of subjective perspectives that shape perceptions of objective reality. Berger explicitly saw his work as drawing on the earlier political scientists who developed the concept of political culture, particularly those who viewed political culture as the result of the interpreted historical experiences of a national elite.

[38] Elizabeth Kier, "Culture, Politics, and Military Doctrine: France and Britain between the Two Wars" (Ph.D. diss., Cornell University, 1992), pp. 27, 34, 47–48, 54, 62.

[39] Sidney Verba, "Cross-National Survey Research: The Problem of Credibility," in *Com-*

tries, their responses may be appropriately interpreted in different ways, variations that affect interpretation of questions posed to local inhabitants may exist within the country, and so on. Strategic culture faces analogous problems plus the obvious fact that direct access to members of the strategic elite is not possible if they are hostile, distant, or long dead. In the absence of access to interview data or private papers, how much can be done to characterize the strategic culture of a particular group?[40]

It is clearly circular to study the behavior of leaders, infer from that behavior certain subjective perspectives, and then use those inferred perspectives to explain the same set of observed behaviors. The alternative is to study what strategic elites have studied and what they have written and to work back from those texts to their internal states of mind. This is a valuable approach in theory. But what is inside peoples' heads may or may not be related to what they read and what they write. Subtle and careful research is necessary to infer from the written record what people actually thought. As Johnston acknowledged, the difficulty with the scholarly application of strategic culture lies in the practical hardships involved in gaining consistent, reliable access to what is inside the heads of people who are not available for questioning and whose private writings have been destroyed or are denied to scholars.

Another problem in the concept of strategic culture reveals itself, however, if we go back to its intellectual predecessor, political culture. Political culture is the system of subjective beliefs that derive from the experience of a society and are used to organize the political life of that society. Beliefs about one's own society are used to bring social behavior into accord with subjective norms. Subjective beliefs and social realities will never be in perfect conformity, but if social life is to be tolerable, they will have to modify each other over time, turning the subjective set of beliefs into a rational set of assumptions about what kind of treatment might be expected from members of that society and about how to operate successfully in that society. But in international relations, the power of the subjective norms of the leaders of one nation to shape the objective

---

parative Methods in Sociology, ed. Ivan Vallier (Berkeley: University of California Press, 1971), pp. 309–323.

[40] As Jack Levy has pointed out, even complete access to private and public papers does not eliminate the difficulty in determining the intentions of actors "with any degree of precision." See Levy, "The Causes of War: A Review of Theories and Evidence," in *Behavior, Society, and Nuclear War*, ed. Philip E. Tetlock, Jo L. Husbands, Robert Jervis, Paul C. Stern, Charles Tilly, vol. 1 (New York: Oxford University Press, 1989), pp. 285–286. For an excellent discussion of how the problem of assessing the impact of ideas and perceptions can be successfully managed by scholars, see the essay by Judith Goldstein and Robert Keohane in *Ideas and Foreign Policy: Beliefs, Institutions, and Political Change*, ed. Judith Goldstein and Robert Keohane (Ithaca: Cornell University Press, 1993).

international environment might be much more limited. In international politics, little tendency may exist for the environment to support subjective ideas that are not consistent with international political realities. In his own reading of the major strategic writings of Ming China, Johnston concludes that those texts do not differ greatly from power political analysis familiar to the West.[41] In addition, sociological studies of many human and primate communities have found some very widely shared, almost universal tendencies among such communities to display patterns of behavior associated with realpolitical behavior, such as coalition building in general, coalition building to balance against an unwanted dominant actor in the community, punishment inflicted by the coalition leader on defecting coalition partners, mobilization of coalition members to display group power in a crisis to deter rival groups, and so on.[42] Indeed, a growing body of anthropology suggests that some broadly defined forms of human social behavior are common to all human cultures because they are the product of a shared evolutionary genetic history. If these findings are supported, they would indicate that while cultural differences in strategic behavior could exist, they would be limited and conditioned by our common human genetic ancestry.[43] This would tend to bound the relevance of the concept of strategic culture by supporting the observation made by Robert Jervis that the patterns of perceptions and misperceptions we see in foreign policy–makers are shared by all humans and are "as far as we can tell . . . a product of the way our brains are 'hard wired' to process information."[44]

But it is important to note that these skeptical questions about the impact of strategic culture apply to specific forms of international political behavior, such as the propensity of a state to form coalitions or to go to war. They do not obviously apply to how a political unit generates military power internally. So while we may have questions about the

[41] "This is not a cross-national study. . . . But it seems fairly evident that what I believe to be the operative Chinese strategic culture (at least up to the Ming) does not differ radically from key elements in the Western 'realpolitik' tradition." Johnston, "Strategic Culture," p. 350.

[42] See for example, Christopher Boehm, "Segmentary 'Warfare' and the Management of Conflict," in *Coalitions and Alliances in Humans and Other Animals*, ed. Alexander Harcourt and Frans de Waal (Oxford: Oxford University Press, 1992), pp. 140, 154, 164; Frans de Waal, *Chimpanzee Politics* (New York: Harper and Row, 1982), pp. 42–45, 128–136, 144–153. For examples of coalition balancing behavior among Native American tribes, see Frank McNitt, *Navajo Wars* (Albuquerque: University of New Mexico Press, 1990). I thank Barry Posen for bringing this work to my attention.

[43] John Tooby and Leda Cosmides, "The Psychological Foundations of Culture," in *The Adapted Mind: Evolutionary Psychology and the Generation of Culture*, ed. Jerome H. Barkow, Leda Cosmides, and John Tooby (New York: Oxford University Press, 1992), pp. 19–136.

[44] Robert Jervis, Richard Ned Lebow, and Janis Gross Stein, *Psychology and Deterrence* (Baltimore: Johns Hopkins University Press, 1985), p. 4.

efforts of the strategic culture theorists to explain variations in the use of power, we still face the problems with the realist assertion that the amount of power that states will generate from a given level of resources will converge. However similar are states with regard to the uses of power, it might be the case that different societies organized themselves differently, and those variations might lead to differences in the amount of military power they could generate. Whether or not culture, defined as the dominant set of beliefs, matters for strategy, domestic social structures could still affect the generation of military power.

Culture versus Domestic Social Structures

What does political science have to say about the way social structures that dominate different societies affect their ability to organize and act collectively? What are social structures, and are they same or different from "culture"?

"Social structure" is a broad term that includes such entities as social classes, occupational specializations, caste organizations, tribes, and perhaps even gender. Such structures are the subunits of society with which people identify and to which they give their loyalties. When and if it is the case that these social structures are purely functional, there is no necessary reason for them to be the product of "culture." Marxists, for example, see class as the result of different relations to the means of production. Class, for Marxists, is the dominant social structure, and they believe the utility of class analysis to be universal, despite cultural differences. Or it might be that social structures such as caste derive from specific sets of beliefs not related to material factors, in which case social structures would be more closely linked to "culture." Whether they are the product of the subjective beliefs of the members of the community or the product of objective economic forces or other factors, social structures have independent, observable existences. One can observe to what groups people belong, with whom they interact socially, and for what goals they are willing to make sacrifices. These domestic social structures can, in turn, affect what Raymond Aron called the "collective capacity for action" of the larger political units in which they reside, including the capacity for economic and military action.[45] The consequences of different social structures will be various. Specifically, social structures that are organized and engage in economic activity will have particular consequences for the economic behavior of the society. Social structures that

---

[45]Raymond Aron, *Peace and War*, trans. Richard Howard and Annette Baker Fox (Garden City, N.Y.: Doubleday, 1966), p. 54.

have military or quasi-military functions will have special importance for the collective capacity for military activity. The political unit thus acquires characteristic strengths and weaknesses that are the result of its internal social structures. Differences in these strengths and weaknesses can become evident when compared with foreign societies with different social structures. Subjective beliefs may still matter for this argument, because they might provide the foundation for social structures, but these beliefs do not have to be assumed or inferred from books but can be observed, as they are embodied in social practice. In short, the dominant social structures of a group of people might lead to characteristic strengths and vulnerabilities of each society when making money or war. Whether or not dominant social structures vary or remain constant across cultural boundaries is an empirical question, not determined a priori or by definition.

The argument that social structures might affect the capacity of a society for economic growth has been made by a number of authors, beginning at least as far back as Max Weber. More recent authors who have studied culture and economic growth have emphasized the impact of social structures on the limits to which members of that society feel they can trust and interact economically with one another, what Lawrence Harrison has called "the radius of trust."[46] The idea that the dominant structures of a society can affect the overall capacity of a society for collective political action can be found in Robert Putnam's study of the effectiveness of the representative organs of regional government in Italy. He found that certain regions of Italy displayed collective behavior that was dominated by family structures that narrowly defined the interests of family members. In other regions, structures larger than the family played a major role in organizing collective behavior. As measured by twelve indicators, interregional differences in the levels of institutional performance found in Italy were explained not by levels of economic performance or educational levels but by levels of participation in voluntary organizations and other indicators of the level of civic community that reflected the relative strength or weakness of family-dominated social structures.[47]

Chie Nakane's influential analysis of Japanese society focused on the ways in which the centuries-old social structures derived from village life in Japan carried over into the institutions and organizations of modern Japan. The structure of village life was reflected, for example, in

[46] Lawrence E. Harrison, *Who Prospers? How Cultural Values Shape Economic and Political Success* (New York: Basic, 1992), pp. 11, 19–21.

[47] Robert D. Putnam, *Making Democracy Work: Civic Traditions in Modern Italy* (Princeton: Princeton University Press, 1993), pp. 83–116, 122–133.

[23]

Japanese businesses long after industrialization. The emphasis on uni-fied, hierarchical relations within the frame of a local, socially hetero-geneous "household," or *ie*, rather than on relations among siblings or horizontal, socially homogenous kinship groups, was replicated, accord-ing to Nakane, in the modern Japanese firm: "A company is conceived as an *ie*." Nakane explicitly compared this with patterns of social organ-ization found elsewhere in Asia, in India for instance, and found striking differences in the structure of day-to-day relations of the bureaucracies of the two countries.[48]

Other intensive studies, such as those of Japanese labor unions and corporations, found that while initially modeled on Western labor unions and corporations, over time they adopted patterns of organization that were more characteristically Japanese. In the case of unions, the pattern shifted from industry-wide unions to company unions, reflecting what was judged to be the tendency of Japanese "associations and organiza-tions of all kinds . . . to be localized and territorially based."[49] Japanese businessmen after World War II deliberately tried to reject "backward" forms of Japanese corporate behavior in favor of models drawn from the United States, but Japanese practices such as lifetime employment, promotion by seniority, and ownership of the company by the man-agers and employees gradually reasserted themselves.[50] Rather than convergence to a single corporate model, increased divergence between American and Japanese corporations was found as a result of the different social milieu in which the Japanese corporations found them-selves.

On the basis of these observations, it may be suggested that govern-ment bureaucracies performing the same functions may or may not con-verge toward the same patterns of organization and behavior. Weber argued that all bureaucracies should in theory have the same character, one derived from their essential nature as purposeful, rational, hierar-chical structures. It is not clear whether in practice all bureaucracies are as nonculturally rational as the Weberian ideal type would lead us to believe. One student of the Japanese police observed that Weber's em-phasis on the common character of bureaucratic institutions tended to be confirmed by studies of *European* bureaucracies, but that in the Japa-

[48]Chie Nakane, *Japanese Society* (Middlesex, England: Penguin, 1973), pp. 5–8, 40–41, 90, 105.

[49]Robert J. Smith, "The Cultural Context of the Japanese Political Economy," in *The Political Economy of Japan*, ed. Shumpei Kumon and Henry Rosovsky, vol. 3, *Cultural and Social Dynamics* (Stanford: Stanford University Press, 1992), pp. 16–19.

[50]Ryushi Iwata, "The Japanese Enterprise as a Unified Body of Employees: Origins and Development," in Kumon and Rosovsky, *Political Economy of Japan*, pp. 170–197.

nese police bureaucracy, initially modeled on the Parisian police force, the pattern of organization gradually diverged from the Western model.[51] Another study of the senior bureaucracy in Japan found its character to be remarkably stable over time, successfully resisting even the efforts of Douglas MacArthur after World War II to democratize its role in Japanese government and society.[52] Although these studies also found elements of bureaucratic organization that were shared across cultures, they could not reduce Japanese bureaucracies to a single Weberian functional-rational type.

Even studies of Western state bureaucracies have suggested that their internal functioning may be affected by the dominant social structures of the host society. Michel Crozier's study of French state monopolies showed that internal bureaucratic structures—in particular, the absence of any self-organizing groups or cooperative behavior—mirrored the atomization of French society observed by anthropologists studying a variety of French communities. This correspondence created for Crozier the possibility that "the basic cultural conditions predetermine[d] the possible scope of authority relationships within bureaucracies," although Crozier acknowledged that "the field is still so unexplored that one cannot make too much of these correspondences."[53]

This review of studies that look at various forms of social structure and their implications for collective behavior is illuminating but highlights an obvious problem. The concept of social structures is broad enough to encompass family-oriented structures, village-based structures, class structure, anomic individualism and many other phenomena. In any given case, how should the general, abstract, and acontextual definition of social structure be defined and applied? How can the problem of circularity be avoided? That is, after having defined and assessed the dependent variable, whatever it might be in a given case, and found it to be large or small, how can we make sure that the study does not then search for just the right definition of the independent variable of "social structure" that makes the theory come out right? There are two ways of handling this problem, one more theoretically clean, one more sensitive to context. An a priori definition of social structure can be defined for all cases, everywhere and at all times, at the outset of the exercise. This will prevent ad hoc adjustments of the independent variable,

---

[51] D. Eleanor Westney, *Imitation and Innovation: The Transfer of Western Organizational Patterns to Meiji Japan* (Cambridge: Harvard University Press, 1987), pp. 11–12, 92–93.

[52] B. C. Koh, *Japan's Administrative Elite* (Berkeley: University of California Press, 1989), p. 65.

[53] Michel Crozier, *The Bureaucratic Phenomenon* (Chicago: University of Chicago Press, 1964), pp. 220–221.

but it will not be sensitive to the enormous variations in behavior across cases separate in space and time. Just how relevant, for example, would it be to ask questions about socioeconomic classes in ancient India? Or about "ethnicity" or "nationality" or functional specializations in periods when those concepts were not entertained or observed by the people who are being studied? The alternative is to adopt context-sensitive definitions of social structure in each case and to avoid circularity by insisting that the application of that kind of social structure to a given case be widely shared by a large number of independent observers. If many people with many different intellectual and political perspectives look at a society and independently agree on what the dominant social structures are, we have at least satisfied the criterion that the chosen definition has been replicated by independent observations. One must then stick with that definition and apply it consistently. There remains the danger that the study will select for those observers who agree on the "right" definition, so the search for independent observations should be broad-ranging. This solution is not perfect, but it may be the only one that allows relevant generalizations while guarding against bias on the part of the investigator.

SOCIAL STRUCTURES AND MILITARY POWER

The literature on culture and development, economic and political, together with comparative studies of military power, may lead us, finally, toward a tentative conclusion. We can suggest that in all cultures, dominant social structures exist that can affect the capacity for collective action in the political entity in which they reside. Those social structures may or may not vary across cultural boundaries. In the military realm, variations in the divisiveness of the dominant social structures can affect the amount of military power that can be generated from a given level of material resources. The impact of social structures on the capacity to generate military power will increase the more the subunits of society engage in activities related to the military, just as the capacity for economic activity is most affected by social structures that engage in activities related to business. Therefore, the ability of the state to suppress or weaken the military power of divisive social structures will affect the amount of power that can be generated. To varying degrees, the military organizations of a society may be separated and isolated from the host society and from the effects of divisive social structures, which will also influence the amount of military power that can be generated. The most salient measure of the ability to generate offensive military power is the ability to generate power surplus to the need to maintain internal order

[26]

so that it can be projected abroad. The most salient measure of the ability to generate defensive military power is the ability to defend successfully against foreign invasion.

This position is far from being new but has been lost sight of in the debate about culture and strategy. The *Muqaddimah* of Ibn Khaldun (usually translated as an *Introduction* [or *Prolegomena*] *to History*) was perhaps the first book to review systematically the relationship in premodern, Arab-speaking societies between social structures—specifically, nomadic pastoral social structures of Arab societies—and the power, offensive and defensive, of the military organizations that arose in those societies.[54] In the nineteenth century, in essays that predate *On War* and in *On War* itself, Carl von Clausewitz developed the argument that the customs, culture, and society of a nation transformed the nature of the wars it will conduct and gave as examples the same nomadic peoples and their armies that Ibn Khaldun had studied, as well as the mass citizen-soldier armies generated by the wars of the French Revolution, armies that, on balance, reduced the importance of the older social structures of social class on the military.[55] Stanislav Andreski provided a brilliant if erratic account of how differences in social stratification affected the ability of a society to generate military power.[56]

The argument that social structures may have consequences for military social structures and military behavior is a general one. Historians have long tried to understand the impact of war on domestic social structures.[57] More recent work by historians has begun to combine a study of more modern European states with analyses of the dominant social structures in those countries at a given time to try and understand how that relationship worked in reverse—how social structures affected military organizations and the conduct of war. William Fuller's work on the military strategy of Czarist Russia, for example, convincingly argued that Russian social structures—in particular, serfdom—had a profound impact on Czarist military capabilities and strategic thought.[58] Historians

[54] Ibn Khaldun, *The Muqaddimah: An Introduction to History*, vol. 1, trans. Franz Rosenthal (Princeton: Princeton University Press, 1967), pp. 11, 12, 77, 249, 251–252, 263–264, 267.

[55] Clausewitz, *On War*, Bk. 8, Chap. 3B, pp. 585–593. See also Gat, *Military Thought*, pp. 187, 189.

[56] Stanislav Andreski, *Military Organization and Society* (London: Routledge and Kegan Paul, 1954). Andreski deliberately decided not to provide any footnotes to his sources for the book, and his account of Indian society and the Indian military would not be accepted by students of India.

[57] See the review of this literature in Bernard Waites, "Warfare and Social Structure in Social Theory and Social History," in *A Class Society at War: England, 1914–1918* (Lexington Spa, England: Berg, 1987), pp. 5–33.

[58] William C. Fuller, *Strategy and Power in Russia, 1600–1914* (New York: Free Press, 1992).

and political scientists have discovered that patterns of military behavior we now associate with "Third World culture" were the dominant patterns in Europe at times in history when certain aspects of the internal social structures of Europe resembled those now associated with countries in the Middle East or Africa. David Kaiser, for example, argued that in European states up until the end of the seventeenth century, the social structures with most military relevance were the great aristocratic families and the plebeian populations organized around them. These families severely constrained the ability of the monarchs to generate offensive military power, a phenomenon exemplified in the memoir of Louis XIV, who wrote that "we find ourselves obliged for the conservation of our state as much for its glory and reputation to maintain . . . in peace as well in war, a great number of troops, both infantry and cavalry, which will be ready and in good condition to act to keep our people in obedience and the respect they owe us, to insure the peace and tranquillity that they have won . . . and to aid our allies."[59] Charles Tilly has made parallel observations.[60] In modern times, the same phenomenon has been found in Third World nations in which loyalties to social structures divide political units and reduce their military power. Steven David noted that in such states, "groups owe allegiance to and act for interests other than the national interest. Instead of identifying with the state, individuals identify with ethnic, religious, or regional groupings. . . . Rather than transcending the differences among these different groups, the state is often simply the representative of the group that holds power in the capital."[61] Adda Bozeman has pointed to a related issue, which is that states aware of the nature of the internal social structures of their enemies are better able to exploit the weaknesses that those structures create.[62]

This way of looking at societies and military power has some advantages. Rather than arguing that Christian, Islamic, Hispanic, or Hindu cultures each have specific, constant, and unique strategic outlooks, we

[59] David Kaiser, *Politics and War: European Conflict from Philip II to Hitler* (Cambridge: Harvard University Press, 1990), pp. 10, 12, 140, 145–146 (quote from p. 145).

[60] Charles Tilly, *Coercion, Capital, and European States, 990–1992* (Cambridge, Mass.: Blackwell, 1992), pp. 68–69: European states built up "fearsome coercive means of their own as they deprived civilian populations of access to those means."

[61] Steven R. David, *Choosing Sides: Alignment and Realignment in the Third World* (Baltimore: Johns Hopkins University Press, 1991), pp. 12–13, and Steven R. David, "Explaining Third World Alignment," *World Politics* 43 (January 1991): 233–256.

[62] Adda B. Bozeman, "Covert Action and Foreign Policy," in *Intelligence Requirements for the 1980s: Covert Action*, ed. Roy Godson (Washington, D.C.: National Strategy Information Center, 1981), pp. 30–32. See also her extended discussion of the historical impact of social structures on international politics in Southwest and Central Asia in Adda B. Bozeman, *Politics and Culture in International History* (Princeton: Princeton University Press, 1960), passim.

can look at each political unit in each culture area and ask what the dominant structures are, what effects they have for the ability to generate military power, what relation the military has to society, and whether those structures and relations are changing. We do not need to and should not assume that every political unit in a given cultural area has the same social structures. We do not have to and should not assume that social structures cannot be replicated across cultural boundaries. By looking at the independent variables, we can understand the ability to generate offensive and defensive military power. We can understand why, in certain cases, changes in social structures have been associated with changes in offensive or defensive military power. Unlike the concept of strategic culture, a focus on the social structures frees us from the assumption central to the strategic culture argument: strategic outlooks are determined by the subjective, interpreted experiences of the leaders of states in international relations, interpretations that are somehow consistently transmitted to disparate individuals over long periods of time. Instead, by focusing on observable internal social structures, we can assume that state leaders do not think in ways that are culturally different from our own but simply observe that foreign leaders may face objectively different internal social realities that affect their ability to generate military power. When those internal realities change, so may their strategic behavior. This perspective can be confirmed or denied by empirical study.

THINKING ABOUT SOCIETIES AND MILITARY POWER

To obtain better answers to the question of how social structures may affect strategy, we can formulate an explicit model of how social structures and military power may interact. On the basis of the above discussion and review of some of the historical record, the following model may be advanced:

(1) Social structures determine how individuals within societies treat one another. These structures will affect the behavior of individuals toward each other in the society as a whole and within the organizations that emerge from that society. Organizations have some freedom to isolate their members from society and to develop internal structures that govern their members, structures that may differ from those found in the society as a whole.

(2) Military organizations will be *less* likely to reflect the structures of the larger society the more they are small relative to society and isolated from their society physically by deployments or by war, temporally

[29]

by long service of soldiers and officers in the military away from society, and psychologically as the result of inculcated professional habits that create Weberian rational discipline which eradicates any loyalties and attitudes that do not contribute to effectiveness in war. Military organizations such as navies and air forces, the structures of which are strongly affected by the nature of their functions—for example, by technological functions—will also be less affected by the general ambient social structures. Military organizations will be *more* likely to reflect the structures of the larger society if the reverse is true: if the military is a mass, nonprofessional army with short terms of service, large relative to society, fighting wars on its own territory among its own people; if it fights wars with high casualty rates that force the military to bring many new soldiers in rapidly as replacements, while limiting the amount of time recruits spend in military training that can socialize the recruits to new norms before they are sent into battle; and if goals other than military effectiveness are allowed to govern the norms and structures of the military.

(3) The social structures of the political unit can affect its ability to generate military power, offensively and defensively, by dividing the society as a whole. Social structures that lead to divisiveness in the society as a whole, in particular, can reduce the military power that can be generated from a given quantity of material resources. The division of society into social structures that do not share common loyalties will be more relevant to the ability to generate military power to the extent that those social structures engage in militarily relevant activities, especially if the social structures are militarily strong relative to the central power that tries to govern the entire society.

(4) The social structures in the political unit also affect the amount of military power that can be generated by creating divisions internal to the military itself if divisive social structures are replicated within the military.

(5) The possibility of isolating military organizations from society creates an additional element that needs to be added to the picture of culture and strategy. The less a military organization reflects the structures of the society, either because it is recruited from subgroups who are not representative of the society as a whole or because the officers and soldiers are socialized by training and discipline to operate within structures that the society as a whole does not accept, the more the military will be perceived as an alien element in society, as a group that is not representative of society. This can lead to distrust of the military by the society or its leaders, which can reduce the military power available to the state.

This picture of the relationship between strategy and culture does not rest on assumptions about or characteristics of any one society or set of cultures in particular. This model can be applied to specific societies and military organizations to generate propositions about the military effectiveness of those societies and military organizations, propositions that can then be examined empirically. The cases initially selected for empirical study should be comparative. One should choose societies that display markedly different social structures to see if military effectiveness varies with change in social structure. If possible, cases should be selected in which the social structures in a given society and civil-military relations vary somewhat over time. Cases should also be developed in which two societies with similar social structures have armies that display different degrees of separation from their societies, to assess the interaction of military organizational structures and social structures and strategic behavior. I attempt such an effort in Chapters 3 through 6.

The case selection was driven by the criteria listed above and by the desire to compare this perspective against that of strategic culture and realism, although, as we noted above, strategic culture focuses more on the uses than on the amount of power observed in different societies. In Chapter 3 on ancient India, I compare the society and armies of ancient India with those of Greece, Macedonia, and the Roman republic. Ancient India was divided by caste structures that were not so rigid as they would later become, and its armies were not separated from society. But some contemporary European societies, including some Greek societies, were also badly fractured. It is worth remembering that each year, the leaders of Sparta formally declared war on the helots living in Spartan territory, helots who were linguistically distinct from Spartan citizens and who could not intermarry or interdine with Spartans. Some European armies were separated from their host societies by prolonged military campaigns abroad, most notably, the army of Philip and Alexander of Macedon. The society of Italy during the Roman republic is described as being relatively coherent and undivided; but this had changed by the late republican period, and the war known as the Social War had broken out in Italy. Throughout this period, the Roman legions remained separated from society by protracted campaigning. The literary culture of India at that time has been noted by Indian and Western commentators as being very different from Western literary culture. If the strategic culture argument is correct, we should see large differences in the uses of military power between India and the West. If realism is correct, we should see convergence in military practices and power. If my perspective is correct, we should see similarities when the independent variables are similar, differences where they vary. In the medieval period, Mughal

India is ruled by a Persian-reading, Turkish elite, as is Ottoman Turkey. Strategic culture would tend to predict similarities in behavior. Both Ottoman and Indian societies were badly divided. But the Ottoman army was radically separated from society, whereas the Mughal infantry armies were not. I argue that the amounts of military power that those two states could generate should tend to differ. In the British period, a comparison can be made with the Mughal period immediately preceding it. Indian society did not change overnight, though it did change gradually; but very quickly, the relationship of the army to Indian society changed. By focusing on the early British period, we can keep the nature of Indian society constant and vary the degree of military separation from society. Finally, by looking at India after independence and comparing it with British India, we can vary the strategic culture variable—since presumably Indian nationalist leaders and British imperial rulers had different mind-sets—as well as the political system variable. Sharp changes in military power behavior should be expected. But the structure of the Indian Army did not change after independence, though the nature of civil-military relations shifted because civilians changed from British imperialists to Indian nationalists. Indian society itself did not change in one generation and so can be held roughly constant. The variations in behavior in Indian history are large enough to allow us, at a minimum, to begin to assess the relative explanatory power of the three different approaches.

But before that can be done, we must first search to discover whether there is a commonly agreed-on, replicable definition of the dominant social structures of India. Happily for the investigator, there are many observations of Indian society made by a diverse set of observers: Buddhist, Muslim, Hindu, and Christian; Bengali, Kashmiri, Chinese, Arab, French, and British; Indian nationalist and British imperialist—virtually all observers agree on the existence of the dominant social structure of India: caste. Explicating that point is my task in Chapter 2.

[2]

India and Caste

India is different, but how and why? Is India different because it is Hindu, with a system of beliefs that affect the perceptions of those who hold them, or because of the system of castes and subcastes that structure social life—or for neither reason? In this chapter, three arguments will be considered. The first is that above all else, India is Hindu, and Hindus think differently from non-Hindus. This statement, of course, acknowledges the presence of non-Hindus in India and has been modified to take into account the existence in India today of an elite that is relatively less traditional in its religious outlook. Political scientists note at least two political cultures in India, one dominated by traditional Hindu beliefs and the other an elite political culture, more modern and national in outlook.[1] But accepting that qualification, is it important that India is Hindu? If it is important, that could form one basis for arguing that there is a Hindu strategic culture.

The second argument is that the caste system fragments Indian social life in ways that have consequences for Indian economic and political life. That argument—and the evidence associated with it—is central to the argument of this book. Like the argument about Hindu beliefs, it is a simplification. It acknowledges that, of course, there are religious, regional, and linguistic divisions in India, as well as caste divisions, but that caste divisions in India are ubiquitous and structure everyday life. Though other social divisions may be overlaid on the system of caste relations, they do not have the same profound impact on day-to-day life,

---

[1]Myron Weiner, "India: Two Political Cultures," in *Political Culture and Political Development*, ed. Lucian W. Pye and Sidney Verba (Princeton: Princeton University Press, 1965), pp. 199–244.

and they do not, by and large, weaken or cut across caste divisions. Special attention will be paid to universal religions such as Islam and Christianity to show that in the South Asian context, they have not weakened the caste divisions among fellow believers but have themselves been "caste-ified" and have acquired internal caste lines of division. The third argument is that caste is a social construct of the imperialist West, the purpose of which is to legitimize the oppression of India. The conclusion of this chapter, based on a wide-ranging consensus that includes scholars—Indian and Western—and Indian nationalists, is that there is ample evidence that the caste system does exist, though its rigidity has probably varied over time and space within Indian history, and that caste structures do have implications for Indian politics. The Hindu religion and its possible intellectual and psychological consequences may be important for the political perceptions of Indians, but the available evidence makes it difficult to reach that conclusion unambiguously.

The discussion of caste in this chapter is quite general. This is deliberate and should not be understood as reflecting the assumption that caste practices in India have always and everywhere been the same. They have not. Precisely because there have been variations, each subsequent historical chapter will attempt to come to grips with the variations in caste practices in its own time period. In this chapter I develop an understanding of caste as a social structure, because social structure is one of the two independent variables in this book and it is important to say what we are talking about in general, and leave it to subsequent chapters to assess variations in that independent variable.

HINDU RELIGION: PRIESTS AND POLITICS

The predominance of Hindu religious beliefs in India suggests one possible reason why Indian political behavior might differ from that of the West. Indian as well as Western analysts have tried to understand the "religious psychology and behavior of the the Hindus."[2] Are there tendencies in that psychology that might be important for the strategic behavior of Hindus? Max Weber found two connected elements of the Hindu religion that he believed distinguished it from those found in Japan and China. The first was the strong component that was not rationally communicable or transferable. That was the knowledge attained by intensive physical training, asceticism, and meditation. This esoteric knowledge gave individuals power over themselves, primarily, and had

[2]Nirad C. Chaudhuri, *Hinduism: A Religion to Live By* (London: Chatto and Windus, 1979), p. xi.

its counterparts in Western monastic traditions. But this knowledge also gave its owners power over others by creating, in Weber's terms, a "redemption aristocracy" composed of those who possessed a "charisma not accessible to all." The men with this knowledge became a class of "living saviors: the *gurus* and their equivalents ... magical dispensers of grace ... [with] often completely unrestricted power."[3] In China, Japan, and Tibet, Weber noted, this belief in living saviors was either restricted by means of force or sublimated and denatured into forms that reduced its secular power. In India, however, the belief not only in miracles, common to all religions, but in magical spells, effective in everyday life and dispensed by gurus, remained strong. As a result, Weber was pessimistic about the development of Western-style capitalism in India. Although the desire for riches was as strong in India as it was in the West, the means that were employed for seeking wealth in India were different from and antagonistic to the means for seeking wealth that arose out of the "inner-worldly asceticism" of Protestantism. In contrast to the Protestant ethic,

> This most highly anti-rational world of universal magic also affected everyday economics. There is no way from it to a rational, inner-worldly life conduct. There were spells ... against enemies, erotic or economic competition, spells designed to win legal cases, spiritual spells of the believer for forced fulfillment against the debtor, spells for the securing of wealth, for the success of undertakings. ... With such means the great mass of the aliterary and even the literary Asiatics sought to master everyday life.[4]

The twentieth-century Indian writer Nirad Chaudhuri assented to this observation. He wrote that for believing Hindus, unlike for Christians, religion was not "an alternative to the world, but primarily the means of supporting and improving their existence in it." Worldly prosperity was the object of prayer, and the essence of the relationship between Hindu gods and mortals was a "social contract between two acquisitive communities," such that the gods who did not respond to devotion by delivering worldly rewards had their temples shut down. To illustrate the results for the relationship between gurus and their followers, Chaudhuri related a conversation overheard between a Calcutta lawyer and a pundit: "The barrister suddenly looked up and appeared to be meditative. Then he remarked as if to himself: 'There is peace in religion.' The

---

[3] Max Weber, *The Religion of India: The Sociology of Hinduism and Buddhism,* trans. and ed. Hans H. Gerth and Don Martindale (Glencoe, Ill.: Free Press, 1958), pp. 331, 335.
[4] Ibid., pp. 336–337.

pundit, who had a blazing vermillion mark on his forehead, replied with a smile that seemed to be compassionate, though he was the younger man: 'Also power.' "[5]

One of the most eminent scholars of the Hindu religion rose to be president of the Republic of India, Sarvepalli Radhakrishnan. He also wrote of the interaction of Hindu belief and politics, emphasizing the role of the Hindu religion in providing solutions to worldly problems not by furnishing material gain but by offering religious means of finding peace in a violent world. He was very clear: "The world in which we live today, the world of incessant fear and violence, of wars and rumours of wars, where we are afraid of everything . . . is nothing but the ordinary life of ignorance hurried up." He was also clear that, for the Hindu, that fear cannot be removed by political action: "The fear which is an expression of man's rationality cannot be removed by any changes in his circumstances," and "True freedom from fear can be reached only by *inana* or wisdom, the truth that casteth out fear." He was equally frank about the consequences for politics of the belief that the proper response to secular violence is a search for spiritual knowledge. According to Radhakrishnan, for four thousand years, India has adored gurus, not soldiers and statesmen, or even scientists, poets, or philosophers. As a result, "India has failed to give political expression to its ideals. The importance of wealth and power to give expression to the spirit, though theoretically recognized, was not practically realized. India has suffered for this negligence."[6] Other scholars have noted the caste element of Hindu religion is such as to emphasize systematically the fears of pollution that are as strong as the fears of death and to emphasize the unique role of religion and Brahmin priests in managing that fear.[7] This reinforces the power of priests and the irrelevance of the state as the source of psychological escape from fear.

The problem with these observations is not that they are clearly false but that they do not make enough of an effort to compare the religious content of the Hindu religion with that of other religions; they also make no effort to compare the social consequences of the Hindu religion with

[5] Chaudhuri, *Hinduism*, pp. 9–10, 14–15, 295.

[6] Sarvepalli Radhakrishnan, "The Supreme Spiritual Ideal: The Hindu View," in Sarvepalli Radhakrishnan, *Eastern Religions and Western Thought* (Delhi: Oxford University Press, 1974), pp. 35, 44, 54–55.

[7] David Shulman, "The Enemy Within: Idealism and Dissent in South Indian Hinduism," in *Orthodoxy, Heterodoxy, and Dissent in India*, ed. S. N. Eisenstadt, Reuven Kahane, and David Shulman (New York: Mouton, 1984), pp. 17–18: "The Hindu order incorporates a dimension of necessary but threatening *disorder*, and one wonders if the Indian preoccupation with boundaries does not, in fact, derive from this basic sense of chaos constantly assailing the fragile defenses erected against it."

the social consequences of religion elsewhere. It is hardly difficult to find examples from the political history of medieval Europe in which Christianity, through the intercession of priests, offered a nonrational means both for managing the material world and for escaping the fear of violent death. Unlike India, it might be argued, the West produced political theorists, beginning with Machiavelli and Hobbes, who argued that the secular power of priests must be broken and that by creating a strong king with a monopoly of power, rational men could find by rational means a worldly solution to the problem of the constant war of all. This would provide answer, if not to death itself, to the fear of violent death. But that is different from saying that India is different because it is Hindu and the West is not. It is an argument that the Indian state did not establish a monopoly on the legitimate use of force and the Western states did. If that is the case, to understand the differences between India and the West, would it not be better to look at the extent to which the state had a monopoly on power and political legitimacy at any given moment in Indian history rather than to assert the general influence of Hindu religious beliefs in all times?

If their importance was difficult to distinguish, might it be the case that Hindu religious beliefs were expressed in or affected Indian political philosophy? The system of political beliefs expressed in the great literary works of India might shed some light on the cultural context from which Hindu strategic thought has and will emerge. This may be true, but scholars of Indian politics have warned that Westerners should not apply the history of Western political theory and practice to India. Westerners are accustomed to the idea that political philosophers can be the autonomous source of political ideas that have gone on to shape Western political and social practice, at a minimum, from Hobbes and Locke to Marx. This appears not to have been the historical experience of India. In Myron Weiner's view, "The absence of analytical continuity among ancient [Indian] political theorists, the relatively small role of political theory in the dense fabric of Hindu philosophical and religious writings, the historical break in this literature caused by the Muslim invasions, the introduction of European political ideas and institutions in the nineteenth century . . . all suggest the irrelevance of classical Hindu thought." He suggested, however, that even if classical Hindu political philosophy did not have an autonomous role in Indian political life, it should still be read seriously as a means of understanding contemporary Indian politics, because both philosophy and contemporary politics were shaped by and reflected deeper Hindu beliefs. Weiner reached the following conclusion about classical Indian political ideas:

Having been so deeply rooted in the realities of India's hierarchical social structure and the country's system of religious belief—both of which continue to exist—it would be surprising if these ideas were totally at variance with contemporary political behavior. . . . [Ideas and behavior both] derived from deeper fundamental assumptions concerning the nature of man—assumptions that mark one culture from another, such that contemporary Indians are more akin to their ancestors than they are to other contemporaries.[8]

But, again, if it is the case that Indian political-religious thought is "so deeply rooted in the realities of India's hierarchical social structure," as it may well be, would it not be better to look directly at Indian social structures as they existed at various points in time in order to understand their political consequences?

THE HINDU EXTENDED FAMILY AND ITS CONSEQUENCES

It has also been suggested that Indians think differently from Westerners because they are Hindu, but not because of the content of their religious beliefs. Comparative, cross-cultural studies of the impact of the Hindu religion on the thought and behavior of Hindu Indians have been done by Freudian and Eriksonian psychologists. They have looked at the impact not of Hindu religious beliefs as such but of the Hindu version of the extended family. What is distinct about Hindus, according to this argument, is the Hindu form of the extended family and the impact of the child-rearing practices of the Hindu extended family on the psychology of the children and adults who emerge from those families. This is an intriguing argument, but one that is very hard to wrestle with theoretically or empirically. It is extremely difficult to utilize Freudian and Eriksonian psychoanalytic concepts and analyses to help explain patterns of Indian politics. Freudian analysts typically deal with small numbers of people who have chosen to go to doctors because they thought themselves to be sick. Generalizing from this small number of self-selected individuals to the politics of a nation must be regarded as a risky business. Eriksonian analyses that focus on stages of individual personality development characteristic of various societies have the potential for providing generalizations about politics that are more broadly based, but even here, much of the evidence found in analyses performed

[8]Myron Weiner, "Ancient Indian Political Theory and Contemporary Indian Politics," in Eisenstadt, Kahane, and Shulman, *Orthodoxy, Heterodoxy, and Dissent in India*, p. 113.

[38]

by the students of Erikson is personal, anecdotal, or the result of the interpretation of popular myths and culture.

Nonetheless, a reader working her or his way through the psychoanalytic literature discussing the "Hindu personality" is struck by the broad agreement in that literature, expressed by Hindus and Westerners alike, about the sources of and consequences of that personality and the fundamental differences between a healthy Hindu psyche and a healthy Western psyche. The basic sources of the Hindu personality identified by many authors include:

- the extreme indulgence of male children until the age of eight, when the *upanayana*, or thread-cutting ceremony, is performed;
- the subsequent radical break with the mother, with whom the boy child has been extremely close;
- the lack of close identification of sons with the father in the Hindu extended family because of the father's obligation to be impartial to all children of the family; and finally,
- the life in the extended family that obliges the child to submerge his personal identity in the identity of the family.[9]

---

[9]See, for example, Philip Spratt, *Hindu Culture and Personality: A Psycho-analytic Study* (Bombay: P. C. Manaktala and Sons, 1966), pp. v, 1, 9, based on thirty-five years of psychoanalytic practice with Indian patients, regarding indulgence of Indian children; Sudhir Kakar, *The Inner World: A Psycho-analytic Study of Childhood and Society in India* (Delhi: Oxford University Press, 1978), pp. 12, 104–105, 114, 134–135, regarding the indulgence of boys, the continued prevalence of the extended family in modern Calcutta (though not in Bombay); Erik Erikson "Report to Vikram: Further Perspectives on the Life Cycle," and B. K. Ramanujam, "Toward Maturity: Problems of Identity Seen in the Indian Clinical Setting," in *Identity and Adulthood*, ed. Sudhir Kakar (Delhi: Oxford University Press, 1979), regarding the absence of an adolescent stage of development for Indian children, pp. 25, 37–55; Ashis Nandy, "Woman versus Womanliness," in Ashis Nandy, *At the Edge of Psychology: Essays in Politics and Culture* (Delhi: Oxford University Press, 1980), p. 36, on the sharp shift from intimacy with to ritual abhorrence toward women that a Hindu boy undergoes during childhood; Lucian W. Pye, *Asian Power and Politics: The Cultural Dimensions of Authority* (Cambridge: Harvard University Press, 1985), pp. 148–150, regarding the differences between the Hindu extended family, in which the mother is dominant, and other Asian extended families in which the father is central, the indulgence and then repression of boy children, and the break with women that boy children experience; Alan Roland, *In Search of Self in India and Japan: Toward a Cross-Cultural Psychology* (Princeton: Princeton University Press, 1988), pp. xix, 7–12, on the difference between the Western individualized self and the Indian familial self based on eighteen Indian patients and review of case records in the Indian National Institute for Mental Health and Neuro Science in Bangalore. For a discussion of the narcissistic and passive aspects of the Hindu personality based on a study of Hindu myth and literary sources, see Dhirendra Narain, *Hindu Character (A Few Glimpses), University of Bombay Publications Sociology Series no. 8* (Bombay: Bombay University Press, 1957).

The consequences of the Hindu pattern of child development, it is commonly argued, are egos and superegos that tend to be weaker than their Western counterparts, the replacement of the functions of the superego by an all-encompassing set of caste rules of behavior, and a tendency for Indians to search in their professional lives for the same kind of highly personalized relations of hierarchical dependency and protection that they experienced in their families. For example, one psychoanalyst who has treated both American and Hindu patients argues:

> To work psychoanalytically with . . . [an Indian patient's] depression is to understand that in traditional as well as contemporary Indian work settings it is well nigh impossible for a highly intelligent Indian man or woman to work creatively without being promoted and protected by a benefactor. . . . Congruent with this hierarchical framework is an inner psychological structure of the familial self, whereby Indian men or women profoundly need the active support, respect, and involvement of senior authority figures. . . . I concluded that the valid psychoanalytical goal . . . was not for him to function independently, in the way one would tend with most American patients, that is, he should *not* have to learn to be on his own with an unappreciative director. . . . [10]

An Indian academic, Sudir Kakar, summarized what he believed to be the social implications in India of a common personality type in which a strong sense of self was absent, one that did not experience strong personal feelings of guilt when violating nonfamilial, impersonal, timeless norms:

> Among the vast majority of tradition-minded countrymen dishonesty, nepotism, and corruption as they are understood in the West are merely abstract concepts. These negative constructions are irrelevant to Indian psycho-social experience, which, from childhood on, nurtures one standard of responsible adult action, and one only, namely, an individual's life long obligation to his kith and kin. Allegiance to impersonal institutions and abstract moral concepts is without precedence in individual developmental experience. . . . Guilt and its attendant inner anxiety are aroused only when individual actions go against the primacy of [extended family] relationships, not when foreign ethical standards of justice and efficiency are breached.[11]

---

[10] Roland, *In Search of Self*, pp. 36–37.

[11] Kakar, *Inner World*, pp. 125–126. See also Spratt, *Hindu Culture and Personality*, pp. 6, 8–9; Pye, *Asian Power and Politics*, pp. 149, 153.

Although rejecting the applicability of Freudian or Eriksonian modes of analysis to Hindu personalities, T. G. Vaidyanathan came to many of the same conclusions about the implications of Hindu ideas concerning authority and identity as the psychoanalysts he criticized. In particular, he saw the model of the highly personalized, loving relation of the guru and his devotees as the key to Indian social and political history. The origin of this pattern of authority and identity has its roots in the extended family, which Vaidyanathan argued still "occupies center stage in India" despite the superficial changes in Indian family arrangements and living habits. The extended family leads to a condition in which "an Indian thinks of himself as being a father, a son, a nephew, a pupil, and these are the only 'identities' he ever has." In Indian psychology, he claims, "there is no intrinsic self." This leads to ideas of proper and improper behavior very different from Western norms. Vaidyanathan claims, for example, that while an Indian audience watching Shakespeare's *King Lear* would empathize with the theme of ungrateful children, "even there, Cordelia, with her unbending notions of honesty and truthfulness would be found repugnant and, worse, disobedient by the millions of Indians now watching the Ramayana in television dosages every Sunday morning."[12]

In general, outside the norms of the extended family and caste regulations, the weakness of the ego, it is argued, leads Hindus to despair about the utility of individual actions. The weakness of the superego tends Hindus toward greater infringement of norms. The importance of family loyalties and personal relations and the relative unimportance of abstract ideas and norms leads to a nonideological politics based on patronage, but even those relations are not likely to be enduring when they are not based on family.[13]

As with the assertions concerning the impact of Hindu religious beliefs, the validity of these cannot be seriously tested without a much broader base of comparative social psychological data. At least one study of Indian strategic thought, or rather the absence of such thought, blamed it on the passivity of the Hindu personality.[14] This judgment may or may not be correct. By the standards of social science, it is simply impossible to resolve this question at this point.

[12] T. G. Vaidyanathan, "Authority and Identity in India," *Daedalus* 118, no. 4 (Fall 1989): 148, 151, 153, 155.

[13] Kakar, *Inner World*, pp. 134–136; Spratt, *Hindu Culture and Personality*, pp. 49, 52; Pye, *Asian Power and Politics*, p. 152. For a judgment concerning the consequences of this pattern of child development for Indian politics, see Richard Sisson, *Politics and Culture in India* (Ann Arbor: Center for Political Studies Institute for Social Research, University of Michigan, 1988), pp. 8–10.

[14] George Tanham, "Indian Strategic Culture," *Washington Quarterly* 15, no. 1 (Winter 1992): 129–142.

In contrast with the fascinating but difficult-to-test assertions about the Hindu religion, the social structures of India embodied in the caste system satisfy the criterion of being objective, in the sense of being perceived in the same way by foreign and indigenous observers. This issue is not trivial, for the entire concept of the existence of objective, indigenous cultures has come into question and is actively debated by, among others, the academic anthropological community in the United States. One school has argued that culture, as opposed to observed behavior, cannot be studied directly. Culture, as a concept, was an intellectual construct and, to the extent that it differed from behavior, did not necessarily reflect social realities but was a tool for elites to justify their domination of a society. Anthropologists who continue to use the concept of culture have argued in reply that the exclusive focus on behavior reflected "an extreme positivism, which at times was and is a 'false' methodological rigor, [which] was only the expression of a scientism that soon dominated most of sociology, linguistics, and anthropology." The proponents of the study of culture argued that it was no more an intellectual construct than any of the other concepts used by social scientists, such as power or politics, and played a useful role in analyzing complex but coherent sets of social activities.[15]

The problem of "natural" categories versus artificially imposed constructs has also come up in the natural sciences. Even the existence of animal species that are "natural" has been called into question, and the claim has been made that species have no existence independent of humanly created concepts. Here, the commonsense criterion has been established that if local observers and outside biologists independently observe a number of animals in their natural setting and independently place them into the same categories, there is reason to believe that the categories so established have some independent existence.[16]

The caste system of South Asia constitutes a set of social structures that appears to meet an analogous criterion, despite academic objections that caste is an artificial category invented by Europeans to simplify and

[15] For a summary of the critiques and defenses of the anthropological uses of the concept of culture, see Aram A. Yengoyan, "Theory in Anthropology: On the Demise of the Concept of Culture," *Comparative Studies in Society and History* 28 (April 1986): 368–374; Kent V. Flannery, "The Golden Marshalltown: A Parable for the Archeology of the 1980s," *American Anthropologist* 84 (June 1982): 265–278; R. A. Foley, "How Useful Is the Culture Concept in Early Hominid Studies?" in *The Origins of Human Behavior*, ed. R. A. Foley (London: Unwin Hyman, 1991), pp. 25–37.
[16] E. O. Wilson, *The Diversity of Life* (Cambridge: Harvard University Press, Belknap Press, 1992), pp. 42–43.

characterize Indian social life for the purpose of establishing European cultural and political supremacy.[17] It is possible, as will be shown, to use an overly simple understanding of caste and to paint a picture of the unchanging role of caste in Indian society that is historically inaccurate. It is equally possible for foreigners who wish to dominate another society to construct a false image of India to justify their own dominance. But unless one adopts the position that all intellectual constructs are suspect (in which case all intellectual discourse should halt), it is reasonable to adapt to social science the criterion of natural science. If there are multiple, independent, reinforcing observations and characterizations of the same social structures, which furthermore are congruent with the observations and characterizations made by indigenous observers who are in the forefront of the political opposition to foreign domination, those observations may be taken as representations of objective social structures. The caste system of India satisfies this criterion. We shall observe that Chinese and Arab travelers to India in the premodern and modern periods, modern European observers, and Indian nationalist leaders of the nineteenth and twentieth centuries have all made the same set of observations with regard to the principal characteristics of the Indian social system.

First, what is caste? One of many acceptable summary definitions is provided by Charles Drekmeier: "When tradition and law support the rigid and continuing separation of social classes we may speak of a caste society. . . . A society possesses a caste system if it is divided into many specialized groups which are graded in status and mutually opposed, and which do not tolerate mixture of blood or change in vocation." Eating together and intermarrying exclusively within a group tend to go together, though there are important exceptions. "Caste provides one of the rare instances of several groups living in close proximity with one another and yet having little direct physical contact."[18] It thus differs from tribes, members of which tend to marry outside the tribe; from social classes, which may or may not interact socially or professionally with other classes; and from guilds, which, again, may or may not marry and eat outside their group. The caste system represents one form of

---

[17]Ronald Inden, *Imagining India* (Cambridge, Mass.: Basil Blackwell, 1990), pp. 31–32, 69: Inden argued that the English used the concepts of Indian "culture" or civilization to deny "that India on her own could ever be the expression of the essence of the West, practical reason, . . . [and to make] the British Empire appear the sole expression of it in Europe." Schlegel and Mill argued, according to Inden, that "India was perennially open to conquest yet was also resistant to total conquest. . . . The reason for this was that India was politically disunited. . . . Mill held that caste led to despotism."

[18]Charles Drekmeier, *Kingship and Community in Early India* (Stanford: Stanford University Press, 1962), p. 72.

social hierarchy. All societies have some form of social hierarchy and limits on social mobility, but that does not mean all societies have castes. Drekmeier notes, "Although stratification is universal and essential to organized social activity, societies may vary greatly in degree of social mobility, in cohesiveness among members of particular groups, in value assigned to different gradations, and so forth."[19]

Social stratification marked by marriage within one group, exclusiveness with regard to members outside the group, and hereditary occupations and social status were not unknown to Europe, as Alexis de Tocqueville noted,[20] and can be weakened or strengthened by the actions of government or by social upheavals such as war or radical changes in population. Therefore, it is important to avoid several errors. First, all societies must not be equated simply because they have social stratification and divisions into subgroups, but second, all periods in Indian history and all regions of India must not be equated and assumed to have the same degree of social stratification and caste rigidity. What matters is the observed strength or weakness of the caste system at a particular time and place, to the degree that this can be known, and the way the government chooses to interact with the caste system: attacking, defending, reinforcing or trying to transcend it.

Attempts have been made to assess the strength of caste divisions at different times and in different regions in India. The major variations in the caste system over time have often been associated with major military invasions and their aftermath. The caste system has been judged to have been in place by the time the Aryan invaders stabilized their rule over the Gangetic plain sometime around 500 B.C., becoming more rigid thereafter, and stabilizing around the tenth century A.D. Fluidity of caste statuses was probably restored somewhat by the frequent wars associated with the early Mughal invasion and consolidation of Mughal rule. Frequent wars made it possible for low-ranking castes to provide soldiers to the emperor and so to upgrade their status. The British conquest paradoxically may have made the caste system more rigid by introducing literacy, newspapers, and reliable transportation,

[19] Ibid., p. 69.

[20] Alexis de Tocqueville argued that feudal France originally had social orders and not a caste system, but "by the Middle Ages it had developed into a caste, by which I mean that membership in [the orders] . . . was essentially a matter of birth and had become hereditary," in contrast to England, where "nobility and commoners joined forces in business enterprises, entered the same professions, and—what is still more significant— intermarried. . . . For when we seek to discover whether the caste system . . . has been definitely eradicated in any country, the acid test is that country's marriage customs. Even in modern France, after sixty years of democracy, we often find the old prejudices surviving." Tocqueville, *The Old Regime and the French Revolution,* trans. Stuart Gilbert (Garden City, N.Y.: Anchor, 1955), pp. 81–96.

all of which facilitated communication and organization among the members of a geographically dispersed caste. The British Empire may also have strengthened caste values by emphasizing the distinctions between martial and nonmartial races. At the same time, the British, like the early Mughals, may have increased social mobility by offering military occupations to some groups.[21] To the extent possible, therefore, it is necessary to assess the strength and weakness of the caste system in given cases. The extent to which this assessment is possible will vary case by case.

One oversimplification concerning caste is to assert that caste relations were and are everywhere and always the same. Another error is one largely of terminology. The broad division of castes in India is not the same as local subcaste structures. Many people know of the broad, hierarchical divisions in India related to caste: Brahmins, Kshatriyas, Vaisyas, and Shudras. But the social hierarchy created by these four major orders, or *varna* (literally, colors), of Indian society cannot be simply transposed onto India's thousands of locally based subcastes or *jatis*, the local endogamous groups with a traditional occupation. Members of a jati in a given locality may identify themselves with the same major varna, but will still be stratified hierarchically relative to each other, will dispute which jati is of higher status, and may or may not intermarry or interdine with other jati of the same varna.[22] This is of consequence because it can affect the level of social cohesion present in a given time and place, since, for example, it cannot be assumed that all jatis that identify themselves as Kshatriya or of the ruler/warrior varna will be united by their common membership in that varna.

In addition, the strength or weakness of the caste system does not necessarily correlate to the strength or weakness of Hindu and non-Hindu religions in South Asia, although the presence of non-Hindu religions may affect the strength of the caste system. This is of importance for comparative purposes. There is no reason to assume, for example, that comparisons between Hindu India and Muslim Pakistan will necessarily reveal the differences between two societies: one in which the caste system is strong and one in which it is weak, respectively. Religions

[21] David G. Mandelbaum, *Society in India*, vol. 1, *Continuity and Change* (Bombay: Popular Prakashan, 1991), p. 7. Drekmeier, *Community in Early India*, pp. 17; M. N. Srinivas, "Caste in Modern India," in M. N. Srinivas, *Caste in Modern India* (Bombay: Asia Publishing House, 1962), pp. 15–16; M. N. Srinivas, "The Caste System and Its Future," in M. N. Srinivas, *On Living in a Revolution* (Delhi: Oxford University Press, 1992), p. 67, on the way the British caste census heightened caste consciousness; Dirk H. A. Kolff, *Naukar, Rajput, and Sepoy: The Ethnohistory of the Military Labour Market in Hindustan, 1450–1850* (Cambridge: Cambridge University Press, 1990), p. 58.
[22] Srinivas, "Varna and Caste," in *Caste in Modern India*, pp. 63–69.

that originated outside South Asia were brought there by foreign rulers and traders. Christianity and Islam did, to varying degrees, take root in what is now India, Pakistan, and Bangladesh. But, notes David G. Mandelbaum, "the foreign merchants and rulers were too few or too aloof to induct converts into a new way of life as well as into a new mode of worship.... Converts lacked any new social base to go with their new scripture and had little alternative but to continue in the pervasive caste system. They became jati-fied ... and reentered the typical struggle for social mobility." The Zoroastrian Parsis were the exception to the rule of jatification, and "their rejection of jati division may help explain why they later took so successfully to modern social models." Islam and Christianity have had important influence in India, but village Muslims and Christians carry on their social relations in ways that are generally similar to those followed by their neighbors of other religions. "Muslims and Christians participate in their local social orders as jati groups." South Asian Muslims resent the use of the word "caste" when applied to their social organizations, but "though their doctrine and their popular theory assert that all Muslims are equal, the actual social practices of Muslim villagers usually parallel those of their Hindu neighbors." Indian Muslims class themselves "into endogamous hereditary groups which are ranked in relation to each other. Hereditary occupations are usually attributed to each group." Muslim untouchables exist and are so treated by Hindus as well. However, all Muslims of a village may interdine and will attend the same mosque, and their views on permanent pollution are vague. Muslims are monotheistic but will often use Hindu shrines, and "riots between Muslim factions have long been reported," from 1838 onward. The partition of India had social consequences, "yet studies of Pakistani villages since independence show a considerable continuity in the traditional social groupings." A 1960 study of Punjabi and Gujarati Muslim villages described a society in which " 'a child learns the caste it belongs to from the time it begins to speak and tells it when he gives his personal name. Very early, the child also learns that it can marry only within its own caste.' " Caste practices with regard to hereditary occupations are acknowledged by Muslim villagers to be borrowed from Hindus but are strongly observed anyway. Striking social similarities among Hindu, Muslim, and Sikh Jats have been observed. The first question a Muslim Jat asked a visitor, for example, was reported to be what his caste was, to determine whether to give him a cot or make him sit on floor and what food to give him. Christian Jesuits and missionaries often focused their efforts on either the Brahmins, in the hope that they would lead the rest of Indian society to Christianity, or on the untouchables, because of their misery. The Brahmins rejected Christianity, by and large, as a result of which Christianity became associated with low-status groups in society.[23]

In short, religious differences were translated into the jati system in South Asia, and levels of social trust and cohesion were not necessarily affected by conversions to Islam or Christianity. Islam added more divisions to Indian society, rather than weakening those divisions, and conflicts among jatis were not necessarily defined by or confined to religious differences.

Finally, neither the forms of economic organization that lead to economic interdependence between castes and jatis nor levels of mass political participation necessarily bring about a weakening or strengthening of relations that cross the boundaries of jati or caste. The traditional forms of agriculture and industrialization do not appear, by themselves, to be necessary for or contrary to the persistence of caste divisions. We cannot assume, therefore, that as India became more industrialized and democratic that it necessarily shifted toward or away from caste-based social norms and structures. Modern economies, it might be assumed, require high degrees of interdependence across occupational groups. This might break down the barriers between them. But traditional forms of agriculture in India also required high levels of interdependence among jatis for the purpose of growing and getting in the harvest. Landowners belonging to one jati, members of service-providing jatis, and artisan jatis: all had and still have to work together toward those agricultural goals, and those interjati relations are called *jajmani* relations. But barriers among jatis still existed, and disputes among jati could and did still arise. When they did, they were handled within the framework of caste. "If the dominant landowners of a village become convinced that one of their service or artisan groups is derelict in its obligations or threatens the power and status of the landowners, the patron families are likely to bring collective pressure on them by withholding payment, by beating their men, or through any number of other means of harassment. . . . Such clashes are apt to spread from one village to others in the locality where jati fellows of the opposed groups live."[24] On the other hand, the breakdown of the network of agrarian interdependence may or may not have led to a weakening of divisions among jatis and castes. M. N. Srinivas has noted that as village life began to break down over the last one hundred years, "caste-sections living in the same village or cluster of villages . . . started competing with each other for access to ed-

---

[23] David G. Mandelbaum, *Society in India*, vol. 2, *Change and Continuity* (Bombay: Popular Prakashan, 1991), pp. 545–549, 551–552, 566.
[24] Mandelbaum, *Society in India*, 1: 173.

ucation, employment, medical facilities, and higher status. As a result, the conflict became more vicious and divisive." As rural labor mobility increased, landlords brought in hired agricultural labor that was cheaper than provided by the local jati, which led to increased hostility among lower-caste agricultural workers and toward higher-caste landlords.[25]

CASTE AND POLITICS IN INDIA

How might the norms and structures associated with the caste system affect the political and social cohesion of Indian society? Here we must work carefully. It is precisely the claim that the Indian caste system led to low levels of political cohesion that has drawn the most criticism as providing, consciously or not, the intellectual justification for European imperialism. Hence, it is necessary to proceed in two stages. First, the most widely respected analyses of the political consequences of the caste system will be reviewed. Then, those analyses will be contrasted with the views of non-European, Indian nationalist leaders, and Indian and non-Indian empirical social scientists.

Two of the most influential and controversial Western works concerning the norms of the caste system and their consequences for Indian political life are Max Weber's *The Religion of India* and Louis Dumont's *Homo Hierarchicus*. Weber's work is best known for its arguments concerning caste practices and their impact on the Indian economy. Following Karl Marx, he argued that those effects "were essentially negative" but acknowledged that his conclusion "must rather be inferred than inductively assessed"—that is, directly obtained by observation—and his conclusion followed from the *assumption* that "a ritual law in which every change of occupation, every change in work technique, may result in ritual degradation is certainly not capable of giving birth to economic and technical revolutions from within itself." What Weber judged to be the antirationalism of the Hindu religion combined with the secular political power of the priesthood to make rational economic activity more difficult in India than in the West. Weber acknowledged, however, that at the time of his writing there were "but scanty materials concerning the participation by castes in modern capitalist business—at least only a few detailed descriptions are available to the outside student."[26] Weber also reached some conclusions about the impact of Indian society on the Indian political system that were also inferred from the "spirit" of the caste system. The division of society into castes and subcastes supported

[25]Srinivas, *Living in a Revolution*, pp. 3, 21–22.
[26]Weber, *Religion of India*, pp. 112, 114, 331–336.

by religious belief, he argued, was far different from any of the guild or class distinctions of European society because Christian Europe was united by a religious and social fraternity that had consequences for other social structures and political life, which led to the notion of a common civic life that included members of all social orders as citizens. "[W]ithout this commensalism—in Christian terms, without the Lord's Supper—no oathbound fraternity and no medieval urban citizenry would have been possible," according to Weber. In contrast, "India's caste order formed an obstacle to this, which was insurmountable, at least by its own forces. . . . [A] profound estrangement usually exists between the castes, and often deadly jealousy and hostility as well, precisely because the castes are completely oriented towards social rank. This orientation stands in contrast to the occupational associations of the Occident." Weber also notes: "The consequences of this difference have been of considerable political importance. . . . For the castes excluded every solidarity and every politically powerful fraternization of the citizenry and the trades."[27]

As he set it forth, Weber's thesis concerning the impact of the structures associated with the caste system is plausible but empirically unproved. If true, it would suggest that, to the extent that it was socially dominant, the caste system would lead to low levels of cohesion in Indian society as a whole. These would create general social vulnerabilities which might be exploited by foreign powers—ones that Indian political-military leaders would somehow have to manage—and which would affect Indian military effectiveness. Because Weber was concerned with political and economic activities that involved society as a whole, his analysis is not relevant to the problems of the Indian military itself, for that military might or might not reflect general Indian social norms and structures.

Louis Dumont essentially extended and developed Weber's analysis of the spirit of the caste system, elevating it to an "ideology" of caste which emphasized a hierarchy of group status and which had its roots in norms concerning ritual purity and impurity.[28] Like Weber, he saw the caste system as being hostile to modern forms of economic activity, which Dumont, unlike Weber, viewed as due to the lack of any element of the caste system that protected the merchant and his property from seizure by higher castes. When the British imposed Western property law and institutions to enforce it, India developed a sphere of indepen-

---

[27] Ibid., p. 38.
[28] Louis Dumont, *Homo Hierarchicus: The Caste System and Its Implications*, trans. Marks Sainsbury, Louis Dumont, and Basia Gulati (Chicago: University of Chicago Press, 1980), pp. 37, 39, 43–45.

dent economic activity.[29] The consequences for politics as understood by Dumont were, however, similar to those inferred by Weber. Indian nationalists, Dumont argued, had created a myth of village democracy in traditional India as a political tool for use against the British claim to rule a people incapable of democracy. The reality, argued Dumont, drawing on intensive studies by Indian authors, was that the village councils, the *panchiyats*, were organs of the locally dominant castes, used to enforce their privileges, collect their taxes, but, most important, uphold the norms of the caste system itself—to prevent and punish transgressions that brought impurity. The European notion of government as an organ to protect individuals and prevent violations of "public order, like murder or theft, that did not jeopardize the caste's status" was subordinate to "infringement of the rules about food." To the extent that politics did not support or threaten the ideology and practice of caste, it was tolerated but also not seen as inherently legitimate. It was simply to be obeyed as the right of the stronger.[30]

This review of Weber and Dumont suggests why there has been some suspicion concerning their possible bias. Key conclusions rest on untested deductions from interpretations of the "spirit" of the caste system. Dumont's work, like Weber's, is primarily an interpretation of texts rather than an empirical work of research, though Dumont also did engage in serious research. Their conclusions are plausible and widespread among some Indian scholars, but they are also rejected by others. Despite their stature, they might represent what critical authors had in mind when they referred to undifferentiated Western generalizations about Indian culture that tended, even if they were not so intended, to justify Western assertions of cultural and political superiority. Therefore, before using their ideas to construct hypotheses about the relation of Indian culture to Indian strategy, it is important to go back and see whether their observations were driven by the dynamics of cultural imperialism or tend to be confirmed by non-European observers, by Indian nationalist leaders, and by modern empirical social science. Did travelers who were not influenced by European political and cultural imperialist tendencies observe the caste system in ways that were congruent with the observations of Weber and Dumont? Did the Indians who were in the forefront of the struggle against British domination of India confirm or deny the inferences about Indian politics that these European authors make from their study of caste? Does empirical evidence support the propo-

[29] Ibid., pp. 165–166.
[30] Ibid., pp. 170–174, 179–180, 196. The Indian scholars on village caste government are R. Sharma, *Aspects of Political Ideas and Institutions in Ancient India* (Delhi, 1959), pp. 1–13; P. V. Kane, *History of Dharmasastra*, 5 vols. (Poona: Bhandarkar Oriental Research Institute, 1930–1962).

sitions that the stronger the caste system, the less cohesive and effective the society and government?

On the first count, from the seventh century A.D. we have the account of the Buddhist monk Hiuen-Tsiang (also referred to as Yuan Chwang), who traveled in Ferghana and Tashkent in Central Asia, Kashmir, Rajapur, and elsewhere in India for sixteen years. His reports noted that "butchers, fishermen, public performers, executioners and scavengers have their habitations marked by a distinguishing sign. They are forced to live outside the city and they sneak along the left when going about in the hamlets." He described the ritual purity of eating, washing of the inhabitants, and noted that "there are four orders of hereditary clan distinctions," the Brahmin, Kshatriya, Vaisyas, and Shudras. "The four castes form classes of various degrees of ceremonial purity. The members of a caste marry within the caste, the great and obscure keeping apart. . . . There are also mixed castes; numerous clans formed by groups of people according to their kinds, and these cannot be described."[31] In the tenth century A.D., the scholar Alberuni, who was traveling with Islamic armies in India, noted the same orders of society, which he indicated were referred to as varna, or colors; the same patterns of endogamy within groups and prohibitions on exogamy; and concerns with ritual purity.[32]

The first Indian nationalist leaders in the late nineteenth century came, for a variety of reasons, from Bengal, which was then experiencing an indigenous intellectual explosion. Caution, however, must be used in extrapolating from this Bengali intellectual output to Indian nationalist thought as a whole. The explicitly political Bengali writers were clearly influenced by the British liberal and utilitarian writers such as Mill, Bentham, and Hume. Because they were writing largely in their vernacular or in English, their work was not accessible to the vast majority of Indians. Perhaps partly for that reason, the Bengali version of Indian nationalism was something of a political dead end, with no clear connection either to Gandhian movement or the Congress Party. Still, it produced Rammohun Roy, the man responsible for both the campaign against widow burning and a modernized version of Hinduism as part of his effort to regenerate Indian political life; Bankimchandra Chatterjee, the author of the novel *Anandamath*, which contains the poem that has been incorporated into the Indian nationalist anthem, *Bande Mataram*; and the Nobel prize–winning poet and novelist Sir Rabindranath Tagore. Their

[31] Thomas Watters, *On Yuan Chwang's Travels in India, 629–645 A.D.* (London: Royal Asiatic Society, 1904), pp. 147, 152, 168. See also Samuel Beal, *Hwui Li, The Life of Hiuen-Tsiang* (London: Kegan Paul, Trench, Truban, 1911).

[32] Alberuni [or al-Biruni], *Alberuni's India*, trans. Edward C. Sachau, ed. Ainslee T. Embree (New York: W. W. Norton, 1971), pp. 100–101.

[51]

views on Indian social and political life may be taken as the analysis of acute, indigenous observers who, while influenced by non-Indian intellectual forces, were vigorous in the search for Indian political autonomy. Their commentaries on Indian political life are striking because they tended to focus on and emphasize the same political tendencies that were identified by Weber and Dumont.

For example, Rammohun Roy, in an essay he prepared to promote the introduction of Indian judges into the British system of justice in India, began by noting that the political division of India into many principalities under Mughal rule, plus the "successive introduction of castes and sects, destroy[ed] every texture of social and political unity" of India. As a result, the country was vulnerable to foreign conquest. The political divisions introduced by the Mughals, in his view, were clearly not the product of caste ideology but did reinforce the political tendencies of the caste system. The legacy of the social and political history of India was a society in which the judicial system could not expect men and women testifying in court to be loyal to their oaths to tell the truth. In Rammohun Roy's words, "The great prevalence of perjury ... has grown so ... that the facts sworn to by the different parties in a suit are generally opposite to each other, so that it has become almost impossible to ascertain the truth from their contradictory evidence." The practice of perjury had led to the widespread practice of forgery of written evidence "to such an extent as to render the administration of justice still more intricate and perplexing." Further, he found the distribution of corrupt practices to differ by religion. A Hindu himself, he wrote that "among the Muhammadan lawyers I have met with some honest men. The Hindu lawyers are in general not well spoken of, and they do not enjoy the confidence of the public." He was careful to note, however, that Hindus who still lived in villages, where they were wholly under the rule of caste government and regulations, "were as innocent, temperate, and moral in their conduct as the people of any country whatsoever."[33] He was categorical about the impact of the Hindu social system on Indian politics: "I regret to say that the present system of religion adhered to by the Hindus is not well calculated to promote their political interest. The distinction of castes, introducing innumerable divisions and subdivisions among them, has entirely deprived them of political feeling, and the multitude of religious rites and ceremonies and laws of purification have totally disqualified them from understanding any difficult enterprise."[34]

[33] "Exposition of the Practical Operation of the Judicial and Revenue System of India and the General Character and Condition of Its Native Inhabitants," 1832, reprinted in Raja Rammohun Roy, *The English Works of Raja Rammohun Roy* (Bahadurganji, Allahbad: Panini Office, 1906), pp. 232–234, 242, 245, 296–297.
[34] The quote dates from 1828 and can be found in Bimanbehari Majumdar, *History of*

His efforts to reform Hindu practice followed logically from this analysis.

Bankimchandra Chatterjee, best known for his novel *Anandamath*, also wrote a number of sociological essays about conditions in Bengal. He too was concerned by the impact of the Hindu religious and social system on Indian politics. In his essay "Kamalakanta," for example, he wrote: "We want politics—politics week after week and day after day; but like the desire of the dumb to be brilliant speakers, like the yearning of the lame to run swiftly . . . it is ridiculous and without fruit. . . . [A] people who have been conquered by seventeen horsemen have no politics. 'Praise to Radha and Krishna! Give me alms!' That is their politics. There is no possibility of any other political seed to take root in this province."[35] He expounded at greater length on the political character of the caste system, arguing that it was a form of oppression that bore striking similarities to the oppression of one race by a conquering race. He noted that in the caste system and in British imperial rule over Indians, members of the dominant group, Brahmins in one case, the English in the other, had separate judicial systems for their own. The caste system would never allow a Brahmin to be sentenced by a Shudra and treated the murder of a Brahmin by a Shudra far differently from the murder of a Shudra by a Brahmin, just as the British would never allow themselves to be sentenced by an Indian. In the British Empire, Indians occasionally rose to high political positions, probably more often than Shudras were allowed to rise to similar positions in Hindu India. He concluded by writing that "many will say it is not valid to compare the supremacy of the English with the supremacy of the Brahmins; since even though the Brahmins and the Kshatriyas oppressed the Shudras, they were of the same race; and the English are of a different race. Our inclination is to reply that to he who is oppressed it is immaterial whether the oppressed be of the same or of a different race. It is not likely that there is something sweet in being oppressed by one's own race."[36]

The best-known of his essays, "Samya," usually translated as "Equality," is even more emphatic than Weber on the consequences of the caste system for Indian economic and intellectual development. Chatterjee noted that social inequality was a universal phenomenon but that an excess of social inequality was "the specific cause of India's long-standing miserable condition." In a sweeping judgment, Chatterjee

---

Political Thought: From Rammohun to Dayananda, vol. 1 (Calcutta: University of Calcutta, 1934), p. 9.

[35] Bankimchandra Chatterjee, *Sociological Essays: Utilitarianism and Positivism in Bengal*, trans. and ed. by S. N. Mukherjee and Marian Maddern (Calcutta: Rddhi-India, 1986), p. 45.

[36] "Vividha Prabandha," in Chatterjee, *Sociological Essays*, pp. 56–58

wrote, "Of all the kinds of social inequality which have developed in the world, none, in any society, have been so serious as the caste inequality of ancient India." The dominance of the Brahmins meant that all intellectual activity was directed to the end of preserving the mastery of the Brahmins. All other intellectual activity was prohibited. "The Brahmins create more sacrifices, increase the incantations . . . , they invent false histories full of the glories of even more deities, and thus bind even more tightly the Indians' bond of ignorance. What is the use of philosophy, science, and literature? Do not turn your minds in those directions. . . . Learning? Let its name disappear in India!" Chatterjee then argued, somewhat idiosyncratically, that it was only the conquest of India by Buddhism that moderated the caste system and produced a golden era that lasted a thousand years.[37] In his time, Chatterjee was concerned that India would remain dependent because it could not develop a strong sense of nationalism given the multiple divisions of Indian society that had their origins in both caste and ethnic divisions and because political power was seen as the exclusive possession of the Kshatriya caste. Only if nationalism could somehow be wedded to religion could it, in Chatterjee's view, become a powerful force in India.[38]

Rabindranath Tagore was a poet and a novelist, but like Chatterjee, he also wrote essays about political questions. In particular, he delivered the lecture "Nationalism in India" in 1916 that reiterated many of the themes taken up by Chatterjee. India was different from European nations because of the problem that had existed from the earliest times: the "race problem" of "caste distinctions." India had solved the problem of a multiplicity of races by creating the caste system that created peace and order by keeping each caste within strict boundaries within which it could have full freedom. But this system, while reducing social violence, had become rigid. In particular, it created a condition in which "India has never had a real sense of nationalism." He criticized the Congress Party of that time for focusing on the issue of independence from the British. This was incorrect, in his view, because "our real problem in India is not political. It is social." The Congress Party "did not recognize the patent fact that there were causes in our social organization which made the Indian incapable of dealing with the alien. What would we do if, for any reason, England was driven away? We should simply be victims for other nations. The same social weaknesses would prevail." The Indian nationalists of the Congress Party "never dream of blaming our social inadequacy for our present helplessness, for we have accepted as the creed of our nationalism that this social system has been perfected

[37] Ibid., pp. 86–89.
[38] Majumdar, *History of Political Thought*, pp. 413–418.

for all time. . . . This is the reason why we think that our task is to build a political miracle of freedom upon the quicksand of social slavery."[39]

The writings of the first generation of Indian nationalists, on balance, analyze the political consequences of the caste system in ways that are congruent with the analysis of India expressed by leading Western scholars. The India they portray is fundamentally divided by castes, and the level of trust among individuals outside the framework of caste law is low. The result is an India easily penetrated and manipulated by foreigners.

What of the views of the leader of modern Indian nationalism, Jawaharlal Nehru? While clearly opposed to British rule, he, like the earlier nationalist leaders, was certainly influenced by the West, especially by his prolonged residence abroad, which, in his own words, affected his outlook so much that when he returned to India in 1936, "I approached her almost as an alien critic, full of dislike for the present as well as for many of the relics of the past that I saw."[40] But if Nehru is rejected as an inauthentic Indian commentator, along with his political and intellectual predecessors in the Indian nationalist movements, it is hard to imagine who would be an acceptable Indian commentator on the Indian social system, other than self-appointed Western academics.

With regard to caste, Nehru's views, written while in prison and first published in 1944, are clear and repeated over and over. Caste was a necessary consequence of the clash of several civilizations in South Asia. It embodied a system that compartmentalized Indian society in order to prevent extraordinarily diverse elements from clashing with one another. In the past, the alternative to the caste system, was conquest by one civilization followed by genocide, or prolonged, constant internal war. The caste system from 500 B.C. to 700 A.D. grew more and more rigid, and in that period "we see that exclusiveness and touch-me-not-ism which were to grow and grow till they became unalterable, octopus like, with their grip on everything—the caste system of modern times. Fashioned for a particular day, intended to stabilize the then organization of society and give it strength and equilibrium, it developed into a prison for that social order. . . . Security was purchased in the long run at the cost of ultimate progress."[41]

The caste system at its best was the means by which tolerance of alternative ways of life within separate spheres could be achieved. But it had a price. This separatism and tolerance in narrow spheres led Indians

[39] Rabindranath Tagore, *Nationalism* (New York: Macmillan, 1917), pp. 117–118, 127, 135–138, 144–145.
[40] Jawaharlal Nehru, *The Discovery of India* (Delhi: Oxford University Press, 1989), p. 50.
[41] Ibid., p. 88.

in ancient time "to attach little importance to the social aspect of man, of man's duty to society. For each person life was divided and fixed up, a bundle of duties and responsibilities within his own narrow sphere in the graded hierarchy. He had no duty to, or conception of, society as a whole, and no attempt was made to make him feel his solidarity with it." The system and its consequences persisted, resisting, Nehru wrote, the efforts by Buddhist and Islamic religious movements; Afghan, Mughal, and British conquests; and the efforts of Hindu reformers like Rammohun Roy. As a result, outside the boundaries of the subcastes was a notion of a common culture that "was weak politically but, socially and culturally, it was strong. Because of its political lack of cohesiveness it facilitated foreign conquest; because of its social strength it made recovery easy."[42]

By the criterion of common, independent judgments by observers from different cultures, one would have to conclude that the observations concerning observable caste structures, the associated norms that must be inferred from behavior, and their consequences for politics did reflect objective realities. The final test is that of modern empirical research. What are the findings of social scientists concerning caste and Indian political life?

Social scientists attempted to measure the degree to which societies are divided along ethnic and linguistic lines, and to assess the impact of these divisions on the ability of political institutions to function. Although not the same as caste divisions, ethnic divisions and caste divisions in India tend to add to each other, rather than cutting across each other. It is important to observe, therefore, that one measure using data from the period 1960–1965 shows an extraordinarily high degree of ethnic fractionalization in India as compared with other Asian and African countries. In this metric, numbers indicate the rank of a country among 136 countries in terms of its fractionalization. Low numbers indicated a high rank in fractionalization. Egypt, for example, with a relatively homogeneous population, scored 121.5. A country like Israel that included several major ethnic groups scored lower, 84.5, while Mexico scored 72.5. India, on the other hand, scored 4.5.[43] As a result, some social scientists have concluded that the Indian government remains weak relative to the powerful leaders of local castes and unable to execute its program of institutional reform even when the national government is elected by lopsided national majorities.[44] This tends to reinforce the conclusion that

[42] Ibid., pp. 95, 246, 251–252.

[43] See table 1.3 in Joel Migdal, *Strong Societies and Weak States* (Princeton: Princeton University Press, 1988), p. 38.

[44] Francine R. Frankel, *India's Political Economy, 1947–1977* (Princeton: Princeton University Press, 1978), p. 4.

postindependence India remains dominated by the social structures that were dominant before independence.

Efforts to analyze Indian politics after independence confirm not only the persistence of caste organizations but also their impact on postindependence Indian politics. Two major studies of the Congress Party, one conducted by Susan Rudolph and Lloyd Rudolph, the other by Myron Weiner, were reviewed by Francine Frankel with regard to just this issue. Rudolph and Rudolph argued that beginning in the twentieth century, Western political ideas employed by Congress Party organizers interacted with traditional Indian caste and subcaste associations. Those Western ideas did not eliminate caste structures but "transformed" them into something the authors called "paracommunities." "Latent horizontal solidarities and interests" were mobilized in India, extending beyond the narrow bounds of subcaste politics, and the paracommunities became "a means to level the old order's inequities by helping to destroy its moral basis and social structure." As Frankel notes: "This is a very provocative thesis. But little evidence appears in this book to demonstrate its validity." Rudolph and Rudolph's book focused on the efforts of two subcastes to upgrade their status by traditional means, a process that took one hundred years of agitation marked with bloodshed. "That these efforts were ultimately successful hardly indicates an erosion of a caste-based hierarchy," Frankel wrote, and in any case involved only small numbers of prosperous businessmen, leaving the lower castes and untouchables out of the picture. Tracing the activities of these groups after independence, the evidence presented by Rudolph and Rudolph suggested that new elites tended to use the older social structures to mobilize support to increase their personal power, not to delegitimize the older social structures. Postindependence political organization, in fact, tended to make caste structures more politically salient. Frankel indicated that "one fact . . . is demonstrated beyond question by the Rudolphs' study. That is the enormous proliferation of district, state, and regional caste associations and the extent to which they now act as pressure groups in local and state politics."[45]

The periodic political instability in India has caused Indian and Western political scientists to search for the reasons why Indian national political institutions have been threatened by violence and have not been able to establish the levels of internal peace common in Western democracies. Atul Kohli found persistent and repeated patterns of political behavior that demonstrated the difficulty of establishing loyalties to political institutions larger than the local caste and the rapidity with

[45] Francine Frankel, "Indian Political Development," *World Politics* 21 (April 1969): 448–468.

which such institutions, if they were created, degenerated into violently warring factions, often defined by caste. The caste system, far from being replaced by modern political parties and interest groups, had been made more divisive by the introduction of democratic political processes. Electoral competition did, indeed, increase the participation of the Indian people in politics, but this led not to European-style ideological or interest group politics but to caste, religious, and ethnic conflict. "Conflicts among traditional cleavages of caste and community have been around for quite some time, but what is new is the . . . intensity of such conflicts." Kohli, in fact, went back to the election districts surveyed by Myron Weiner in the early 1960s and found that the Congress Party as a political institution had "declined in all the districts analyzed." The social heterogeneity of India and repeated decisions by Indian political leaders to build political power on the basis of their personal popularity and influence had combined to weaken "modern" political institutions at the local and national level and to elevate the salience and importance of "traditional" social distinctions.[46] However, poverty, political mismanagement, ethnic conflicts, and other non-caste-related factors might all be the causes of the failure of stable, nonpersonal political institutions to take root in India. Can it be fairly claimed that it is the persistence of the caste system that continued to divide loyalties and to create an environment in which loyalties to larger communities or institutions have difficulty surviving? In a brilliant piece of analysis, Kohli examined the politics of West Bengal, an Indian state that since 1977 has been the exception to the problems of governability because of a stable, institutionalized party. Why was West Bengal more governable? Nearly half the population of that state was *not* mainstream Hindu. There were essentially no members of the two castes between the Brahmins and the Shudras, and the Brahmins themselves did not observe the caste distinctions common elsewhere in Hindu India, being willing, for example, to take water from members of the lowest caste. Landholding was not dominated by the upper castes. In short, despite its extreme poverty, West Bengal was more politically stable than its neighboring Indian states because "the absence of dominant castes at the state level opens up the possibilities for political parties to forge coalitions along lines other than caste." In West Bengal, further, "caste identities simply were not as deeply embedded . . . and did not mold the political behavior of Bengalis to the same extent as, say, those of Biharis."[47]

Given the frequent eruptions of violent political instability in India, the

---

[46] Atul Kohli, *Democracy and Discontent: India's Growing Crisis of Governability* (New York: Cambridge University Press, 1990), pp. 15–18, 184–188.
[47] Ibid., pp. 269, 271.

question arises, Why has there not been an India-wide revolution since independence? Weiner has suggested that it is precisely the fragmentation of India into small communities reinforced by the federal political system that has prevented the emergence of any coherent national revolutionary movement: "Social structure and constitutional forms thus combine to quarantine violent social conflict and political instability at the state level."[48]

By studying the ability of various states in India to improve the rates of literacy in their jurisdictions, Weiner also tried to assess the varying impact of Indian social structures on the ability of government organizations to perform their tasks. He began his study by noting that India, unlike many other poor Asian and African countries, "is a significant exception to the global trend toward the removal of children from the labor force and the establishment of compulsory, universal primary-school education. Poverty has not prevented governments of other developing countries from expanding mass education or making primary education compulsory. Many countries of Africa with income levels lower than India have expanded mass education with impressive increases in literacy." He cited figures showing that sixteen poor African countries now have literacy rates of between 50 percent and 75 percent, and reports from 1989 showed China having an adult literacy rate of 73 percent. India's literacy rate was 41 percent. "India is the largest single producer of the world's illiterates." Why? Weiner's argument is that low per capita levels of income cannot explain these striking comparative figures. They cannot explain why, relative to other poor countries, India spent a smaller fraction of its state education budgets on primary school education. Instead, what was decisive, in Weiner's judgment, was a set of beliefs, widely shared in India, "concerning the respective roles of upper and lower social strata, the role of education as a means of maintaining differentiations among social classes, and the concerns that 'excessive' and 'inappropriate' education for the poor would disrupt existing social arrangements. Indians reject compulsory education, arguing that primary schools do not properly train the children of the poor to work, that the children of the poor should work rather than attend schools that prepare them for 'service' or white collar occupations."[49] His evidence for this conclusion took many forms, including extensive interviews with state officials responsible for education policy. But most impressive were his findings that within South Asia, including the Indian

[48]Myron Weiner, "The Indian Paradox," in Myron Weiner, *The Indian Paradox: Essays in Indian Politics* (Newbury Park, Calif.: Sage, 1989), pp. 21–37.
[49]Myron Weiner, *The Child and the State in India: Child Labor and Education Policy in Comparative Perspective* (Princeton: Princeton University Press, 1991), pp. 4–5, 160–161.

state of Kerala and the country of Sri Lanka, literacy and higher budgets for primary schools did not correlate with per capita income but were associated with strong Christian and Buddhist influences. Weiner does not argue that these non-Hindu religions necessarily led to the dismantling of the caste system in the areas where they were strong. But in Kerala, Christian missionaries did set up schools that taught reading and writing to help convert children to their religion. This posed a challenge to the Hindu rulers, who saw the possibility of a shift in power to literate Christian Indians in their area. As a result, the rulers funded their own schools to teach reading and writing. Competition among castes to improve their own literacy emerged. At the time of Weiner's study, Kerala had a literacy rate of 70 percent, and Sri Lanka had a literacy rate of 86 percent.[50] The norms associated with the caste structure did appear to have an impact on the ability of the government to perform one basic function, but strong external challenges to those norms could weaken their effects.

Unless all these studies are misleading, they reinforce the view of European and Indian observers that the norms and structures of the caste system do reduce the cohesion of Indian society above the level of sub-caste and do impede the ability of the state to pursue a political agenda that does not support, much less challenge, those norms and structures, but also the view that the strength of those norms and structures can vary in India regionally and, conceivably, over time. The extent to which caste existed and affected Indian strategic behavior, however, must be studied on a case-by-case basis.

[50] Ibid., pp. 93, 172–177.

[3]

Society and Military Power in
Ancient India, 500 B.C.–A.D. 500

Given the perspective of this book, what questions can we ask about ancient India that might lead us to some conclusions about the impact of that society on the military organizations of that time and place? In general, we want to know, How divisive were the the dominant social structures of the period, and to what extent were the armies of the time separated from their society? In terms of ancient India, this means we would like to know about the nature and strength of the caste system in the ancient period in South Asia, after the Aryan conquest of the north Gangetic plain had been consolidated but before other foreign conquests by Arabs, Afghans, Turkish peoples, and others had an impact on Indian social structures. Most particularly, we would like to know if the caste structures of ancient, agrarian India were significantly more or less divisive than the social structures of other ancient, agrarian societies, in Europe or elsewhere. As for relations between society and the armies of ancient time, we know from a variety of sources that European armies of ancient times sometimes, but not always, took the form of aristocratic mounted soldiers supplemented by an infantry that was composed of farmers serving temporarily as soldiers as the need arose. The internal structure of such armies tended to mirror the structures of their host societies. But this was not always the case. Some ancient European armies were in various ways divorced from their societies. What was the case in India? Finally, we would like to know how well Indian armies performed in ancient times, preferably against non-Indian armies that either came from societies that had less divisive social structures or had a different relation to their own host societies. If these questions can be answered, even imperfectly, we can begin to understand the historical question of why ancient India, when invaded by Alexander the Great,

[61]

was conquered. We can then test the answer to that question by looking at ancient Greece and Rome. Those ancient societies were also invaded by powerful foreign armies, from Persia and Carthage, respectively, and they were not conquered. Are the factors that allegedly explain the defeat of India adequate to explain the successful defense of non-Indian societies? Altogether, these questions will suggest what kind of case can be made for associating Indian social structures with their comparative strategic strengths and weaknesses in this period.

THE DIFFICULTIES AND BENEFITS OF STUDYING ANCIENT INDIA

The problem with studying ancient India is that of reliable data. The benefit is that this period is the one for which the idea of strategic culture, as opposed to social structures, is most important from the standpoint of the writers who say that there is an Indian strategic culture.

There is no question that the data concerning the social structures and military performance of ancient India are poor, consisting primarily of Indian political texts. In general, we can date these sources with a margin of error of only several hundred years. In addition to these texts, there are epic poems, written and oral; laws inscribed on Indian monuments; some archeological data; and the accounts of foreign travelers, ambassadors, and invaders. Historical texts, of even the possibly biased and partisan kind, exemplified in the Western tradition by Thucydides and Polybius, are not available for ancient India. The epic poem the *Mahabharata* is more like the *Iliad* than *The Peloponnesian War*, and the *Arthasastra* is more like Machiavelli's *Prince* than his *Florentine Histories*. Administrative records that assist scholars of Rome or of later periods in Indian history do not exist for this period of Indian history.

Despite these difficulties, efforts, which will be discussed below, have been made repeatedly to study ancient Indian texts and poetry in order to find a "primordial" Hindu strategic culture in ancient India that could be used to explain its strategic behavior in ancient but also in modern times. It is important, moreover, to study the ancient period even if an enduring Indian strategic culture turns out not to exist. Study of this period might help us understand the origins and character of military thought and behavior in ancient India, even if it told us little about subsequent periods. Whatever their weaknesses, the political and literary texts of India were written by intelligent local observers who cared deeply about their subject. They might well have had some understanding of ancient Indian military strengths and weaknesses from which we can benefit. G. D. Bakshi and P. Sensarma, both Indian military officers, have gone back to the *Mahabharata's* description of the Kurukshetra War, an event for which there is no independent historical or archeological evidence, because, they argued, even as myth, the *Mahabharata* provided insight into ancient and modern Indian military psychology. They go on to claim that the continued power of that myth as demonstrated by the popularity of productions of the *Mahabharata* for Indian television demonstrated its continued relevance for understanding the perspective of Indians on political and military affairs.[1] Other Indian scholars have argued that the different reactions of contemporary Indians to the ancient epic poems and to Western literature revealed very non-Western attitudes toward the relation of the individual to the family and to political authority.[2]

In addition to military matters, social scientists who have studied India have also argued that the study of ancient Indian political writings can tell us much about what is enduring about Indian social structures. Myron Weiner, for example, after noting the very different and less powerful or autonomous role that Indian political thought had played, compared with Western political thought, in shaping political practice, emphasized that "the fact remains that ancient theory should not be lightly dismissed. . . . Having been so deeply rooted in the realities of India's hierarchical social structure and the country's system of religious belief—both of which continue to exist—it would be surprising if these ideas were totally at variance with contemporary beliefs and behavior." Ancient Indian political thought was not the cause of modern behavior, but the similarities between ancient injunctions and modern practices "is enough to make us consider the possibility of similar underlying premises . . . derived from deeper fundamental assumptions concerning the nature of man—assumptions that mark one culture from another, such that contemporary Indians are more akin to their ancestors in some respects than they are to other contemporaries."[3] In some sense, this period in Indian

---

[1]G. D. Bakshi, *Mahabharata: A Military Analysis* (New Delhi: Lancer, 1990), pp. ix, xxii. Priyadarsan Sensarma, *Kurukshetra War: A Military Study* (Calcutta: Naya Prakash, 1982), pp. 39–41, noted the great problem of foreign exploitation of Indian internal social weaknesses for the purpose of espionage and suggests that "the present Indians should also take lessons from those lapses and be more conscious about this weakness of the Indian character."

[2]See, for example, T. G. Vaidyanathan, "Authority and Identity in India," *Daedalus* 118, no. 4 (Fall 1989): 154–155, comparing the reaction of modern Indians to television productions of the Ramayana with their reaction to Cordelia's treatment of her father in *King Lear*.

[3]Myron Weiner, "Ancient Indian Political Theory and Contemporary Indian Politics," in *Orthodoxy, Heterodoxy, and Dissent in India*, ed. S. N. Eisenstadt, Reuven Kahane, and David Shulman (New York: Mouton, 1984), p. 113.

history and thought, it has been argued, reveals what is indigenous and "authentic," in the sense of not deriving from foreign influences or Indian reactions to them, about India.

It makes sense to study this period to assess the general arguments concerning strategic culture. To go back, strategic culture is the subjective state of mind that arises from the interpreted strategic experiences of the people making strategic decisions. Common strategic experiences may lead over time to common strategic cultures. But certainly if two groups have almost no shared strategic experiences, as was the case for India and Europe in this period, then the strategic cultures of the two areas should differ greatly.

The strategic thought of the ancient period is also relevant to the thought of subsequent periods. Understanding the strategic culture of India in later periods may require us to understand the interaction of preexisting subjective states of mind with subsequent historical events. Understanding the state of mind in any given period, therefore, requires us to understand the subjective states of mind in the preceeding period, a process that pushes the analysis back as far as possible. The earliest differences in the subjective perspective of Indians on their conduct of war should matter, according to the strategic culture argument, especially if they are distinctively "Indian," with their roots in a period before India had extensive contacts with other civilizations. The differences between Indian and non-Indian strategic thought and practice might well be most marked at this time.

If, however, Indian social structures and their relation to Indian armies are what matter for the Indian practice of war, as I argue, then the fact that Indian thinking is most "exotic" and most "Hindu" during this period matters less, but the period still contains a particular set of social structures that might influence Indian military effectiveness, not necessarily for all time, but for that period. Those social structures and strategic behavior can be compared with those that existed elsewhere at the same time and in subsequent periods in Indian history. If ancient Indian social structures led to certain levels of social division, if ancient armies distanced themselves from ancient society in certain ways, and if those same levels of social division and military distance from society are found in the West in ancient times, then, according to this model, ancient Indian military strengths and weaknesses should resemble ancient Western military strength and weaknesses. Strategic differences should exist only to the extent that social structures and army-society relations differ. By studying ancient India, we can begin to compare the predictions of the strategic culture model with the predictions of the model of the relation between armies and social structures and cohesion made here.

A final reason exists for examining ancient India. During this period

[64]

in selected areas of Europe, societies began to emerge which were not representative of Europe as a whole but which are thought of as laying the intellectual, political, and social foundations that shaped modern Europe. The rise of Greece and Rome took place during the first half of this period, and their social and military characters have been as intensively studied as the data permits. The availability of studies of Greece, Macedon, and Rome form the basis for a comparative assessment of Indian military effectiveness, which is all the more interesting because the Macedonian army under the command of Alexander the Great initiated the military interaction of India with the West in the fourth century B.C. That interaction was cut short, but it offers a direct comparison of one particular form of European military organization with that of ancient India. Not less interesting is the fact that both ancient Greece and republican Rome were invaded by powerful foreign armies, as was ancient India, but the reaction of the armies and societies of Greece and Rome to Persia and to Carthage was very different from the reaction of the armies and societies of ancient India to Alexander the Great.

THE SOCIAL STRUCTURES OF ANCIENT INDIA

Direct evidence concerning the extent to which the caste system had become established in India at the beginning of this period is scant, and what we know comes from secondary sources. These include the generally useless fragments from the observations of the Greek ambassador (306–298 B.C.) to India, Megasthenes, and the more factual observations from the chronicles of the Buddhist traveler, known as Hieun-Tsiang or Yuan Chwang, in India preserved in Ceylon/Sri Lanka.[4] From this body of evidence, the consensus of scholarly opinion is that although Indian society was stratified by subcastes, this division was less pronounced than it would become after Aryan rule had become stable and of long duration. Ancient India was composed of people who identified their interests with those of their caste, but the power and rigidity of caste divisions—the degree to which caste narrowed the social and political radius of trust of Indian peasants and the higher castes—increased toward the end of the ancient period. At this time the challenge of Buddhism to the Brahminic forms of the Hindu religion had been met and, at the political and religious level, successfully resisted, and the Mauryan dynasty, which dominated North India and which had converted to Bud-

[4]Samuel Beal, *Hwui Li, The Life of Hiuen-Tsiang* (London: Kegan Paul, Trench, Truban, 1911); Thomas Watters, *On Yuan Chwang's Travels in India, 629–645 A.D.* (London: Royal Asiatic Society, 1904), pp. 147, 152, 168, 170–171.

dhism, had been overthrown by a Brahmin-led counterreform, after which land grants to Brahmins became common, providing them revenue, the right to govern their land, and, in general, greater social and political power.

At the beginning of the early period, social mobility, particularly in cities, was not unknown, and individuals could raise themselves to the status of Brahmin by study. Kingly rule by men from lower castes is sanctioned by the *Mahabharata*. Low-caste members are known to have been employed as soldiers by the Mauryan dynasty that became dominant in India by the fourth century B.C. For the life of rural villagers, Indian caste divisions were important, but perhaps not in ways so different from the isolation and fragmentation experienced by rural villagers outside India. William McNeill, for example, commented that in contrast to urban life, "the peasant village community of the Middle East was in many respects comparable to an Indian caste. A man was born into the village and seldom left; a sharp line was drawn between members of the village and outsiders; a strictly defined series of expectations and attitudes defined the relationships between the members of the community; and their relationships with outsiders were defined by a scarcely less well-defined code."[5]

Although detailed pictures of the social life of ancient India are scarce, texts advising Indian rulers on how to govern their people have survived and have provided the basis for descriptive analyses of Indian politics as well as for the Indian normative perspective on politics. For many of the key texts, the relationship between prescription and actual practice has been assumed. This assumption seems warranted by the fact that the internal textual evidence clearly indicates that the authors of these texts did not advise Indian rulers to try and change Indian society; rather, they educated rulers to their responsibilities in maintaining and protecting the social order that already existed, conceiving of "the state as both an expression of the social order of hierarchy and as an instrument for maintaining that order." The state in particular is seen—for example, by Beni Prasad and other Indian authors who have interpreted those texts— as insuring that the individual will "fulfill the function assigned to him from the moment of birth in the social order of which he forms a part."[6]

---

[5]Charles Drekmeier, *Kingship and Community in Early India* (Stanford: Stanford University Press, 1962), pp. 5, 80, 82, 166, 173, 179, 181; William H. McNeill, *The Rise of the West* (Chicago: University of Chicago Press, 1991), p. 176.

[6]Weiner, "Ancient Indian Political Theory," p. 119, citing Beni Prasad, *Theory of Government in Ancient India*. For a review and dissent to the view that the Indian state in ancient times was seen as a force to maintain but not to interfere in the division of society into occupational orders, the position asserted by Prasad and Radha Kumud Mookerji

THE LITERARY TRADITION, CULTURE, AND STRATEGY
OF ANCIENT INDIA

In the absence of a great deal of data about Indian social structures, scholars have studied the great political texts and poetry of this period, trying to gain from them insights concerning the nature of Indian society and its impact on war as conducted by armies drawn from that society. This kind of analysis cannot prove any relationship between culture and strategy: if the same texts are used simultaneously to develop a model of Indian society and of Indian military behavior, it will not be surprising if the model winds up being consistent with the textual descriptions of Indian society and Indian military behavior. But while this kind of analysis will not prove hypotheses, it may suggest them, and other methods may then be sought to test them.

The most important single text in Hindu political philosophy is Kautilya's *Arthasastra*. Conclusive evidence as to when Kautilya wrote this work has not yet been unearthed, nor is it absolutely clear that the book had a single author. It has been claimed that Kautilya was a historical figure also known as Chanakya, about whom a play, *Mudra-Rakshasa*, was written, describing him as an adviser to the Mauryan kings.[7] Most Indian scholars, on the basis of their interpretation of the internal evidence, date the book from the fourth century B.C., although the Indian author Nirad Chaudhuri casts doubt on whether any important Hindu texts existed earlier than the fourth century A.D.[8] The book is a practical guide for kings on the management of their affairs, not an abstract discussion of politics, and is written for the most part in the form of a commentary on earlier advisers to kings, to whom Kautilya collectively refers as "the teachers." The first book of the *Arthasastra* is on the training to be given to kings. Beginning in book 1—and constantly reappearing throughout the entire work—is an obsession with spies, secrets, and treachery. When listing the virtues of a king, Kautilya includes, along with energy, controlling his sensual nature, cultivating his intellect, and

<hr />

(see n. 7, this chapter), see M. V. Krishna Rao, *Studies in Kautilya* (New Delhi: Mushiram Manohartal Publishers, 1979), pp. 34–36, 42, 48–50. Supporting Prasad, see Usha Mehta and Usha Thakkar, *Kautilya and His Arthashastra* (New Delhi: S. Chand, 1980), pp. 10, 18.

[7] See, for example, Radha Kumud Mookerji, *Chandragupta Maurya and His Times: Madras University Sir William Meyers Lectures, 1940–1941* (Delhi: Motilal Banarsidass, 1966), pp. 426–427.

[8] Contrast, for example, Mehta and Thakkar, *Kautilya and His Arthashastra*, p. 3, which places the book between the fourth century and the third century B.C., and Nirad C. Chaudhuri, *Hinduism: A Religion to Live By* (London: Chatto and Windus, 1979), pp. 40, 60–63, who claims that there has been systematic exaggeration of the age of all Hindu texts.

associating with his elders, keeping "a watchfull eye by means of spies."[9] Who should be the counselors of kings? Those whose "integrity or the absence of integrity" has been ascertained "by means of secret tests." Those tests would include discharging a minister and then using a secret agent to approach the sacked minister to propose the overthrow of the king. The loyalty of the minister must be tested by attempting to subvert him by appeals to impiety, material gain, lust, and fear.[10] An establishment of spies must be created to serve the king and should include "the apostate monk, the seeming householder, the seeming trader, the seeming ascetic, as well as the secret agent, the bravo, the poison-giver, and the begging nun." In addition to these spies, there should be roving spies, including magicians, poor widowed nuns of the Brahmin caste, who, because they can with ease penetrate the households of high-caste officials, are said to be ideal couriers for messages. These roving spies should spy on "the councillor, the chaplain, the commander-in-chief, the crown-prince, the chief palace usher, the chief of the palace guards, the director, the administrator, the director of stores, the commandant, the city judge, the director of factories, the council of ministers, the superintendents, the chief of the army staff, the commandant of the fort, the commandant of the frontier-fort, the forest chieftain in his own territory" and so on. Songs, music, poems, and concealed writings should be used as the means of secretly conveying information. Double agents should be employed, and their families kept hostage.[11]

That is the beginning. Kautilya then says, "When [the king] has set spies on the high officials, he should set spies on the citizens and the country people." These spies, like the spies on high officials, are not merely passive observers, but agents provocateurs. Secret agents should stage disputes in public places, with one agent saying the king is good, the other that he is bad, so that the enemies and friends of the king may be drawn out. After having found who the enemies of the king are among the common people, he should make them unpopular by giving them odious jobs, such as tax collection. After they have incurred popular displeasure, these enemies of the king can then be safely eliminated by "secret punishment" or by seizing their families and sending them to the mines.[12]

Only after this extensive discussion of the need to "keep watch over the seducible and non-seducible parties in one's own territory" does

---

[9] *The Kautilya Arthasastra: An English Translation with Critical and Explanatory Notes,* trans. and commentary R. P. Kangle (Bombay: University of Bombay, 1963), vol. 2. Hereinafter, reference will be given to the *Arthasastra* by book and paragraph number (e.g., 1.7).

[10] Ibid., 1.10.

[11] Ibid., 1.11, 1.12.

[12] Ibid., 1.13.

Kautilya discuss the use of spies against foreigners. This use involves seeking out the malcontents in other kingdoms or those subjects enraged against their own foreign king and recruiting them for the purpose of espionage. Given this emphasis on secret agents, it is not surprising that of the eight periods of the day set aside for work, Kautilya says the king should devote three of them to the interviewing and dispatching of spies.[13]

Just as the king uses secret measures against his enemies, so should he expect those methods to be used against him. What modern analysts would call counterintelligence is also discussed by Kautilya, with specific sections about how to prevent the king's children from betraying him, how to protect the king against assassination attempts made by the queen, and how to guard against poisoning and the infiltration of weapons and assassins into the palace.[14]

The discussion of the uses of secret agents and betrayal recurs in book 2 on the activities of the heads of departments, which should include the use of spies to check on the honesty of those departments.[15] Book 5 is entirely devoted to "Secret Conduct," in which the proper ways to entrap unreliable officers in crimes are discussed, as is how such unreliable officers might be sent to their deaths in battle by giving them command of military units that are weak and full of assassins. Book 7 on foreign policy sets out as a rule that the key to the decision on whether to go to war lies in finding out whether the disaffected subjects of the enemy will betray their king and come over to you if you invade.[16] In book 9, the king about to march on an enemy is instructed how to incite revolts among the enemy's border troops, how to win over traitorous kings, and how to deal with treacherous allies, treacherous commanders, and treacherous ministers.[17]

When finally coming to book 10, "Concerning War," the reader is not surprised to find the primary distinction that Kautilya makes in military affairs is between secret, or covert, war and open warfare. Open warfare is simply conventional battle, for which Kautilya gives a number of standard battle formations useful for engaging different kinds of enemies. Secret warfare includes identifying the treasonous elements in the forces of the enemy and attacking the portions of the enemy line that such elements defend; instigating rebellion among enemy troops, especially by means of what modern analysts would refer to as psychological warfare; and methods of instilling terror in the enemy by means of ruses,

[13] Ibid., 1.19.
[14] Ibid., 1.19–1.20.
[15] Ibid., 2.35.
[16] Ibid., 7.3, 7.4.
[17] Ibid., 9.3, 9.8.

assassins, occult practices, or elephants. Secret and open warfare are then compared with each other, with advice given as to when to employ each. Open warfare is clearly "most righteous," Kautilya says. So, when a king is superior to the enemy in the number of his troops, when he is also fighting on terrain favorable to himself, and when, simultaneously, the enemy is also stricken by a calamity and is on unsuitable terrain, then a king may employ open warfare. If the king is not so happily favored, he should employ secret warfare. Open warfare under most circumstances is risky and inefficient, whereas secret warfare is certain and efficient. Kautilya's judgment is summed up thus: "An arrow discharged by an archer may kill one person or may not kill even one; but intellect operated by a wise man would kill even children in the womb."[18]

There is more to the *Arthasastra* than the discussion of spies, assassination, and secret warfare, although a Western reader may see only those elements that seem strikingly different from the modern Western political tradition. The Western reader may even overlook those elements found in the Western tradition that resemble elements in Kautilya—in Machiavelli, for example. It is noteworthy, therefore, that *Indian* commentaries have focused on the fact that Kautilya seems to base his political advice on the assumption that the loyalty of subjects of the Hindu state could not be taken for granted—that subjects must be assumed to be untrustworthy and treacherous when it was in their interest to be so. Most important, the Hindu commentators on Kautilya found no reason to believe that there could be circumstances in which Hindu society and state would escape from the condition of domestic war of all against all. In their 1980 commentary on Kautilya, Usha Mehta and Usha Thakkar suggested that since he wrote during the fourth century B.C., it was reasonable to assume that during his lifetime, the Macedonian army was or had recently been on India's borders. This external threat did not increase the cohesion of Indian society. Rather, "the loyalty of the foreigners in the Punjab and adjoining regions was doubtful, and a dangerous example of insecurity and perfidy was set by Alexander." It was the nature of Indian domestic society that kept the state weak and divided. "The state was conceived as an aggregate of several loosely knit organizations," one that nonetheless saw itself as having jurisdiction over all aspects of Hindu life. Kautilya seemed to accept the central idea of the preeminence of the caste system over the political system, a relationship of social structures to the state that permanently weakened the state and perpetuated the conditions that divided Hindu political loyalties. While Machiavelli saw disorder in the Italy of his time, he also envisioned a

---

[18] Ibid., 10.3, 10.5. The quote is on p. 525.

way to escape this disorder. The actions of a strong prince could create a state that brought with it domestic peace. Kautilya saw his ideal prince as a man of power as well, but "unlike as in Machiavelli, in Kautilya we find several checks put on the authority of the king. . . . Like almost all other Hindu thinkers, he, too, has accepted the *varnashramic* [caste-oriented] superstructure of Hindu society, and his king had mainly to function as a preserver of *Dharma*. . . . Thus, whereas for Machiavelli, the state was all in all, for Kautilya, it was subordinated to the society which it did not create." This social structure had implications for the systemic disloyalty of the subjects to the central state. As a result, again from the perspective of Mehta and Thakkar, Kautilya, unlike Machiavelli, did foresee "the possibility of impoverished and disaffected persons going to the side of the enemy and destroying their own king."[19]

This is not an idiosyncratic Indian interpretation of Kautilya nor of the difference between Kautilya and Machiavelli. U. N. Ghoshal, who wrote one of the standard works on Hindu political thought, also reviewed Kautilya's emphasis on the potential for treachery in the Hindu polity at great length and Kautilya's consequent advise to kings to create "an elaborate system of espionage on the widest scale and with a high degree of technical perfection" to guard the king against his own subjects and ministers. Kings, Ghoshal noted, were advised to seek out the parallel weaknesses in enemy states and to exploit them "by means of treacherous murder by the application of the methods of unscrupulous diplomacy. This anticipates the policy of totalitarian states of our own times." For Machiavelli, this commentator indicated, the aristocrats of Italy were the source of treachery, and it was they who had to be repressed. For Kautilya, treachery was more broadly based, arising from "the anti-social elements of the population and the clandestine public enemies and enemies of the state as well as the enemy outside." Ghoshal concluded: "A more fundamental difference may be observed in between the objectives of the two sets of policies. In Machiavelli there lay behind all his thought the urge of burning patriotism which sought passionately for the deliverance of his unhappy motherland, and the picture of Italy that he draws in the closing chapter of the *Prince* is one of the most moving on record. The aim of Kautilya's statecraft, by contrast, was more limited and self-

[19]Mehta and Thakar, *Kautilya and His Arthasastra*, pp. 9–10, 18, 29, 57, 81–82. M. V. Krishna Rao lays out the similar interpretations of Kautilya developed by Radhaumud Mookerji and Beni Prasad with regard to the disaggregated nature of the classical Hindu polity and of the primacy of Hindu society over the state. Rao himself dissents from this view. Though he agrees as to the existence of divisions in Hindu society, he argues, with no visible new evidence, that disorder led classical Hindu society to create a "plurally determined monism." Rao, *Studies in Kautilya*, pp. 34–39, 42, 48–50.

ish, for it consisted in ensuring the security and stability of the king's rule inside the kingdom."[20] Machiavelli hoped that the ruthlessly intelligent use of power might end the state of constant domestic factional disputes. Kautilya hoped that the ruthlessly intelligent use of power might simply help his king survive in a society that would be perpetually intriguing against him.

Equally interesting, modern Indian commentaries on other Hindu political texts from roughly the same period as Kautilya find in them many of the same key elements regarding the cohesiveness of one's own society and that of the enemy. The *Smritis* of Manu and Yajnavalkya, for example, advise the king to use "spies as his eyes" to seek out open thieves, among whom he includes high officers of the state who abuse their trusts. War should be resorted to only after conciliation, bribery of the enemy, and efforts to create dissension within the enemy's forces have been tried and have failed.[21]

Though not explicitly political, the *Mahabharata*, one of the great epic poems of India, has powerful political implications on which Hindu authors have remarked. Nehru ranked it, not the *Ramayana*, as the Indian literary work that was of world stature. The events it refers to may have occurred long before the ancient period, but the poem itself has been dated within the period 400 B.C.–A.D. 400.[22] The *Mahabharata* is in considerable measure the account of the protracted Kurukshetra War and contains a number of discussions among mythical figures about the ways to fight and win wars. As such, it may provide some insight into the cultural factors influencing the conduct of war in Hindu society. Certainly, the *Mahabharata* continues to be a widely popular literary work in India, and there has been no effort within India to reject its teachings. Because it is not explicitly political, it is possible for a Westerner to misinterpret it when searching for its political implications because the Westerner might not be familiar with the cultural context and nuances that allow the Indian reader to understand which of the statements and actions of the characters in the poem is meant to reflect behavior that are socially acceptable or admirable. One could completely misinterpret Western views on kingship, for example, by assuming that the statements and actions of Shakespeare's Richard III represent English views on how a king should behave. For that reason, it is important to consider Indian interpretations of the *Mahabharata*.

One of the important and explicit distinctions in the *Mahabharata* is

[20] U. N. Ghoshal, *A History of Indian Political Ideas* (London: Oxford University Press, 1959), pp. 132–134, 154.
[21] Ibid., pp. 221–222.
[22] *The Mahabharata*, vol. 1, *The Beginning*, trans. and ed. J. A. B. Buitenen (Chicago: University of Chicago Press, 1973), p. xxv.

between *Dharma Yuddha* or *Nyaya Yuddha*, translated as open, chivalric warfare, and *Kata Yuddha*, or secret or unethical warfare. In his commentary devoted to the military study of the *Mahabharata*, Sensarma concluded that while the winning clan resorted only reluctantly to *Kata Yuddha* after having been advised to do so by Lord Krishna, its victory depended on the use of unethical war. Unethical war in the *Mahabharata* included conveying to the enemy king the false idea that his son has been killed, in order to demoralize him so that he could be more easily defeated; flattering an enemy commander so that he revealed his army's plan of battle; using agents to create dissension in the enemy army; and, most important, espionage. Espionage was depicted as being widely practiced by each army against both its enemy and itself, with spies set by the king against his own sons, ministers, princes, friends, and queen. The winning clan had the most extensive system of spies, based on a network of men who supplied meat to the enemy. Most interesting, Sensarma then went on to note that in the *Mahabharata*, counterespionage seems not to have worked as well as espionage. That is, efforts to prevent the infiltration of spies and the betrayal of secrets had generally failed. Generalizing from this, Sensarma concluded that "the present Indians should also take lessons from those lapses and be more conscious about this great weakness of the Indian character."[23] Once again, both the poem and the commentary on it tend to suggest that the expectation of loyal behavior from Hindu military and state personnel was and is low.

Ghoshal concluded that the *Mahabharata* reiterates the teachings of Kautilya with regard to the superior effectiveness of deceit and secret war over open battle. Specifically, one character, Bhisma, is noteworthy in that in his speeches, "the cult of violence is accompanied . . . by that of calculated distrust and treachery." After reviewing seven separate extracts from the *Mahabharata*, Ghoshal went on to note that in the work as a whole, the reader will find "a vigorous plea for total war against the enemy. . . . The king is asked in effect to wage a war of complete extermination against the enemy as well as a cold war preparatory to attacking the enemy. . . . This policy is to be carried through with methods of unscrupulous diplomacy and calculated treachery based on unquenchable distrust of the enemy." The enemy should be corrupted by bribery, dissension should be created in his army and among the counselors of the enemy king, and "poison and stupefying drugs" should be employed, as well as fire. Members of the warrior or princely caste, the Kshatriyas, had the obligation to fight well on the battlefield to satisfy the obligations of their caste. Other than that, there were few moral constraints on their actions in war. For the Kshatriya in the *Mahabharata*,

[23]Sensarma, *Kurukshetra War*, pp. 18–19, 31–40, 41.

"what is unrighteous in the case of others is unavoidable in the case of Kshatriyas: the Kshatriya, it is explained in terms of unblushing egoism, should act in such a way that he may not suffer in his religious merit (*dharma*) . . . but he should by all means rescue his own self." After listening to Bhisma explicate this doctrine, his interlocutor, Yudhishthira, asks, "'bewildered and grief stricken, 'is there any rule of conduct among robbers left to shun?' " To which the reply is, kings "were created for performing cruel acts."[24]

Searching for the root of this approach to war, Ghoshal cited passages in the *Mahabharata* in which it is noted that families or clans are the constituent units of monarchies and republics both and that dissension in those larger communities is the result of the greed of those families, greed that can be exploited by the bribery and intrigue of the enemy.[25] Reviewing this commentary in light of the earlier analysis of caste obligations versus political obligations, we can also note the *Mahabharata*'s emphasis on the caste obligation of warriors to fight well on the battlefield but the absence of any notion that their political obligations constrained their self-interested behavior in ways that were not related to religious merit.

In addition to the great literary texts of ancient India, there is the oral tradition of the *Puranas*, folktales which deal with many of the same characters and themes of the epic poems but which were accessible to those non-Brahmins who did not read Sanskrit and to those barred from the study of sacred texts.[26] The dates of origin of an oral tradition are everywhere hard to determine, and the extent to which the versions that were ultimately transcribed resembled the original oral versions is always questionable. Dating the *Puranas* is, therefore, difficult, but the versions of the *Puranas* analyzed for their military contents are estimated to date from 600–800 A.D., that is, toward the very end of the period we are considering. Scholars generally enumerate thirty-six *Puranas*, of which three, the *Agni Purana*, *Matsya Purana*, and *Visnudharmottara Puranas*, are particularly concerned with war. In these, a distinction is made between *Prakasa*, or declared war, and *Aprakasa*, undeclared war, which parallels the distinction between Dharma Yuddha and Kata Yuddha found in the *Mahabharata* and Kautilya. *Sama Niti* and *Dana Niti* are further identified as ways of winning against an enemy without fighting. These involve conciliation and gift giving. If these fail, *Bheda Niti* is to be employed "to erode the strength of the enemy through dissensions and divisions in the

[24] Ghoshal, *History of Indian Political Ideas*, pp. 221, 222, 224, 225, 228, 232.
[25] Ibid., p. 238.
[26] Priyadarsan Sensarma, *Military Wisdom in the Puranas* (Calcutta: Naya Prokash, 1979), p. 2.

enemy armed forces." This is accomplished by breaking the ties of affection between the enemy king and his soldiers, and by causing mutual mistrust. Specifically, eleven types of individuals are identified and described in order to help those looking for men willing to betray their king for reasons of injured pride or self-interest. For purposes of gathering information as well as for intrigue, "the Puranas lay much emphasis on the importance and effectiveness of the *caras*—the spies."[27] Perhaps because of the constant problem of ensuring the loyalty of one's own forces in the face of pressures on common soldiers to flee or defect, "the Puranas consider that the leader of the troops is of paramount importance in the battlefield. In this connection, the Agni Purana says the leader is the life of war, a leaderless war ends in defeat. By implication, it means that with the death of the leader, the war ends. Therefore the King and the generals should always be protected by select troops. . . . Actually, most of the military literature of ancient India is of the same opinion. The military history of medieval India also highlights that the morale of the troops was then directly linked with the presence of the leader on the battlefield."[28]

From the seventh century A.D. until medieval Mughal times, there is general agreement that few new strands appeared in Indian political thought. One of the new intellectual currents to emerge between the eighth and the sixteenth centuries was the Jainist movement. Much less political than Kautilya or even the *Mahabharata*, the Jainist authors of the ninth century to thirteenth, when they did speak about politics and war, reiterated much of the Kautilyan attitude. One Jainist author, Somadeva, depreciated war as a tool of statecraft because it was so uncertain in its outcome, to be resorted to only when intrigue had been tried and had failed. He advised rulers instead to engage in *kutayuddah*, translated in this context as "treacherous fighting," and *tushnidanda*, translated as "silent fighting," involving the uses of poison and intrigue. Another Jainist author, Hemachandra, similarly advised against the risks and costs of open war, favoring the use of bribery, conciliation, and efforts to promote dissension in the enemy camp.[29]

The views of Indian society and their implications for warfare in the more popular literary tradition of Hindu India seems, therefore, to parallel closely those of the great Sanskrit epic poems, the *Arthasastra*, and other ancient Indian religious-political writings. In all these literary works, there appear to be low expectations of political loyalty to leaders when those loyalties are not supported by the obligations of the caste

---

[27] Ibid., pp. 14–20.
[28] Ibid., p. 116.
[29] Ghoshal, *History of Indian Political Ideas*, pp. 456, 490–491.

ideology. The only loyalties other than caste loyalties that seem important are highly personalized loyalties to the king or commander that do not appear to survive the death or disappearance of the leader. Smaller units of society—in particular, the family or clan—look to command more enduring loyalties than do political institutions, which creates the potential for divisions and factional disputes within a political community, disputes that can be engendered, exacerbated, and exploited by enemies at war with the community. If the personal loyalties to the commander can be destroyed by killing him or by destroying the respect that his followers have for him the political and military institutions he commanded can be expected to collapse. Reading these texts suggests but does not prove that the social structure of caste, though not as rigid as it was to become, produced a mode of warfare which, for offensive and defensive purposes, reflected a lack of cohesion among groups larger than the subcaste and which created weaknesses that had to be defended against or exploited. Forms of warfare that required high levels of cohesion for its conduct are less favored than covert warfare, which was executed by isolated individuals and which did not require cohesion across caste lines.

TESTING THE HYPOTHESES CONCERNING INDIAN SOCIETY AND INDIAN ARMIES

To review, there is some, but not a lot, of historical evidence, mostly from foreign travelers and nonhistorical Indian texts, that caste structures existed in India in this period, though they were weaker than they would become, and might not in rural areas have been dramatically different from village life out of India. Caste structures tended to divide society into subgroups which displayed internal loyalty but which did not encourage significant loyalty across caste lines. Literary sources suggest but do not prove that those caste structures affected Indian military capabilities. How might we begin to test whether the connection between Indian social structures and military strengths and weaknesses actually existed and, if it existed, whether it was significantly different from the strengths and weaknesses of other non-Indian armies of that era? The first step, clearly, would be to review the available primary-source accounts of Indian military activity. From these accounts one would try to tease out information about the extent to which the armies did or did not reflect the structures of their host societies, the extent to which they had developed separate functional structures within the army unrelated to the broader social structures, and how well they fought. What questions, specifically, should one ask?

First, very roughly, how large were those armies? The larger they were relative to the population, the more likely they would tend, other things being equal, to be representative of the broader social patterns of their host societies. Persistently large military populations that included elements of society from high and low strata might also indicate expectations that wars would be frequent and threatening. In the absence of foreign invaders, those large military populations would suggest high levels of violence internal to Indian society, as Indians armed themselves against one another. This would indicate serious internal divisions and conflicts within Indian society.

Second, were those armies always in the field fighting? To the extent that they were, the soldiers would tend over time to become physically and socially isolated from their own societies and could become more loyal to one another than to the norms and structures of their host society. Such would increase their military effectiveness but also alienate them from their own society.

Third, how did the Indian armies fight? Warfare in ancient times was not as complex as modern warfare, but it did display varying modes that tell us something about the relation of the components within those armies to one another. For example, did the Indian commanders fight alongside their infantry or remain physically aloof? Commanders who chose to fight unmounted, shoulder to shoulder with the peasants, were demonstrating very powerfully how they had chosen to ignore social structures and norms that divided the various subgroups in society in order to enhance the effectiveness of the army. If many commanders, not just extraordinary captains, fought alongside their men, it would suggest that social divisions had not carried over into the army engaged in battle. Did the components of the army that were filled by the upper classes, typically the mounted forces, cooperate to support the infantry that came from lower social orders, or did each military element fight on its own? Did the infantry and the cavalry display the ability to conduct complex maneuvers with each other on the battlefield? If they did, high levels of confidence, mutual understanding, and cohesion among the components of the army likely existed, despite the fact that they came from different social orders, tribes, or castes, because a unit that undertook, for example, a maneuver to outflank the enemy has to believe that the rest of the army will fight hard at the right time to support it, not leaving it to be isolated and destroyed. A unit that was hated because it was from another social group would expect that after it initiated an attack, the rest of the army would have gone home or be holding back. Complex maneuvers also suggest much practice or battle experience, both of which require sustained absences from civilian life, creating the possibility of alienation.

After asking these questions of Indian armies, one would ask the same questions about non-Indian armies. If one examines Greek, Macedonian, or Roman armies and if the answers to the questions above suggest that Indian and non-Indian armies of this period were equally removed from their host societies, having the same degree of functional integration of their components, the prediction would be that whether or not societies differed, armies that were similar in their separation from society yielded similar levels of military effectiveness on the battlefield. If armies from one ancient European society were more distant from their host society than were the contemporary Indian armies, we would then look to see if they fought better Indian armies and if there were plausible links from Indian military effectiveness back to Indian social structures.

What do we know of the size of Indian armies of this period? Reports of their battlefield strength are the usual basis for estimates of the sizes of the armies. But those reported battlefield strengths are, unfortunately, so large as to be more than somewhat suspect, and independent confirming evidence for these figures, such as payrolls or muster rolls, are absent. One scholarly estimate of the combined armies of the eight major kingdoms in India at the time of Alexander the Great's invasion was 1,078,000 infantry and 216,000 cavalry. The army of the major imperial power, Chandragupta Maurya, is put at 600,000.[30] Another estimate of Chandragupta's army included all his military personnel and arrived at a slightly higher figure of 690,000.[31] Both figures derived ultimately from references to the reports of the Greek ambassador to India, Megasthenes, that have survived in other Greek histories, not on any Indian sources. Reports of battles fought by subsequent kings in the Mauryan dynasty are even less credible. Memorial inscriptions credit the king Asoka with having fought battles in the area of the Bay of Bengal in which the slain numbered 100,000, and the captured, 150,000.[32] As Martin Van Creveld has pointed out, given the roads, transport, and food storage technologies, the physical impossibility of feeding, let alone controlling, a field army much larger than 20,000 makes these ancient Indian battlefield troop strengths and casualty reports difficult to believe,[33] unless they referred not to battles but to cumulative strengths and casualties during the course of protracted wars.

The historical material, however, includes other data that may be of more use. Chandragupta Maurya's army certainly appeared to include

---

[30] Bimal Kanti Majumdar, *The Military System of Ancient India* (Calcutta: Firma K. L. Mukhopadhyay, n.d.), pp. 48, 54.

[31] Mookerji, *Chandragupta Maurya*, p. 165.

[32] Majumdar, *Military System of Ancient India*, p. 75

[33] Martin Van Creveld, *Supplying War* (Cambridge: Cambridge University Press, 1977), pp. 11–16, and Martin Van Creveld, *Command in War* (Cambridge: Harvard University Press, 1985), p. 24.

large numbers of foot soldiers, charioteers, and soldiers mounted on elephants. Stirrups and horse-mounted archers do not appear on Indian coins until the very end of the period 500–900 A.D., seemingly after contact with the Parthians. Hence, professionalization of the Indian soldiers, in the sense of being a hereditary profession, also does not appear to have emerged until after this period had ended, in the seventh century A.D. This is consistent with foreign accounts. Finally, Hindu sacred texts, the *Brahminas* and the *Ṛg Veda*, refer in this period to armed peasants being the military equal of nobility, and in fact, accounts survive of nobles beseeching the peasants to come to their military assistance, for members of the Vaisya varna to come to the aid of the Kshatriyan troops. Thus armies do not seem to have been standing armies but drawn as needed from the community as a whole, and military training for soldiers was individual training, not training that accustomed soldiers to fighting together as a disciplined military unit.[34]

Taken together, these data have suggested to historians the following: first, although something like a protocaste system was in place in India during this period, it was far less rigid with regard to the division of society into warriors and nonwarriors than it was to become by the time of the Arab conquests in the eighth century A.D. Peasant militia fought alongside charioteers and elephant-mounted aristocrats, whose armor has survived to demonstrate some military divisions of labor. This is not much, but it is something. Indian armies of this period were not separate or isolated from society—by deployments, term of service, or discipline. They were not grossly unrepresentative of Indian society in terms of the strata from which soldiers were drawn. The society from which the soldiers were drawn was marked by caste but also by social mobility in war and by mutual military need across caste boundaries.

How did these Indian armies fight? The best firsthand historical data we have come from the letters and accounts written by the nineteen contemporaries of Alexander the Great who fought under his command or who accompanied him during his invasion of India in 326 B.C. These, along with other sources, form the basis from which Arrian wrote his history of the campaigns of Alexander.[35] Alexander's invasion of what is now the Punjab and his fighting withdrawal from India does not provide us with a direct military view of the Mauryan dynasty dominant at that time in India. Although it is known that Chandragupta Maurya was a

---

[34] Sarva Daman Singh, *Ancient Indian Warfare with Special Reference to the Vedic Period* (Leiden, Netherlands: E. J. Brill, 1965), pp. 14–15, 17, 19, 63, 140; Majumdar, *Military System of Ancient India*, pp. 15–16, 97, 102.

[35] For a review of the reliability of the Greek sources concerning Alexander in India, see J. W. M'Crindle, *The Invasion of India by Alexander the Great* (Westminster, Great Britain: Archibald Constable, 1896), pp. 7–10.

contemporary of Alexander, their armies did not encounter each other, the revolt of Alexander's armies having taken place before he reached Mauryan territory. The invasion does provide us with accounts of the battlefield performance of several kingdoms in that area, the armies of which resemble the descriptions of the armies of Chandragupta provided by the literary and archeological sources reviewed above.

Alexander's invasion had three major phases: his initial victories, the battle of Hydaspes, and his withdrawal. Alexander first encountered Indian soldiers who were in Persia to fight for the Persians, who controlled the territory to the west of India up to the Kabul River valley. Alexander was approached with offers of assistance by Indian rulers who hoped to use him for their own purposes before he reached India.[36] He faced an Indian army for the first time after crossing the Indus River near the city of Taxila, which archeologists have located and excavated northwest of the present-day city of Rawalpindi. Neither the ruler of Taxila nor the other Indians of that district were inclined to fight against Alexander, and they offered him their help, for which he "granted them, in return, as much of the territory bordering on their own as they asked for." Alexander met with and also successfully negotiated with the king of the Indian hill tribes in that area. The Indian tribes in the Indus River area provided Alexander not only with easy access to India but also with additional troops, bringing his troop strength up from eleven thousand mounted and on foot to about thirty thousand.[37] One Greek source noted that in this initial invasion across the border, Alexander's force was blocked in a pass by twenty thousand Indian troops under the command of a leader referred to as Erix, but after winning an initial victory, Alexander was welcomed by the Indian soldiers who "either from disaffection to their chief or to court the favor of the conqueror, set upon Erix during his flight and killed him. They brought his head and his armor to Alexander."[38]

Their lack of social and military solidarity appeared to have affected the military effectiveness and behavior of the Indians. This lack of solidarity was consistent with the picture of a divided Indian society—in which stable patterns of loyalty did not extend beyond the limits of small social groups—that has been inferred, as we have seen, from Kautilya and other sources. Whether this pattern of behavior is unique to India and whether armies were necessarily affected by broader social divisions in this period will be explored below.

---

[36] A. B. Bosworth, *Conquest and Empire: The Reign of Alexander the Great* (Cambridge: Cambridge University Press, 1988), p. 119.

[37] Arrian, *The Campaigns of Alexander*, trans. Aubrey de Seligncourt (London: Penguin, 1971), pp. 159–160, 165, 170, 259, 266; Bosworth, *Conquest and Empire*, pp. 127, 142.

[38] M'Crindle, *Invasion of India by Alexander*, citing Curtius Rufus, p. 200.

The major battle fought by Alexander took place in May of 326 B.C. after he crossed the river known in the ancient sources as the Hydaspes and today as the Jhelum, most probably near the modern-day Jalapur, against an Indian king known in the ancient Greek sources as Porus and by Indians as Paurava. The dominant facts concerning the performance of Indian forces at the battle of Hydaspes come from the firsthand account of Ptolemy, who fought under Alexander's command, and from Alexander's own letters.[39]

Alexander's principal problem was to cross the Hydaspes in the face of Porus's assembled army. He succeeded in doing so by means of a tactical deception, which succeeded well enough that one portion of his army was able to get across the river before a portion of Porus's force could challenge him with a force of infantry and charioteers. Arrian noted that the Indian charioteers declined to dismount from their chariots to fight Alexander's forces on the muddy banks of the river as those forces emerged from the water.[40] Advancing against the main body of Porus's army, which numbered approximately thirty thousand, Alexander initiated his attack with his mounted archery against the left and right flanks of the Indian army and then attacked the center of the Indian forces with his armored infantry. Porus positioned his three hundred elephants every hundred feet to intimidate the enemy and to protect his own infantry. The cohesion of the Indian army and Porus's ability to command it quickly broke down once the Macedonian phalanx engaged the elephants and the Indian infantry around them. According to Arrian, "The king's [Porus's] authority was in these circumstances unheeded, and, as usually happens when ranks are broken, and fear begins to dictate orders more peremptorily than the general himself, as many took command upon themselves as there were scattered bodies of troops. . . . No common plan of action was after all concerted." Porus's elephants, pushed back into the Indian infantry, began to trample Indian troops, and "Porus, meanwhile, being left in the lurch by the majority of his men," fought on alone. The Indian cavalry in this crisis did not assist the Indian infantry against the enemy phalanx but dealt as best it could with the Macedonian cavalry. Compressed into a mass, the Indian army was subjected to attack by arrows, heavy infantry, and cavalry raids, succumbing after perhaps two-thirds of its troops had been killed. Porus, treated magnanimously by Alexander, joined him as a friend.[41]

The third phase of the campaign came when Alexander's troops, un-

---

[39] Plutarch, *The Lives of the Noble Grecians and Romans*, trans. John Dryden (New York: Modern Library, n.d.), p. 844.

[40] Arrian, *Campaigns of Alexander*, p. 274.

[41] Ibid., pp. 276–278; see also M'Crindle, *Invasion of India by Alexander*, pp. 210–211.

defeated but facing the prospect of unending war in India, demanded of Alexander that he return home. He did so, but his way was not entirely unopposed. In his withdrawal, he first encounterd a group of thirty-seven towns, of which the smallest is said to have had a population of five thousand. Their leader had promised to fight alongside Porus at Hydaspes but had not shown up, and now he offered his surrender to Alexander. Alexander then encountered the Indian armies of the Sud-racae—referred to as the Oxydrakai by Arrian—which were united with the tribes of Cathei and Malli in the mountain stronghold of Sangala. In a strong defensive position, they refused to come out to fight Alexander, who surrounded their fortress. He was told by a traitor inside the fort that the Indians would try a night escape, and "at approximately the fourth watch the Indians, just as Alexander's informants had said they would do, opened the town gates . . . and made their way." Alexander then sprang his prepared ambush and killed all the Indians. Next he encountered the Sabsarcae, whose army is said to have numbered sixty thousand but who broke and ran on the battlefield when faced by Alexander. He also encountered and occupied a Brahmin village, which revolted against him, leading Alexander to kill all the Brahmin priests.[42]

This is history written by the victor about the vanquished. But it is history based on the accounts of multiple independent firsthand observers and has not been challenged by historians, European or Indian, and it provides us with a picture of Indian society and its armies. First, the Indian armies reflected the society from which they came. They were not professionalized, they were not fighting away from their home society, and functional integration of the components of the army that could have reduced the power of social divisions originating in the host society was not visible. As a result, the coordination among the various components of the Indian army that were drawn from different strata was poor, with charioteers refusing to fight as infantry and cavalry refusing to aid the infanty. Cohesion between Indian commanders and their troops was poor, most strikingly after initial reversals or injury to the commander. In Indian society as a whole, cohesion and trust among groups of people were low, and cohesion within one group was not reliable. Rather, betrayal could be expected and was exploited by the enemies of the Indians for strategic gain.

These patterns of social behavior and their military implications have long been noted by Indian military historians. Indian military authors writing about this initial period of Alexander's invasion have been con-

[42] Arrian, *Campaigns of Alexander*, pp. 281, 283, 286, 288–289, 309–310, 324; see also M'Crindle, *Invasion of India by Alexander*, pp. 236, 252–253.

cerned about the lack of solidarity among the Indian tribes or cohesion between soldiers and their officers in the presence of a foreign invader, lamenting the absence of any Indian protonationalism, which has been attributed to the effects of the caste system.[43] After reviewing the battle of Hydaspes, Jadunath Sarkar, the foremost Indian historian of ancient and Mughal military affairs, wrote that at the battlefield level, the Indian army was a "tribal levy, improvised for national defence under threat of invasion," and while "the Indian defenders of the Punjab were brave, . . . each man fought to the death in isolation . . ." The soldiers were "unable to make a mass movement in concert with their brethren of other corps." At the strategic level, the population of the Punjab was "disunited, narrowly self-centered, [and] mainly rustic." Their leadership was composed of disunited tribal leaders. The net effect was that "divided we fell." Sarkar also believed that the Indian armies of that time were significantly different in the level of military cohesion they displayed relative to roughly contemporary European armies. The only evidence he presented, however, was a quotation from book 2 of *The Iliad*, comparing the Asian Trojan army to the European Achaians: "The Trojans marched with clamour and shouting like birds. . . . But on the other side, the Achaians marched in silence, breathing courage, eager at heart to give succor man to man."[44]

The comparative question is the central one. Indian society had its military weaknesses but also its strengths. Although defeated by the foremost general of the time, Indian empires toward the end of this period were also strong enough to defeat the Epthalite Huns who had invaded as far as Kabul and were able to deter further attacks.[45] Are there reasons to believe that Indian military behavior displayed systematic characteristics which were the consequence of the nature of Indian society and of Indian military organizations that, by all accounts, were representative of that society? Or were Indian armies of variable quality, sometimes good or bad depending on individual military leaders and circumstances, and not significantly different from the armies generated by other societies of the same time?

[43]See, for example, Lt. Col. S. K. Sinha, "Compulsory Military Training," *United Service Institution of India Journal* 407 (April–June 1967): 114–126: "It is an unfortunate fact of our national history that we seldom repelled an invader. . . . The failure to offer suitable resistance may be traced in no small measure to the pernicious caste system."

[44]Jadunath Sarkar, *Military History of India* (Calcutta: Sarkar, 1960), pp. 8–10, 20–23. See also Mookerji, *Chandragupta Maurya*, p. 26, and Majumdar, *Military System of Ancient India*, p. 46.

[45]The empire in question was the Gupta in the years 460–470 A.D. See Rene Grousset, *The Empire of the Steppes: A History of Central Asia*, trans. Naomi Walford (New Brunswick, N.J.: Rutgers University Press, 1970), pp. 69–70.

THE SOCIETIES AND ARMIES OF GREECE AND MACEDON

It is not difficult to find numerous accounts of the breakdown of social cohesion along class lines in ancient Greece or to find historical examples of how these social divisions could have been and were exploited by Greek and non-Greek belligerents. Despite this, military historians have tended to emphasize noteworthy examples of solidarity within Greek armies and among Greek city-states when confronted with foreign invaders. The father of ancient Greek social history, Fustel de Coulanges, wrote about the division within Greece into city-states that formed "completely separate societies," between which intermarriage was, with some exceptions, illegal and beyond which "the ancients were never able to establish, or even to conceive of, any other social organization" than temporary military alliances.[46] Did this have consequences for warfare as practiced by the ancient Greeks? In what is probably the most systematic review of the evidence concerning the internal levels of solidarity displayed by Greek city-states in war, Luis Losada found that instances of internal betrayal of a city-state to the enemy with which the city-state was at war could be found as early as 490 B.C., when the Persians besieging a Greek city-state were assisted by disaffected citizens within the wall of the city. Focusing on the Peloponnesian War, Losada counted twenty-seven instances of planned or actual betrayals, of which thirteen were successful, twelve never came off, and two were thwarted. The plots were divided roughly evenly between the two warring coalitions, with fifteen pro-Spartan plots and twelve pro-Athenian plots. Losada, following Thucydides, accounted for these plots by referring to the social structures of the cities—to the division between oligarchic and democratic factions—to what Solon, Thucydides, and Plato called *stasis*, civil war or factional strife, "the condition resultant when the parties no longer feel bound to operate within constitutional limits . . . [and] resort to illegal means; e.g. open fighting, assassination, and expulsion of their opponents." Going beyond Thucydides, Losada argued that social divisions could also have a quasi-ethnic as well as a class dimension. Cities settled by different groups could split along the resulting ethnic lines: the Athenian expedition against Sicily hoped for success because of the belief that Sicily would split along the Dorian/Ionian lines of its population.[47]

Losada does not discuss what is arguably the most important division

[46] Numa Denis Fustel de Coulanges, "The Municipal Spirit," in *The Ancient City: A Study of the Religion, Laws, and Institutions of Greece and Rome*, trans. Willard Small (Garden City, N.Y.: Doubleday Anchor, n.d.), pp. 201–205.

[47] Luis A. Losada, *The Fifth Column in the Peloponnesian War* (Leiden, Netherlands: E. J. Brill, 1972), pp. 1–4, 25, 47, 66–70.

in the society of one Greek state, one that led, in effect, to the end of the first phase of the Peloponnesian War with the Athenian victory at Pylos and the subsequent Peace of Nicias. Spartan society rested on a system of agricultural slavery that provided each full Spartan citizen with a plot of state-owned land, called a *kleros*, and a cohort of state-owned slaves, called helots. The slaves and the land functioned to make of the full Spartan citizens, the Spartiates or *homoioi* (Equals), something unusual in Greece: a class of men who did not themselves have to farm or engage in commerce to support themselves and who were, as a result, free to engage in full-time military training and prosperous enough to be able to buy the armor and weaponry of the hoplite heavy infantry. The nine thousand *kleroi* originally supported a maximum of nine thousand hoplites, a number that decreased over time for various reasons. These slave-supported hoplites were the basis of Spartan military prowess.[48] As full-time professionals, the Spartiates were able to train together in peacetime, developing their loyalty to one another. They lived and ate in barracks in exclusively adult male society. This made possible the development of organized unit warfare—the infantry phalanx—in which individual combat was replaced by warfare executed by disciplined, cohesive units. The Spartan system thus rested on a society that was divided between full Spartan citizens and the helotry and a military organization that was professional and separate from the society as a whole. The society was divided, but the army was separate and cohesive.

It was this kind of collective military behavior that caught the eye of Western and Asian observers. Persian soldiers were not foot soldiers armed with swords and lances but with bows and arrows—or they fought from horseback. Hans Delbrück noted: "It is not only the difference in arms, however, that distinguishes the Persians from the Greeks. The power of the phalanx rests . . . on the steadfastness of the whole of the tactical formation." In contrast, "the Persians do not form a tactical body. . . . By their very nature they tend to spread out rather than to form a unit." A conversation between the commander of the Persian forces, Xerxes, and the exiled Spartan king, Demaratus, on the military strengths and weaknesses of the Spartans and Persians turned on this difference. Xerxes boasted that one Persian soldier was the equal of three Greeks, to which Demaratus answered that the real Spartan "strength lies in their joint steadfastness, and the law commands them to conquer and die

[48]See Paul Cartledge, *Sparta and Lakonia: A Regional History, 1300–362 B.C.* (London: Routledge and Kegan Paul, 1979), pp. 96–97, 164–165, 167–169, 176–177, 243, 248; M. I. Finley, *Economy and Society in Ancient Greece* (London: Chatto and Windus, 1981), pp. 27–28; Alvin H. Bernstein, *Soviet Defense Spending: The Spartan Analogy* (Santa Monica, Calif.: Rand Corporation, N-2817–NA, October 1989), pp. 6–36.

standing together in rank and column. We stress this point specifically: the Greek hoplites formed a closed tactical body; the Persian warriors do not."[49] It was this form of military organization that defeated the Persians at Marathon and at Platea, despite the betrayal of the Greek Ephialtes who showed the Persians a way to bypass the Spartans at Thermopylae and despite the fact that the Greek army as a whole came from twenty different and bickering communities. At both battles, the Persians were maneuvered into positions in which the individual prowess of their soldiers was rendered useless because they could not find space to deploy, while the solid phalanx of the Spartans could and did hold steadfast.[50]

But Spartan military virtue, based on the segregation of the full-time male soldiers from helot, female, and family societies into permanent military organizations, had its price. First, the Spartan military system was highly elitist, which kept the size of the Spartan army drawn from the Spartan citizenry small and sensitive to casualties. Although there were a maximum of nine thousand full Spartan citizens in early years, only five thousand Spartan citizens faced the Persian at Platea, and a generation after the Peloponnesian War, only one thousand full Spartan citizens were at the battle of Leuctra. All commentators have noted that the capture of only 120 Spartan citizens at the battle of Pylos contributed to the Spartan decision to seek peace in order to secure their return.[51] But the Spartan system had an even more serious weakness in the form of very serious tensions between the slave population that formed the basis of Spartan society and the Spartan military. By the time of the Peloponnesian War, helots were almost entirely Messenians and thus territorially, ethnically, and linguistically distinct from the Spartans. Since these helots were owned by the state, they could not be freed by their individual masters, nor could their loyalty be obtained by promises of manumission for them or their children in return for their faithful service. The Spartan citizens dined in military messes and did not eat with helots. Helots could not intermarry with Spartans. The consequence, according to Aristotle, was that "the helots were constantly on the watch for Sparta's misfortunes, just as if they lay in ambush." Sparta's neighbors, which

---

[49] Hans Delbrück, *History of the Art of War*, vol. 1, *Warfare in Antiquity* , trans. Walter J. Renfroe Jr. (Lincoln: University of Nebraska Press, 1990), pp. 67–69.

[50] Ibid., pp. 79, 92, 112–116.

[51] Spartiates declined in number over time for a variety of reasons, and more and more Spartan soldiers had to be drawn from the nonlandholding classes known as the *perioeci* and from the sons of Spartiates who no longer qualified for full Spartiate rights. But even with these additions, there was a limited pool of men, and only 4,480 Spartan soldiers of all sorts fought at the battle of Leuctra. See Bernstein, *Soviet Defense Spending*, p. 32.

did not have similar systems of slavery, all became its enemies because of the danger that foreign armies might ally with the helots against the Spartans.[52] The solution to the pathologies of this social structure was the Spartan institution of every year having the newly elected Spartan leaders, the ephors, ritually declare war on the helots, and having Spartan youths engage in a secret campaign of terror, the *Krypteia*, against helot leaders who became too prominent. These measures could keep the helots under control so long as no foreign army appeared in the Peloponnese to challenge the Spartans and aid the helots.

This is precisely what happened at the battle of Pylos during the Peloponnesian War in 425 B.C. The Athenian commander Demosthenes, having brought with him Messenian troops that could speak the same language as the helots, found himself forced by storm to land on the coast of the Peloponnese in helot territory, where, as Thucydides noted, "the Messenians, whose country this used to be and who spoke the same dialect as the Spartans, were capable of doing a lot of damage if they had this place as a base." The Athenians won the battle at Pylos, isolated and captured a number of Spartans on the offshore island of Sphacteria, and caused great fear of helot uprisings among the Spartan leadership. The Spartans took recourse to the infamous subterfuge of asking each helot whether he thought his service to Sparta had earned him his freedom. Having found two thousand helots who said yes, as Thucydides recounted, the Spartans caused them to disappear: "No one ever knew exactly how each one of them was killed." The Athenians, however, retained control of Pylos and continued their raids into Spartan territory. Thus, "the helots were deserting, and there was always the fear that even those who remained loyal might gain confidence from the others and take advantage of the situation to make a revolution, as they had done in the past." The Spartans also signed the Peace of Nicias, in which the Athenians and Spartans exchanged captured cities and returned prisoners and in which Athens agreed that "in the case of a rising of the slaves, the Athenians are to come to the aid of Sparta with all their strength, according to their resources."[53]

We are now in a better position to judge the case of ancient India in comparative perspective. It may reasonably be stated that both ancient India and ancient Greece were subject to social divisions that reduced the levels of trust that could be expected across community boundaries—

[52] Aristotle, *The Politics*, trans. Carnes Lord (Chicago: University of Chicago Press, 1985), pp. 73–75 (2.9.1269a, b).

[53] Thucydides, *History of the Peloponnesian War*, trans. Rex Warner (London: Penguin, 1986), pp. 313, 356. See also Donald Kagan, *The Archidamian War* (Ithaca: Cornell University Press, 1990), pp. 221, 239, 248.

castes in the case of India, cities in the case of Greece. Internal betrayals from within a community at war could and did occur regularly in both Greece and India, producing similar modes of warfare that deliberately exploited those betrayals. We can say that in Greek society the city-state with the most severe internal divisions related to its social structures had the most severe problems maintaining social cohesion in war, though the tensions between rich and poor were present in democracies as well as in the Spartan oligarchy. The special fighting power and character of Spartan military institutions were not a direct reflection of Spartan society but the result of the purposeful, insistent segregation of the Spartan army from the larger Spartan society—based economically on the helots—that supported it. The Spartan army did not represent the agricultural bulk of the Spartan population but was literally at war with it. Demographically, the Spartan army was not representative of the whole of Spartan society. It did reflect and embody the hierarchical norms of Spartan society, and the ruling elites of Spartan society were not estranged from the army, but the army as a whole was estranged from society as a whole and lived in fear of its rebellion. As a result of this relationship between the army and society, strong cohesion existed within Spartan military units, which led directly to both battlefield and strategic success; cohesion between the army and the political leadership, which led to treaties to ransom small numbers of Spartiates who had been taken prisoner at Pylos in the Peloponnesian War; but also fissures between the army and society, which, when exploited militarily, forced the Spartans to negotiate a compromise peace, despite a general run of victories.

Rather than an Indian versus a "Western Way of War" that at least Victor Davis Hanson has identified after studying ancient Greece,[54] we instead see the importance of divisions within a society and of forms of military organization that did or did not separate an army from its society. Greek society could produce powerful armies, but it did not seem to have been free of social divisions within and among city-states. Surviving muster rolls and other evidence indicate that in non-Spartan Greek armies, members of tribes were deployed in phalanxes with their fellow tribe members, alongside soldiers from their own town or residence.[55] This indicated that loyalties to units larger than the tribe were

---

[54] Victor Davis Hanson, *The Western Way of War: Infantry Battle in Classical Greece* (New York: Oxford University Press, 1989), pp. 9–18. Hanson emphasized the importance of a common Greek language in unifying the military units from various parts of Greece and a common ethos in Greece that believed in fighting battles and wars to murderously decisive finishes on the battlefield; see pp. 10, 16, 107.

[55] Ibid., pp. 119–122. Captured muster rolls from 415 B.C. Syracuse show, for example, that tribesmen were deployed together in units.

not sufficiently strong to make tribal loyalties dispensable in organizations for war. Greek society and Indian society were fragmented, perhaps one more than the other, but what seems to have been decisive in explaining the important differences in their military behavior in the face of foreign invasion was the relationship chosen by the different societies between their armies and themselves. The Indian armies mirrored their large societies, the Spartan army did not. Sparta thus generated an army that had high levels of military effectiveness but at the price of a tension within Sparta that led to a set of strategic liabilities.

These conclusions are reinforced when we examine in detail the ancient Western army that actually encountered and defeated Indian armies—the army of Alexander the Great. The available historical evidence strongly suggests that although the military capabilities of Alexander's army were clearly superior to contemporary armies, this was not the result of the absence of divisive social structures in the society from which Alexander's army emerged. The military power of this army derived from the close cooperation within and among the branches of the army, branches which came from different social strata and ethnic groups and which under other circumstances might have been expected not to trust and support one another. But this collective cooperation appears to have been the product of specific forms of military organization and the length of time the army spent in the field, dependent on itself and isolated from its social origins.

Hans Delbrück has written that the Macedonian army inherited by Philip II, Alexander's father, was composed of poor Macedonian farmers and shepherds, too poor to own heavy armor or weapons. According to Thucydides, Brasidas, a Spartan contemporary of that army, indicated that the Macedonian infantry did not display any notable cohesion or other military capabilities: "In hand to hand combat they are worthless, for they do not remain in formation and feel no shame in falling back out of position." The Macedonian cavalry was drawn from the aristocracy and was probably more cohesive than contemporary Greek cavalry because Macedonian aristocrats had less power relative to their monarch, and all had to submit to his orders, which led to less unruly military behavior. Philip II, however, took this army of disparate elements and transformed it into an army in which the cavalry, which had been dominant for military and social reasons, became militarily subordinate to the infantry on the battlefield. He constructed a new form of infantry organization based on the phalanx in which soldiers fought with long spears as a cohesive unit. So great was the shock value of this mass formation that rather than being used to soften the enemy for the coup de grace in the form of a cavalry charge, the cavalry was now used to pin down the enemy force by raids on its flanks to prepare for the de-

[89]

cisive attack of the infantry phalanx. Archers and special elite infantry units were also used to protect the rather unwieldy and tactically inflexible phalanx from attacks designed to exploit its lack of maneuverability.

What is important is not the details of ancient warfare but the ability of Philip II to construct a complex military organization with combat specialization in which all of the units trusted one another sufficiently to come to one anothers' aid, even though they came from different social strata and from different groups in society. This was a massive advance on armies composed simply of groups of tribesmen fighting alongside one another, or small military elites like that of Sparta. As Delbrück noted, "The progress made by the Macedonians lies in the organizational blending of all branches of the arms in unified cooperation."[56] A. B. Bosworth echoed this judgment and remarked that the Macedonian phalanx enjoyed "a cohesiveness and weight of offensive armament that was unmatched in the contemporary world."[57] This cooperation could be seen on the battlefield when Alexander faced Porus. Alexander's fast-moving cavalry found the Indian troops first. Any other cavalry of antiquity would have simply attacked: well into the nineteenth century, cavalry officers wrote that a cavalry element that hesitates to engage an enemy it has found has lost its purpose. Alexander, however, "checked the advance of his cavalry to allow the infantry to come up with him. Regiment by regiment they made contact, moving swiftly until the whole force was again united." The cavalry harassed the Indian army, as we saw, until the time was right for the infantry attack, and it then supported the infantry instead of seeking battle with its aristocratic counterpart on the enemy side.[58]

How was this integration achieved? The Macedonian army began with a tribal form of organization, but Philip II made a decisive innovation by separating his infantry from the tribal society from which it came. Tribal militia were replaced with standing infantry units manned by peasant conscripts, who were constantly in training or in battle and were given a status within the military equal to the cavalry, in part to check the political power of the aristocracy. The economic basis of the standing army, of necessity more expensive than occasional tribal levies, was likely related originally to the devastation in Greece caused by the Peloponnesian War, which impoverished many farmers and led them to seek military employment. After that, the standing army seems to have

---

[56] Delbrück, *Warfare in Antiquity* 1:175–180. Delbrück repeats Thucydides' reference to Brasidas's comment on the Macedonians on p. 175; the reference to the Macedonian infantry is on p. 180.

[57] Bosworth, *Conquest and Empire*, pp. 259–271. The quotation is on p. 261.

[58] Arrian, *Campaigns of Alexander*, p. 276.

been paid from the revenues generated by successive wars of conquest, particularly Alexander's conquests in Persia. As the army expanded to include foreign allies, the constant campaigning kept the ethnic additions to Alexander's army far from home, isolated from their home societies, and dependent on the army organization for their survival.[59] None of this suggests that Macedonian society or Alexander's empire was any more or less cohesive than Indian society, but it does indicate that a combination of circumstances, partly contrived, partly accidental, allowed the army of Macedon to develop into an organization that divorced soldiers from the loyalties created by the social structures of their larger societies so that the army became a self-sustaining society of its own. Because it had weak connections to the societies from which it came, the army, like the empire, could not survive the death of Alexander and the constant campaigning which he insisted on and of which even his army grew tired.

The Spartan and Macedonian armies were divorced from societies with divisions not hugely different from those of Indian society. They were militarily successful on the battlefield, but precisely because they were isolated from their societies, they created larger vulnerabilities for themselves. The Indian military of this time, which was, in contrast, drawn from its society, reflected the weaknesses of that society and met defeat on the battlefield but was easily regenerated by that society as well. A kind of iron law of society and military power seems to have existed under the conditions of ancient life: it held that military links to society had to be traded off for military effectiveness, the effects of the surrounding culture had to be eliminated for the sake of military strategy. But this solution was unstable because an army that was divorced from its society could not be easily regenerated by that society, and so the army could not afford to lose major battles. An army that was drawn from society could easily be regenerated, but it was inferior militarily. Was it possible under the conditions of ancient societies to create armies which did not become segregated from their societies but which were also militarily cohesive? In particular, was it possible to construct an army that had social roots and military capabilities such that the army and the society together were able to do what the Indian army and society were not able to do—maintain its cohesion in the face of a military genius leading an army of professionals who penetrated into the homeland, inflicted repeated defeats on the defenders, and sought to win the war by eliciting

---

[59] John Frederick Charles Fuller, *The Generalship of Alexander the Great* (New York: Da Capo, 1989 [facsimile of 1960 Rutgers University Press edition]), pp. 15, 42, 47–51; Bosworth, *Conquest and Empire*, p. 243.

defections from the subunits of the defender's society? This question inevitably draws us to the armies of the Roman Republic and to Rome's reaction to the invasion of Hannibal in the Second Punic War.

THE ARMY OF THE ROMAN REPUBLIC

Let us begin by asking to what extent Roman society was divided into subgroups that displayed castelike characteristics that might have fragmented Roman society and the Roman army. One potential source of division in Roman society was the division between the citizens of Rome and the inhabitants of the communities which were ethnically and linguistically separate from Rome but which were allied with Rome. Laws governed the groups into which Roman citizens could marry (the *ius conubi*), but intermarriage between Romans and the inhabitants of the communities allied with Rome has been claimed by some scholars to have been extensive, a judgment based largely, in the absence of marriage records, on evidence of extensive Roman colonization into allied communities. Evidence also exists of the systematic reduction of barriers between Romans and citizens of allied communities, for example, by the practice common among noble families in allied communities of sending their sons to schools in Rome and by intensive efforts to spread Latin and make it the common language of Italians.[60]

Other studies have also suggested that in the period of the later Republic (249–50 B.C.), the social structures dividing Roman society into hereditary classes were weak. Keith Hopkins, for example, argues:

> There was continuous movement into and out of the Roman political elite during the last two centuries of the Republic. This conclusion is based on a study of consuls, the chief elected offices of the Roman state. One third (35%) of all consuls elected in the period 249–50 B.C. had no direct consular ancestor in the previous three generations . . . ; barely one third (32%) of all consuls had a consular son. Political success did not guarantee political successors. We extended our investigations to cover praetors, the elected magistrates who ranked second to consuls. Praetor's chances of having politically successful sons were much lower than consuls' chances. The results of our research imply that the Roman senate was wide open to outsiders, that is, to men who were not themselves the sons of senators.

---

[60]See William V. Harris, *Rome in Etruria and Umbria* (London: Clarendon, 1971), pp. 160, 170–174, for what is known of Roman/allied social integration and the scholarly debate on this subject.

In addition, Hopkins determined that there were frequent intermarriages between senatorial and the older equestrian classes and that the upper class recruited from Italian outsider families recently assimilated to Rome.[61]

Historians of the Roman republic have even looked at the works of modern political scientists such as Edward C. Banfield, who argued that "anti-community patterns of behavior" could be found in modern Italy, to see whether similar patterns could be found in Republican Rome. As Stephen Dyson put it: "Clearly, investigations of this sort are of considerable interest to ancient historians, who often are dealing with communities deeply split by social tensions and family ambitions. The lurid picture that Cicero paints of family fighting in first-century B.C. Larinum well illustrates this point." Analysts must be careful to distinguish between the early and late republican times when assessing "anti-community patterns of behavior," because the early Roman republic experienced a period of Italian solidarity against Hannibal, but the late republic lived through the murderous internal Social War of 91–89 B.C., during which Romans killed perhaps twice as many Romans as did Hannibal. But when looking at the second century B.C., Dyson found evidence to contradict "many traditional reconstructions of Roman rural history which have tended to picture the Roman countryside as a place of extreme economic stratification and major social strife, a world which by the late Republic had lost most of its sense of community. . . . I would argue that cohesive communities did survive in rural Italy." Dyson reviewed the archeological evidence and found that it did not support a picture of unrelieved rural poverty. For the Roman provinces in this period, there is archeological evidence of large projects funded by aristocrats for the benefit of the entire community, such as communal baths in Stabia. Other theaters and baths found in Campanian cities date from second and first centuries B.C. Capuan religious inscriptions enable scholars to identify and to some extent track the social origins of Italian elites. Dyson adds: "Some sixty percent of those whose origins can be identified were freeborn, while forty percent were freed slaves. Some of the collegia were composed of persons drawn from one status group, but others were a mixture of freeborn and freed." Another record "indicates that the new Roman Mediterranean economy offered opportunities to the ambitious slave."[62]

If these scholarly pictures of Rome before the first century B.C. are at

---

[61] Keith Hopkins, *Death and Renewal: Sociological Studies in Roman History* (Cambridge: Cambridge University Press, 1983), pp. 32, 108, 111–112.

[62] Stephen L. Dyson, *Community and Society in Roman Italy* (Baltimore: Johns Hopkins University Press, 1992), pp. 17, 44–46. The reference to Edward Banfield is on p. 14.

all correct, they suggest a society that, while scarcely a modern egalitarian society, was far less marked by divisive linguistic, ethnic, or hereditary structures than ancient India. What of the armies of Republican Rome? Here, we should ask the same questions we asked of the Indian and Greek armies. How large were they relative to society and how reflective of the social structures of those societies? How much did they fight, and were they likely to be divorced from their societies by their organization or by frequent campaigns? Did they fight as conglomerations of individuals or as cohesive units in which military discipline had reduced the influences of the social structures from which the soldiers came?

The Roman army was originally composed both of legions, filled with volunteers drawn from only the ranks of Roman citizens who could afford the cost of their own armor and weapons, and of army units drawn from the allies of Rome, which were not formed into legions. The size of the allied contingent of the Roman army was confined to half the entire army.[63] The Roman army as a whole thus included Romans and other Italians. The best estimates of the size of the Roman population and of the army of Republican Rome have been assembled and assessed by P. A. Brunt from Roman census figures. He concluded that in the years before 225 B.C., the Roman census counted only men eligible for military service. These census numbers cross-check well with assessments that begin with estimates of the total Roman population and then work back on the basis of reasonable demographic assumptions to calculate how many freemen of military age could have been available for service. Both figures converge toward 270,000 men eligible for military service in 234 B.C. before the Second Punic War and the invasion of Hannibal, out of a total free population of Rome of 923,000 and a total free population of Rome and its allies of 2,750,000. During the war with Hannibal and afterward during the prolonged occupation of Spain, a Roman soldier in the legions would probably serve an average of six or seven years continuously in the field, some serving as many as twelve years away from home. On the basis of evidence from Livy and of archeological evidence, such as the identifying numbers that Roman legions inscribed on the lead slugs they used in their slings, the number of legions in the field can be estimated. In 212 B.C. at a high point of the war with Hannibal, twenty-five Roman legions were in the field with eighty thousand Roman legionnaires. This declined to eighteen legions with fifty thousand Roman soldiers. Roman legionnaires were not the only Italian military personnel during the war with Hannibal. If Italian soldiers allied

---

[63] Delbrück, *Warfare in Antiquity*, p. 263.

to Rome are added, if the thirty-five thousand Romans serving in the Roman navy are included, if some number of Italian soldiers are assumed to have been fighting alongside Hannibal, and if allowances are made for the number of soldiers lost to disease and battle casualties, the number of Italians under arms during the Hannibalic War rises to a maximum of 225,000–240,000, the great majority of whom were fighting for Rome, and a minimum of 125,000–100,000 as the war wound down. The number of Italians under arms remained high in the twenty-five years after the war, ranging from 95,000 to 212,000.[64]

These estimates are reconstructed from incomplete and imperfect records, and too much emphasis should not be placed on exact numbers. The point of the exercise is to establish that during and after the Hannibalic War, external military pressures led Rome to keep 20 to 30 percent of its free adult males of military age in the legions (50,000–80,000 out of 273,000)[65] This meant that about 8 percent of all Italians were engaged in military affairs during the Hannibalic War (240,000 of 2,750,000 free Romans and allies), declining to perhaps 3 percent thereafter (95,000 out of a Roman and allied population which had grown to over three million by the end of the second century B.C.). The demand for military manpower gradually led to an enlargement of the pool eligible for service in the legions. Originally composed as a citizen's militia drawn from those wealthy enough to buy their own military equipment and eligible to vote, it became a force drawn also from the proletariate, whose equipment was paid for by the state. By the time conscription of proletarii into the legions was legislated by Marius during his consulship in 107–100 B.C., nothing was left of the citizens' militia. The officer corps was drawn extensively from the upper classes, inasmuch as service in the military was the prerequisite for participation in Roman political life.[66]

Thus at the time of the invasion of Hannibal, the Roman legions and the Roman army as a whole were seemingly both very large relative to Roman and Italian society—and so likely to include a representative sample of Italian society—*and* divorced for long periods of time from Roman society, such that legionnaires developed their own characteristic

[64] P. A. Brunt, *Italian Manpower, 225 B.C.–A.D. 14* (Oxford: Clarendon, 1971), pp. 44–45, 54, 59, 418, 422, 424–425.

[65] An independent analysis by William Harris puts figures of men of military age mobilized for the legions between 18 and 24 percent in 250 B.C., before the Second Punic War and the invasion of Hannibal. See William V. Harris, *War and Imperialism in Republican Rome, 327–70 BC* (Oxford: Clarendon, 1979), p. 44.

[66] Emilio Gabba, *Republican Rome, the Army, and the Allies*, trans. P. J. Cuf (Berkeley: University of California Press, 1976), "Origins of the Professional Army," pp. 11–12, and "The Roman Professional Army from Marius to Augustus," pp. 22–23; Harris, *War and Imperialism*, p. 11.

point of view on politics that was not clearly linked to the concerns of the segments of Roman society from which the soldiers originally came.[67] All this makes it difficult to make clear-cut judgments about the relationship of the Roman army to Roman society. Drawing heavily over long periods of time on Roman society for its manpower, the legions might well reflect the social structures of the republic. Fighting so long, in many cases in distant theaters, they might equally well form a separate military society no longer reflective of the society that first called it into existence. It thus becomes difficult to argue whether and to what extent the cohesiveness of Roman military organizations reflected the cohesiveness of Roman society that has been said by historians to have existed or whether that military cohesiveness existed independently of the character of Roman society because of the nature of its military organization. What can be done to refine our understanding of the relationship of Roman society to Roman military strengths and weaknesses?

By looking more closely at the army and at Roman society over the course of the republic, we can posit that the cohesiveness of Roman society may have aided in the formation of the legions, but it was the internal organization of the legions that created their effectiveness and maintained it even when Roman society clearly ceased to be cohesive, in part during the war with Hannibal, totally during the period of the Social War, and thereafter toward the end of the republic. That internal organization of the army, along with its physical separation from society did isolate the army from society and create cohesive military units, but it also led to fissures between the army and society that altered the nature of Roman politics.

Hans Delbrück has traced the origins of the legions. Key to the fighting power of the legions, which were originally drawn from the twenty tribes of Rome, was intense discipline, inculcated by drill and enforced by severe punishment. Organized into phalanxes, the legions would have had the same shock force as the phalanxes of the army of Macedon but also the same rigidity on the battlefield. Hundreds of men marching shield to shield simply had difficulty keeping in ranks over anything but a flat field, much less turning around on a battlefield while their enemies were pelting them. The Roman solution was to break the phalanx down into sections and then into maniples. There would be spaces between the men in a maniple, and space between the maniples. On the march, each maniple would keep a fixed distance from the one in front but could maneu-

---

[67]Gabba argues that by 100 B.C., Roman "soldiers now came from classes which did not entertain sincere and clearly defined political views. This, together with the fact that their demands as soldiers were purely of an economic nature, had drained the army of all political character." Gabba, *Republican Rome*, p. 33.

ver independently. To fight an enemy, the maniple behind would march up into the spaces in the maniple in front of it to form a solid phalanx, which could be decomposed if necessary. The result was a unit as strong as a phalanx but with much more maneuverability.

The point of this description is to suggest just how well drilled and disciplined the maniples had to be if they were to execute what we have come to think of as parade ground maneuvers on the battlefield and just how high the levels of trust among the men in separate maniples must have been. The men in the front units, if they were not to break and run when attacked by a powerful enemy, had to have absolute confidence that the units behind them would close up with them in an orderly fashion. The entire idea of war as individual combat had to be eradicated. Military discipline as we know it was born in the legions for this reason. As Delbrück noted in his summary discussion of the legions, "All the differences between the Greek and Roman military system can be traced back to the difference in discipline." Along with prolonged drill, elaborate written records were kept to insure that orders were obeyed, and failure to carry out orders was punished by death by stoning the next day.[68] These legions were constantly at war. During the period 327–241 B.C., there were at most four or five years in which Rome was not at war.[69] Drill, discipline, and constant war created the military system with which Rome made its conquests.

The military system of Rome was tested, however, by an equally cohesive army that did not come from a cohesive society. The army of Hannibal was composed of North Africans but also of Gauls and other allies hostile to Rome, and it won its most famous victory against Rome at Cannae because of its cohesiveness. The famous double envelopment of the Romans was set up by the withdrawal of the center of Hannibal's line, manned by Gauls. The key to the battle was putting as few troops as possible in the center of Hannibal's army, allowing the Romans to push them back so that the Romans could be attacked in the rear by the troops taken from the center of the Carthaginian line. Easy to say, as Delbrück noted, but the tactic relied on the troops in the center not breaking, despite the fact that, outnumbered, they would be taking the brunt of the attack and casualties, they would be retreating in the face of the enemy, and they were ethnically and linguistically alien to Carthage.[70] Hannibal's army was cohesive for the same reason as Alexander's. Led by a great captain, it was constantly at war and had become a self-sufficient independent military society.

[68] Delbrück, *Warfare in Antiquity*, pp. 272–275, 283–289.
[69] Harris, *War and Imperialism*, p. 10
[70] Delbrück, *Warfare in Antiquity*, pp. 322–324.

With that army Hannibal hoped to defeat republican Rome precisely by attacking the bonds that held it together, in exactly the same manner that Alexander brought about the defeat of the Indian forces. Before setting out against Rome, Hannibal sent emissaries out to the Celtic allies of Rome whom he would encounter along his route to Italy. Hannibal, as Polybius notes, "had thoroughly acquainted himself with the fertility and populousness of the districts at the foot of the Alps . . . but most importantly with their hostile feelings towards Rome. . . . When his messengers returned with a report that the Celts were ready to help him and all eagerness for his approach," he decided to march. News of his march immediately prompted one Gallic tribe, which "had long been lying in wait to throw off their loyalty to Rome," to revolt. Once over the Alps in Italy, Hannibal's strategy was clearly to elicit defections from Rome's allies by offering favorable terms to those who helped him and massacring those who resisted him, again, very much along the lines employed by Alexander in India. This strategy succeeded in leading a "Celtic contingent of the Roman army, seeing that Hannibal's prospects looked the brighter of the two," to mutiny and kill the Roman soldiers with whom they were deployed. Hannibal continued to advance in Italy, in part with the aid of the treachery of the commander of the Roman garrison of Clastidium, a city in which large quantities of food had been stored, treating all the Italian allies of Rome with great leniency, "wishing by this policy to attract the inhabitants of Italy to his cause and to alienate their affections from Rome and to awaken the resentment of all those who considered themselves to have suffered by the loss of harbours or cities under Roman rule," saying that "he was not come to fight against the Italians, but in behalf of Italians against Rome." Until that point, however, no city of Italy had defected to Hannibal, despite the Roman defeats at Trebia and Lake Thrasymene, "a fact which may show us the awe and respect which the Republic had inspired in its allies."[71] However, following the Roman defeat at Cannae, Italian cities did revolt from Rome, most notably Capua and Tarentum, the second and third largest cities of Italy, as well as numerous smaller cities.[72] Italian society, as opposed to Roman society, seemed no more cohesive than that of the Punjab when faced with an invader who could inflict repeated defeats on the dominant local power.

How, then, did Rome win? All commentators note that Rome and Roman colonies in Italy remained loyal during the war, continuing to

---

[71] Polybius, *Polybius on Roman Imperialism*, trans. Evelyn S. Shuckburgh, ed. Alvin H. Bernstein (South Bend, Ind.: Regnery/Gateway, 1980), pp. 115–118, 125, 131, 137, 138–139, 145, 151, 155 (book 3, 34–40, 48, 60, 67–69, 77, 85, 90).

[72] Delbrück, *Warfare in Antiquity*, p. 339.

supply the legions with soldiers. But Hannibal had defeated eight of eighteen legions and was picking up Italian support. What becomes clear here is the importance of the Fabian strategy, which is usually described as a strategy of attrition in which the Roman legions dogged the militarily superior army of Hannibal to wear him down while avoiding pitched battles that Hannibal would win. But why would a strategy of endurance not benefit Hannibal? The real importance of the Fabian strategy lies in what it displays about the relationship of the legions to Italian society. The Fabian strategy succeeded not simply because the legions wore Hannibal down but also because they were ready to make war on the potentially rebellious portions of Italian society. The Roman army stayed close to Hannibal both to harass him and to be close to any Italian city that was thinking about joining Hannibal when he showed up to "liberate" it from the Romans, ruthlessly punishing any Italian state that did dare to revolt. As a result, the defections to Hannibal did not bring permanent increases in his power, because as soon as Hannibal's army left the defecting city, the Roman legions would appear, besiege and then destroy the rebellious city. So great were the reprisals taken by Rome against Italian defectors that one scholar has attributed the decline in Italian agriculture not to the Hannibalic War itself but to the mass confiscation of lands from rebels which Rome dealt out as punishment, and which created a whole new class of landless rural inhabitants. If the Italian countryside was impoverished by land confiscations and not by the physical devastation that might have accompanied the Hannibalic War itself, this would explain the otherwise puzzling absence of archeological evidence of physical destruction in Italy, despite the existence of trustworthy accounts of rural poverty in the second century B.C.[73] To execute this strategy, the legions had to be the disciplined tool of Rome *against* parts of Italian society. The legions did emerge from a cohesive Roman society, but the Roman army as a whole emerged from an Italian society that did fragment when the fear of Rome was reduced by the appearance of a military challenger. Despite that fragmentation, the Roman legions were able to *enforce* cohesion on Italy by means of their internal organization.

What other evidence is there to help us analyze the relationship between Italian social structures and the Roman army? If cohesiveness in both the legions of Rome and the Roman society from which they were drawn makes it difficult to understand which was the cause of which, it is important to look for periods in Roman history in which cohesion in the society as a whole broke down, to see if the cohesion of the army

[73] Ibid., pp. 341–343; Brunt, *Italian Manpower*, pp. 277, 279–284; Dyson, *Community and Society in Roman Italy*, pp. 26–27, 44–45.

was affected. This brings us naturally to the period of the Social War in 91–89 B.C. While there is much debate about the causes of the Social War—the rise of new mercantile elites; radical stratification of the rural population in the aftermath of the Hannibalic War, which led to large plantations worked by slaves and large numbers of landless farmers; and so on—there is no doubt in the minds of scholars that the society of Rome and its allies was consumed by a war of all against all during this time. Estimates of the casualties suffered by Italians in the Social War put them at almost twice those suffered in the war against Hannibal (300,000 as opposed to 175,000), while archeologists have found that massive new construction of city walls, suggesting a rise in the perceived levels of violent danger, dates from this period. The proportion of Italians under arms during the Social War was probably equal to the maximum percentage of Italians under arms during the peak of the war against Hannibal (175,000 Roman soldiers fighting 130,000 rebels out of a total Italian population of about 3.5 million, or nine percent).[74] However high the levels of social cohesion in Italy earlier, internal warfare on this scale must have reflected and caused social conflicts that set Romans against their Italian allies, but also Romans against themselves.[75]

There is no sign, however, that the legions lost their internal cohesion during this period. Rather, all indications are that they became more divorced from society, with a stronger sense of their own community as soldiers, not as Romans. This is the period in which legionnaires who were veterans of foreign wars presented themselves to generals, seeking the *fides*, or the loyalty and protection of patrons and offering their *pietas*, or acknowledgment of their dependence as clients. These military clientele were composed, in the words of Emilio Gabba, of veterans "who are . . . homogenous in their social condition and their outlook. These men . . . have a heightened consciousness, either individually or collectively, of their own ability and their own rights which they have derived from their lives as soldiers and from their military experience." This shift in loyalties and in the soldiers' sense of their relationship to the larger society brought about a profound change in Italian politics in which "the army thereby ceases to be the state's army, but becomes in practice a private army." Within the legions the "various races of the peninsula" had become unified, but "while the army saw an accelerated trend towards fusion of various Italian races, the Roman *populares* on the other hand, operating in a strictly political sphere, collaborated with the rebel

[74] Dyson, *Community and Society in Roman Italy*, pp. 62, 63 n. 49, 67; Brunt, *Italian Manpower*, pp. 94–97, 436–438.
[75] As vivid a picture as any of the divisions within Rome can be found in Machiavelli's *Discourses on Livy*, book 1, discourse 37. See, for example, Niccolò Machiavelli, *The Discourses*, trans. Leslie J. Walker (London: Penguin, 1983), pp. 200–204.

Italian peoples and went so far as to participate ... in residual separatist tendencies, aiming at the independence of regional political groups." Given the solidarity and poverty of the legionnaires, the fragmentation of Roman and Italian society, the breakup of Roman elites into competing factions, and the willingness of generals to forge alliances with popular leaders, the ease with which Sulla persuaded the legions to march on Rome in the immediate aftermath of the Social War in 88 B.C. cannot be surprising.[76] The legions, cohesive when Roman and Italian society was cohesive, remained cohesive when the society became divided, given their existence as separate military communities divorced from society. The price, however, was that the legions became increasingly alienated from that society, which had now become a target for conquest.

But the cohesiveness of the legions did not mean that the changes in Roman and Italian society were strategically irrelevant. As the bonds of trust and loyalty within the political community of Italy broke down in the late Republic, changes in strategic emphasis also changed. Roman strategies in the period of the early Republic displayed only a minor emphasis on the exploitation and management of the internal divisions of opponents. The Roman strategy for the First Punic War, for example, relied simply on massive naval construction programs that allowed Rome to bring its land forces to bear against the maritime forces of Carthage. The legions themselves were the embodiment of a strategy for the "ferocious" application of highly organized force, unusual even for its time, against an enemy army or people.[77] Machiavelli, in his commentaries on Livy's history of early Rome, noted that it was advisable to use subterfuge against an enemy army, but he provided examples primarily of Roman generals doing the reverse and fighting their enemies to the finish on the battlefield.[78] By the late republic, however, written Roman strategies emerge that emphasize the uses of deception, betrayal, intrigue, and treason. The writings of the Roman general Frontinus (A.D. 40?–103), the governor of Britain, include a list of forty-three principles of war, fourteen of which are clearly directed at deceiving the enemy, inducing treachery, or protecting against deception and treachery.[79] Polybius contrasted the open warfare of the earlier Roman times with the more frequent use of stratagems and deceit observable in his life toward the finish of the second century B.C.[80] Machiavelli, observing retrospec-

---

[76] Gabba, *Republican Rome*, pp. 25–29.

[77] Harris, *War and Imperialism*, pp. 51–53.

[78] Machiavelli, *Discourses*, book 3, discourse 37 (p. 443).

[79] Neal Wood, introduction to *The Art of War*, by Niccolò Machiavelli (New York: Da Capo, 1965), pp. lix–lxi.

[80] See the discussion of the shift in modes of warfare in J. K. Anderson, *Military Theory and Practice in the Age of Xenophon* (Berkeley: University of California Press, 1970), pp. 1–

tively the changes in Roman society and reflecting on their strategic implications, noted that fortresses were constructed by rulers who did not trust either the people or their aristocratic rivals, but that precisely under those conditions, fortresses could be taken "through treachery of their keepers." It was far better to rely on "faithful troops," according to Machiavelli. "So long as Rome enjoyed freedom and was loyal to her institutions and to her efficient constitution, she never held cities or provinces by means of fortresses."[81] But when the troops had become alienated from society and its rulers, when the bonds that held society together had become weak, different strategies became more prevalent, ones that took into account the changes in social structures and the relationship of the army to society. By the end of the republic, Italian society had become at least as fragmented as Indian society, though for different reasons, and Machiavellian strategies resembling Kautilyan strategies had appeared to replace the strategies appropriate to earlier times in which both the army and the society had been more cohesive.

The propositions concerning the relationship between social structures and military power laid out in Chapter 1, as applied to ancient India and to ancient Greek and Roman societies and armies, would suggest that to the extent that both ancient India and ancient European societies were fragmented along linguistic, ethnic, or other lines, they would be vulnerable to enemy strategies that tried to exploit these social vulnerabilities. Further, under the conditions that prevailed at the time, mass militia–type armies that drew in large numbers of soldiers for intermittent periods of war would reflect those social vulnerabilities, which would then have consequences for the cohesion and capabilities of those armies on the battlefield. The armies that escaped the divisions of their societies by keeping their soldiers in the army and fighting for long periods of time could develop superior battlefield capabilities, but at the price of tensions between the army and society, which would have different strategic consequences. Specifically, ancient India, marked by protocaste structures, if it did employ mass militia armies, should have had armies that did not display cohesion among the elements that drew from various communities that did not cooperate closely in the larger society. According to the model, those vulnerabilities should have been reflected in the strategic thought of ancient times. The Indian militia-type armies

---

12. For the breakdown in order in Roman society somewhat later as measured by the varying levels of banditry during the empire, see Ramsay MacMullen, *Enemies of the Roman Order: Treason, Unrest, and Alienation in the Empire* (Cambridge: Harvard University Press, 1966; reprint, London: Routledge, 1992), pp. 193, 197, 255–268.

[81] Machiavelli, *Discourses*, books 2, discourses 10 and 24 (pp. 300–302, 352–357).

should have been inferior to armies that had divorced themselves from their societies to form cohesive armies, but they should not be radically weaker than other mass part-time armies.

This appears to have been the case. The army of Alexander had become cohesive via long campaigns that made it self-sufficient, even though the societies from which Alexander drew his soldiers were not noticeably cohesive. The ancient armies were able to deter the armies of the Huns as long as there was not open civil war in India. The societies of Greece—Sparta in particular—were marked by social structures that divided society at least as severely as the protocaste system divided India. Both ancient Greece and ancient India did have strategically relevant social vulnerabilities in war. The relatively cohesive society of Rome and its allies did help generate somewhat more cohesive armies that were better able to stand up to the challenges of foreign invasion. Yet the organization of the legions that separated the soldiers from their society did enable those legions to remain cohesive even when society fragmented, but at the price of alienation of the legions from society, which had an impact on Roman strategy.

Although the historical analysis tends to support the predictions generated by the general propositions, the record is not perfectly clear. Life and history are never as simple as theories. Data on the social structure of India are fragmentary, as are data on its military organization. Information on the social structures of Greek city-states and on their military structures is imperfect. The Roman legions were clearly the result of both a cohesive Roman society and of their organization, which makes the independent role of either hard to assess.

But the observation that emerges from this comparative analysis is that the strategic outlook of ancient India was not uniquely Indian. Other societies that displayed or developed similar fissures evidenced similar social vulnerabilities and developed "Indian" strategies. The armies that escaped their social origins tended to develop similar problems of army-social relations that affected strategy. The Indian army did not try to escape its social origins and paid a different price.

[4]

The Medieval Period in India: Mughal Rule, 1526–1707

In the Mughal Empire, a foreign military elite ruled a society with local structures indigenous to the area. The character of the Mughal political and military system had its origins in the system of rule that began with the Sultanate of Delhi, which was ethnically Afghan, and continued with modifications under the rule of the Mughals, who were Chaghtai-speaking Turks from Ferghana in what is now Uzbekistan. If we want to understand the military behavior of the Mughal armies, what mattered more—the mind-set of the elite or the nature of the military drawn from Indian society? How can one begin to ask the right questions about society and military power to assess how these layers of civilizations might have affected each other and the military performance of that empire? These are the questions central to this chapter. They will be asked about the Mughal Empire at the peak of its power, before decay and decline affected its character.

Because of the possible importance of the culture of the Mughal elite, this chapter will begin with an investigation of Central Asian Turkish ideas about war, the military, and society. Then, following the pattern laid down in Chapter 1 and applied in Chapter 3, I ask a series of questions. These will also be the questions we will ask in Chapter 5 about the British Empire and its army in India. These questions should lead to some conclusions about the nature of Indian society in a given period. In this period, there were differences in the character of the dominant social structures in different parts of India. However, Indian society, though differing between the Aryan-conquered north and the south and between the more highly caste-structured east and the more egalitarian Marathi-speaking areas, was divided by local subcaste and by religion. As for the nature of the Mughal armies, I will try to determine what

degree of separation existed between the Mughal army and Indian society by asking questions similar to those asked in the preceeding chapter. How big was the Mughal Empire relative to society? How was it
recruited? Was it used and deployed in ways that increased its distance
from society or the reverse? Was it professionalized? The data for the
Mughal period are better than for the period of ancient India, and reasonably robust answers to these questions can be obtained. For example,
because of the existence of administrative records from this period, we
can examine the composition and behavior of the Mughal military elites.
How many Mughal military chiefs were Turks or Muslims or Hindus?
Were there significant differences in the behavior of the Mughal elites
depending on the cultural identity of the members of the elite? Were, for
example, Hindu officers more or less likely to disobey orders than Turkish officers?

Finally, what differences can we see in military organization and in
the relationship of the military to society if we compare seventeenth-
century India to seventeenth-century Europe? In the case of Europe, we
know that there was a revolution in military organizations that not only
produced much more powerful armies but also transformed the relationship of the army to society by giving the professional armies and the
states that controlled them an effective monopoly on the instruments of
organized destruction within the boundaries of the nation or empire. Did
this happen in Mughal India? If not, why not? The Mughal armies were
large, and there was no successful effort in this period to separate them
from society or to professionalize them. The Mughal armies did reflect
the social divisions of Indian society. They were not able to project power
out of South Asia, despite the explicitly stated desire of the Mughal emperor to do so. Finally, the chapter will compare the Mughal and Ottoman Empires. Both were ruled by Turkish military elites, but the relation
of the Mughal army to Indian society was very different from the relation
of the Ottoman army to Ottoman society.

This is the simple version of the answer. The full answer is more complicated because the Mughal political and social system was far from
simple. When dealing with ancient India, our major problem was the
weakness of the primary data on the social structures, military organization, and military performance of the dominant culture. In the case of
medieval India, the opposite is the case. There is a wealth of administrative histories and official imperial histories, of varying quality, as well
as a few campaign diaries kept by Mughal generals and regional records
that provide some picture of the system of government and military organization. There are scholarly surveys, also of varying quality, of the
sociology of portions of Indian society in this period. These data reveal
enormously complicated social structures and political responses to those

social structures. Trying to understand what caused what is hardly easy. Crudely put, when we observe medieval Indian patterns of military behavior, are we seeing the influence of Turkish patterns of military thought imposed by the dominant elite; the impact of Hindu social structures on the Mughal military, which over time submerged the Turkish elite in Indian social realities; or simply the development of patterns of military technology that are common to all military organizations that are making the transition from traditional patterns of warfare to patterns characteristic of the era of gunpowder warfare?

To make sense of the extraordinarily complicated society and military of medieval India, we must make very clear what questions we are asking and how we mean to answer them. In the case of ancient India, the central question we posed was whether ancient India was relatively more easily penetrated by the invading army of Alexander the Great in comparison with ancient Greece and Republican Rome. In the case of medieval India, the comparative question that strikes an observer at the outset is, Why was the Mughal Empire not able to expand outside South Asia, even to regain control of the homeland of the Chaghtai elite in Ferghana? The Mughal emperor Jahangir wrote his memoirs after the emperor Akbar had consolidated Mughal control of northern India and before the rebellion and constant wars of the emperor Aurangzeb had exhausted and destroyed large portions of the empire. Even in this period of comparative peace and power, Jahangir was militarily unable to do anything more than keep his existing possessions more or less under control. In 1607, he expressed in his memoirs the desire to project Mughal military power outside South Asia: "As I had made up my exalted mind to the conquest of Mawara'a-n-nahr [Transoxiana], which was the hereditary kingdom of my ancestors, I desired to free the face of Hindustan from the rubbish of the factious and the rebellious and . . . to undertake the conquest of my ancestral dominions."[1] He found himself unable to do so and suggested the reasons why. As he toured his empire, he noted local political conditions in Afghanistan and the Punjab, where local warfare was endemic, and commented: "This tribe is wonderfully like animals; they are always squabbling and fighting with each other. Although I wished to put an end to this fighting, I was unable to do so." He visited another area in which one group systematically oppressed its neighbors while raiding the highways. He received reports on the lack

---

[1] Jahangir, *The Tuzuk-I-Jahangiri, or the Memoirs of Jahangir*, Alexander Rogers translation of the Henry Beveridge edition (London: Royal Asiatic Society, 1909), p. 89. This translation is based on the 1863–1864 Rogers translation with additions and corrections made by Beveridge on the basis of comparisons with additional Persian manuscripts, and it should not be confused with translations based on the 1829 Price translation to which I also refer.

of progress of the imperial army against the rebellion in the area of central India south of the Narmada River known as the Deccan, on the rebellion of the Afghan population of Bengal, and of the wars against the Hindu population of Rajasthan.[2] In a different version of Jahangir's memoirs, the origins of which are disputed, the emperor lamented the constraints imposed on the Mughal rulers by Indian internal social problems: "Notwithstanding the frequent and sanguinary executions which have been dealt among the people of Hindustan, the number of turbulent and disaffected never seems to diminish; . . . ever and anon, in one quarter or another, will some accursed miscreant spring up to unfurl the standard of rebellion; so that in Hindustan never has there existed a period of complete repose."[3] The Afghan province of Qandahar was taken by the Mughals before they conquered Delhi but was lost to the Persians in 1649. In 1656, while still the Mughal viceroy in the Deccan, Aurangzeb repeatedly tried to organize a campaign to reconquer Qandahar but was just as repeatedly told that he could not because the empire had not yet consolidated its control over the Deccan in southern India.[4]

This inability to develop a surplus of military power beyond that which was necessary for internal control of existing possessions is noteworthy. As Marshall Hodgson has noted, both the Ottomans and Savafid Iranian Muslim empires could and did make use of their imperial revenues to purchase an overwhelming amount of artillery, which they used first to overwhelm internal opposition and then to expand, despite the divisions among religious and ethnic groups within their empires.[5] But contrary to Hodgson, students of the Mughal Empire have argued that the empire in India was not able to consolidate its internal control and expand outward in the way that the Ottoman Empire did.[6] During the

---

[2] Ibid., pp. 77, 99–100, 178–183, 209–212, 249–250.

[3] Quoted in Dirk H. A. Kolff, *Naukar, Rajput, and Sepoy: The Ethnohistory of the Military Labour Market in Hindustan, 1450–1850* (Cambridge: Cambridge University Press, 1990), p. 14. This quote is from the disputed Price translation.

[4] Jagdish Narayan Sarkar, *The Life of Mir Jumla: The General of Aurangzeb* (New Delhi: Rajesh Publications, 1979), p. 163. For the siege of Kandahar by Shaibani Khan, a Mughal general serving Babur, see *Memoirs of Zehir-el-din Muhammad Babur*, vol. 2, trans. John Leyden and William Erskine (London: Oxford University Press, 1921), p. 54. For a persuasive discussion of the internal factors that forced the Mughal emperors to remain preoccupied with the internal matters of unrest in the Deccan, see M. N. Pearson, "Shivaji and the Mughal Empire," *Journal of Asian Studies* 35 (February 1976): 221–236.

[5] Marshall G. S. Hodgson, *The Venture of Islam*, vol. 3, *The Gunpowder Empires and Modern Times* (Chicago: University of Chicago Press, 1974), pp. 6–7, 24–25, 30, 47.

[6] See, for example, the discussion in Douglas E. Streusand, *The Formation of the Mughal Empire* (Delhi: Oxford University Press, 1989), pp. 68–70. See also the summary chapter in John F. Richards, *The New Cambridge History of India: The Mughal Empire* (New Delhi: Cambridge University Press, 1993), pp. 282–283.

same period of time that Mughal rule was seeking to consolidate itself in India, the societies of Europe were also plagued by incessant internal warfare, including the Thirty Years' War. But they developed political-military institutions that enabled them first to establish domestic peace and then to generate and project surplus military power with which they established overseas empires. As we noted at the outset in Chapter 1, this contrast between European success and Indian failure cannot be explained by differing levels of iron, steel, or weapons technology, because at the beginning of the eighteenth century, Mughal India was the equal of Europe in these areas and was in some areas superior. Yet Mughal India did not develop the same military strengths as contemporary Muslim empires or the West. Why?

Some answers have nothing to do with Indian social structure. Did the Mughal Empire have weaknesses because of the political culture of its elite? Central Asian pastoral nomads shared certain laws of political succession. The absence of any fixed law of political succession among the Mughal nobles did lead to constant rebellions among the heirs to the throne and among the tribal leaders, all of whom claimed to have as much royal blood running in their veins as the ruling princes. Did this aspect of the social structures of the Chaghtai Turks explain the internal debilities that hobbled the Mughal Empire? If so, why did it not cause similar debilities in the Ottoman Empire, which had similar problems of succession? Or did the problems of the Mughal Empire come about as the result of the fact that an alien elite could not and did not establish effective control over a massive indigenous population with different languages and religion? Or were the social structures of Hindu India the most important factor, since in the final analysis, it was Hindu society that provided the financial and human resources on which the Mughal Empire was based? Or if, as is most likely, the problems were the result of some combination of all these factors, roughly what did that combination look like? How did it work?

TURKISH SOCIETY AND MILITARY THOUGHT

There is not a great deal of information about the relationship between the society and armies of the Turkish-speaking peoples of Anatolia and Central Asia before the establishment of the Ottoman Empire. The bulk of the literature from this period is laudatory poetry,[7] but social-military

---

[7]See the introductory essay by Reuben Levy in Ibn Qabus ibn Washmgir [Kai Ka'us ibn Iskandar], *A Mirror for Princes: The Qabus Nama*, trans. Reuben Levy (London: Cresset, 1951), p. xii.

relations can be traced through the contemporary sociological studies conducted by Ibn Khaldun and the written advisories, known as "mirrors for princes," to the ruler of Turkish/Persian kingdoms. The reasons for seeking out these few sources is that students of the Mughal Empire in India agree that its political practices had their origins in the political practices of the nomadic Turkish peoples of Central Asia, having far more in common with that society and its political norms than it did, for example, with feudal Europe.[8] In India, but elsewhere as well, these nomadic peoples became sedentary and set up empires with relatively fixed capitals, and their behavior may help us establish a reference point from which we can observe possible deviations in Mughal India.

Ibn Khaldun's *The Muqaddimah* stands out as the great work of analytical sociology of the medieval Islamic world. It was based on the study not only of the Arab and Berber peoples of the western Islamic world but also of the Persians, Kurds, and Turks. The behavior he observed in the Arabs and Berbers he considered to be the purest form of pastoral nomadic societies, but similarities could be observed between their behavior and that of the other groups he studied.[9] The economic conditions of pastoral nomads in harsh climates were such, he argued and observed, as to have created fiercely loyal tribal units bound together by *asabiyah* or what we would call "group feeling" or "cohesion."

> Their defense and protection are successful only if they are a closely-knit group of common descent. This strengthens their stamina, since everybody's affection for his family and group is more important (than anything else). . . . Those who have no one of their own lineage (to care for) rarely feel affection for their fellows. If danger is in the air on the day of battle, such a one slinks away and seeks to save himself, because he is afraid of being left without support. . . . Nothing can be achieved in these matters without fighting for it . . . and for fighting one cannot do without group feeling.[10]

The cohesion that began in family groups and blood relations was extended to patron-client relations in pastoral societies. "Clients and allies belong in the same category," Ibn Khaldun argued, as blood relations.

---

[8] See the discussion in Ishtiaq Husain Qureshi, *The Administration of the Mughal Empire* (Patna, Bihar, India: N. V. Publications, n.d. [1974]), p. 113; and *Formation of the Mughal Empire*, Streusand, p. 31: "The Timurid polity was one of a series of pastoral nomad confederations in the Islamic world; in other words, much or most of the military power rested in nomad tribes."

[9] Ibn Khaldun, *The Muqaddimah: An Introduction to History*, vol. 1, trans. Franz Rosenthal (Princeton: Princeton University Press, 1980), p. 252.

[10] Ibid., translator's note, pp. lxxviii–lxxxiv.

"The affection everybody has for his clients and allies results from the feeling of shame that comes to a person when one of his neighbors, relatives, or blood relation in any degree is humiliated. The reason for it is that a client-master relationship leads to close contact exactly or approximately in the same way as common descent." The consequence of these highly cohesive but narrow social subunits was intense competition among rival tribal leaders, or *fitmah*, variously translated as "rebellion" or "disorder," which constituted, according to Ibn Khaldun, the basic political dynamic in such societies.[11] Constant conflict internal to nomadic societies was the norm and was only occasionally suppressed by leaders who could claim religious authority or who could found a dynasty to overawe the other tribes. Neither of these solutions was stable, because they led to sedentary life for the rulers, the pursuit of luxury, and to the decay of their fighting abilities, from which followed Ibn Khaldun's most famous generalization that "dynasties have a natural lifespan like individuals," usually living a maximum of three generations or 120 years, and occasionally lasting twice that long, a span which neatly bracketed the period of Mughal rule in India.[12]

The implications of this analysis for the conduct of war were, in Ibn Khaldun's eyes, clear. He disputed the argument that what was decisive in war was the number of soldiers, either of masses of men or of individual heroes. What mattered was cohesion, and where cohesion was absent, ruses of war would be more important than battle. These ruses could panic soldiers who did not have feeling for one another and could lead them to defect.

What is the fact proven to make for superiority is the situation with regard to group feeling. If one side has a (single) group feeling comprising all, while the other side is made up of numerous different groups, and if both sides are approximately the same in numbers, then the side that has a single (comprehensive) group feeling is stronger than, and superior to, the side that is made up of several groups. These different groups are likely to abandon each other, as is the case with separate individuals who have no group feeling at all, each of the groups being in the same position as an individual. Thus, the side composed of several different groups cannot stand up to the side whose group feeling is one. This should be understood.[13]

---

[11] Ibid., pp. 263–267, 304–305; Streusand, *Formation of the Mughal Empire*, pp. 34–35.
[12] Khaldun, *The Muqaddimah*, pp. 332, 336–340, 343.
[13] Ibid., 2:87, disputing the claim that victory goes to the army with the most knights. For the discussion of what Ibn Khaldun calls the "hidden factors" of war relating to

In terms of the propositions that structure this book, in nomadic pastoral societies, the society and the army were coextensive. Thus the army reflected all the strengths and weaknesses of that society, especially the patterns of *asabiyah* (or tribal group cohesion), and *fitmah*, which seems to correspond well with the *stasis* (or perpetual civil war), overt or latent, discussed in Chapter 3 in the context of ancient Greek society.

What were the consequences for military affairs conducted by such societies? Two relevant works from these nomadic societies have survived from the period before the founding of the Ottoman Empire, both written toward the end of the eleventh century A.D. after nomadic tribes had established sedentary empires and political systems influenced by Persian monarchies. Both display an intense concern with the divisions internal to their own societies and with the need for strategies that took those internal divisions into account. *A Mirror for Princes* was written by Ibn Qabus ibn Washmgir, who ruled the Ziyarids peoples who lived the area south of the Caspian Sea, to instruct his son, and it was heavily influenced by the events of his own dynasty. Ibn Qabus's father had been killed after a revolt by his slave soldiers, and Qabus himself was forced to kill his own bodyguards to escape and collect an armed force with which he could retake his throne. Not surprisingly, in his book, much attention was given to the task of avoiding or detecting military revolts by means of generous pay and a close watch of the military elite, respectively, and to the task of managing the royal bodyguard, which should be multiethnic in composition, such that each of the several races held the others in check. "Most of all, be on your guard against the enemy who is within your own household; no stranger has such opportunities of informing himself concerning your affairs and of spying upon them as fall to the members of your own household."[14] The advice concerning external enemies was, in contrast, perfunctory and banal: remain informed of the doings of your enemies, win them over to your side if possible, fight to the finish if war begins.

The second work from this period is *The Book of Government of Rules for Kings*, or the *Siyasat-nama*, by Nizam al-Mulk, an adviser who was ultimately assassinated[15] and who lived and wrote at Baghdad, which was, in the late eleventh century, the western capital of the Seljuk Turks

---

cohesion and the ways in which trickery and ruses can play on armies lacking cohesion, see ibid., 2:85–86.

[14] Ibn Qabus, *Mirror for Princes*, "On Taking Thought Concerning the Enemy," pp. 132–139, "Rules for Vizierate," pp. 211–218, "The Art of Controlling an Armed Force," pp. 219–221, "Conduct of Kingship," p. 230.

[15] Nizam al-Mulk, *The Book of Government of Rules for Kings*, trans. Hubert Darke (London: Routledge and Kegan Paul, 1978), pp. ix–x.

and the center of a well-developed system of military and postal communications.[16] In this book again, a modern Western observer finds a striking imbalance between the attention devoted to internal and to external security. Indeed, only three pages were written specifically on the army, and they were devoted exclusively to the importance of regular pay to secure loyalty and to "having troops of various races." Nizam al-Mulk recommended that armies be composed of units, each of only one race, such that they guarded against one another in peacetime and competed for glory against one another in battle.[17] In contrast, fifty-six pages of the book are devoted to the management of spies directed against the king's own officials, the ways to gain knowledge of and guard against their corruption, and the means of guarding against the peasantry and army and the ways to discover their legitimate grievances and win their loyalty. It was the necessity for mechanisms to obtain information relevant to internal security, Nizam al-Mulk wrote, that led kings to create the aforementioned internal postal system connecting officials throughout the country, "through whom they have learnt everything that goes on, good and bad." The king's spies should be sent out in all manner of disguises to penetrate all levels of society because "in the past it has often happened that governors, assignees, officers and army commanders have planned rebellion and resistance, and plotted mischief against the king; but spies forestalled them and informed the king, who was thus enabled to set out immediately with all speed and coming upon them unawares, to strike them down and frustrate their plans; and if any foreign king or army was preparing to attack their country, the spies informed the king and he took action to repel them." Without adequate spies, heretic priests had committed treachery unknown to the king and had gone undetected in their efforts to subvert the king.[18]

Adda Bozeman has argued on the basis of these texts and other information that Turkish-Iranian societies developed a culturally specific approach to politics that differed significantly from that of the West.[19] As seen from the evidence presented in Chapter 3, however, a strategic emphasis on espionage, covert action, and internal security can be found in ancient Greek and Roman societies, not to mention ancient India, where social structures created severe divisions and tensions within a society. Thus, the contents of *A Mirror for Princes* and *The Book of Government* may

---

[16] Ahmad Y. al-Hassan and Donald Hill, *Islamic Technology* (Cambridge: Cambridge University Press, 1988), p. 105.

[17] Nizam al-Mulk, *Book of Government*, pp. 99–100, 100–101.

[18] Ibid., pp. 47–58, 63–71, 74–87, 187–190, 190–206. The quote concerning the postal system is on p. 64. The discussion of spies is on pp. 74–75.

[19] Adda B. Bozeman, *Politics and Culture in International History* (Princeton: Princeton University Press, 1960), pp. 9, 43–47.

be taken less as an indication of culturally specific behavior and more as indication of the presence of the internal social divisions that were directly observed by Ibn Khaldun, but also by Kautilya, Thucydides, and Livy. The texts also suggest what Ibn Khaldun does not specifically discuss, which is the emergence of tensions between military institutions—specifically, slave armies—and societies after nomadic tribes established sedentary empires.

This discussion of the Turkish societies and military thinking before the Ottoman Empire provides an incomplete but interesting picture of the environment in which that empire was created. But the Ottoman Empire clearly rose above its political predecessors in the development of military power. The Ottoman rulers built a larger empire from which more military power was extracted. This discontinuity appears to be linked both to changes imposed on Turkish society by the Ottoman rulers and with the creation of Ottoman military institutions that were deliberately divorced from society, which led to relations between the army and the host society different from those between nomadic societies and their armies. These new Ottoman military institutions provide a useful reference point against which to assess the Turkish Mughal Empire.

In discussing the relation of the Ottoman armies to the society of the Ottoman Empire, we must distinguish between the patterns prevalent in the fifteenth and sixteenth centuries, at the height of Ottoman power, and those in the seventeenth and eighteenth centuries, when cohesion within the Ottoman ruling elite had broken down, leading to intra-elite conflicts and the development of regionally based centers of political and military power.[20] Because we will be considering the Mughal Empire in India during the time of its greatest strength, it is appropriate to examine the Ottoman Empire at the time of its greatest strength—the fifteenth and sixteenth centuries.

The standard histories of the Ottoman Empire agree on three points central to our concerns with the nature of Ottoman society and the relationship of the military institutions to that society.[21] First, the traditional tribal elites of Anatolia whence the Ottoman ruling elite came were just as prone to internal rivalries and civil war as the analyses of Ibn Khaldun and the prescriptions of Ibn Qabus and Nizam al-Mulk had suggested.

---

[20] Abou-El-Haj Rifa'at Ali, *Formation of the Modern State: The Ottoman Empire, Sixteenth to Eighteenth Centuries* (Albany: State University of New York Press, 1991), pp. 12–17, 53–54.

[21] The following section relies on the volume of essays edited by M. A. Cook, *A History of the Ottoman Empire to 1730: Chapters from the Cambridge History of Islam and the New Cambridge Modern History* (Cambridge: Cambridge University Press, 1976), which contains essays by M. A. Cook, Halil Inalcik, and V. J. Parry.

For example, before the institutions of Ottoman rule had been firmly established, the Ottoman ruler Bayezid I died, and his empire was divided into three parts by his sons, who promptly began a civil war lasting from 1405 to 1413, a period known as the interregnum. Wars among the sons of deceased emperors continued well into the fifteenth century, for example, after the death of Mehmed II. But by the middle of the fifteenth century, the Ottomans had conquered Constantinople and were expanding into Serbia and Italy in the west and toward the Euphrates in the east. If Ottoman pastoral nomads were capable of this concerted action, what had become of the influence of the social structures that were earlier considered a source of military weakness?

The answer given by historians is that Ottoman rulers systematically leveled and reduced the social structures in their domains that could serve as the source of organized social or military opposition to their rule, and constructed a state apparatus populated with slaves deliberately divorced, ethnically and professionally, from the host society. In the words of M. A. Cook: "The striking thing about the Ottoman Empire is the relative absence of those accredited structures which in post-feudal Europe so densely populated the social and political space between the state and its subjects. Two closely related aspects of this contrast are particularly noteworthy. The first is the absence of 'nations' in the Ottoman context. Absorption into the Ottoman Empire was very much more likely than absorption into a European state to strip a subject people of its traditional political structures." Hungary, Cook noted, remained a nation under Hapsburg rule, and Czechoslovakia might have: "But in Ottoman Anatolia, by contrast, the survival of the pre-Ottoman polities was purely nominal. The second aspect of the contrast is the lack of an Ottoman aristocracy. Where Europe made a fundamental social distinction between noble and commoner, the Ottomans made a fundamental political distinction between members and non-members of the state apparatus." There were rural fief holders, the *sipahis*, but they were not a gentry. "The obverse of this was of course . . . the role of slaves in constituting the military and administrative backbone of the state."[22]

The Ottoman state emerged from a society in which tribal social structures gave great power to military chiefs on the periphery, the beys of the march with their troops, but Ottoman rulers steadily stripped them of their control of taxes on the peasants and of their role in the military, replacing them with direct, centralized taxation and a system of slave soldiers and administrators whose self-interests were tied directly to the

---

[22] Ibid., p. 7. See also the discussion of how decentralized contractual patterns of military obligation were replaced with a centralized military patronage state in the Ottoman Empire, in Hodgson, *Venture of Islam*, p. 25.

centralized administration and who were the natural enemies of the rural elites. According to Halil Inalcik: "To understand why the Ottomans succeeded in re-establishing the unity of their state, one must remember above all that Bayezid had abandoned the traditions of the marches and had introduced the highly developed classical Turkish-Islamic system of central government into the administration of the state. Provincial land and population surveys, fiscal methods developed in the Il-Khan state in Persia, a central treasury and bureaucracy which sought from the capital to regulate affairs of the state throughout the provinces were introduced." "Above all instrumental in establishing the absolute authority of the sultan in the provinces," was the use of sultan's personal slaves as administrators, a practice that "came to dominate the administration in the time of Bayezid I." Military commanders were chosen from among slaves, "and even the majority of timar fiefs in the provinces were granted to the sultan's slaves. . . . The military units made up of the sultan's slaves came to number 7,000 men." As long as there were rivals to the sultan, the slave class could not be sure of holding on to their fiefs if the reigning sultan were defeated. "The rights and influence which they had acquired could only be guaranteed by a stable centralized administration. It is they who supported first Mehmed I and then Murad II. . . . They defended the absolute authority of a single sultan against the divisive tendencies of the marches."[23]

These slaves were the Janissaries, who were selected from among Christian boys captured in campaigns and raised to serve the state and who increased in number to a force of ten thousand. As a result, although Ottoman emperors did have to worry about the revolt of these slave administrators, they had at their disposal a force that could overpower any individual bey. It was not only the tribal leaders who were deprived of their revenues and power. The religious organizations, the *waqff*, which had earlier been given grants of state land or had received private land from private landowners seeking to escape state taxes, found their land confiscated by the Ottoman state, with the ulema being the primary victims. The right of the ulema to interpret and apply religious law was maintained in principle, but in practice the sultan assumed the right to interpret religious laws according to precedents, which resulted in a set of legal institutions that was under secular control. The political threat of religious leaders with secular power was thereby reduced. In conquered Islamic and non-Islamic areas, military strongholds that might serve as centers of resistance and opposition were either destroyed, as in Serbia and Bosnia, or placed under the control of Janissaries. They were

---

[23] Halil Inalcik, "The Rise of the Ottoman Empire," in Cook, *History of the Ottoman Empire,* p. 28. See also pp. 46, 49.

not turned over to local governors. The peoples who lived in mountainous areas or other areas difficult to police by mounted troops were relocated to the plains, where they could be easily controlled. As a result, Bosnia and Serbia, which before Ottoman times had been marked by constant violence and banditry, became safe for overland commerce.[24]

For comparative purposes, what is important is that the Ottoman Turks were able to vitiate the impact of the preexisting social structures on their military by means of revenue and military institutions whose officers were deliberately alienated from society, which militarily dominated society, and which did not depend on preexisting social orders for support. This made possible internal military control and external military expansion. Indeed, to some extent, the system depended on external military expansion to provide career opportunities for the officers of the state. While this radical divorce of the military and state institutions from the host society brought long periods of stability that the host society would not have otherwise experienced, the Janissaries, like the Roman legions, developed, precisely as a result of their own homogeneity and psychological separation from society, a sense of corporate identity that, over time came to feature the protection of its own privileges as of greater importance than service to the state. In short, Turkish social structures did create some problems for the creation of military power and the centralization of military power in the hands of the state, but the effects of those social structures could be and were minimized by the separation of the military from society. The question for Mughal India will be, Could the Mughal Turks develop the same separation of their military from Hindu society, and if not, why not?

AFGHAN AND EARLY MUGHAL RULE IN INDIA

The discussion of the society and military of the Turkish peoples of Central Asia and Anatolia served to establish a picture of how Turkish institutions functioned in a non-Hindu context, to enable us better to see what might be different and special about the relationship between a ruling Turkish culture when it interacted with Hindu society under the Mughal emperors. One additional reference point may help us identify what is Turkish and what is Hindu in Mughal India. Delhi and the surrounding area were ruled by Afghan dynasties before they were ruled

---

[24]Hodgson, *Venture of Islam*, pp. 100–103, 108–110; Franz Babinger, *Mehmed the Conqueror and His Time*, trans. Ralph Manheim, ed. William C. Hickman (Princeton: Princeton University Press, 1992), pp. 433–434. Babinger cites the observation about the safety of Balkan roads in Ottoman times made by C. J. Jirecek regarding the routes into the Balkans from Istanbul.

by the Mughals, and they were ruled briefly by the first Mughal emperor, Babur, before he died and his son Humayun lost control of his territories to another Afghan ruler, Sher Shah. By looking at Afghan rule and the rule of Babur, we may be able to see how Islamic, nomadic, tribally organized societies first operated in India, before enough time had gone by for them to have been penetrated or affected by Hindu society. It will also help us identify which forms of Islamic military organization and military-social relations were already present in India and which may have continued into the Mughal Empire.

Hindu rule in Kabul ended in 870 A.D. when it was conquered by Yaqub Ibn Layth, who originally came from Seistan in Persia. The ability of Ibn Layth to conquer easily the Hindu rulers of Afghanistan—who had successfully resisted Arab military pressures for over two hundred years—has been explained by Hindu historians in terms of the increasing rigidity of caste divisions and caste hostility between Kshatriyas and Brahmins. In fact, a Brahmin rebellion against the Kshatriya rulers in Kabul gave Ibn Layth his strategic opportunity. The Brahmin usurper, who had weak domestic support, accepted Ibn Layth's offer of military assistance and was promptly betrayed by him.[25] Numerous Turkish raids on the Punjab followed in the tenth and eleventh centuries, with Turks and Hindus exchanging control of frontier territories until 1206, when Turkish rule was permanently established in Delhi.

Indian scholars have debated why these numerically small Turkish groups were able to establish control of northern India. Even those Indian scholars skeptical about the divisive impact of increasing caste rigidity on the strategic cohesion of Indian society agree that increasing Hindu conservatism in this period led the Hindu elites to regard the peoples of the border territories, who had become racially and culturally mixed, as "repugnant" to Hindu sensibilities and not deserving of assistance. The same growing Hindu conservatism alienated the large Buddhist, Jat, and Med populations of the border area in Sind, leading them to shift their allegiance to the Islamic enemy. One Indian historian concluded, "The political result, therefore, of the Brahmanical orthodoxy

---

[25] A. L. Srivastava, "A Survey of India's Resistance to Medieval Invaders from the Northwest: Causes of Eventual Hindu Defeat," part 2, *Journal of Indian History* 43 (August 1965): 354–356: "The main causes of the loss of modern Afghanistan by the Hindus are evident on the face of the narrative.... The internal disunity brought about by a Brahmanical revolution against the Kshatriya ruler must be said to have been the most prominent factor." See also Jadunath Sarkar, *Military History of India* (Calcutta: Sarkar, 1960), pp. 25, 32–37, on the confrontation between Turkish people and Hindu states, which were "disunited by love of local independence and ... torn by the jealous feud of clan against clan, caste against caste. Hindu religious philosophy may be sublime, but it does not teach the social solidarity and equality of the faithful which is the noblest gift of Islam" (p. 25).

was the destruction of the social solidarity the presence of which is reck-
oned as the best guarantee of the preservation of political independence."[26]

From 1206 until 1526, there followed a succession of Afghan dynasties
ruling the Sultanate of Delhi. The dominant characteristic of these Turkish sultans from Afghanistan was their lack of substantive administrative
control over the Hindu and Muslim societies they governed in India. The
everyday life of the people was beyond the control of the sultan because
"he could not interfere with the personal and religious laws of his subjects, for both the Muslims and the Hindus had their system of law with
which they would not brook interference even at the cost of their lives."
This unwillingness to allow state intrusions into society was enforced
by periodic armed insurrections of the population of Delhi, which made
and broke the power of sultans. In the words of Ishtiaq Husain Quereshi,
the modern historian of the Sultanate of Delhi, ". . . the Indian populace
during the Middle Ages was by no means timid or forebearing; on the
other hand, the people were mostly warlike, refractory, and rebellious.
Besides, those were the days of dense forests and limited means of communications; and the difference between an army and armed rabble was
proverbially very little. The hostility of the people seldom proved fruit-
less."[27]

Nor was the fiscal basis of the sultanate under the control of the state,
as opposed to the intermediate social orders rooted in the host society.
The primary tax was on the assessed agricultural production of the land
and was collected by a variety of middlemen and tax farmers who were
not under the regular control of the sultan.

> [First were] the old Hindu chiefs who had long traditions of authority and
> could command the loyalty and support of the peasantry. . . . These fami-
> lies were semi-independent even under Hindu rulers and kings, and were
> by no means easy to control; they were left in the same state by the early
> Muslim rulers on the promise to pay the fixed tribute. Whenever he could
> defy the central government, the chief withheld the tribute. . . . The tribute
> they paid to the state . . . was often decided by armed conflict, and thus
> depended on their strategic position or fighting power. . . . Less powerful
> were village headmen who helped the officials assess and collect taxes for
> the sultan, for which the headmen received a commission. Sometimes they

[26] Srivastava, "Survey of India's Resistance," p. 365. See also A. K. Majumdar, "India's
Resistance to Medieval Invaders," part 2, *Journal of Indian History* 44 (August 1966): 475–
482; and A. L. Srivastava, "India's Resistance to Medieval Invaders: A Rejoinder," part
1, *Journal of Indian History* 45 (April 1967): 181–186.
[27] Ishtiaq Husain Qureshi, *The Administration of the Sultanate of Delhi* (Karachi: Pakistan
Historical Society, 1958), pp. 49, 52.

agreed to pay fixed amount to the state, at which point they became tax farmers.

Then there were the overt tax farmers, who collected taxes over a wide area for a fee. Initially knowing little of local conditions, sultans employed the existing tax farmers in India, though the sultans tried periodically and unsuccessfully to do without them.[28]

What was the nature of the army of the Afghan rulers of Delhi? Contemporary histories and records indicate that soldiers were of four different kinds.[29] First, slave soldiers, like the Janissaries, were drawn from youths captured from peripheral areas, predominantly Muslim, but including Hindus and trained for service and loyalty only to the sultan. Their numbers are uncertain, but one account claimed the sultan possessed fifty thousand slave boys. Second, there were foreign soldiers from outside India who were largely Turks and Afghans and who were attracted by the prospect of loot. Closely related were the Muslim mercenary troops, referred to as *ghazis*, who opportunistically volunteered for service in the sultan's army on the eve of campaigns. Finally, there were Hindu troops, who were almost entirely foot soldiers or workers serving the military in the field. Accounts of the total number of soldiers serving the sultan consistently place the number of mounted cavalry troops between 475,000 and 900,000. Although these enormous numbers of cavalrymen seem too large to be factual, we should consider several factors when assessing those counts. First, the number of cavalry troopers available was carefully monitored by a system of branding horses and keeping detailed written descriptions of individual soldiers, who had to be presented for review when serving the sultan. Branding and detailed descriptions prevented horses and men from being presented more than once by their commanders, who would receive payments from the sultan on the basis of the number of men and horses they could present at muster. Thus, despite a systematic incentive for commanders to try to overstate their troop strength, systematic efforts also guarded against fraud. Troops were presented in groups of ten to facilitate counting, and one account of a review noted that it took fourteen days to process one group of soldiers. Second, the revenue necessary to support troop strengths of this size has been estimated to have been the equivalent of 50 percent of the agricultural revenue of the sultans: large but not financially impossible sums. Budgetary records from this period have not survived, however, denying us payrolls that might reduce our uncertainties.

---

[28] Ibid., pp. 119–122.
[29] In this section I draw heavily on K. S. Lal, "The Striking Power of the Army of the Sultanate," *Journal of Indian History* 55 (December 1977): 85–110.

Third, the trade in horses necessary to support a mounted army of this size was enormous. One port among many that supplied horses to independent Hindu rulers in India in this era recorded the arrival of ten thousand horses in one year. The sultan's stables at Delhi alone had seventy thousand horses. Fourth, the troop strengths claimed are not demographically unreasonable. The combined populations of Asiatic Turkey, the Caucasus, Russian Turkestan, Iran, Iraq, and Afghanistan in 1200 have been estimated to have been in the range of 18–19 million.[30] The population of the Indian subcontinent is estimated to have been between 83 and 86 million during this period.[31] Not all the populations of all these areas were available to supply troops to Delhi, but the wealth that could be obtained from military service was a powerful attraction that did draw soldiers from many parts of Asia. A cavalry of five hundred thousand would have represented 2.5 percent of the population of non-Indian sources of soldiers. This percentage is high—roughly 10 percent of the adult male population of military age—but not so high as the figures for the Italian armies at their peak during the rule of the Roman republic, as we saw in Chapter 3. And, finally, the total *available* mounted strength was not the same as the strength that was maintained as a standing army, nor was it the same as the number of troops who would show up for battle. The useful debunking of premodern claims to huge armies in the field discussed in Chapter 3 is, therefore, probably not relevant to these claims concerning the pool of available cavalrymen.

Given the uncertainties associated with the information about the armies of the Sultanate of Delhi, what conclusions can be drawn? First, even if taken at face value, figures for slave soldiers—the troops who owed their loyalty exclusively to the sultan and were paid only by him—were some very small fraction of the military strength on which the sultan depended. The bulk of the armies of the sultans were temporarily drawn from the host societies of central, south, and southwest Asia as needed for battle. In the words of K. S. Lal, "A large portion of the army of the Sultanate remained temporary, with loot as its only source of sustenance."[32] Those soldiers constituted a substantial percentage of the adult males of military age, which would have reduced the likelihood that they were grossly unrepresentative of the larger population from which they were drawn. These soldiers, in consequence, are not likely to have been socially or psychologically divorced from their host societies, in which they would live

---

[30]Colin McEvedy and Richard Jones, *Atlas of World Population History* (New York: Penguin, 1980), pp. 135, 151, 153, 155, 159, 163. The population of each country in 1200 was 6 million for Turkey in Asia, 1.5 million for Iraq, 5 million for Iran, 2.5 million for Afghanistan, 1 million for Caucasia, and 2.5 million for Russian Turkestan.

[31]Ibid., p. 183.

[32]Lal, "Army of the Sultanate," p. 109.

for the great bulk of their lives. Second, the army was not physically divorced from society by military deployments out of the country, as were the Roman legions, but was dispersed in garrisons within the sultanate under the control of provincial governors. Third, like the host population of the sultanate from which it was drawn, the army was heterogenous, composed of Hindus and Muslims, Indians, Afghans, Turks, and others. Fourth, it was not a highly trained or disciplined army. Such training as there was focused on the development of individual skills, not unit performance. The ferocity of the individual warriors was what provided the striking power of the armies of the sultan.

In sum, it is reasonable to conclude that the size, recruitment, deployment, training, or discipline of the armies of the sultan were *not* such as to divorce them from the norms and structures of the host society. Rather, it seems fair to say that they were representative of and integrated into the societies from which they were drawn, *unlike the armies of the Ottoman Empire*. They should, therefore, be expected to display the strategic strengths and weaknesses of those societies, and they did. Drawn from heterogenous societies in which the bonds of loyalty did not extend past local levels, the armies of the sultanate were also heterogenous, and K. S. Lal has noted that "ethnic and racial tensions and jealousies were rampant in the Sultanate's army." Hindu infantry were commonly put in the front rank of an attack, where they would be killed first and from where they could not flee or defect, being trapped between the enemy in front of them and the mounted Islamic troops behind them. The armies of the sultans could and did conspire against their own rulers to make or break them.[33] Therefore, to the extent that the armies of the Mughal Empire, once established in the territory of the Sultanate of Delhi, were shaped by their military inheritance from the immediately preceding regime, they would tend to reflect the prevailing social structures of northern India and southwest Asia.

The Lodi dynasty was the last Afghan dynasty to rule in Delhi before the invasion of the Mughal emperor Babur, who defeated the army of the sultanate in the battle of Panipat in 1526. What were the characteristics of the army the first Mughals brought with them into Hindustan? To begin with, Babur's own army, drawn from his tribal area in Ferghana, was small—very small relative to the armies of the sultanate. In Babur's own estimate, the revenues of Ferghana could support only three to four thousand troops.[34] The troops were badly disciplined, would

---

[33] Lal, "Army of the Sultanate," p. 88 n. 20, 108; Quereshi, *Administration of the Sultanate*, pp. 143–144.
[34] Babur, *Memoirs of Zehir-el-din-Muhammad Babur*, vol. 1, trans. John Leyden and William Erskine (London: Oxford University Press, 1921), p. 9.

break ranks to loot after or during a battle, and would not easily or quickly reassemble when ordered to do so. Only when Babur assembled an elite fraction of his army could he count on a highly disciplined fighting body.[35] And, like the pre-Janissary Ottoman Turkish armies, it was full of the internal divisions stemming from the social structures of the Turkish society from which it came, internal divisions that were consistent with the descriptions of divisions in the writings of Ibn Khaldun, Ibn Qabus, Nizam al-Mulk. It is impossible to read Babur's memoirs without noting how much of his time is devoted not to fighting his external enemies but to dealing with plots against his rule by his tribal chieftains. When he moved into the frontier areas of India in Sind, his chiefs (*begs*) tried to induce Babur's brother to usurp him, with their support. While fighting in Afghanistan, he "gained information" that some of his nobles in his army "had formed the plan of deserting. I instantly had them seized and . . . delivered to the executioner." His chief subordinate noble was urged to sedition against Babur by the sons of other nobles. After having subdued Kabul, Babur departed to continue his campaign, only to find that his nobles in Kabul had declared him dead in order to put his cousin on the throne, forcing Babur to march back to reconquer Kabul from his own forces. The Uzbeg tribes following Babur rebelled, and at one point, Babur, opposed by his own ethnic group, the Chaghtais, the Uzbegs, and other Turks, chose to advance into Hindustan because he felt he would be safer on enemy than on friendly ground.[36]

With internal divisions as debilitating as this, the question naturally arises as to how Babur managed to conquer anything. At least a partial answer can be found in his memoirs. As often as he faced his own internal threats, he found people from the hostile local societies who were willing to help him with information and soldiers. In Sind he noted that several local headmen marched with him for "the benefit of their advice regarding the roads and the country." In Afghanistan, local tribal leaders pledged their support to Babur, and "persons perfectly acquainted with the whole routes represented to me that Dasht was near at hand; that the inhabitants were wealthy and the roads good; and it was firmly established that . . . we should plunder Dasht." On his order, Babur's no-

---

[35] Babur, *Memoirs*, 2:17, where he notes that it could take over thirty days to reassemble men who had dispersed to loot, adding, "When five or six thousand men set out on a pillaging party, it is extremely difficult to maintain discipline" (p. 38). He also discusses how he picked a force of one thousand soldiers who were well trained and disciplined, noting, "Perhaps on no other occasion had I my troops in such perfect discipline" (p. 48).

[36] Ibid., 1:266, 276, 284; and 2:26, 35, 55.

bles used the money obtained from loot to enroll soldiers from the local Jat and Gujer tribes.[37] When he advanced for the first time into India proper in 1519, "some persons who were acquainted with the country and the political situation of the neighboring territories ... who were old enemies of the Gakkars represented to me that Hati the Gakkar had been guilty of many acts of violence ... therefore, it was necessary either to effect his expulsion ... or at least to inflict on him exemplary punishment," and provided their assistance against the Gakkars. By the time Babur advanced into India again in 1525, this time to defeat the forces of the sultan and to take Delhi, his force was no longer three to four thousand troops but thirty to forty thousand, soldiers who must have come from allies Babur acquired on his march and with whom he faced the army of the Sultan Ibrahim Lodi, which numbered, according to Babur's estimate, some one hundred thousand soldiers.[38]

Thus, at the very beginning of the Mughal Empire in India, both the core Mughal army and the Hindu society it was trying to rule suffered from internal fragmentation. The early armies of the Ottoman rulers and Anatolian society were also fragmented. How did Turkish elites in Turkey succeed in creating a state and an army that escaped the divisions of the host society? Did the Turkish elite in India not try to create such military institutions? Were the Mughal rulers somehow blocked by the nature of Indian social structures from creating an army and a state, like that of Ottoman Turkey, which by virtue of its strength and its monopoly on the means of organized violence could generate an exportable surplus of military power? To answer this question we must turn to the information available on the nature of Indian society at that time and to the military policies of the Turkish rulers in India.

INDIAN SOCIETY IN THE SIXTEENTH AND
SEVENTEENTH CENTURIES

It is difficult to make useful generalizations about the nature of social structures in any society that spans a subcontinent, and Mughal India is no exception. It is, therefore, useful to make some distinctions about Indian society on the basis of the regions of India. To be sure, even within regions there were significant differences in social structures, as numer-

[37] Ibid., 1:252–255, 258, 278–280.
[38] Ibid., 2:20, 28. John Dowson, ed., "Tuzuk-I Babari," in *The History of India as Told by Its Own Historians: The Papers of Sir H. M. Elliot* (Calcutta: Susil Gupta, 1953), pp. 20, 28, 34.

ous sociological surveys of modern India show. But given the purposes here and the absence of the equivalents of modern social science surveys of Mughal India, analyses at the regional level may be the best we can hope for. If some generalizations about Indian social structures appear to hold in Mughal India across regions, those will make the analysis of the interaction of Indian society and Mughal military institutions somewhat easier to perform.

Mughal India can be roughly divided into its core and the south. The core area was composed of the northern-western Gangetic plain, which included Delhi and Agra, Rajasthan, and the Hindu states of Mewar, Marwar, and the Hindu Rajput states. One of the more systematic accounts of Rajasthan and the western and central Rajput states of this region is James Tod's chronicle written in the nineteenth century on the basis of his own surveys between 1818 and the 1820s and on the basis of the local histories written by the various court historians of the region that were made available to Tod.[39] While he was struck, like most Westerners, by the differences between nineteenth-century India and Europe, he had enough historical self-consciousness to juxtapose his impressions of contemporary Indian social structures against his knowledge of European social structures of earlier times. For example, he noted the increase in the power of the Indian clergy relative to the power of the state, which was the result of the gifts of large blocks of land by Indian princes to priests who had influence over them. Rather than simply attributing this to Hindu religious beliefs, Tod remembered the medieval struggles between the French state and the Catholic Church for control of land, which French kings had transferred to the Catholic Church on their deathbeds to avoid damnation.[40] Tod was therefore in a better position to recognize what was genuinely distinctive about India and to reach some tentative conclusions about the causes of some of the phenomena he observed. Because of his direct access to Indian society and Indian

---

[39] James Tod, *Annals and Antiquities of Rajasthan or the Central and Western Rajput States of India*, vol. 2 (London: Oxford University Press, 1920), bk. 4, chap. 27, p. 825, recounting how Raja Man Singh presented Tod with manuscript histories of Jodhpur.

[40] Ibid., chap. 19: "The antiquary who has dipped into the records of the dark period in European church history can have occular illustration in Rajasthan of traditions which may in Europe appear questionable" (p. 591). "Yet let the reader check any rising feeling of contempt for Hindu legislation and cast a retrospective glance at the page of European church history, where he will observe [citing Hallams's history] in the time of the most potent of our monarchs that the clergy possessed one-half of the soil: and the chronicles of France will show Charlemagne on his death bed, bequeathing two-thirds of his domains to the church, deeming the remaining one-third sufficient for the ambitions of four sons. The same dread of futurity, and the hope to expiate the sins of a life, at its close by gifts to the organs of religion is the motive for these unwise alienations whether in Europe or in Asia" (pp. 596–597).

histories as well as his self-consciously comparative perspective on Indian society, Tod is a credible observer.

For our purposes, Tod's detailed accounts of Indian society can be searched for the same kind of information that we sought about ancient Greek, Roman, and Hindu societies and about medieval nomadic pastoral societies. What were the groups to which men gave their loyalties? How strong were the bonds of cohesion that extended beyond the groups related by marriage or ancestry? What were the levels and character of conflict within that society? Tod did find significant differences in the nature of caste structures in different parts of India. What he did not find were structures or institutions that ameliorated the social divisions created by different kinds of caste structures. Focusing primarily on the states of Mewar, Marwar, and Bikaner in the west, he noted the far-flung marriage connections among the Rajputs—which has has also been described by modern sociologists—for whom "not only is intermarriage prohibited between families of the same clan (*khanp*), but between those of the same tribe (*got*); and though centuries may have intervened since their separation . . . a marriage between any of the branches would be deemed incestuous. . . . Every tribe has therefore to look abroad, to a race distinct from its own, for suitors for the females." This insistence on outmarrying or exogamous marriage practices was combined with strict insistence on observance of status distinctions governing suitable marriage partners, to the extent that the infanticide of baby Rajput girls was observed when warfare had reduced the number of husbands of the proper status. These prohibitions had their exceptions in practice, as when "in the most tempestuous period of the history of Mewar, when the Ranas broke asunder the bonds which united them to the other chiefs of Rajasthan, and bestowed their daughters on foreign nobles incorporated with the higher class of their own kin." But more frequent were the accounts of female infanticide, the refusals of high caste women to marry lower-caste rulers, their suicides, the wars that resulted from marriage into other castes, and the immolations of women in Rajput villages to prevent their abduction and rape by conquerors.[41] Tod's account strongly suggests that although Rajput states had geographically extensive marriage practices, loyalties to the Rajput subcastes were strong to the point of deterring marriage alliances and limiting the growth by intermarriage of political units that could command Rajput loyalty.

Second, Tod noted the prevalence of civil war within the Rajput states, a state of affairs that he likened to the period of the War of the Roses in England and France. He gave detailed accounts of persistent intra- and interdynastic conflicts in which the Indian clergy played an important

---

[41] Ibid., chap. 23, pp. 712, 727–728, 741, 743–744.

secular role, with consequences for civil society similar to those which Thucydides ascribed to civil war in ancient Greece. Tod noted that "civil war is the parent of every crime, and severs all ties, moral and political; nor must it be expected that Rajputan should furnish an exception to the rule. . . ."[42]

These observations tend to suggest that conditions in northwest India reflected low levels of social cohesion within units larger than the sub-caste and enough armed men at the disposal of small subregional leaders to make possible endemic internal warfare. But these observations are fragmentary. What picture has modern social scientific analysis been able to reconstruct concerning the social structures of this region of India? One analysis of state-society relations in preindustrial India looked at Rajput groups, noted the persistence of loyalties to geologically defined corporate groups and the absence of loyalties to a territorially defined state, and concluded that "ideological" commitment to caste identities, reinforced by marriage patterns, "meant a continued belief in the worth of claiming to be a Rajkumar, Chauhan, or Rajput. . . . Identities in terms of caste, sub-regional varna, and thus geneological reckoning were not threatened by the behavioral sabotage of the kin system by the state. . . . The continued ideological identification at regional levels could never be effaced by the state in traditional northern India."[43] This social scientific account does not seem to differ greatly from Tod's narrative account.

What of southernmost India, the areas of present-day Kerala and Tamil Nadu—the areas least touched by the succession of foreign invasions from the north and conquered last by the Muslim rulers of India? This area of India may or may not have been more or less "authentically" Hindu, but were its social structures different from north India? The absence of foreign invasions and influences, or perhaps other factors, does appear to have given the Brahmins an unusual role in south India. One study of its society observed that medieval south India had three special characteristics relative to the rest of medieval India. First, "Brahmans were strongly entrenched in the localities where they lived as a result of the prestige which attached to their sacerdotal functions, and this power was backed in many places by the power which they possessed by virtue of their direct control over land and those dependent on land. . . . In respect to Brahman locality power associated with land control, South India appears quite unique" in medieval India. Temples, for example, were often endowed with villages which supported them and which they controlled. Second, in addition to the division of local

---

[42] Ibid., chap. 28, p. 871.

[43] Richard G. Fox, *Kin, Clan, Raja, and Rule: State-Hinterland Relations in Preindustrial India* (Berkeley: University of California Press, 1971), pp. 167–169.

society into subcastes found in most of India, the lower castes of southern India were further divided into left- and right-handed subgroups, and sometime after the fifteenth century, relations between these subcaste groups became "deeply competitive and conflict ridden" and often violent. Finally, "territorial segmentation of society and culture in the south Indian region is the third characteristic of social structure. . . . Social groups have tended to maintain a low order of significant and persistent relationships with groups at any substantive distance from their locality. . . . Marriage and descent systems in South India operate in quite narrow territorial areas" in contrast with the geographically extensive marriage patterns of Rajput clans.[44] That is, the caste system in south India was more narrow and rigid by virtue of being associated with geographically compact and discrete areas of territory.

Although there is debate on the extent to which South Indian kingdoms established centralized, standing armies, the judgment by Burton Stein is that "there is no evidence of the basic means of supporting a large [central] army any more than there is for maintaining an elaborate bureaucracy. Neither, of course, was needed. Just as locality institutions provided most of the administrative functions required at the time, so, too, it must be supposed that the major forces involved in the wars . . . were supplied from the existing organizations of locality-based society of the time." The major kingdoms of South Asia did not have a monopoly of military power in their respective areas. Surviving inscriptions richly document local institutions, but central armies have "a poorly documented and often tortuously argued existence."[45] The result, Stein concluded, was that South India had a "segmentary" form of political organization. This form of political organization was marked by local territorial sovereignty, the distribution of administrative functions from the center to the periphery, shifting networks of allegiances among the power centers on the periphery, and a nominal monopoly on armed forces claimed by the central government. The reality of military power was a distribution of "legitimate force . . . at all the peripheral focuses." In less tortured language, the political system was based on local subcaste chiefs who lived in armed opposition with one another, with no effective central government to check them. When kings did try to exert centralized authority, they were opposed.

The dominant basis of opposition . . . would include opposition between families of chiefs and dominant castes from which they had come, between

[44] Burton Stein, *Peasant State and Society in Medieval South India* (Delhi: Oxford University Press, 1980), pp. 52–55.
[45] Ibid., pp. 190–191, 256–257.

[127]

locally dominant landed groups and subordinate ones; between agricultural and non-agricultural groups, between established castes of a locality and newcomers and outsiders, and among sects and cult groups. Many of these oppositions took concrete form in the right and left caste groups.[46]

Each of the local chiefs had his own forces to support his local claims against opposition. The territorial boundaries of local polities were fluid and constantly shifting. Supralocal empires existed, such as the kingdom of Vijayanagar, but are " 'best looked upon as a military confederation of many chieftains cooperating under the leadership of the biggest among them.' "[47]

This survey of northern and southern Indian society at the time of the Mughal Empire strongly suggests a varied society in the subcontinent within which caste practices differed but which, overall, had a high degree of internal social divisons based on subcastes. In addition to the divisions among Hindu subcastes were the divisions between Hindus and Indian Muslims and the sectarian divisions among Hindu Muslims, all of which became embodied in caste practices. The Indian historian Jadunath Sarker has characterized the religious tensions in Mughal India in these words:

> The lower classes, after some fighting between Hindus and Moslims [*sic*] or Shias and Sunnis . . . at last came to a settlement in every locality, recognising the boundaries, rights and limitations of each creed. . . . Thus they lived amicably within their own narrow limits. But this religious truce held good only so long as the local society was static. With the least change in the relative strength of the two sects or in their temper . . . the sleeping volcano of mob-passions would again wake to fury.

As evidence, Sarkar cited the massacre of Shias at Srinagar in 1685 and the anti-Muslim riots after the emperor Aurangzeb ordered the destruction of Hindu temples.[48]

Did these internal divisions lead only on occasion to internal violence, as may happen in any society, or to high and endemic levels of conflict? Since all societies have some internal divisions, is there evidence of the degree of fragmentation of Indian society? Two important sources of evidence come from accounts of public order and landholding practices

---

[46] Ibid., pp. 265, 270–271.
[47] Ibid., pp. 281, 406, quoting Nilikanta Sastri, *Sources of Indian History*.
[48] Jadunath Sarkar, *History of Aurangzeb*, vol. 5 (New Delhi: Orient Longman, 1952), p. 376. This multivolume history made use of private written histories, the manuscript newsletters put out by the Mughal court, and six thousand private letters written by Aurangzeb and others.

in India included in the authoritative modern study of the agrarian system of the Mughal period by Irfan Habib.

First, Habib recorded the numerous references to the problems of public order in Mughal India. Although the intensive, long-distance caravan trade in Mughal India could not have been possible without the suppression of private violence along the trade routes, Habib noted that this order "was true only of the plains and the territories closely controlled by the imperial government. In or near the hills, ravines and desolate country," imperial order enforced by "vicious reprisals" broke down, "and here, robbers and rebels often became indistinct, levying what might be regarded either as ransom or tribute upon the merchants passing through their territories."

Second, Habib analyzed the nature of the social order created by the impact of the caste system on landholding practices. What were the origins of landholding rights in India—the rights of the landholders, the zamindars? Habib argued that private landholding rights in India before and during the Mughal period were caste-based. By surveying the caste censuses and landholding records from the Mughal period, Habib concluded that patterns of landholding were dominated by "the *zamindar* class as consisting of a number of castes which monopolized *zamindari* holdings in different areas." Each administrative unit, called a *pargana*, was associated in the censuses with a single caste. "We must suppose, therefore, that there were well-marked blocks of territory each consisting of a single *pargana* or group of *parganas* under the *zamindari* of members of the same caste." Habib noted that the boundaries of the *parganas* seldom coincided with any natural physical boundaries and were representative only of caste landholdings, though records indicate that land could be and was sold to members of other castes.

Third, Habib noted that the administrative records contained information on both the distribution of landholdings and the locally based armed forces. "In this testimony," Habib wrote, "we find that the one great instrument by which every caste could establish its possession of *zamindari* was the armed force it could command. Indeed, armed force appears as the first historical pre-requisite for the establishment, as well as the retention, of *zamindari* rights." The development and maintenance of the landholding system resting on caste rule of agricultural territories led to the creation of local armies commanded by the landholders. The sizes of all local armies or militias in the Mughal Empire were enumerated, region by region, in the administrative history of the reign of the emperor Akbar, the *Ain-i Akbari* of Abul Fazl. In the 1590s, the total number of soldiers in the empire, including the local militias, totaled around 4.4 million, mostly peasant foot soldiers. There were also numerous small forts built by landholders and used by them not only to maintain control during times of peasant rebellion but also to defy the tax collections of whatever central government was in power.[49]

Habib's account of the nature of the agrarian system of India that was present before and during the Mughal period tends to support the conclusion that Indian society at the local level was fragmented into caste-related, armed territorial segments. He also called attention to the large number of locally available soldiers in India. The 1993 authoritative history of the Mughal Empire presented the same conclusion about the connections between caste, landholding, and military power. John Richards notes that in India in the 1560s, "in one *pargana* after another, armed, potentially hostile warrior lineages—Rajputs, Jats, and other locally rooted caste elites—ruled the cultivating peasantry.... *Parganas* in the north were miniature kingdoms.... These chiefs or *zamindars* as the Mughals called them, maintained substantial military forces."[50] How substantial were these forces?

LOCAL INDIAN ARMIES AND THEIR RELATIONSHIP WITH INDIAN SOCIETY

The number of soldiers accounted for in the *Ain-i Akbari* is high and strategically important. We saw in Chapter 3 that during the Social War in Italy, roughly 9 percent of the Italian population may have been at least temporarily in service as soldiers on both sides of the conflict, a fraction that was roughly the same as that which served in the legions abroad during the most active periods of foreign war. The total population of the Indian subcontinent in 1600 has been estimated to have been about 135 million.[51] A military population of 4.4 million would have been about 3 percent of the total population. The administrative control of the Mughal Empire in 1600 did not extend to all south India at this time, so the effective percentage would have been somewhat higher, at least 4 percent. In addition, the figure of 4.4 million is a static snapshot of the military manpower pool, and in times of prolonged internal conflict (which appear to have been usual, as the observations of the emperor Jahangir cited at the beginning of this chapter would suggest) there would have been dynamic military manpower burdens created by the need to replace casualties with new soldiers. This is a factor to remember later in this chapter when making comparisons with estimates of the

---

[49] Irfan Habib, *The Agrarian System of Mughal India, 1556–1707* (London: Asia Publishing House, 1963). pp. 68–69, 160–168. See also Abul Fazl, *Ain-i Akbari*, 2d ed., trans. H. Blochmann (1927; reprinted, Lahore, Pakistan: Qausain, 1975), book 2, "The Army," p. 241.

[50] Richards, *Cambridge History of India*, pp. 79–80.

[51] McEvedy and Jones, *Atlas of World Population History*, p. 183.

fraction of European manpower under arms in medieval times. If around 4 percent of the Indian population was engaged from time to time in local armies fighting local wars within India, it would help explain why Mughal India did not project military power externally. It is important, therefore, to see what other evidence exists to confirm or deny the accuracy of the figures concerning the number of soldiers said to have existed in Mughal India.

Because the number of soldiers a rural chief could present for service in the imperial Mughal army was related to the amount of cash payments made by the emperor to the landholder, was there a systematic bias upward in the number of *zamindar* troops reported to the imperial census? Ishtiaq Husain Qureshi argued that such was not the case: these local militias were composed largely of peasant foot soldiers, without mounts, who could not easily travel long distances and be used out of their area or report for imperial musters at which they would be counted and their descriptions recorded, as under the Afghan sultans of Delhi. In the administrative history, a distinction is made between the number of mounted soldiers in the empire and the number of foot soldiers. The number of mounted soldiers is far smaller, amounting to only 340,000 horsemen.[52] At the same time, the *zamindar* troops were exempt from *jiyazah*, the Islamic poll tax imposed intermittently on the non-Muslim residents of a Muslim polity, in this case, Mughal India, who did not assist in the common defense. The Mughal administrators, therefore, had a general motive to *undercount* the zamindar troops so as to limit tax avoidance, Qureshi argued, although during the period covered by this specific census—the reign of Akbar—the jiyazah was imposed only occasionally and finally suspended. It was subsequently reimposed under the reign of Aurangzeb, some fifty years later.[53]

Are there more focused looks at the local military forces in various regions that would help test the validity of the overall figure of 4.4. million soldiers in India? Tod estimated the population of the state of Marwar in northwest India in the early nineteenth century at about 2 million, which is approximately the same figure as the 1911 British imperial census figure. Of that 2 million, according to Tod, 500,000 were Rajputs, of whom 50,000 were men capable of bearing arms. Tod provided figures on the revenue of Rajput chiefs and the number of troops supported by one chief. Extrapolating from these numbers, the eight major Rajput chiefs in Marwar may have had about 32,000 cavalry troops under arms at the beginning of the nineteenth century. This would have been 6 percent of the entire population, or 64 percent of the men capable of bearing

[52] Kolff, *Najput, Rajput, and Sepoy*, p. 3.
[53] Qureshi, *Administration of the Mughal Empire*, pp. 115, 133–134, 141, 143.

arms. Tod also provided census information about the state of Bikaner and a detailed roster of the troop strengths of the thirty-seven major chiefs of that state. His 1820 estimate of the total population was 539,000, which is consistent with the 1911 census figure of 574,000, and the roster of troops in the service of the chiefs totaled 44,000 foot soldiers and 5,000 cavalry troops.[54] This would represent 9 percent of the total population of this region.

Other early, independently collected data against which we can cross-check Tod's figures come from northeast India, from the area in Bengal around Calcutta, where the British police activities were first established. The figures from the Bengal area can serve at least as a rough check on the possibility of an armed population as high as those suggested by Tod's figures. In the early nineteenth century, the British East India Company surveyed the area governed by a large zamindar in Bengal, who controlled an area seventy-three miles long and forty-five miles wide, described as being "well stocked with inhabitants." A letter written by a British magistrate on October 1788 was cited in which the magistrate estimated that this zamindar commanded, exclusive of other police or soldiers belonging to the state, a force of pike men "stated by the Magistrate to have been in number no less than nineteen thousand" who could be called up to maintain public order.[55] The Mughal emperor Jahangir, who followed Akbar on the throne, stated in his memoirs that in the time of his reign, the rulers of Bengal commanded 20,000 horsemen and 100,000 foot soldiers. Jahangir also gave detailed accounts of two areas in northwest India governed by Rajput chiefs: Ajmir, which was west of Agra and south of Delhi and north of Gujarat, and Malwa, which was east of Gujarat and Ajmir and north of Baglana. Ajmir, Jahangir wrote, could generate 86,000 horsemen and 304,000 Rajput soldiers in time of war, while Malwa, which was described as being particularly fertile, could generate "when needful" 473,000 foot soldiers and 9,300 horsemen.[56] Like Tod's reports, this would suggest that private armies in the northern Gangetic plain of India were indeed very large.

Figures on the size of the armies of South India from the period before their conquest by the Mughals are scanty, though figures on the sizes of the armies that fought against the Mughals in the late seventeenth century have been reported. Muhamad Said, a wealthy Shia Persian who rose to become prime minister of the South Indian kingdom of Golkonda

[54] Tod, *Annals*, bk. 5, chap. 16, pp. 1105–1106, 1120, bk. 6, chap. 1, pp. 1147, 1160, 1162.

[55] Percival Griffiths, *To Guard My People: The History of the Indian Police* (London: Ernest Benn, 1971), pp. 59–60, referencing the *Report of the Fifth Select Committee of the House of Commons to Inquire into the Affairs of the East India Company, 1812.*

[56] Jahangir, *Memoirs of Jahangir*, pp. 207, 341, 349.

and who is better known as Mir Jumla, ruled as his own property a territory in South India three hundred miles long and fifty miles wide, which supported in the mid–seventeenth century his private army of 5,000 cavalry and 20,000 infantry, a force larger than that of the king of Golkonda, who commanded only 4,000 cavalry.[57] When Mir Jumla commanded the royal army of Golkonda in a war against the declining empire of Vijayanagar in 1642–1643, his force numbered 40,000 infantry and 4,000 cavalry.

Other reports that tend to confirm the large numbers of troops in India are the accounts by historians of the ease with which troops could be raised in the hinterland, or even at the heart of the empire. The Mughal emperor Aurangzeb, Indian historian Jadunath Sarkar wrote, wished to subdue the province of Gujarat, where "the roads were unsafe to traders and travelers alike. . . . Any rebel or bandit leader could in a few days raise a large body of fighters by the promise of plunder. . . . Indeed, Gujarat bore the evil title of *lashkar-khez*, or a land 'bristling with soldiers.' " Aurangzeb also reversed the policies of religious toleration that had begun under Akbar, reimposing special taxes on Hindus and banning Hindu assemblies. As a result of these and other measures, there was a rebellion of one subcaste, the Jats, in Mathura, a city not far south of Delhi. The Jats in Mathura mustered twenty thousand troops at the heart of the Mughal Empire to do battle with the Mughal army in 1669 and 1670.[58] A Mughal commander whose campaign diaries have been preserved and who is known as Mirza Nathan was sent on campaigns in Bengal in 1607 and later in Kuch/Bihar, also in northeast India. On two occasions he lost his army, once to desertion and once to defeat in battle and then to desertion, and in both cases he was able to recruit another force—one of one thousand and the other of fifteen hundred—on the spot from locally available soldiers.[59]

The ability to raise new troops on the spot from local sources became of critical importance in the twenty-year war waged by Aurangzeb against the Marathi-speaking people of the highlands in South India, the Deccan, under the leader of Shivaji and his successor, Shambuji. A European soldier of fortune who commanded artillery for Aurangzeb esti-

[57] Jadunath Sarkar, *History of Aurangzeb*, two vols. in one (New Delhi: Orient Longman, 1973), pp. 121, 142.

[58] Jadunath Sarkar, *History of Aurangzeb*, vol. 3 (New Delhi: Orient Longman, 1972), pp.183, 195.

[59] Mirza Nathan (Mirza Natula), *Baharistan-I-Ghaybi, or A History of the Mughal Wars in Assam, Cooch, Behar, Bengal, Bihar and Orissa during the Reigns of Jahangir and Shahjahan*, trans. M. I. Borah (Gauhati, Assam: Department of Historical Records and Antiquarian Studies, 1936), 1:30 and 2:611. For another, summary translation of Mirza Nathan's campaign diary, see Jadunath Sarkar, "A New History of Bengal in Jahangir's Time," *Journal of the Bihar and Orissa Research Society* 7 (March 1921): 1–8.

mated that the emperor lost one hundred thousand men and three hundred thousand pack animals a year in the peak years of fighting, all of which had to be and were replaced locally.[60]

How does the size of the armed peasantry in India compare with contemporary non-Indian societies? The period of the Mughal Empire included much war, including local wars resulting in part from prolonged struggles between Muslim conquerors and Hindu kingdoms. It may be the case that this pushed the size of the military population above historical norms, though it might be just as easily argued that the census conducted during the reign of the emperor Akbar, a tolerant and peace-loving ruler, provided a picture of Indian society at relative peace in comparison with some of his successors, Aurangzeb in particular. Perhaps the most relevant comparison is with Europe during the period of the Thirty Years' War, when religious conflicts led to civil and international war that extracted all the available military manpower for protracted war. What portion of the European population was under arms in this period?

The number of European soldiers fighting in that war has been derived from fragmentary muster roles that have survived and estimates of casualties. In his 1991 history of the Thirty Years' War, Geoffrey Parker made a series of estimates and assessments. Estimates of the total number of French forces on all fronts in 1634–1636 range upward from 9,500 cavalry and 115,000 infantry, "but it is difficult to be sure that even these forces were actually mobilized, because no series of muster rolls survive." On some fronts, the French forces took heavy casualties to death, disease, or desertion. In the Low Countries campaign of 1635, French forces fell in strength from 26,000 to 8,000. At the time of the signing of the peace of Westphalia, all opponents of Emperor Ferdinand III (France, Hesse-Kassel, Sweden) maintained 140,000 troops on the soil of the Roman Empire, to which must be added the Scots who fought for the Protestant Germans (25,000), the estimated French casualties (117,000, or the difference between the size of the entire French army at its peak and at its nadir), and the estimated Swedish casualties of about 150,000 (50,000 in the period 1621–1632; 100,000 in 1633–1648) during the entire war. The imperial forces peaked at about 150,000 and declined by war's end to 70,000. We may assume the difference between 150,000 and 70,000 to have been the result of wartime losses.[61] This comes to a total of 550,000 soldiers who participated in the war. In 1650 the population of Europe

---

[60] Niccolao Manucci, *Storia do Mogor, or Mogul India, 1653–1708*, vol. 4, trans. William Irvine (London: John Murray, 1907), p. 96.

[61] Geoffrey Parker, ed., *The Thirty Years' War* (New York: Routledge, Chapman, Hall, 1991), pp. 100, 147, 191, 193.

west of the Urals, including Scandinavia, Britain, European Russia, Spain, and the Balkans, was 105 million.[62] Thus the ratio of soldiers to total population was on the order of 0.5 percent.

This estimate is not the only one available. Drawing on a variety of sources, Charles Tilly pulled together estimates of troop strength, with a high of 2.5 percent of the total population for Spain in 1600, down to 0.7 percent in 1700; France, 0.4 percent in 1600 and 2.1 percent in 1700; England and Wales, 0.7 percent in 1600 and 5.4 percent in 1700; and the Netherlands, 1.3 percent in 1600 and 5.3 percent in 1700.[63] In the case of England and France, these figures are consistent with the estimates based on data from the Thirty Years' War. Where Tilly's estimates are higher, as in the case of Spain, they diverge upward from estimates of army sizes of the major European powers made by Parker, who put the size of the armies of the great powers in 1630 at about 150,000 men each.[64]

In addition to acknowledging the dispute about the figures, in making this comparison we must remember that the Indian figure counts part-time peasant soldiers, whereas the European armies were becoming professionalized. Is it legitimate to compare the number of Indian soldiers, including peasant soldiers, with European professional soldiers? Despite this professionalization, conditions of the Thirty Years' War also tended to draw many peasants into military service who would not ordinarily have served. The war was a series of bitterly contested, local religious conflicts that led to a population reduction in the Holy Roman Empire of about 20 percent.[65] In this kind of total war, which transformed European international and social politics, it was not unlikely that many European peasants, who would otherwise have been farmers, were drawn into the armies. Furthermore, the figure of 0.5 percent of the European population under arms includes battle casualties and their replacements. It pushes the estimate of the number of European soldiers up. The figures for India are static figures and do not account for casualties and their replacements. This pushes the estimates of the number of Indian soldiers down. If we adjust the Indian figures to account for the 100,000 casualties a year reported during the wars of Aurangzeb, the figure of 3–4 percent for India might well be higher.

The bottom line is that even with conservative estimates of the number of Indian soldiers and liberal estimates of the number of European soldiers, the incidence of Indian soldiers per capita in the sixteenth century

[62] McEvedy and Jones, *Atlas of World Population History*, p. 18.

[63] Charles Tilly, *Coercion, Capital, and European States, 990–1992* (Cambridge, Mass.: Blackwell, 1992), p. 79.

[64] Geoffrey Parker, *The Military Revolution: Military Innovation and the Rise of the West, 1500–1800* (Cambridge: Cambridge University Press, 1988), p. 24.

[65] Parker, *Thirty Years' War*, p. 211.

[135]

is at least as high as it was in Europe during the Thirty Years' War and might well be closer to ten times the incidence of soldiers per capita in Europe during that war. There can be no doubt that India was heavily militarized during this period and that the central political authorities controlled only a small portion of the total military forces in India.

To find times and conditions in non-Indian societies in which the incidence of soldiers relative to total population approaches that of Mughal India, one must look at periods of severe internal warfare. During the Hundred Years' War, for example, the English king relied primarily on musters of his subjects who were paid to fight. These men were not knights but infantry armed with bows and arrows. From the fragmentary records, scholars have learned that at the end of the thirteenth century, Edward I in England had requested money for sixty thousand foot soldiers and forty-seven thousand were actually on the payrolls in the field in 1294. The total population of England and Wales in 1300 was approximately 4 million, and on the assumption that at least as many English and Welsh soldiers were fighting against the king or sitting on the sidelines, there may have been a total of one hundred thousand soldiers in 1300, or about 2.5 percent of the total population. This level of militarization is thought to have been "so exhausting for both sides that it discouraged the normal development of the apparatus of the state."[66] Philippe Contamine's estimate of the number of men under arms in England in 1298 is somewhat lower, "perhaps 5 percent of the adult male population had been called to arms," or about 1.3 percent of the total population, but he assumed that all soldiers were in fact fighting in the field. He also notes that the general rise and fall of the size of European armies was associated with fluctuations in the level of public order or the lack of it.[67] Estimates of the armed population of Europe in the tenth century are even more sketchy. But scholars have noted the gradual shift in western Europe from a society in which the peasant culture was one of "war and aggression," in which "the status of freedom was first of all defined as fitness to participate in military expeditions" against other peasants, to a culture in which warfare was increasingly restricted by religious and political authorities. These restrictions had their origins in movements such as the "Peace of God" which were reactions to the endemic violence in society, and which placed restrictions on who could serve in armies, reducing the number and role of armed peasants

---

[66] See Richard W. Kaeuper, *War, Justice, and Public Order: England and France in the Later Middle Ages* (Oxford: Clarendon, 1988), pp. 17–25, 121; McEvedy and Jones, *Atlas of World Population History*, p. 43.

[67] Philippe Contamine, *War in the Middle Ages*, trans. Michael Jones (New York: Blackwell, 1985), pp. 117, 123–124.

and where and when nobles could fight, as well as restricting the scope and targets of war. Domestic peace was also pursued over centuries in Europe by bans on private aristocratic wars, by confiscation or neutralization of private fortresses, as noted above, by exporting surplus aristocratic knights on crusades and other external military missions, and by professionalizing the remaining warriors.[68] None of these restrictions on warfare appear to have been operating in Mughal India, in which endemic warfare and service in armies were seen by peasants as promising avenues of social mobility.[69]

There are other indications that Mughal India was highly militarized at the local level and different from Europe during the same period. Consider the incidence of military fortifications. The area of south India, like north India, was heavily fortified in general. One survey of the forts in India built during that period noted that "Military defences are practically innumerable throughout India. Almost every hill in the range running north-east through the south of Rajputana has a fortification on its summit; the same may be said of the Deccan . . . and of the hilly districts of south India. . . . They were all built by the absolute ruler of the state in which they stand, well knowing that they were subject to attack at any moment by the monarch of an adjoining or far-off state—an event which was of frequent occurrence."[70] Another survey of the fortresses of south India noted that Shivaji, the most famous commander of the Marathi-speaking people of the central highlands or Deccan of South India, constructed over one hundred forts in his territories.[71] The area of south India in which Mir Jumla conducted his military operations was heavily fortified. In one strip of coastal territory one hundred miles long, Mir

[68] See Georges Duby, *The Early Growth of the European Economy: Warriors and Peasants from the Seventh to the Twelfth Century*, trans. Howard B. Clarke (Ithaca: Cornell University Press, 1978), pp. 48–49, 162–163, 167; Contamine, *War in the Middle Ages*, p. 249; Jean-Pierre Poly and Eric Bournazel, *The Feudal Transformation, 900–1200* (New York: Holmes and Meier, 1991), pp. 23–24, on the early prevalence of peasant soldiers in Normandy, and pp. 147–155, 160, on the restrictions on peasant soldiers and scope of war; Kaeuper, *War, Justice, and Public Order*, pp. 200–203, on monarchical restrictions on knightly private warfare, pp. 211–215, on the dismantling of private forts, and p. 229, on the development of the idea of treason as private warfare against the king; R. C. Smail, *Crusading Warfare, 1097–1193* (Cambridge: Cambridge University Press, 1989), p. 102, on large demands for knights in the Crusades relative to their numbers in Europe; Norbert Elias, *The Civilizing Process: State Formation and Civilization* (Oxford: Basil Blackwell, 1982), pp. 40–41, on early rapid population growth in Europe, the resulting number of "surplus" knights, and the solution found by exporting them on expansionist Crusades.

[69] Kolff, *Naukar, Rajput, and Sepoy*, pp. 58, 71–73, 84.

[70] Sidney Toy, *Strongholds of India* (London: William Heinemann, 1957), pp. 1–2. Toy surveys in detail twenty-three fortresses in India.

[71] Virginia Fass, *The Forts of India* (London: Collins, 1986), p. 196.

Jumla captured a minimum of seventeen forts in thirteen months. When in 1656 he marched his private army out to meet the Mughal imperial forces, they numbered 6,000 cavalry and 15,000 infantry.[72] The Mughals themselves established sixty-four forts in their four Deccan provinces.[73] In addition to elaborate fortresses, small village fortresses were ubiquitous.

This level of fortification was true of Europe at an earlier time, but by the seventeenth century, systematic state efforts to remove the military bastions from which central state power could be challenged by local chiefs had had considerable effect. Even after religious conflicts had grown in intensity, central Germany remained unfortified, even into and during the Thirty Years' War. Small-scale wars among local garrisons manned by regional forces for local security were characteristic of French religious wars and the English civil war but came to an end with the demolition of local strongholds. In 1593 Henry IV destroyed forts and castles as he pacified provinces. In the 1630s, Richelieu razed over one hundred fortresses in the south after the suppression of Huguenot and aristocratic rebellions. In Great Britain, the eighteen fortresses in Shropshire were reduced to two in 1645–1647. "However, all this was as nothing compared with the systematic demilitarization of central France under Louis XIV," according to Parker. More important "was the creation of a virtually demilitarized zone in the inland provinces, through the destruction or studied neglect of 600 or so other walled cities and fortresses in the interior of the kingdom—including Paris, whose fortification the government ordered to be demolished in 1670."[74]

No great precision can be expected in figures from Europe or India from this period. But if the consensus of these estimates is roughly correct, then Indian society was more heavily populated with soldiers than was France or the Netherlands during the Thirty Years' War, though less than one-half as heavily populated with soldiers as was Italy during the Social War. Mughal India was also heavily fortified, and the local bastions were not controlled by the central government. The implications were profound. Indian social structures in this period caused and reflected severe internal conflicts, legitimized by caste rights, which regularly became military in nature and which led to widely distributed local military capabilities that denied the central state a monopoly on the legitimate use of force. In consequence, the emergence of a strong, Turkish-style centralized state and military that were free to pursue external military activities was inhibited. John Richards noted in his history of

[72]Jagdish Narayan Sarkar, *The Life of Mir Jumla*, pp. 32–34, 121.
[73]Jadunath Sarkar, *History of Aurangzeb*, 1:23.
[74]Parker, *Military Revolution*, pp. 26, 41–43.

the Mughal Empire that "disarming and subduing regional aristocracies or converting them into officials was a formidable task that was rarely accomplished by early modern states. The Timurids [Mughal rulers] were not prepared to execute policies more reminiscent of various Ottoman efforts than those characteristic of Indo-Muslim regimes."[75]

The consequences for Indian politics and military policies of this militarization of Indian society at the local level were immense. In the words of the historian Dirk Kolff: "in such a society, no government, however powerful, could even begin to think of achieving a monopoly on the use of arms. In some respects, the millions of armed men, cultivators otherwise, that the government was supposed to rule over, were its rivals rather than its subjects.... Historical sources often refer to peasants and townspeople assaulting soldiers, and not only in the hills and inaccessible places far from the well-subdued plains."[76] Arthur Wellesley, later the duke of Wellington, noted his personal observations of warfare in India in 1804: "Whenever the largest and most formidable bodies [of enemy soldiers] are hard pressed by our troops, the village people attack them upon their rear and flanks, cut off the stragglers and will not allow a man to enter their village."[77]

As these accounts and histories make clear, the 4.4 million soldiers counted in the census of the Mughal Empire were not a standing professional army, nor were they all mobilized at the same time. Most were peasants who farmed when they could and fought when it was profitable, honorable, or necessary to do so. The cavalry which was the striking arm of the empire and which has received the bulk of scholarly attention until more recently was much smaller. But the armed peasants could and did rebel against tax collection, could and did assist military adventurers who challenged the empire, and, in general, prevented any Indian state during this period from "the achievement of a central monopoly, or something nearly approaching it, on the use of arms."[78] Qureshi notes that "peasants were not averse from taking up arms if they felt that they were being unjustly treated. They could resort to such resistance because the difference between an army and an armed rabble was proverbially too small, especially when the peasant bore arms almost as part of his dress.... The tradition of self-governing village communities date back to pre-historic times.... The Mughals ... respected them."[79]

As a result, the interaction between the Muslim Turkish elite with the population in India was far different from the interaction between the

[75]Richards, *Cambridge History of India*, p. 87.
[76]Kolff, *Nankar, Rajoput, and Sepoy*, p. 7.
[77]Ibid., p. 9.
[78]Ibid.
[79]Qureshi, *Administration of the Mughal Empire*, p. 177.

Turkish elite and the local population, Muslim and non-Muslim, in the Ottoman Empire. The Ottoman rulers had succeeded in constructing a highly centralized system of revenue in conquered territories, in which taxes were directly assessed and collected by officers of the state. One cavalryman would routinely be dispatched to each conquered village in the Ottoman Empire to collect the taxes based on the land surveys conducted by the central government. "But in India," as Douglas Streisand stated, "the swarms of infantry meant that one cavalryman could not cope with a village, much less a *zamindar* with his own army. The Mughal Provincial army thus confronted a series of private *zamindar/* peasant armies."[80]

Revenue in the Mughal Empire was formally extracted by a series of nonhereditary, revocable grants of land to Mughal officials who would collect the taxes and pass them on to the emperor. In practice, the rotation of Mughal officials, intended to prevent them from developing local power bases and to keep them dependent on the emperor, made the Mughal officials dependent on local hereditary officials who performed the land surveys and actually collected the taxes for the official in return for a fee. The local officials in charge of the land surveys, the *qanungos*, dealt with imperial officials who had no knowledge of the locality. "The *qanungo* was therefore often placed in a position which he could greatly exploit for his own gain." The local officials who collected the taxes— *chaudhuris*—were invariably zamindars themselves and often the leading local *zamindars* backed by their own army. To enforce even this decentralized collection of revenue, in the first half of the seventeenth century the emperor Shah Jahan required an army of about two hundred thousand solely for tax collection.[81] Because of the armed nature of Indian society, the Mughal rulers did not have direct access to the sources of revenue, which were in the hands of the local military chiefs, in complete contrast to the system of the Ottoman Empire. As Jadunath Sarkar put it, "the activities of a modern State were left to the community, to society or the caste brotherhood. . . . The aim of government was thus extremely limited, materialistic, almost sordid."[82]

Efforts to Create a Modern State in Medieval India

How can we know that it was the caste-based local political and land-holding system, backed by local armed forces, that led to the weak cen-

---

[80] Streusand, *Formation of the Mughal Empire*, pp. 68–70.
[81] Habib, *Agrarian System of Mughal India*, pp. 168, 273–293.
[82] Jadunath Sarkar, *Mughal Administration* (Calcutta: Sarkar, 1952), p. 5.

tral government of the Mughal Empire? That weak government might simply have been the result of an incompetent imperial government that never sought to establish a monopoly on the use of legitimate force and on the collection of revenue. History is full of contingent outcomes, and nothing in this chapter or book is meant to suggest that social structures predetermine the emergence of a strong central state or its failure to emerge. Social structures do create the context in which any government will pursue its objectives, but they cannot tell us which policies a state will try to pursue. Did any rulers in medieval India try to create a strong state and military? If we can establish that there were such efforts and they failed, we can better assess the limits imposed on the state by the nature of Indian society at that time.

There were at least two periods in medieval Indian history during which Indian rulers did try to create something resembling a modern state, and their failure can be linked back to the impact of Indian social structures. The first period was the reign of Sher Shah. In 1540–1545, there was a brief interruption in the Mughal rule of India when Humayun, the son of Babur, was unable to hold on to his father's Indian conquests as the result of several separate conspiracies mounted against his rule when Humayun proved not to be up to the military challenge posed by the Afghan ruler, Sher Khan, later Sher Shah.[83] Sher Shah gained control of the area of the Sultanate of Delhi and made a clear effort to replace the existing decentralized rule with a system that centralized financial and military power. In many ways, his efforts resembled those of Richelieu in France. Sher Shah introduced regular land assessments for tax purposes, placed heavy emphasis on Turkish professional soldiers who were the descendants of Mamluk slave soldiers, and tried to build an army that did not depend on the revenue or the men controlled by local chiefs. Instead, he used the money gained from conquest to hire soldiers directly and to pay them regularly. The major study of his rule summarized his administrative efforts to overcome the challenges to centralized rule posed by the society in which he was operating: "The challenges of ethnic loyalties . . . and of . . . segmentary, aristocratic politics were largely overcome by direct recruitment based on merit, a leadership that owed little to ascribed status" financed by revenues gained through conquest."[84]

But he failed. Why? First, the wealth that Sher Shah could acquire from conquest could and did buy him soldiers, but it did not buy him legitimacy, either in the eyes of the Muslim faithful or the Hindu Rajput

---

[83] Jouher, *Private Memoirs of the Moghul Emperor Humayun Written in Persian by Jouher,* trans. Charles Stewart, (Delhi: Idarah-I Adabiyat-I Delhi, 1972), pp. 7, 15, 26, 34, 47.

[84] Kolff, *Naukar, Rajput, and Sepoy,* pp. 54–56, 67.

chiefs. The Muslims were offended by Sher Shah's religious eclecticism and the practice of some of his Rajput allies of capturing and sexually exploiting Muslim women. The Rajput warrior clans could and did make frequent alliances with Sher Shah, but they also occasionally practiced *jauhar,* or the ritual killing of their women and children before a final battle, rather than surrender when faced with military defeat at the hands of non-Rajput conquerors. Second, though Sher Shah could enter the market for military manpower directly, he could never buy up all the numerous available soldiers or eliminate the other demands for soldiers. As a result, the incentives for the leaders of the warrior bands to improve the terms on which they could sell their services by dealing, counter-dealing, and treachery between Sher Shah and his rivals continued. This complicated playing-off of sides usually took the form of a deal between a Rajput warlord and Sher Shah, while the same Rajput leader would send his son to cut a separate deal in support of another local leader.[85]

The second period of attempted state building occurred during the reign of the Mughal emperor Akbar, who, in many senses, was the true founder of the dynasty in India. He too made a determined effort to develop a political base in India that was not under the control of independent lords, and he too found it impossible to do so because of the nature of Indian social structures. The circumstances of his rise to power were such as to provide him with a vivid picture of the dangers of relying too heavily on his Mughal nobles. The emperor Humayun died while Akbar was a child and the regent was a prominent noble, probably of Iranian descent, Bayram Khan. Faced with rebellion among the Mughal nobles, Bayram Khan executed one of their leaders and appears to have favored Shiite nobles at the expense of the Sunni nobles. In 1559, he attempted what amounted to a coup d'état to gain complete control of the Mughal court. In all this, he neglected to cultivate and secure the approval of young Akbar. He failed because of this and because, having alienated the Sunni Mughal nobles, he had no plausible allies in India itself among the Indian Muslims. His only other possible source of support would have been the Rajput chiefs. Although not impossible, such relations took time and care to develop, which Bayram Khan did not have.[86] From Akbar's perspective, this episode carried with it two lessons: first was the danger of relying on nobles who could grow too powerful, and second, the need to and possibility of developing an independent base of power among the Hindu Rajputs. Akbar did make

---

[85] Ibid., pp. 70, 91, 93, 96–101, 108, 126, 143.

[86] Iqtidar Alam Khan, "Mughal Court Politics during Bairam Khan's Regency," *Medieval India: A Miscellany* 1 (1969): 22, 33, 37–38. See also John Dowson, ed., "Akbar-Nama of Shaikh Abu-l Fazl," in *The History of India as Told by Its Own Historians: The Papers of Sir H. M. Elliot* (Calcutta: Susil Gupta, 1953), p. 24.

serious efforts to increase his power relative to his Mughal nobles and to expand the base of his support in Hindu India, but he ran into opposition from both camps.

Winning greater support among the Hindu Rajputs required that Akbar both display tolerance of Hindu religious beliefs and control the reaction of the Muslim faithful to what would appear to them as heresy. Akbar did seek instruction in Hindu beliefs, shaved his beard, publicly adopted Hindu practices and wives, protected cows, and banned the eating of beef. At the same time, in the words of Badaoni, a contemporary historian, "His Majesty was anxious to unite in his person the powers of the State and those of the Church; for he could not bear to be subordinate to any one." Consequently, he had chosen religious leaders draft a document that declared that in the interests of peace and security, the emperor would be the final arbiter in Islamic religious disputes:

> Should therefore, in the future, a religious question come up, regarding which the opinions of the Mujtahids are at variance, and His Majesty in his penetrating understanding and clear wisdom, be inclined to adopt, for the benefit of the nation and as a political expedient, any of the conflicting opinions which exist on the point, and issue a decree to that effect, we do hereby agree that such a decree shall be binding on us and on the whole nation. Further, we declare that, should His Majesty think fit to issue a new order, we and the whole nation shall likewise be bound by it, provided always that such an order be not only in accordance with some verse of the Qu'ran, but also of real benefit for the nation.

Akbar signed and proclaimed this document in 1579. He further decided "publicly to use the formula, 'There is no God, but God, and Akbar is God's representative.' But as this led to commotions, he thought better of it and only used this formula to a few people in the Harem."[87] There is some debate about whether this proclamation was somehow designed to woo the Indian Muslims to whom Akbar wished to turn for support in order to reduce his dependence on the Mughal nobles. What is not in dispute is that the proclamation provoked a hostile reaction among Akbar's Mughal nobles, who now had a religious basis on which to rebel against Akbar, whom they opposed because of his general efforts to reduce their financial power.[88] This pushed Akbar toward greater reliance on the Hindu Rajput chiefs, but these were the leaders who had their

---

[87] Abul Fazl, *Ain-i Akbari*, pp. 188–193, 194–197, all quotes are Blochmann citing Badaoni.

[88] Iqtidar Alam Khan, "The Nobility under Akbar and the Development of his Religious Policy, 1560–1580," *Journal of the Royal Asiatic Society of Great Britain and Ireland* (1968): 34–35; Streusand, *Formation of the Mughal Empire*, pp. 6, 100–102.

own local sources of revenue and military power. The question then became whether Akbar or subsequent Mughal emperors could develop a set of relationships within India that would allow them to develop stable military institutions that owed their loyalty to the emperor and not to their local subcaste leaders.

THE MUGHAL ARMY AND INDIAN SOCIETY

In the sections above, we sought to understand the nature of Indian society, the local armies it generated, and the implications of both for the Indian state. But in addition to the local armies that might serve or oppose the Mughals, the Mughal Empire had its own military institutions as well. What was their size, their relationship to society, and their battlefield strengths and weaknesses? The available answers to these questions suggest that the imperial Mughal armies were profoundly affected by the military context of Indian society described above.

The heart of the Mughal army was its cavalry, which in turn was supported by what was known as the *mansabdari* system. *Mansabdar* is best translated as rank holder, and the mansabdari system involved the grant of a rank to a Mughal officer. It entitled the holder to pay from the imperial treasury or to rights to the revenue of an assigned area of land known as a *jagir*. The rank carried with it the obligation to present a certain number of horses and mounted troops. Neither the rank nor the land was granted to its holder as a hereditary possession, and both could be withdrawn by the emperor at his pleasure. The ranks themselves were simply numbers, nominally corresponding to the number of mounted horsemen the *mansabdari* were obliged to produce. In practice, ranks became inflated in competitions for prestige, and the rank, for example, of five thousand did not correspond to a force of five thousand that could be mustered. On average, the number of mounted troops that a *mansabdar* would actually present tended to be about one-fourth to one-third his nominal strength. This much is known because of the elaborate system of counting men and horses (branding and counting horses, recording the descriptions of mounted soldiers) used by the Mughal emperors.

Units of the Mughal cavalry were predominantly homogenous by ethnic group, with units commanded by Turkish Mughals containing only Mughal Turks.[89] Iranian-led units were at least two-thirds Iranian in their

---

[89] "Each mansabdar was free to recruit men of his own ethnicity and religion. Later regulations tended to codify this by stipulating that commanders might not employ more than a fixed proportion of men outside their group." Richards, *Cambridge History of India*, p. 64.

composition, and Hindu Rajput units contained only Rajputs. Supplies of soldiers were provided by intermediate military jobbers who had, de facto, established areas within which they regularly recruited from certain groups, on the basis of personal relations with local leaders developed over time. The size of the cavalry, as estimated by European observers and as it has been reconstructed from administrative records, varied during the period 1560–1707 between three hundred and four hundred thousand. It had a much larger infantry component that drew on local sources of manpower, as noted above.[90]

Entire books have been written about the mansabdari military system of the Mughal Empire. Here the purpose is to determine whether and to what extent it created an army that was loyal to the state or the emperor, as opposed to Mughal chiefs or local Indian leaders, and whether it reflected the social structures of India. It was designed to prevent the establishment of local bases of military power independent of the emperor by keeping the grants of revenue or land at the pleasure of the emperor and by changing the assignment of *jagirs* from time to time. Did it do so?

The first question to be answered is the identity of the mansabdars. How many were drawn from within India and how many from non-Indian sources? Even an approximate answer to this question would begin to help us understand the relationship of the Mughal imperial officer corps to Indian society. A number of scholars have gone back to contemporary histories and records to survey the mansabdars. One such survey found, not surprisingly, that in 1555, near the beginning of the Mughal period, no Hindu or Indian Muslim mansabdars could be identified. Twenty years later, only 8 percent of high-ranking mansabdars were Hindu, and 9 percent were Indian Muslims, as distinct from Mughal Turks or Iranians. Toward the end of Akbar's rule in 1595, the role of the Mughal and Persian mansabdars had dropped considerably, whereas the fraction of high-ranking Indian Muslim and Hindu mansabdars had each risen to 16 percent for a total of 32 percent. The representation of Indians among high- and low-ranking mansabdars was only slightly higher, 35 percent.

Were the Hindu mansabdars more or less loyal to the emperor than their Muslim counterparts? Hindu officials do appear to have been more

---

[90] For the Mughal military and the mansabdari system, see among many sources Abdul Aziz, *The Mansabdari System and the Moghul Army* (Delhi: Idarah-I Adabiyat-I Delhi, 1972), pp. 13–14, 26, 82, 156; William Irvine, *The Army of the Indian Moghuls: Its Organization and Administration* (London: Luzac, 1903), pp. 11, 13–15, 36, 38, 53–55, 57; Kolff, *Naukar, Rajput, and Sepoy*, pp. 175, 178–179; Raj Kumar Phul, *Armies of the Great Mughals, 1526–1707* (New Delhi: Oriental Publishers, 1978), pp. 126–134; Qureshi, *Administration of Mughal Empire*, pp. 88–89, 92–93, 96, 106–107, 119–123.

loyal to the emperor than were Mughal officers in the rebellion of 1580–1581, which was triggered by Akbar's efforts to reduce the power of the Mughal nobles and to increase his control over Muslim political-religious life. Forty-five Mughal mansabdars rebelled, and sixty remained loyal; six Hindu officials rebelled, while thirty-seven remained loyal; and three Indian Muslims rebelled, while forty-one stayed loyal.[91] Akbar seemed to have moved successfully toward an officer corps which was more representative of Indian society as a whole and which was more loyal to his state than his own kin. However, the rebellion of 1580 was one in which the material interests of the Mughal nobility were threatened, whereas Hindu officialdom stood to profit. There were other occasions and issues that would test the loyalty of the Indian officials. Other Mughal emperors were less tolerant of Hindus, most noticeably, Aurangzeb. But despite his intolerant policies, a survey of the high-ranking mansabdars under Aurangzeb reveals that the number of Hindu mansabdars grew throughout his reign, as did the number of mansabdars who were Indian Muslims.[92]

In sum, solid evidence shows that the military leadership and units of the central Mughal cavalry army were increasingly representative of the ethnic composition of the portions of India that it ruled. The foot soldiers of the Mughal military had always come from and represented Indian society. Over time, the heart of the Mughal military, the cavalry, also came to represent Indian society. What were the consequences of the fact that the Mughal army did in this way reflect Indian society? Were there tensions among the Mughal army officers that mirrored tensions that existed in the society of Mughal India? If those internal military tensions did exist, did they have any impact on the military performance of the Mughal army?

The administrative history of the reign of Akbar known as the *Ain-i Akbari* contains a list of 415 mansabdars who served the Mughal Empire as officers of high and low rank, along with their biographies. This list is not complete with respect to high-ranking officers of the empire. To it can be added six officers who are known to have been deliberately excluded by the author of the *Ain-i Akbari* because they had fallen into disgrace or had rebelled as well as some members of the royal family who were not listed as mansabdars. The biographies of these additional

[91] Iqtidar Alam Khan, "Nobility under Akbar," Appendices 1 and 4, pp. 35–36.

[92] M. Athar Ali, "Provincial Governors under Aurangzeb: An Analysis," *Medieval India* 1 (1968): 98–101. See also M. Athar Ali, *The Mughal Nobility under Aurangzeb* (Bombay: Asia Publishing House, 1970), p. 31, where a table shows that of total mansabdars, Hindus represented 22.5 percent of those serving Akbar in 1595; 22.4 percent of those serving Shah Jahan, who ruled from 1628 to 1658; 21.6 percent of those serving from 1658 to 1678; and 31.6 percent from 1679 to 1707.

officers are also avaliable. The brief biographies of each *mansabdar* can be coded along relatively unambiguous lines for a number of factors. From this coding, a picture of the Mughal officer corps as a whole might be developed to determine and assess the extent and nature of the internal tensions of the officer corps, thus providing an overview of the tensions that affected military effectiveness of the Mughal army. In particular, this analysis could shed light on the consequences of the most obvious social tension in Mughal society and the officer corps—that between Hindu and Muslim officers. Of the officers listed, fifty-one are identifiable as Hindus. Only 16 Hindus are identifiable in the 137 higher-ranking mansabdars, those with ranks of one thousand or higher.

How can the existence of tensions within the higher ranks of the officer corps be extracted from the biographies? It is always clear from the histories when a mansabdar had been assassinated, when he had participated in a major rebellion, when he had been guilty of a failure to obey imperial orders or had conducted unauthorized military actions sufficiently offensive to the emperor to have been banished from the imperial court for a period of time. The most common offense was failing to report to court when ordered to do so by the emperor, an order that would usually be issued when an officer was suspected of disobeying commands. Ordering him to return to court would either put the officer in the hands of the central government or, if the order was refused, indicate clearly that the officer was rebelling. Finally, it is relatively clear from the histories when a mansabdar has been betrayed by his own troops or officers. The results of the examination of the administrative history are set out in tables 1 and 2 below. What emerges from this sample is proof of the obvious. The Mughal officer corps was affected by larger social conflicts. Hindu officers defected or disobeyed orders nearly three times as often as Muslim officers (13 percent of the Muslim mansabdars defected versus 36 percent of the Hindu mansabdars), but they also rebelled less often (in fact, not at all) against the emperor. A separate study of Akbar and his Hindu officers by an Indian scholar, C. M. Agrawal, provides an independently conducted survey against which to check that based on the *Ain-i Akbari*. Agrawal enumerated thirty-one Hindu officers and gave their biographies. Of these thirty-one, eleven, or 35 percent committed easily identifiable acts of disobedience against the emperor.[93] These findings are consistent with the observation that Hindu officers did not participate in the 1580 rebellion, since rebellion, active participation in a conflict against the empire, was different from defying or ignoring imperial orders.

What was different about Hindu officers of the Mughal Empire? The

---

[93] C. M. Agrawal, *Akbar and Hindu Officers* (Jalandar, India: ABS, 1986), passim.

Table 1. Non-Hindu high-ranking mansabdars (N = 142)

	Number	%
Assassinated	18	13
Rebelled	19	13
Defected, disobeyed	19	13
Betrayed	23	16

Source: Data from Abul Fazl, *Ain-i Akbari*, 2d. ed., trans. H. Bloch-mann (1927; reprint, Lahore, Pakistan: Qausain, 1975), pp. 32–484, 596; coding and calculations mine.

review of the landholding, revenue, and military manpower system showed that the imported Mughal Muslim elite was dependent on local social structures and elite for their support. The Hindu elite—the Rajput chiefs who were recruited into the Mughal officer system—on the other hand, emerged from and were part of the local social system and structures that yielded money and men. The Rajput chiefs who became mansabdars were usually allowed to remain in their own locales. Although the land and revenue that had traditionally belonged to them would officially become part of the Mughal system, the Rajput chiefs would in effect continue to retain the revenues and hire the soldiers they had always hired. Unlike the imported Muslim elite, the Rajput chiefs had independent power bases that simultaneously allowed them to defy the emperor and to remain, with some major exceptions during the reign of Aurangzeb, uninterested in rebellions to unseat the emperor. Although Mughal emperors relied more on Rajput chiefs over time, the ability of those chiefs to control land revenues and their access to abundant military manpower gave them considerable freedom to defy the emperor, despite the mansabdar system—more freedom than the non-Indian Mughal mansabdars, who did not have the same links to Indian society. In short, as the Mughal officer corps absorbed more Hindu officers, it became more representative of Indian society as a whole, less divorced from Indian society, but less controllable by the central government.

What were the military characteristics of the Mughal army? Much of its early military character had nothing to do with the nature of Indian society. To recall, at the beginning of the period, the Mughul army was largely Turkish and Persian. Much of the behavior of the Mughal army in the early days can be understood in terms of its reflection of the norms and social structures of nomadic Turkish society, in which each tribal leader felt himself to have as much a right to be king as any other. Babur himself noted that he conquered Afghanistan in 1511 and tried to invade

Table 2. Hindu high-ranking mansabdars ($N = 16$)

	Number	%
Assassinated	0	0
Rebelled	0	0
Defected, disobeyed	6	36
Betrayed	2	13

Source: Data from Abul Fazl, *Ain-i Akbari,* 2d. ed., trans. H. Bloch-mann (1927; reprint, Lahore, Pakistan: Qausain, 1975), pp. 32–484, 596; coding and calculations mine.

India four times but was denied victory until his fifth effort, "sometimes . . . from the misconduct of my *amirs* [chiefs] and their dislike of the plan, sometimes from the cabals and opposition of my brothers."[94] Because the organization of the Mughal military units was based on the principle described by Ibn Khaldun of loyalty to individual chiefs, the deaths of those chiefs in battle would often lead to the disintegration of those units.[95] Babur's successor, Humayun, increasingly lost the support of his own chiefs and family, and so became more dependent on other sources of support.[96]

The first battle of Panipat in 1526, which secured for the emperor Babur control of Delhi and which toppled the Afghan Lodi dynasty, was a set-piece battle in which Babur set up a fortified defensive killing zone into which he lured the young and inexperienced Afghan commander Ibrahim Lodi. So elaborate were Babur's field fortifications that one of his commanders told him, " 'You have fortified our ground in such a way that it is not possible he [Ibrahim Lodi] should ever think of coming here.' I answered, 'you judge of him by the Khans and Sultans of the Uzbeks. . . . But you must not judge of our present enemies by those who were then opposed to us. They have not the ability to discriminate when it is proper to advance and when to retreat. . . . ' It happened as I foretold." Lured into the pursuit of Babur's advance party, the Afghan army could not halt its advance and perhaps fifteen thousand of its nominal one hundred thousand initial soldiers were killed.[97]

[94] Cited in ibid., p. 46.

[95] The accounts of Akbar's rule provides four examples of rebellious Mughal forces collapsing when their leader is killed during the imperial war against Bengal. See Abu-l Fazl, *Akbar-Nama,* pp. 47–55, 71, 75–81, 92–93. Phul provides examples from battles in 1556, 1568, and 1658 in which the disappearance of a Mughal commander in battle led to the collapse of his army. See his *Armies of the Great Mughals,* p. 257.

[96] Jouher, *Memoirs of the Moghul Emperor Humayun,* p. 51. Jouher was the eyewitness.

[97] John Dawson, ed., *Tuzuk-I-Babari,* pp. 39–43.

At its height, the Mughal army adopted military practices that have been associated with a "Roman" or "American way of war"—a brute force, engineering approach to military affairs. The Mughal army on the march would level forests and build its own bridges over the Ganges as well as massive roads to permit the passage of its armies, spending as long as twenty-five days constructing elaborate field fortifications before attempting to subdue an enemy fortress.[98] This engineering approach had its own weaknesses, for it meant that large numbers of slaves who served as construction troops would accompany the army. Present on the battlefield on the day of battle, those slaves, if they panicked, could cause disorder that could lead to the disruption and rout of their own army.[99]

But there was much in the behavior of the mature Mughal army that can only be understood in terms of the divisons of Indian society and their reflection in the Mughal army. To begin with, the internal organization of the mature Mughal army in the field reflected the needs of a multilingual army in which active coordination among units taken from different parts of society could not be expected. The standard historical description of the Mughal battlefield formations—not at the beginning of the empire, when the army was essentially a fast-moving body of Turkish cavalry, but at its height—are complex because of their numerous ranks and subunits. This complexity becomes simple and illuminating if the internal problems of cohesion and coordination of such an army are taken into consideration.

Even a simple description of the Mughal army in the field is bewildering. The army would first have a skirmish line called a *qarawal*, with about two thousand troops; second, a vanguard called a *harawal*, which was broken down into center, left, and right components, with a total of fourteen thousand troops; third, an advance of center called the *iltimish*, also broken down into left, right, and center, with eighteen thousand troops; fourth, a center called the *qol*, broken down into left left, left, center, right, and right right sections, with a total of twenty-nine thousand soldiers. The center would have cavalry flanking parties on each side with fourteen thousand troops.[100] In war, this array would move

[98] Ibid., pp. 57, 64–65, 69–70.

[99] John Dawson, ed., "Tariki Rashidi of Haidar Mirza Doghlat," in *The History of India as Told by Its Own Historians: The Papers of Sir H. M. Elliot* (Calcutta: Susil Gupta, 1953), pp. 99–103. Mirza Doghlat was a contemporary of Humayun and describes one such rout. Five thousand engineering troops were taken on one Mughal expedition to Kashmir in 1586. See Phul, *Armies of the Great Mughals*, p. 234.

[100] Phul, *Armies of the Great Mughals*, pp. 245–248. See also Jagdish Narayan Sarkar, *Some Aspects of Military Thinking and Practice in Medieval India* (Calcutta: Ratna Prakashan, 1974), pp. 21–22.

very slowly, not exceeding eleven miles *per day*, usually half that distance until it encountered the enemy.[101]

Stepping back from the details and incorporating a knowledge of the social origins of the army, these details fall into place. This was a big army of separate, socially based components, none of which could be expected or needed to cooperate with one another. No complex maneuvers were expected from or were within the capabilities of this army. Massive but not integrated, it was essentially three sets of armies—vanguard, advance of center, and center—each with its own separate armies horizontally arrayed and commanded. No coordination was or could be expected from these armies. The vanguard would move ahead until it encountered the enemy and either won or lost. If it lost, the advance of center would next encounter the enemy and would win or lose. If it failed, the center, the strongest component, would then encounter the enemy simply by continuing to march along.[102] No unit would be called on to maneuver in a way that made its survival dependent on the actions of any other part of the army. Success depended not on coordination among different units but on weight and inertia, with the simplest set of orders possible. The Mughal emperor would march in the center and would establish his position with the artillery pieces chained together in a line, with his brothers on his left and right, to keep them out of danger unless necessary but also to command the forces in the rear, which prevented the Mughal forces in front from running away. It was the only possible formation for an army with such disparate elements and internal tensions. The fact that this type of formation was not dictated simply by its size is shown by the fact that similar formations were observable in much smaller Mughal forces.

The Mughal army made the best possible use of the elements that it imported from Indian society, given that those components could not be integrated into a functional whole. The weaknesses of maintaining this kind of unintegrated organization, however, were revealed when they were stressed in combat. Simply put, Hindu and Muslim troops serving together in the Mughal army did not trust each other, killing each other on the battlefield. This was a consequence of the existing tensions between the Hindu and Muslim elements of Mughal society. To recall, even the tolerant emperor Akbar had ordered the massacre of the Rajput garrison of the fortress of Chitor after he captured its fort in 1568. The continuing tension between the Mughal state and Rajput leaders was such that "neither the honors from a Muslim monarch nor the intensive nature of their service relationship with the Timurid [Mughal] dynasty affected

---

[101] Irvine, *Army of the Indian Moghuls*, pp. 219–220.
[102] Phul, *Armies of the Great Mughals*, p. 242.

the Hindu character of the Bundela [Rajput] kingship in the least."[103] This did have consequences when the Rajput armies served alongside Muslim armies.

For example, one particular Mughal army in the field about which we have detailed information contained ten thousand soldiers. It included ethnically distinct Rajput infantry, sayyids, and Central Asian soldiers, all organized into separate and independent units and dispatched to fight a Hindu army from a different clan of Rajputs at the battle of Haldighat in 1576. When the armies closed and the two opposing groups of Hindu Rajput infantry engaged, the Muslim Mughal cavalry simply circled the mass of foot soldiers shooting arrows into them at will. Their commander told the historian Badaoni that "on whatever side a man falls, it is a gain to Islam because it is one Hindu the less."[104]

In times of chaos, the Hindu Rajput soldiers returned the mistrust. When Aurangzeb rebelled and imprisoned his father, the emperor Shah Jahan, Aurangzeb depended on fourteen thousand Rajput soldiers who had defected from the imperial camp to support him.[105] At the Battle of Dharmat in April 1658 between Aurangzeb and the troops of his father, there were also some Rajput generals and soldiers fighting for Shah Jahan. They were distrusted and disliked by their Muslim imperial generals, some of whom were secret supporters of the rebellious Aurangzeb. The casualties inflicted in that battle suggest that Muslim officers on both sides conspired to kill the Rajputs. When the battle was over, twenty-four Rajput generals from the imperial army were dead, but only one Muslim imperial general had died.[106]

The social tensions affecting battlefield organization and behavior were not confined to those between Hindus and Muslims. That was simply one of the distinctions that fragmented Indian society. Subcaste divisions within Hindu Rajput units had the same consequences in this period. Two different Rajput clans allied to deal with an invasion of an army composed of Marathas, a people from the southern plateau of India, the Deccan. The Maratha army had artillery guns manned by Europeans. One Rajput clan defected before the battle, and the remaining Rajput cavalry unit attacked and was annihilated.[107] Of the Battle of Dharmat noted above, Jadunath Sarkar wrote that "the various Rajput clans were often divided from each other by hereditary feuds and quarrels about dignity and precedence." Casting aside the plan that had called for them

---

[103] Ibid., p. 259; the quote is from Kolff, *Naukar, Rajput, and Sepoy*, p. 136–137.

[104] Jadunath Sarkar, *Military History of India* (Calcutta: Sarkar, 1960), pp. 75, 77–78, 80.

[105] Ibid., p. 115, referring to the events of January 1659 before and during the battle of Khawaja.

[106] Sarkar, *History of Aurangzeb*, 1:222.

[107] Tod, *Annals*, bk. 4, chap. 28, pp. 878–890.

to stay on the defensive, the Rajput cavalry charged, but "being divided into many mutually antagonistic clans, could not charge in one compact mass; they were broken up into six or seven bodies, each under its own chieftains and each choosing its own point of attack." All six Rajput chiefs in the charge were killed. None of the Muslim troops assisted them.[108]

Mughal battlefield organization was designed to reduce but did not eliminate the problems stemming from the divisions of Indian society that the Mughal army reflected. Quereshi noted serious flaws in the Mughal army: "The first was a lack of cohesion. The troopers were personally brave . . . but they only knew how to fight in a big mass or as individuals. The impact of ten thousand troopers riding *en masse* was not only a formidable sight to behold, but its impact upon the foe was great; but if, by some device, this mass could be broken into fragments, it became helpless. They did not know how to form ranks again after a dispersal or to muster the support of a small group which might have become isolated."[109] In retreat, the Mughal army would usually disintegrate into chaos.[110]

The most detailed firsthand account of a Mughal army in the field is provided by the history of Mirza Nathan, which is essentially a diary of his campaigns as a Mughal commander in northeast India in the years 1608–1624. In exhausting detail, this diary shows what it was like to command a Mughal army within which there could be little expectation of cohesion among the Mughal and Hindu officers and what problems the military environment of society in northeast India created for a Mughal military commander. The significance of the numerous events recorded by Mirza Nathan is best conveyed quantitatively. His history refers to twenty-five separate incidences in sixteen years in which Mirza Nathan was dispatched with an army to subdue rebel chiefs or armies, eighteen of which were large enough to warrant extensive description. It describes twelve acts of conspiracy against him by other Mughal officers, all Muslim, including withholding reinforcements; sending reinforcements but instructing the commanders of the units not to support Mirza Nathan if he got into trouble; reporting his weaknesses to an enemy army; sending orders to Mirza Nathan's troops that deliberately put them in vulnerable positions, the locations of which the enemy had been informed about; and one outright incidence of military defection. Mirza Nathan himself twice conspired against other Mughal officers, once refused to obey the governor of the province of Bengal, and thrice refused

[108]Sarkar, *History of Aurangzeb*, 1:226–228.
[109]Quereshi, *Administration of the Mughal Empire*, pp. 126–127.
[110]Phul, *Armies of the Great Mughals*, p. 258.

to obey orders to subordinate himself to another commanding Mughal general.[111]

Of the eighteen chronicled battles, at least eight are clearly described sieges of rebel forts, four are battles in the field, and the rest appear to involve either attacks on Mirza Nathan's forces while they are in a fortified camp or pillaging/punitive raids.[112] The nature of the advance of the imperial forces by boat into Bengal was dictated in large measure by the nature of the terrain. The countryside was dominated by rivers, ravines, and dense jungles and was in many areas impassable to cavalry. Thus infantry and artillery were brought by boat, and a series of forts—nineteen in all—were constructed along the imperial line of advance to safeguard supply lines and to dominate the countryside within which the rebels had their villages and could move freely.[113] The nature of the war as a whole was clearly what would be called in modern times a war of counterinsurgency, designed to subdue an armed and hostile people whose armies could not stand up to the heavy imperial cavalry in the few cases in which those forces could be brought to bear,[114] but armies that could raid and harass the imperial army, particularly in the rainy season, when the artillery and cavalry of the Mughals were entirely useless. In those respects, Mughal warfare in northeast India shared the same general characteristics as would be recognizable to other heavy armies fighting guerrillas in the jungle. The structure of Indian society may have been of less importance in this regard than the balance of capabilities between the opposing armies and the nature of the terrain.

But the nature of the composite Indian society with Mughal officers and a rank and file drawn from the indigenous society did have its impact on Mirza Nathan's conduct of the war. In one campaign near Dacca, Mirza Nathan bribed some emissaries sent by his enemy, and they revealed that twenty-five of Mirza Nathan's horsemen were spies for the opposing sheikh. Having been bribed, they then supplied the sheikh with "news about your every movement. They have also promised that on the day of battle, they will throw you down from your horse and will give your head to the Shaykh." As a result, Mirza Nathan redeployed these horsemen to his far right flank, where they could neither help nor

[111]Mirza Nathan, *Baharistan-I-Ghaybi*, 1:xiii, and 2:903–909, annotated index.

[112]For accounts of sieges, see ibid., 1:128–130, 135–137, 222–223, 231–232, 339–343, and 2:526, 571–577, 661. For open battles, see 1:180–189, and 2:462–475, 556–558, 562–565.

[113]Ibid., 1:108–109.

[114]For a description of encounters between the peoples of the northeast and the Mughal armies of the later part of the seventeenth century, including the use of Mughal cavalry, see K. N. Dutt, "Military Strategy of the Ahoms," part 2, *Journal of Indian History* 41 (August 1963): 459–464.

hurt him.[115] Mirza Nathan observed that it was impossible for such an army, whose officers were a "selfish group of people who laid greater stress on disunion than unity," to conduct an orderly retreat without having the army fall apart. The dissension within the Mughal officers was known to their enemies in the field, who waited for an opportunity to exploit it. The strategy of advancing and constructing forts was hit on at least in part to keep the Mughal army in the field, entrenched in a series of blockhouses, so as to reduce the opportunities for defection from the Mughal army.[116] The fighting power of the Mughal army was reduced because there was no contact or interaction between the officers and the men. In one campaign against the zamindars of Bahirband and Bhitarband, successive assaults by imperialists failed because quarreling imperial units did not support each other. Mirza Nathan rebuked his troops: if the assaults had been properly led, "the victory would have been attained on the first day; it would not have been necessary to spend three months and a half on it." He then ordered the officers to take their place alongside their men in the front lines of the trenches: "[Now] every one of these [imperial] trenches should be assigned to the different Sardars who should take their stand with a strong determination either to attain victory or to die." When this was done, the infantry assault, elephant assault, and imperial artillery were closely coordinated. The infantry reached the fort, while artillery suppressed the enemy's fire, and then "as soon as a noise was raised by the people in the glacis, as previously planned, all the four regiments . . . rushed forward with the elephants in their front and entered the fort, giving no opportunity to the enemy to oppose them."[117]

This last incident suggests that Mughal military organization and commands could on occasion overcome some of the tendencies that derived from the fact that the Mughal army reflected the divisions of Indian society. But as a rule they did not. Historians have not been able to discover any indication that the Mughal army used training or drill that would lead groups of men drawn from disparate elements of society to act and fight as disciplined units, as opposed to individual warriors.[118] Such training and discipline could and did have a dramatic impact on the fighting abilities of European armies and of Indian armies serving European commanders in India. It was inconsistent, however, with a social order in which the foot soldiers were generated by and for local conflicts and in which each chieftain had his own legitimacy as a leader.

[115] Mirza Nathan, *Baharistan-I-Ghaybi*, 2:468.
[116] Ibid., 1:104–105.
[117] Ibid., pp. 231–232, 236–238.
[118] Irvine, *Army of the Indian Moghuls*, pp. 183–185.

Detailed histories of the armies of the Mughals some fifty years after the campaigns of Mirza Nathan show that the internal tensions of Indian society, as reflected in the Mughal armies, still exerted a powerful effect on Indian military capabilities and strategies. In a famous incident, the emperor Aurangzeb used these divisions to defeat the army that his own rebellious son Akbar had put into the field against him. Aurangzeb forged a letter he allegedly sent to Akbar, in which he praised Akbar for carrying out his, the emperor's, orders to assemble all the Rajputs in his army in the forefront for the battle the next day, where they could be attacked by Aurangzeb's troops from the front and Akbar's troops from the rear. Matters were contrived so as to have the letter fall into the hands of the Rajputs, who bolted on the eve of battle, leaving Akbar without an army.[119]

The war by the emperor Aurangzeb against the Maratha people of the Deccan led by Shivaji provides some equally famous incidents in which both sides used the internal divisions of the other for military purposes. Shivaji is now perhaps best known for his assassination of a Mughal general during the course of negotiations with Shivaji, when he was supposed to be unarmed. This assassination was planned and arranged by a Hindu adiviser to the Mughal general to whom Shivaji had secretly appealed for help, on the grounds of Hindu solidarity.

The Mughals could and did use similar tactics, as when the Mughal general Mirza Rajah Jai Singh sought out Shivaji's enemies among the Deccani chieftains. "Everyone who bore a grudge to Shivaji or envied the sudden rise of the Bhonsles [Shivaji's dynasty] had been approached by the Mughal general's spies." Jai Singh analyzed the army of an ally of Shivaji, noted its multiethnic composition, and wrote back to his emperor Aurangzeb that "it is necessary to detach [these] three races from the enemy," which he did by means of bribes. Jai Singh had troops of his own that were unreliable, which he coped with by forming them into an independent column that was sent out to raid the Marathas. Overall, in the thirty-year period from 1659 until 1688, only three major battles were determined by the fighting between openly opposed Mughal and Deccani forces. The most common form of fighting was for the Mughals to besiege an enemy fort and then bribe it to surrender. This strategy of Jai Singh provoked a quarrel between him and Aurangzeb, who objected to the amount of money being spent in bribes. The average cost of a bribe to induce a Maratha fortress commander to give up his position was established at 45,000 rupees.[120] Aurangzeb's other principal general

---

[119]Sarkar, *History of Aurangzeb*, 3:241–242.
[120]Sarkar, *History of Aurangzeb*, 4:33–35, on the 1650 assassination by Shivaji followed by the rout of the Mughal army; p. 46, on the 1663 infiltration of the palace of the Mughal

in the Deccan, Mir Jumla, notoriously obtained the surrender of an inaccessible hilltop fortress of Golconda by bribery and betrayal, not open siege, and suborned numerous opposing generals. He too demanded that Aurangzeb provide him with large amounts of money for bribes, 1 million rupees a year, equal to one-third the annual budget of the viceroy of the Deccan. His own troops, a mixed lot of Hindus, Europeans, and Deccani troops, were so unreliable that he required them to carry passports so that their movement in the area of his encampments could be monitored.[121]

Nor was the Deccan unique. The extended campaigns in the Deccan drained imperial money, soldiers, and treasure away from the rest of the empire. There were, as a result, widespread peasant uprisings and guerrilla war at the heart of the empire. Rajputana in the northwest experienced endemic guerrilla war in the sixteen years from 1681 to 1707 between Mughal forces and the Hindu population, such that "an hour before sunset, every gate . . . was shut. The Muslims held the strongholds, but the plains obeyed Ajit [Ajit Singh, ruler of Marwar]. . . . The roads were now impassable." The Jat people near Agra rose up in 1669 and in 1685–1688, at which time they raided the tomb of Akbar, and were still not suppressed in 1707 when Aurangzeb died.[122]

CONCLUSIONS: MILITARY ORGANIZATION IN INDIA AND EUROPE
IN THE 17TH CENTURY

This review of the social composition and military behavior of the Mughal army has been set forth in great detail to make one irrefutable point. The armies of the Mughal Empire reflected the composite char-

---

viceroy by Shivaji, unopposed by any of the ten thousand Mughal troops present; p. 60, on the 1665 siege of Vajragarh, which surrenders suspiciously after only two weeks; p. 61, on Jai Singh's use of Marathi defectors to induce other Marathi garrisons to surrender; p. 87, on Mughal bribes and suborning of officials at court of Bijapur in the Deccan and major open battle in 1665; pp. 97–98,on bribery and defection of Shivaji's top general and then his redefection back, followed by major battle; p. 103, on the dispute between Jai Singh and Aurangzeb on cost of bribes; p. 323, on the siege of Golconda ended by bribery, 1688; and Sarkar, *History of Aurangzeb* 5:345, on the average cost of a bribe.

[121] Jagdish Narayan Sarkar, *Life of Mir Jumla*, p. 38, Mir Jumla takes Vijayanagar fortress of Udaygiri by "treachery," 1646; pp. 48–50, takes Golconda fortress by treachery; p. 82, on the need for his own troops to carry passports within thirteen leagues of his camp; pp. 106–109, suborns generals of Qutb Shah, ruler of Golconda; p. 167, death of ruler of Bijapur leads to his increased efforts to encourage the defection of Bijapuri generals, 1656: "My whole endeavour is to see that the Bijapuris come to this side by any means, so that famous generals will themselves come over to us even with a little encouragement"; p. 168, on the figure of ten lakhs (10 x 100,000 rupees) for bribes.

[122] Sarkar, *History of Aurangzeb*, 5:205–212, 222–230.

acter of Mughal society. Society and army were divided between Hindu and Muslims, among various Hindu subcastes. The Mughal army was not separated from Mughal society, in terms of its ethnic composition, training, recruitment, or deployment. It did reflect Mughal social structures, and as a result, its military capabilities were severely hampered.

Was it necessarily the case that a fragmented society of this time had to produce a fragmented army? If we now look at the society and armies of contemporary Europe, we can assess whether Mughal India had to have the army that it did because of the nature of the society it governed or whether different forms of military organization might have mitigated the effects of larger social divisions. Was the Mughal army weak because it ruled Indian society or because it was poorly organized in ways that imported into the army the weaknesses of the host society?

Were social structures in Europe any less divisive than those in India at the same time? Was the performance of seventeenth-century European armies any better than that of the Mughal armies? Much effort has gone into the study of the changes in European armies at this time that led to increases in their military effectiveness. Some European armies were emerging as national armies, such as the Swiss army and the Swedish army of Gustavus Adolphus, but many were not. German and French armies existed in a social context in which they were subject to divisive religious pressures. Nations that we think of today as ethnically and linguistically homogenous were far more heterogenous three hundred years ago. France was one of the first states to emerge as a nation, yet in his political testament, Cardinal Richelieu recalled for his king the conditions that existed in 1624: "I can truthfully say that the Huguenots shared the state with [Your Majesty], that the *grands* behaved as if they were not your subjects, and the governors of the provinces as if they were sovereign powers."[123] In his memoirs, Louis XIV suggested that the internal cohesion of France as a result of the *Fronde* was not much better:

> But one must present things as they really were. There were dreadful agitations throughout the realm both during and after my majority [in 1651 at the age of thirteen]. There was a foreign war in which domestic discord had lost France all kinds of advantages. There was a prince of my own family and of great renown at the head of my enemies and a host of plots in the state. The parlements were in the habit of (and enjoyed) usurping authority and in my court fidelity was hardly to be seen without some

[123] Cited in J. H. Elliott, *Richelieu and Olivares* (London: Cambridge University Press, 1984), p. 64.

accompanying self-interest. Thus, my superficially most submissive subjects were as much a burden and a fear to me as the most mutinous.[124]

France was exceptional only in that it was among the more cohesive societies. Spain experienced Portuguese and Catalan revolts in this period, and foreign intervention in internal national conflicts was the norm. As C. V. Wedgewood wrote, "Although the term nation existed, and although some nation-states—England, Denmark, Sweden, Spain—were already recognizable entities, the modern conception of the nation . . . had hardly developed. Older loyalties contended perpetually with the comparatively new idea of loyalty to the nation: loyalty to rank, or religion, even to the orders of chivalry."[125]

In some parts of Europe, these social divisions had led to patterns of domestic insecurity and to a militarization of society that seems not altogether different from that which we have seen in India. In discussing the problem of organized banditry in the sixteenth century, Fernand Braudel noted:

No region of the Mediterranean was free from the scourge. Catalonia, Calabria, and Albania, all notorious in this respect, by no means had a monopoly of brigandage. It cropped up everywhere, in various guises, political, social, economic, terrorist. . . . At the other end of the Mediterranean in Spain, the scene is the same. I have already mentioned the notorious condition of the roads in Aragon and Catalonia. It is quite unthinkable, writes a Florentine in 1567, to take the post between Barcelona and Saragossa. . . . His solution was to join a caravan of armed noblemen.

Braudel adds: "Towards the end of the sixteenth century . . . banditry was on the increase. Italy, a mosaic of states, was a brigands paradise: driven out of one place, they would take refuge somewhere else." Deep social fissures were emerging between rich and poor. The number of soldiers multiplied. The kingdom of Naples in the mid–sixteenth century had an army of ten thousand men and could if necessary find twenty thousand.[126]

Nor were intrigue and betrayal in time of war unknown in European

[124]Cited in François Bluche, *Louis XIV*, trans. Mark Greenglass (New York: Franklin Watts, 1990), pp. 29–30.

[125]C. V. Wedgewood, *Richelieu and the French Monarchy* (New York: Collier, 1962), pp. 10, 31, 33.

[126]Fernand Braudel, *The Mediterranean and the Mediterranean World in the Age of Philip II*, vol. 2, trans. Sian Reynolds (New York: Harper Colophon, 1976), pp. 744–746, 752, 755, 852.

armies of this era. The general of the Holy Roman Empire, Albrecht von Wallenstein, engaged in negotiations with Gustavus Adolphus, his Protestant adversary, that might have led to Wallenstein's defection if the Swedish king had not broken them off. Wallenstein himself was assassinated by an Englishman after the emperor had relieved him of his command and had made known his desire to be rid of Wallenstein.[127]

And yet there were significant differences in the military behavior of European and Indian armies. The nature of these differences is highlighted by early discussions between European and Indian military officers. Niccolao Manucci served as an artillery officer in the armies of Aurangzeb, and while on the march in 1666, he was asked by his Rajput colleagues to describe European warfare. He undertook to explain infantry tactics that made the infantry capable of withstanding cavalry charges: "When I was giving this account, finding some pikes or spears there, I exhibited how the spearmen stood in front of the companies to hinder the cavalry from getting in and throwing into disorder the well ordered ranks of the infantry. Thus the battle would commence with great order and discipline, the cavalry helping wherever it was necessary to repress an onslaught of the enemy.... Upon this he set to laughing, assuming us to have no horses in our country, and thus we could know nothing of fighting on horseback."[128] In his journal, Manucci described two Indian armies in terms that he did not use with his Indian colleagues: "Be it known to the reader that these two armies were not ordered in the disposition obtaining in Europe.... The only soldiers who fought were those well to the front. Of those more to the rear, although holding their bared swords in their hands, the Mughals did nothing but shout *Bakush, Bakush* and the Indian *Mar, Mar*—kill, kill. If those in front advanced, those behind followed the example; and if the former retired, the others fled—a custom of Hindustan quite contrary to that of Europe."[129]

What was so different about European armies as to be unimaginable to Indian officers was the cohesion of European infantry in battle: its ability to resist fragmentation when attacked and to act coherently as a unit. There is general agreement among historians that this was the result not of a sudden shift in the character of European societies that made them and their armies more cohesive but of a "military revolution" that transformed the relationship of European armies to their host societies and multiplied their military effectiveness. Self-consciously modeling

---

[127] Russell F. Weigley, *The Age of Battles: The Quest for Decisive Warfare from Breitenfeld to Waterloo* (Bloomington: Indiana University Press, 1991), pp. 26, 35.

[128] Manucci, *Storia do Mogor*, 2:124.

[129] Cited in Parker, *Military Revolution*, p. 129.

themselves on the Roman legions, with which they were familiar from Roman texts, military leaders such as William of Nassau began the process of professionalizing their armies, which meant the inculcation of discipline in the infantry, the use of drill to make the units capable of military action as units, and the separation of the soldiers from society by longer periods of service and regular salaries.[130] Formed into cohesive units, infantry became much more powerful and capable of withstanding cavalry charges and defeating armies that had not been so transformed. The professional armies also became much more reliable. While mutinies still occurred, historians have judged that during the Thirty Years' War, "the firm allegiance of senior officers . . . was of more than usual military importance . . . because of . . . the financial weakness of the governments involved in the war." The professional mercenary armies also tended to be faithful to their employers: "On the whole it is surprising that clear treason was so rare, and that no military enterpriser is known to have raised a force without a valid commission" from his prince.[131] European society did not transform itself overnight, but the armies of Europe did change dramatically during the years from 1594 to 1648. Disciplined, militarily dominant, and more reliable, their behavior was less reflective of European society and more reflective of their own military structure. Defeating them in battle, as opposed to suborning their commander or mobilizing a dissident prince and his peasant subjects against their king, became the focus of military strategy. Such a revolution had not, by the same time, occurred in India, where the armies did still reflect the nature of their host societies. These two factors—the differences in Indian and European societies and in the nature of their military organizations and their relationship to the host society—accounts for the difference in military performance. Whether it would be possible to apply European methods of military organization to create in India an army that was cohesive and separate from Indian society is the subject of the next chapter.

[130] Ibid., pp. 19–20, 51; Parker, *Thirty Years' War*, pp. 205–206; Weigley, *Age of Battles*, pp. 5–12; Neal Wood, introduction to *The Art of War*, pp. xviii–lix.

[131] Parker, *Thirty Years' War*, pp. 195–196.

[5]

The British Empire
and the Indian Army

The British military role in India and its impact on Indian society cannot be surveyed or analyzed in its entirety in one chapter. A 1976 bibliography by an Indian historian S. N. Prasad, after dismissing pre–nineteenth-century military history as a "blank," went on to present a sixty-three page, single-spaced listing of books and articles concerned almost exclusively with the military history of British India.[1] This chapter will limit itself to the first fifty years of British rule, from the middle of the eighteenth century to the early nineteenth. In this period, the British built armies in India that were so much more powerful that they could be used to conquer the other armies in India. The British accomplished this by separating their armies from Indian society, not by changing Indian social structures. Having conquered portions of India, the British were then able to institute changes that did have a substantial impact on the indigenous social structures. This two-stage process can be observed in the period examined in this chapter.

There are some obvious reasons for focusing on this period, given the analytical purposes of this book. First, during this time the British established military predominance in India. One of the puzzles raised in Chapter 1 was how this could have been accomplished, given the rough equality of British and Indian military technology at that time, and the gross imbalance in the numbers of soldiers available to the British and the local Indian rulers. How could several thousand European soldiers, together with a larger number of Indian soldiers under European control,

---

[1]S. N. Prasad, *A Survey of Work Done on the Military History of India* (Calcutta: K. P. Bagchi, 1976).

conquer the armies of India, which numbered, as we saw in the last chapter, over 4 million? How could those same small forces then rule the historic core of the British Empire in India in Bengal and the surrounding areas in eastern India that initially included 50 million Indians?[2]

Second, if it is the case that the British did not alter the social structures of India in the first few years of their rule, the argument set forth in Chapter 1 would suggest that something fundamental must have changed in the relationship between the Indian army and Indian society under the British. By looking first at the period at the beginning of the British presence in India, we are, as best we can, holding constant the variable of social structure while focusing on changes in the variable of the relationship of the army to Indian society. Can we look back at the formation of the armies serving the British East India Company and observe this change? If Indian society was not restructured between the collapse of the Mughal Empire in the 1730s and 1740s and the emergence of British dominance by the 1790s, we should see major differences in British and Mughal military practices, and their consequences. How could the British conquer and then maintain internal order within India—and afterward export surplus military power from India—as early as 1800? What changed? Both British and Mughal political systems represented empires in which a religiously distinct foreign military elite claimed to rule an enormous indigenous population without political institutions that allowed for mass political participation or representation. If neither the form of the political institutions nor the local social structures varied significantly during this period, why and how did the military outcome change so markedly?

There is little doubt that this outcome did change in unmistakable ways from the very beginning of British rule. In the previous chapter, we noted how Mughal emperors indicated with frustration that though they ruled India, they could not generate enough military power even to reconquer portions of their Central Asian ancestral territories outside India proper. But as early as 1789, Lord Cornwallis asked for and received sepoys, native Indian soldiers trained and deployed under British command,[3] who would volunteer to serve in

---

[2] Lord Castlereagh, for example, wrote in 1804 about the difficulties of ruling 50 million Indians in the area of Bengal with a total of thirty thousand European civil and military servants, of which twenty-four thousand were the King's troops. See Lord Castlereagh to Richard Wellesley, 21 May 1804, in Montgomery Martin, ed., *Despatches, Minutes, and Correspondence of the Marquess Wellesley* [hereinafter *Despatches*] (London: William Allen, 1837), 4:222–227.

[3] The British were careful to distinguish between Indian soldiers "trained as Europe-

Sumatra.[4] The Governor General of the East India Company (EIC) in Calcutta, Richard Wellesley, responded to the news that the French army had established itself in Egypt and might be headed for India by writing the EIC Board of Control back in London that "if the French should be established in Egypt, it might be advisable to consider whether an expedition might be fitted out from India to cooperate by way of the Red Sea with any attempt which might be undertaken from the Mediterranean." If Wellesley was ordered by England to dispatch such an expedition, that order "will be executed with alacrity and diligence, by not only me, but by the whole army in India." Troops from India did arrive in Cairo in 1801.[5] In the early days of EIC rule, sepoys from India were sent as well to Sri Lanka and Aden. From being an area into which soldiers had to be sent in order to maintain control, it became within two generations a limited exporter of military power. What had happened?

Both the nineteenth century and the twentieth saw the emergence of conventional explanations for this shift, neither of which is satisfactory. For the British of Thomas Macaulay's day, the explanation was clear: the moral superiority of British civilization as embodied in the men sent out to conquer and rule India. In Macaulay's famous moral hierarchy laid out in his essay on the impeachment of Warren Hastings, the men of the world could be ranked in terms of their courage and honesty, beginning with the British; descending through other Europeans, with a pause to note the special depravity of the Italians; then going down to the Asians; then to the South Asians; then to the Bengalis, who were the initial subjects of British rule; and finally, at the very bottom, the individual adversary, Tippoo Sultan, who fought the British. But this was the view of the British conqueror, which must be suspect. It can easily be juxtaposed with eighteenth-century Indian observations of European vice, which were equally vivid. Indians saw, with as much justice as the Brit-

---

ans," whom they referred to as sepoys, and Indian soldiers who kept their own weapons and mode of warfare, which "undisciplined troops" they referred to by the Indian word for peasant militia, *Peons*. See Robert Orme, *History of the Military Transactions of the British Nation in Indostan* (1803; reprint, Madras: Athenaeum, 1861), pp. 80–81.

[4] Amiya Barat, *The Bengal Native Infantry: Its Organization and Discipline, 1796–1852* (Calcutta: Firma K. L. Mukhopadhyay, 1962), pp. 42–43.

[5] Richard Wellesley to Dundas, 16 May 1799, in Edward Ingram, ed., *Two Views of British India: The Private Correspondence of Mr. Dundas and Lord Wellesley, 1798–1801* (London: Adams and Dart, 1970), pp. 149–150. As part of his ongoing struggle with the authorities in London to extract more military resources from the EIC, Wellesley would later say that he could send troops from India only if more European troops were sent to him first. See his letter to Dundas, 13 July 1800, ibid., pp. 277–279. But Indian troops were dispatched and arrived in Cairo in the spring of 1801. See Edward Ingram, *In Defence of British India: Great Britain in the Middle East, 1775–1842* (London: Frank Cass, 1984), p. 60.

ish observers of India, the moral corruption of their European adversaries—and European friends, for that matter. Of one French intermediary with whom he had dealt, the so-called Ripaud, a minister of Tippoo Sultan wrote, "From first to last, the language of this man has been that of self-interest and falsehood. . . . From the erroneous statements of this scoundrel, the strongest doubts have arisen. . . . When so much chicane, covetousness of money, artifice and deceit are apparent" with Ripaud in Tippoo's court, what might one expect from the Europeans when they were out of sight and not under Tippoo's control?[6]

As for the moral behavior of the British, the papers of EIC officials show clearly that in campaigns against hostile Indian kingdoms, the British deliberately engaged in the systematic destruction of undefended villages of the enemy, a fact highlighted in the charges brought by the English against their own EIC officers, such as Warren Hastings. One commander serving under Warren Hastings wrote during one of his marches that "there are destroyed upwards of a thousand villages. Had not rain etc. prevented us, which occasioned our return, we should have done very considerable more damage."[7] It may have been that the British were morally superior to the Indians, or vice versa, but considerable care would be needed to show in what way, exactly, that superiority manifested itself and why it might be thought to have had militarily decisive consequences.

The twentieth century offered a different explanation of the easy European conquest: the technological superiority of the West. This, too, is subject to doubt. Careful historical studies have shown the technological advantages enjoyed by the Europeans over the Indians at the middle and end of the eighteenth century to have been marginal, if they existed at all. Indian troops were equipped with domestically produced flintlocks by 1663, using the same techniques for fabricating gun barrels as were used in the best European factories at that time. The iron produced in India was better than European iron, probably because the surface ore available in India was the best in the world. Indian steel was exported worldwide because of its high quality. Indian field artillery was inferior to that made in Europe, though Arthur Wellesley, later the duke of Wellington, noted of the Indian artillery that he captured after the battle of

---

[6]See "Observations of the Five Departments of Government to Tippoo on Negotiations with the French," paper No. 8, in *Asiatic Annual Register for the Year 1799* (London: Debrett, 1800), p. 189. The British regularly captured, translated, and published the documents of the Indian courts that they conquered, usually to justify British actions in India.

[7]Quoted from the letter of Colonel Champion during the 1774 campaign against the Rohillas, the Afghan settlers of northeast India; see C. Collin Davies, "Warren Hastings and the Rohilla War," *The Army Quarterly* 36 (July 1938): 273–288.

Assye in 1803, "The ordnance is very fine, but I have destroyed the iron guns, and shall put the brass guns in a place of security."[8] It would, therefore, be difficult to argue that European technology played a decisive role in the conquest and military transformation of India.

PROFESSIONAL ARMIES AND FRAGMENTED SOCIETIES

What might have been at work? The analytical framework that I laid out in Chapter 1 suggests changes in the nature of Indian social structures which were then reflected in the Indian army and which then improved the performance of that army under British rule. Alternatively, the nature of the relationship between the Indian army as organized by the EIC and Indian society might have changed, increasing the separation between the two in ways that reduced the impact of the divisions within Indian society on the Indian army. In the next section, we will examine the state of Indian society in the middle and late eighteenth century when EIC rule was established over Bengal. This examination will strongly suggest that Indian society did change toward the end of the Mughal Empire but that those changes should have decreased the military effectiveness of the armies emerging from Indian society even further. The decline of the Mughal Empire did affect Indian society, but in ways that increased the divisions and levels of hostility among groups within this society. Despite these adverse changes in Indian social structures, the British built effective armies. The question will then become whether and how the EIC changed Indian military organization to increase the separation of the Indian soldiers from their own society.

Why might we expect the European-created armies in India to be more distant from Indian society? The general character of the separation of the Indian army under Western rule from its own society may be suggested by a review of other cases in the eighteenth and nineteenth centuries in which other non-European countries adopted Western European modes of military organization. Understanding the impact of the introduction of European modes of military organization into non-European societies requires some knowledge of the revolution that had occurred in European militaries in the seventeenth century, because in the extra-European cases, military innovations were introduced that followed the example of the revolution in military organization that took place within Europe itself. The European military revolution will be dis-

---

[8]See Irfan Habib, "The Technology and Economy of Mughal India," *Indian Social History Review* 17 (January–March 1980): 1–34. Arthur Wellesley to Richard Wellesley, 30 September 1803, in Martin, *Despatches*, 3:385.

[166]

cussed at greater length below. Here it is sufficient to note that the decisive innovation for offensive warfare was the development of armies that systematically trained and disciplined professional soldiers, enabling them to act in a cohesive, coordinated, and directed manner on the battlefield. Soldiers were no longer sustained in war by loot and left in peacetime to support themselves by nonmilitary occupations and peacetime roles in society.[9] The revolution was valuable to rulers because the increase in military power it made available, relative to that which could be generated by even very large numbers of brave but undisciplined warriors fighting as individuals, was tremendous and was seen as such by the rulers of Russia, Turkey, Japan, and elsewhere.

But in these extra-European cases, importing Western—that is to say, foreign—military modes of organization also brought with it severe internal cultural tensions. Western armies very visibly carried with them foreign symbols such as uniforms, were based on ideas about the rational organization of human military behavior, and affected the internal distribution of power in ways that were not consistent with indigenous social structures. Each of the non-European countries adopting European military organization saw a hostile cultural reaction toward the new armies. This was inevitable. As David Ralston wrote, "How people prepare for and wage war, and the organizations they create for that purpose, are in fact closely related to the ways in which they deal with the other, more peaceable aspects of life in society. That was certainly true in Europe. There the armed forces were the embodiment of qualities characteristic of its civilization: technicalism and functional rationality." The problem in non-European societies often was that European military organizations were grafted onto societies which had not on their own generated them and which had ideas about how people should behave, ideas that were embodied in social structures that might or might not be compatible with the imported military institutions. In Russia, according to Ralston, "the acceptance by the nobility of the rationalistic norms of the military-bureaucratic state and the re-shaping of their outlook in accordance with its demands had the effect of deepening the gulf dividing them from the great mass of the Russian people." In Turkey, the result of the new military organization was that the men in the new military elite felt "estranged from those they are meant to rule. And because the populace has little appreciation for the modern modes of government or administration, not really accepting the criteria by which the new elite has been designated, the latter has little legitimacy in its eyes." The Turk-

[9] For a discussion of the historiography and the substance of the European military revolution, see Geoffrey Parker, *The Military Revolution: Military Innovation and the Rise of the West, 1500–1800* (Cambridge: Cambridge University Press, 1988), pp. 6–44.

ish officers of the new armies "were estranged intellectually and psychologically from their natal roots, [and] . . . had little in common with" non-Europeanized officers and citizens. They thus became a separate group in society, a new "professional caste."[10]

If we relate this perspective to the army in India under British rule, we see the relevance of the model developed in Chapter 1. In the Mughal Empire, the armies of India were generated by society and were hardly distinguishable from it. Pervasive internal tensions among groups, including subcaste groups, led to constant internal violence—largely about the control of land—and to large numbers of armed militias. These armed militias could serve the Mughal state if they chose to, but they could, and often did, serve local landholders against the Mughal state and army. The Indian army of the Mughal period was not estranged from Indian society and social structures but their product. The division of Indian society into smaller structures was militarily relevant because the smaller structures had armies at their disposal. This limited the strength of the Mughal state relative to society as well as its ability to develop and extract a surplus of military power above that which was necessary to maintain a minimum of control over that society. The British imported a new and more powerful mode of military organization. The experience of other societies suggests that this new military might not have been comfortably included within the indigenous Indian social structures. If that were the case, our model would suggest that improved military performance may have been possible in India because the army was separated from Indian society, but that separation would create a tension between the military and society, tension that much stronger because it was imposed by a foreign imperial government. At the same time, there would be little tension between the Indian army and civilian British rulers because both were imperial institutions serving the same interests. The question then is not only, How did the British defeat the Indian armies? but, How and why could the Indian army maintain itself and British rule against the resistance of Indian society? Although the explanation focusing on the power of an army separated from a badly fractured society would help us understand the initial British conquests in India, the development of a new, more powerful army separated from society would make it more difficult, perhaps, to understand how the British, supported by the Indian army, could sustain itself against a hostile, armed population. By itself, a powerful army that was minuscule in

[10] See the discussion of the development of Western-style, regular army organization in Russia and Turkey in David B. Ralston, *Importing the European Army: The Introduction of European Military Techniques and Institutions into the Extra-European World, 1600–1914* (Chicago: University of Chicago Press, 1990), pp. 16–22, 39, 49–51, 69, 70, 178.

comparison with the size of the population it governed might be expected to have considerable difficulty in maintaining its dominance.

This raises the question of whether, contrary to what might initially be expected, British rule somehow did change Indian society in ways that made it more tractable and more amenable to imperial rule. There have been extensive debates about whether British imperial rule strengthened or weakened Indian social divisions defined by subcaste. This chapter will not resolve that debate, but it will suggest that the answer might lie elsewhere. The perspective of this book indicates that social structures that decrease social cohesion are most relevant to military affairs when those social structures have their own military capabilities. To recall the discussion in the last chapter, European countries in the fifteenth and sixteenth centuries suffered from their division into smaller factions led by aristocrats with their own fortresses and armies. This had consequences for the ability of protonational governments to maintain domestic peace and effective central governments and for their military power. In Europe in the seventeenth and eighteenth centuries, the division of society into social orders did not end, but these social orders did cease to have their own independent military capabilities. It was not that caste divisions went away under British rule in India. The EIC, however, introduced a number of changes, economic as well as military, that had the effect of systematically disarming the Indian population. What happened under British rule was the elimination of the huge numbers of militia-like groups of soldiers subject to nonstate control.

INDIAN SOCIETY ON THE EVE OF BRITISH RULE

In Chapter 4 considerable effort was made to establish the existence and character of the internal divisions within medieval Indian society and to review the extent to which those divisions led to the organization of the Indian people into part-time local armies that were available for local self-defense or predation. Those local armies could assist or attack Mughal military commanders operating in their areas. We looked at the Mughal Empire at its zenith, under the rule of the most powerful Mughal emperors: Akbar, Jahangir, and finally Aurangzeb, who died in 1707. The more or less continuous wars waged by Aurangzeb against the political leaders of southern India, primarily the Marathas, left the imperial government of India militarily and financially impoverished[11] and, in many areas of the south, physically desolate and politically weak, because local

[11] See Nirad C. Chaudhuri, *Clive of India: A Political and Psychological Essay* (London: Barrie and Jenkins, 1975), pp. 16–17, 20–21, and in general for the argument that

kingdoms were destroyed by Aurangzeb but not replaced by effective imperial rule.[12] When Aurangzeb died and the inevitable struggle for succession among his heirs broke out, Indian imperial institutions, already weakened by war, became weaker. Given the reduced strength of the central imperial institutions, we would not be surprised to learn that there was a reemergence of more intense conflict among the groups that composed Indian society. That is, in fact, what contemporary Indian historians recorded.

First published in 1789, the *Siyar-ul-Mutakherin* (translated as *The History of Mohamedan Power in India*) is a detailed chronicle of the struggles for power within India after the death of Aurangzeb.[13] It describes an immensely depressing state of affairs in which all imperial institutional and family loyalties have broken down and in which political alliances are formed only to be immediately destroyed by betrayal. The sons of Aurangzeb fought one another, each taking with them one component of the imperial army. When two of the sons of Aurangzeb were killed, war was made in the name of their children, who were, from time to time, killed or kidnapped. When an emperor was finally established after Aurangzeb's death, he was deposed by his own prime minister, who installed another youth, who then died and was succeeded by another child. Two ambitious brothers at the capital, the Seids, employed assassins to kill imperial viceroys at court, then backing an alleged descendant of Timur to be their candidate for emperor. This all took place within some fourteen years, between 1707 and 1721.

The consequences were predictable. Each leader of each subgroup within Indian society sought to break free of central control, either to increase his local power or to try and claim imperial authority. This took place most noticeably on the imperial periphery, in Lahore, and, most important in the Deccan in southern India, where Mughal rule even at its height had been weak. The imperial military strongholds established in the Deccan, "which had cost a siege of many years to the victorious Akbar, surrendered without a blow" to the now independent viceroy of the Deccan, Nizam-ul-mulk. Local fortresses sprang up to challenge imperial troops and to raid on commerce. Armies based on personal and communal loyalties fell apart when their leader died or sold out to the enemy.[14] Local power based on local social structures was unchallenged

---

the conquest of India by the British was not the result of British strength but Indian anarchy.

[12] Ghulam Hussain Salim, *Riyazu-s-Salatin* (A History of Bengal), trans. and ed. Abdus Salam (1903; reprint, Delhi: IAD Oriental Series no. 26, 1975), p. 253 n. 3.

[13] Mir Gholam Hussain Khan (also Ghulam Husain Tabatabai), *The History of Mohamedan Power in India (Siyar-ul-Mutakherin)*, trans. John Briggs (Delhi: n.p., 1973).

[14] Ibid., pp. 8–10, 28–29, 94–95, 121, 128, 138–141, 160–161, 181.

and dominant. Hyder Ali Khan established himself in 1746 in the south Indian state of Mysore, conquering Coorg and territory on the Malabar Coast by 1765.[15] The Marathas, in particular, long at war with the empire, benefited from the state of anarchy to expand their power and their ability to resist outside control. The size of the total Maratha army was assessed by English and Indian contemporaries in the 1650s at more than one hundred thousand troops. These were divided between infantry and cavalry, with infantry probably predominating, given the very hilly nature of the Maratha territories. By 1787, Portuguese reports put the size of a single Maratha field army at over one hundred thousand men. The founder of the Maratha military system, Shivaji, left budgetary records that list 22 fortress construction projects, and by the eighteenth century some 240 forts and strongholds were counted in Maratha territory.[16]

The decline of imperial control on the periphery also benefited the Sikhs, who were able to evict Mughal imperial officials from Amritsar in 1748.[17] Less well defined groups within India also increased their military power in response to the conditions of anarchy at the end of the Mughal period. The expansion of bandit groups in the Telegu-speaking portions of southern Indian was noted by the Dutch around the time of the death of Aurangzeb. One prominent Telegu bandit chief was independently reported by three Dutch sources to have had a force of between ten and twelve thousand soldiers; another chief was said to have three thousand infantry and perhaps five hundred cavalry.[18]

The demise of the Mughal Empire in the first half of the eighteenth century took place before the British began to play a militarily significant role on the subcontinent, and it created such conditions of internal anarchy that Alexis de Tocqueville, in his draft history of the struggle for empire in India between the British and the French, argued that it was not necessary to look for any unusual power in the European forces to explain the conquest of India. The subjugation of India was best and most easily explained by the internal divisions of India, which he believed to be based squarely on the caste organization of Indian society. By the late eighteenth century and early nineteenth century, those social structures had become thoroughly militarized, with, for example,

[15] Extract from Shah Nuaz Khan and Nuab Sum-fam-ud-dowla, *Meafer-al-Omra, or Memoirs of the Nobility*, in *Asiatic Annual Register for the Year 1800* [trans. not named] (London: Debrett, 1801), pp. 4–7.

[16] Surendra Nath Sen, *The Military System of the Marathas* (Bombay: Orient Longmans, 1958), pp. 16–17, 64, 88, 90.

[17] J. S. Grewal, *The Sikhs of the Punjab* (Cambridge: Cambridge University Press, 1990), pp. 88, 90.

[18] J. F. Richards and V. N. Rao, "Banditry in Mughal India: Historical and Folk Perceptions," *Indian Economic and Social History Review* 17 (January–March 1980): 95–120.

mounted troops of bandits in one province (Oudh) numbering twenty-five to thirty thousand. To quote Tocqueville: "There are a multitude of castes in India, but not any nation, or rather each of the castes forms its own little nation, with its own separate spirit, habits, laws, and government. . . . Their caste is for the Indians their country, countries for which one can look in vain anywhere else in India, but which is alive and well in the caste."[19]

But the state of Indian society alone is clearly insufficient to explain either the success of the EIC or its subsequent ability to create order and a surplus of military power. The conditions of anarchy could and did enable the British to make alliances with local Indian powers against their rivals. But with only small military forces of their own, it is not clear why the British would be able to influence decisively the outcome of contests for power in India. Among so many well-armed local powers, however fragmented, how did EIC military power emerge as the dominant fact in political struggles in India in the second half of the eighteenth century?

THE ESTABLISHMENT OF SEPOY ARMIES AND THE CONSEQUENCES, 1740–1817

The key to understanding the military revolution which took place in India in the eighteenth century and which gave the European-trained and European-led armies their great advantage over the existing Indian armies is understanding the military revolution that took place in Europe beginning in the sixteenth century. Historians of this revolution in offensive land warfare have noted the massive increase in the power of infantry troops, with or without firearms, when they were kept under discipline for periods of time long enough to train them to act in unison under the command of their leader on the battlefield and who would remain loyal to their military unit and to their comrades even under enemy attack. Infantrymen so disciplined and trained could withstand cavalry attacks even if they were armed only with pikes. When armed with muskets, the effect of massed, coordinated musket fire wielded by units, which could have some men fire in unison while others reloaded their weapons and which could maneuver so as to bring that massed firepower to bear on a series of targets in different locations on the battlefield, was devastating on armies not so trained and disciplined. The

[19] Alexis de Tocqueville, "Ebauches d'un Ouvrage sur l'Inde," in *Oeuvres complètes*, vol. 3, *Ecrits et discourses politiques*, ed. J. P. Mayer (Paris: Gallimard, 1962), pp. 447, 449, 448–451. Translation by the author.

military parade ground exercises now useful primarily for ceremonial performances had their origins in one of the most significant revolutions in human organization. Close-order drill and maneuvers were a self-conscious revival in Europe of the practices of the Roman legions, which, as we saw in Chapter 3, had given the Romans a decisive military advantage over their competitors.

But acting in unison at the command of an officer while being attacked at close quarters by an enemy throng, was not natural to the soldiers of Europe of the sixteenth century. Achieving the kind of military performance made possible by battlefield discipline and group cohesion, as opposed to individuals fighting as individuals in a military horde, first "exposed more men to the challenge of face-to-face combat, calling for superior courage, proficiency, and discipline in each individual soldier. Second, it placed great emphasis on the ability of an entire tactical group to perform the motions necessary for volley-firing both swiftly and in unison. The answer to both problems was, of course, practice."[20] Practice meant long-term, full-time service in the military, that is, a professional army filled with men who did nothing but train to be soldiers. By definition, it was a military that by its occupation had set itself off from the rest of society.

There was absolutely no reason in theory why this revolution could not be employed outside Europe. The power of the new military system was that its intense training could take men from disparate groups and even nations and mold them into a fighting force. One of the first practitioners of this military revolution in Europe was the Swedish king Gustavus Adolphus, who began with a professional army based on Swedish militia-men, but who successfully expanded his army as the need and opportunity arose by incorporating mercenary soldiers of many countries, so that by the climactic battle of Breitenfeld, only one-fourth of his force was Swedish, with few of those Swedes in the infantry[21] Properly done, the military revolution could be applied to groups of people who did not yet form a cohesive society or nation. In short, it could be and was applied in India.

The British were not the first to do so. The French were the first Europeans to apply European military methods in India, according to British contemporary accounts, raising four or five native Indian infantry companies in 1746 and providing military training to ten thousand infantry serving the king of Travancore in 1755. But before the British and the

---

[20] Parker, *Military Revolution*, p. 20.
[21] Russell F. Weigley, *The Age of Battles: The Quest for Decisive Warfare from Breitenfeld to Waterloo* (Bloomington: Indiana University Press, 1991), p. 6.

[173]

French, the Maratha army based in the southwestern areas of India began to adopt European military practices, though not without difficulty. By the second half of the seventeenth century, the Maratha army was the dominant military power in those parts of India not under Mughal control. The Marathas under Shivaji began to construct a modern military, as far as can be determined, without any European guidance. Shivaji's military reforms resembled early modern European military reforms. The first step was to make the soldiers independent of particular elements in society, such as large landholders, but dependent on the state. Shivaji insisted that his soldiers be paid in cash out of his central treasury. They were kept under tight discipline in military camps, with little contact with the local society and none with their women. Soldiers were recruited from all social strata, including the Mahars, the untouchables in Maratha territory. In creating a disciplined, coherent army, Shivaji benefited from the nature of Maratha society, the social structures of which appear to have been less divisive than elsewhere in India, with inter-marriage among high- and low-caste families common and not penalized. When European military officers became more common in India, they were hired by Shivaji's successor, Sambhaji, to provide European military training. Perhaps the earliest European documentary record of this is a July 1686 British royal edict ordering all British subjects who had entered into the military service of "the Country Powers, particularly the Mogul . . . and Sambagee [Sambhaji] Rajah to return to the [East India] Company's settlement at Bombay or Madras." The prohibition was not effective because the British were not the only source of European military professionals in India, and records indicate that European officers were being hired up through the middle and end of the eighteenth century.

This attempted professionalization was not without problems. Maratha society had long produced its own military men who were cavalry soldiers famous throughout India. While the Maratha infantry was being professionalized, the cavalry, with deep roots in Maratha society, resisted such efforts, and the Maratha military regularly relapsed into medieval Indian military patterns of organization. The result as late as the third battle of Panipat in 1759 was a disciplined infantry combined with un-disciplined cavalry that could not be relied on to guard the flanks and rear of the infantry systematically, a fact that contributed to the Maratha defeat at Panipat to Afghan troops. The lesson drawn by the Marathas from that defeat was the need for them to continue and extend their efforts to utilize European—in particular, French—military officers. By the 1780s, the Marathas had some seventy thousand trained and disciplined infantry men in three armies. The army under the command of Sindhia Rao (referred to by contemporary British as Dowlut Row Scindiah) was judged by the British to be the best army in India commanded by an Indian ruler.[22]

The Maratha example indicates what might have been predicted: professionalization of Indian sepoy armies and their separation from the influences of Indian social structures was a slow and uneven process, even when it was undertaken by indigenous Indian political leaders. The same was true for sepoy armies raised by the Europeans. Initially, these units were not radically separated from the Indian society from which they came. Sepoys, wrote Robert Orme, "in taking our arms and military exercise do not quit their own dress or any other of their customs. The Sepoys are formed into companies and battalions and commanded by officers of their own nation and religion." But they were distinct from the mass of Indian soldiers, also employed by European powers in India, who kept their own mode of warfare and "retain[ed] the names they bear in their several countries." The recruitment of the first sepoys began, but by no means completed, their separation from society and transformation into professional soldiers whose obedience and loyalty was given to their military units and commanders as opposed to their social groups into which they were born. This modest level of professionalization was matched by modest improvements in military performance. Yet the professional European soldiers in India still outperformed European-trained Indian forces, so much so that Orme argued, "The actions of a single platoon [of European professional soldiers] in India may have the same influence on general success, as the conduct of a whole regiment in Europe; and to give a just idea of European arms, when opposed to those of Indostan, is one of the principal intentions this narrative."[23]

The level of superiority claimed for European troops (10:1 or better) against untrained Indian soldiers was not based on racism but on military reality observable in Europe as well as India. For example, the same ratios in military power between professionally disciplined Spanish troops and undisciplined but highly motivated Dutch imperial subjects were recorded in Europe in the sixteenth century.[24] In addition, the small units of European troops benefited from the fact that large Indian armies, drawing confidence from their numbers, would often attack the European units on battlefields suited by their terrain for defen-

---

[22]Sen, *Military System of the Marathas*, pp. 5, 7–8, 11, 13, 16–18, 111, 114–117, 124.

[23]Orme, *Military Transactions*, pp. 80–81, 98–99 on the less than striking performance of sepoys at Pondicherry against the French, 219, 400. See also Parker, *Military Revolution*, pp. 133–136, and Stephen P. Cohen, *The Indian Army: Its Contribution to the Development of a Nation* (Delhi: Oxford University Press, 1990), pp. 7–8.

[24]Philip Mason, *A Matter of Honour* (New York: Holt, Rinehart, and Winston, 1974), pp. 58–59.

sive operations or in areas without enough room to bring all the Indian soldiers to bear against the Europeans. In one battle, some fifteen thousand Indian troops, not under tight battlefield discipline, came within sight of a detachment of three hundred English soldiers and simply charged. Employing massed musket fire and field artillery on a narrow front behind natural defenses, the English troops were able to rout the enemy.[25]

The separation of the sepoys from Indian society and their professionalization increased over time. In the Bengal army under the command of the Calcutta Presidency, the increasing financial power of the EIC drawn from its monopoly on trade enabled it to directly recruit and regularly pay sepoys instead of contracting to hire them through local leaders as the Europeans had initially done, following the practice of the Mughal army. English-style wool uniforms, completely unsuitable for soldiers in the Indian climate, were insisted on not entirely out of sadism or perversity but as a means of visibly setting off the sepoys from other Indian soldiers who were not part of the English military establishment. The stability of EIC finances made sepoy pay—though not greater than that offered by Indian princes—more regular, giving the sepoy a long-term interest in staying with his profession. The EIC directors were conscious of the importance of regular pay and even reduced the size of the sepoy force in 1785 to ensure the regularity of pay to those who remained, writing "the leading principle of the Company's Government should be that the pay of the soldier ought never to be in arrears; while there was a rupee in the treasury, he was to be paid, every other article of expenditure being postponed to that consideration."[26]

This long-term perspective on soldiering was accentuated by a promotion system linked, after the reforms of 1796, to length of service, plus a pension system that rewarded those soldiers who stayed in the army long enough (twenty years or more) to reach jemadar or subedar, ranks for Indian noncommissioned officers roughly corresponding to lieutenant and captain. Pensions could take the form of retirement pay or uncultivated unowned land that was increasingly brought under cultivation as the result of EIC policies.[27]

The separation of the Indian soldiers was also the result of another mode of military organization which was indirectly connected with the need to professionalize the soldiers, and which, in varying degrees, clearly had the effect of increasing the social separation of the troops

[25]Captain Ironside, "A Narrative of the Campaign in Bengal in 1760," in "Miscellaneous Tracts," *Asiatic Annual Register for the Year 1800*, pp. 7–13.
[26]EIC directors dispatch of 11 April 1785, cited in Amiya Barat, *Bengal Native Infantry*, p. 41.
[27]Mason, *Matter of Honour*, pp. 62–65. Barat, *Bengal Native Infantry*, pp. 51–52.

from their social origins. The linguistically and socially fragmented nature of Indian society was reflected in Indian military organization under the British, but in ways that created socially autonomous, inward-looking groups within the military, groups that reduced the strength of the soldiers' ties to Indian society as compared with the ties that Indian soldiers had to Indian society in the Mughal military system. As noted above, the sepoys were formed into companies and battalions and were commanded at the unit level by Indian officers from the sepoys' own social groups. The need to have military subunits which spoke the same language and which were commanded by officers who also spoke the language of the men and understood their social customs was basic. This was formalized into a system of recruiting men for battalions and regiments exclusively from single subcastes—such as Jats or Dogras—and by recruiting soldiers for given units from the same villages year after year.[28] Given the conditions of full-time, long-term service, these narrowly based, homogenous military units of men living together, slowly replenished over time by men similar to themselves, developed into new social units removed from their origins. The character and degree of social separation of these autonomous military societies varied within the Indian army.

The EIC army of this period, as is generally known, was composed of three armies: the Bengal army of the Calcutta Presidency, just discussed, and the armies of the Bombay and the Madras Presidencies in India. Each had different internal organizations, which affected their levels of professionlization. Despite its name, the soldiers in the Bengal army were not from Bengal but overwhelmingly from the neighboring areas of Oudh and Bihar, which had had large local armies before the British period. It was largely Hindu, despite the large Muslim population of Bengal (9:1 Hindu to Muslim ratio among the sepoys in the Bengal army), and generally high-caste, either Brahmin or Kshatriya (fifty-four thousand high-caste Hindu sepoys out of a total of seventy thousand). Because of this dominance of high-caste Hindus, it has been argued that in the Bengal army, "the victory of caste was complete," producing small, company-sized units and large, battalion-sized units that were homogenous by caste.[29] For the purposes of this analysis, more significant is that in the Bengal army, the Hindu sepoys lived in communities that they literally built for themselves—as groups of newly enlisted sepoys banded together to build a hut, and became part of the sepoy military village. As Amiya Barat, historian of the Bengal infantry, noted, this was representative of how the Bengal "army authorities encouraged the

---

[28] Cohen, *Indian Army*, pp. 32–56.
[29] Mason, *Matter of Honour*, p. 125

growth of family or village ties *within the army*, handing over their duties toward and their control over the recruits to the semi-autonomous body of sepoys."[30] This socially autonomous organization of sepoys reduced but did not eliminate their ties to their original villages. Soldiers living in the military with men from their old village tended to be mindful of the social distinctions that had affected their lives back in the village. This could and did lead to conflicts within the military because separation of soldiers from their social origins was imperfect.[31] This was clearly inconsistent with the professionalization of the military and may, as we shall see, partially explain the special behavior of the Bengal army in the Great Mutiny of 1857.

In the Bombay army, the social organization of the sepoys was different in ways that tended to increase further their separation from society relative to that found in the Bengal army. Based in the western areas of India that had been dominated in the very recent past by the hostile Maratha military, the Bombay army was initially unable to recruit soldiers locally because of the continued hostility of the Maratha population. Recruitments into the Bombay army came from the large military populations of the Punjab, Oudh, and Rajputana. Because of this and possibly because of the example of the relatively egalitarian Maratha military, in the eighteenth century the Bombay army included "all classes and castes down to the most humble," including Jews and the Mahar outcastes. By the late eighteenth century and beginning of the nineteenth century, the clear defeat of the Maratha regular armies and the irregular Maratha guerrillas lead to an acceptance of British rule and an influx of Marathas into the Bombay army, though recruitment from the areas far from Bombay continued. So did the pattern of relatively classless and caste-blind military organization, though Jews and outcastes were gradually excluded. Sepoys worked with one another regardless of caste and were promoted by merit, not by caste or seniority. The consequence of this can be captured by the statement of a high-caste sepoy who left the Bengal army to join the Bombay army. The soldier had resigned from the Bengal army because, contrary to the usual practice in that army, he had been forced to serve alongside a low-caste sepoy. He was then asked why he enlisted in the Bombay army, in which he would have to serve with low-caste soldiers as a matter of standard practice. His reply was that what was honorable—or dishonorable—in Bengal was different from what was honorable in Bombay: "In Hindustan it is pride of caste; in Bombay, pride of regiment."[32]

---

[30] Barat, *Bengal Native Infantry*, pp. 119–125, 130; emphasis added.

[31] Barat goes so far as to say that the sepoy of this period in the Bengal army "remained a civilian at heart though becoming a soldier by profession." Ibid., p. 126.

[32] Patrick Cadell, *History of the Bombay Army* (London: Longmans, 1938), pp. 12–15, 161, 200.

In short, the professionalization of the Bombay army seems to have been more advanced than in the Bengal army. Greater professionalization meant more attention to military discipline and performance of military functions and less attachment to nonmilitary considerations such as the old loyalties and divisions of the sepoys' original village. In this manner, the social separation of the Bombay army was more advanced than that of the Bengal army. This separation appears to have been augmented by the practice in the Bombay army of allowing the wife and children of a sepoy to relocate to the area where the sepoy was stationed. The Bombay army sepoy thus brought his family and community with him into foreign territories within India. In the Bengal army, the sepoy's family and community were left behind, intact in the sepoy's home village, keeping alive in the most personal way the links of the sepoy back to his social origins.[33]

The natural and desired consequence of professionalization was increasing obedience to military authority and some decline in the attachment of the sepoys to the usages of Indian society. The service of sepoys outside India, that is, beyond the Indus River or overseas, offended caste law, but by using bonuses and by carefully catering to the caste laws that could be obeyed during such deployments, the EIC was able to find sepoys who would volunteer for duty abroad. When such care was not taken or when units were simply ordered abroad, mutinies could and did occur. But the success in alienating sepoys from their caste practices was sufficient that the Governor General of India could write to the directors of the EIC praising the sepoys for "sacrificing their prejudices to their duty and . . . overcoming natural reluctance when the state had occasion for their service."[34]

Because the professionalization of the sepoy armies was uneven within the Indian army up through the first half of the nineteenth century, the reaction of the sepoys to military orders that were contrary to the dictates of Indian society was also uneven. We would expect the most highly professionalized armies of India to be less likely to disobey orders that offended the sensibilities of Indian civilian society than were the less highly professionalized armies. The three armies of the EIC thus give us a chance to see a natural experiment in action in the Great Mutiny of 1857. The official history of the mutiny, which was commissioned by the Indian government for the mutiny's centennial, puts the blame for the mutiny squarely on the offensive and insensitive rule of the EIC, which had consistently violated all the religious principles of Muslims and Hindu Indians alike. "Fifty years of ill-timed and ill-judged legislation

---

[33]Surendra Nath Sen, *Eighteen Fifty-Seven* (Calcutta: Government of India Publications Division, 1958), p. 20.
[34]Barat, *Bengal Native Infantry*, pp. 42–45.

drove the people crazy and convinced them there was no infamy of which the faithless Firingi was incapable." The history further asserted that "the Mutiny was inevitable. No independent nation can for ever reconcile itself to foreign domination." But the same history noted some striking anomalies. All Indian sepoys may have been offended by new British military practices affecting their religions, such as the infamous cartridges greased with unclean fat, but only the Bengal army mutinied. The history noted fifty-two regiments in the Bengal army that mutinied, rebelled, or had to be disarmed because their British officers thought the regiment to be unreliable. Not one unit from the Bombay or Madras army was noted for such behavior. This was even more striking because it was during the mutiny that the Peshwa, a traditional leader of the Marathas, raised the flag of rebellion only to face the indifference of the Maratha civilian population and the staunch loyalty of the Maratha soldiers in the Bombay army.[35] Other factors relevant to the separation of armies from society also help explain the different behavior of the Bengal army. Mutinies occur more easily when soldiers are stationed among civilians who are their own people, who can encourage them to revolt and hide them if they do mutiny.[36] The Bengal army, composed of men from Bihar and Oudh, was stationed in Bihar and Oudh. Units of the Bombay and Madras armies, more heterogeneous in their composition, tended not to be stationed among their own people. The combined factors of separation of society by professionalization and by physical deployment goes far to explain the differences in behavior of the armies of India in 1857.

The EIC and the Demilitarization of Indian Society

The military success of the EIC was the result of two other innovations. One was within the military and is not closely related to the arguments of this book but was crucial to British success—the professionalization of logistics. Together with the development of militarily powerful infantry units, the mobility of the EIC army gave it the power to defeat any other regular army in India but also the power to defeat irregular, guerrilla forces that continued to fight the British after the regular armies had been defeated. The other factor was EIC agricultural policy, which led to, in the language of modern counterinsurgency, the pacification of the Indian countryside. This factor is closely tied to the themes of this book

---

[35] Sen, *Eighteen Fifty-Seven*, pp. xx, xxiii, 2–16, 17, 407–409, 417, 463–464 (index entries).
[36] Stephen Peter Rosen, "Mutiny and the Warsaw Pact," *National Interest* 2 (Winter 1985/1986): 74–82.

because EIC agricultural policy did affect the character of Indian society. It may have altered caste structures. It certainly demilitarized them.

The area within which any army could fight a battle in India was in large measure determined by how far it could march from its base and still feed itself. The area an army could control was determined by how long an army could besiege an enemy fort and still feed itself. Much has been written about how European powers improved their ability to fight campaigns over long distances by routinely buying and stockpiling non-perishable food and by planning the march of their armies such that different units would follow different routes to a single destination so that each could systematically extract all the food along its way without starving its fellow units.[37]

In Mughal India, armies were of two kinds: the huge, slow armies described in the last chapter that carried with them all the people necessary to supply the soldiers and their servants with food, or fast, lightly equipped armies such as the Maratha armies. The first type could operate over long distances and defend itself against local military forces, but it could always be evaded. The latter could raid villages and small military units at will, but it could not stand and fight a battle against a Mughal imperial army. The Mughal army, as a result, could never really bring hostile local armies to battle, force them to fight, and pacify a hostile area for a long period of time. A system of modern logistics made it possible for the EIC armies to be fast and powerful and thus to extend their reach against other big armies but, equally important, against lightly armed, very mobile local forces as well.

From the beginning, English commanders had to operate in areas where the agricultural surplus was small, when it existed at all. As a result, as early as 1765, Clive, best known for his victory at the Battle of Plassey, broke up the Bengal army into three brigades because deploying his entire force in any one area would lead to grain shortages, increases in the price of food, starvation for the local peasants, and unrest among the sepoys who had to pay for their own food.[38] Some thirty years later, the EIC army had the capability to move and feed an army of eight thousand infantry through arid land hundreds of miles from Hyderabad in the south to Poona to encounter and fight a professionalized Maratha army trained and equipped by French officers. This army was still large, with ten noncombatant support personnel for every soldier, but discipline and routine made it capable of movement through hostile territory

---

[37] See Martin Van Creveld, *Supplying War: Logistics from Wallenstein to Patton* (Cambridge: Cambridge University Press, 1977), Chaps. 1 and 2, pp. 1–74. See also Parker, *Military Revolution*, pp. 76–78

[38] Barat, *Bengal Native Infantry*, pp. 25–27.

where the climate ensured that there would be little in the way of local food supplies.[39]

To understand the true magnitude of the importance and impact of professional logistics to warfare in India, however, one need only read the correspondence of a military genius engaged in the task of operating his army in India. Arthur Wellesley's letters during his campaigns against Tippoo Sultan and then the Marathas at the end of the eighteenth century and the beginning of the nineteenth are obsessed with the problem of obtaining supplies, particularly grain. He took immense pride in obtaining grain for his army of thirty thousand without upsetting the prices in local markets, flying into a fury when his pursuit of a band of Maratha guerrillas was delayed because grain had not been stockpiled and packed so as to make possible his rapid mounted movement. After successfully hunting down and killing the head of the Maratha guerrillas, he immediately ordered that the newly established garrisons be stock-piled with grain so as to make possible the sustained military control of the areas to which other guerrillas were expected to return. Observing this performance, Lord Mornington wrote to Wellesley, "We have now proved (a perfect novelty in India) that we can hunt down the lightest footed and most rapid armies as well as we can destroy heavy troops and storm strong fortifications."[40]

After their initial victories, more important for the British than logistics was how to prevent the Indians from using the techniques of professional armies against them. We have already outlined how the Maratha army had begun to professionalize itself in the seventeenth and eighteenth centuries. If the British were to avoid eventual defeat by professionalized Indian armies, they would have to employ their initial advantage in organized military power in ways that would not only defeat existing Indian armies before they improved too much but also preclude their creation in the future. By radically increasing the military power of the EIC state and by denying the Indian rulers access to the same military power, the EIC was able to establish something that was new in India: the monopoly—or near monopoly—of the state on the legitimate means of violence.

The effort by Indian rulers to professionalize their armies did not go unnoticed by EIC officials in India, and they worried that the easy EIC

---

[39] William Thorn, *Memoir of the War in India Conducted by Lord Lake, Commander in Chief, and Major General Sir Arthur Wellesley, 1803–1806* (London: T. Egerton, 1818), pp. 25–28, 56, 84–87.
[40] Letter to Henry Wellesley, 7 January 1799, letter to Colonel Barry Close, 30 June 1800, and letter to Lt. Colonel John Sartorus, 18 September 1800, in Antony Brett-James, ed., *Wellington at War, 1794–1815: A Selection of His Wartime Letters* (London: Macmillan, 1961), pp. 22, 37–38, 41–42, 44.

victories that continued up through the middle of the eighteenth century might not continue. The policy adopted by several EIC governor-generals in India of aggressively expanding the area of EIC control was criticized by EIC officials in London at the time, and afterward by historians, as costly and irrational land grabbing.[41] It is interesting, therefore, to read the strategic justification for the expansion by its proponent, Governor-General Richard Wellesley. Written while on his voyage to India in 1798, Wellesley's first dispatch to Henry Dundas was an effort to formulate a strategic rationale based on the military and political intelligence available to him. What figured most prominently in his thinking and, it appears, in the minds of his superiors in London was the development of rival armies in India with European training: "You particularly urged the necessity of my attending with the utmost degree of vigilance to the system, now pursued almost universally by the native princes, of retaining in their service numbers of European or American officers, under whom the native troops are trained and disciplined in imitation of the sepoys in the British service." He noted the reports of Major Kirkpatrick, the EIC resident at the court of the Nizam of Hyderabad who had earlier been in residence with the Maratha chief Scindiah. Those reports documented the Nizam's use of American, Irish, and particularly French officers and the growth in the number of European-trained troops from fifteen hundred men in 1792 to eleven thousand in 1795, a number which was to be raised to fourteen thousand. The Nizam was so training his army not simply in imitation of the British but in competition with the Marathas. Wellesley noted that Scindiah had twenty thousand troops under French and American officers. The result of this trend might well be the end of British military influence in southern India.

> The institution of the corps proceeded from an admiration of the successful policy of Mahdajee Scindiah. . . . The result in my mind is a decided opinion, that the continuance, and still more the further growth of the corps . . . ought to be prevented by every means within our power, consistent with the respect due to the Court of Hyderabad. . . . The dangers to be apprehended from the existence of this corps are not to be estimated by a consideration of its actual state of discipline, or even of its actual numbers. . . . If we are to look to the settlement of peace, can it be possible to provide a more ready channel for the intrigues of France, than would be offered by the existence of a body of 10,000 men, united by military discipline, and stationed in the dominions of one of our principal allies, and on the borders of our own?[42]

[41] Ingram, *British India*, pp. 1–14.
[42] Martin, *Despatches*, 23 February 1798, 1:1–15

The Nizam would not give up this army if simply asked to. Sending British officers to train troops for the Nizam would not remove the independent military power of the French-trained army, which might well be expected to attack the British if and when its military position became precarious.

The only solution that Richard Wellesley could see was to send a British army to the Nizam to defend him against the Marathas, in return for which he could be asked to disband his other armies. It was not sufficient for the EIC to continue making alliances with local Indian powers who could be left militarily independent. The EIC strategy of forging local alliances had not ended the local military competitions that were generating armies that would eventually be powerful enough to make the EIC forces irrelevant. "The balance of power in India no longer exists on the same footing on which it was placed" by the alliance between the EIC and the Nizam. The Indian armies were growing too strong. "The question must therefore arise how it may best be brought back again" into balance. The EIC system of alliances had to be supplemented by the extension of British military control. In war with Tippoo, ruler of Mysore, the EIC objective, Wellesley argued, must be to deprive those powers of the financial resources with which they could build an army and to make "the perpetual exclusion of all Frenchmen, both from his army and from his dominions, the conditions of any treaty of peace." In his orders to his commanders in the war with Tippoo, his intent was explicit: "The military power of Mysore must be broken; or absolutely identified with that of the [East India] Company." On the borders of the EIC territory in Bengal, the army of the Vizier of Oudh, allied with the EIC, had to be broken up. Any instances of bad behavior by a unit of the Vizier's army were to be seized upon and used to justify a demand that the unit be disbanded. Over the longer term, the EIC borders could never be secured except "by dispersing his [the Vizier's] useless rabble and forming an army to be kept up and disciplined under our immediate superintendence." To reinforce the British military monopoly, Wellesley was willing to be lenient when that served his purpose. While at war with the Marathas in 1803, Wellesley instructed his military commander to offer safe conduct and passage back to Europe to the French officer who had trained the Maratha army in order to get him out of that army as soon as possible.[43]

This single-minded attention to creating a monopoly on regular mili-

[43] Ibid., dispatches from Wellesley to Dundas, 28 February 1798, 1:17–34, and 6 July 1798, 1:80–83; Richard Wellesley to Arthur Wellesley and the members of the Army Commission, 20 May 1799, 2: 12; Wellesley to Lt. Colonel W. Scott at Lucknow, 18 June 1799; 2:53–54, Dundas to Wellesley; 21 March 1799, 2:108.

tary organizations led Wellesley into conflict with his superiors, because it involved a series of costly wars. Wellesley justified his conduct to London in a letter of resignation he submitted in January 1802:

> To the exercise of those powers which the Court would now subvert, I attribute the fall of Tippoo Sultaun, the conquest and settlement of Mysore; the extinction of the French influence in the Deccan; the establishment of the British influence in that quarter on the solid foundation of military strength and territorial possession. . . . the substitution of a powerful British force on the northwestern frontier of Oudh in the place of the undisciplined and disaffected army of the Nabob Vizier; the destruction of the power of Zemaun Shah . . . ; the means of contributing to the maintenance of Egypt by the army of India; the tranquillity of the Mahrattas, and finally, the seasonable occupation of the Portuguese possession in the East Indies.[44]

Richard Wellesley's efforts to utilize the British military advantage to defeat or disestablish the emerging professional armies of India was by no means premature. The Maratha army, which had been at work longest on its professionalization, had by 1803 increased its fighting power to levels near that of the British. General Lake, commander in chief of EIC forces, commented after his battle with Scindiah's Maratha army at Laswaree in October 1803 that the Marathas "fought like devils, or rather, like heroes. . . . I was never in so severe a business in my life or anything like it." At the Battle of Assye in September of that year, Arthur Wellesley commanded 4,500 regular EIC troops against a force of 10,500 regular troops under Scindiah's command in a set-piece battle in which EIC troops in close order attacked a line of Maratha troops drawn up in a European line of defense. Wellesley won but suffered 50 percent casualties and wrote afterward that "Scindiah's infantry behaved remarkably well, and stood to their guns to the last."[45] In the areas that remained outside EIC rule until the 1840s, local Indian rulers continued their military development. By 1831, the Sikhs in the Punjab had an army of twenty thousand regular infantry and were able to defeat the British at Mudki in 1845. They were later defeated only because of dissension among rival Sikh leaders.[46]

Beyond creating a monopoly on the regular armies in the areas of India under their control, the British used their military capabilities plus their

[44] Ibid., extract of letter from Wellesley to Addington 10 January 1802, 3:xxiv.

[45] Thorn, *Memoir of the War in India*, pp. 273–280; Brett-James, *Wellington at War*, Wellesley to Major Merrick Shawe, 24 September 1803, pp. 72, 81.

[46] Grewal, *Sikhs of the Punjab*, pp. 104, 123.

agricultural policies to reduce radically the number of irregular soldiers operating in the Indian countryside. In the chapter on the Mughal period, considerable attention was directed toward the evidence documenting the large numbers of troops available in the Indian countryside before the British established a political-military presence in India. The number of Indian irregular soldiers only increased as the British forced Indian political leaders to accept British military protection and domination. They acceded to British demands that they disband their existing armies. As a result, many soldiers formerly employed by Indian rulers were now unemployed and more than willing to make war independently to maintain their way of life. In addition, Indian rulers, defeated in battle by the British, fled with their troops to conduct guerrilla warfare against the British. The disbanded regular Indian soldiers, equipped with modern weapons and extracting resources from the countryside, were known generally as Pindaris.[47] In cooperation with the lightly armed local militias, these forces confronted the British with a military challenge at least as great as that posed by the modernizing Indian regular armies.

Once again, it is clear that the British fully understood this problem and had a self-conscious strategy of following up their battlefield victories with campaigns to wipe out all effective armed forces in the Indian countryside. For example, after the major victory over the Marathas at Assye, the British forces under General Lake continued to pursue surviving Maratha forces, under the leadership of Maratha chief Jeswunt Rao Holkar, who had fled and were operating in the area between the Ganges and Jumna Rivers (referred to as the Doab, the general term for the area between two rivers) in north India. He explained the purposes of his campaign in the area dominated by a local subcaste, the Rohillas, in a letter back to Governor-General Richard Wellesley:

My principal reason for coming into the Doab was from knowing the consequence my presence would be of in this quarter. . . . I was convinced from . . . the inclination of the Zamindars [the large landholders] etc. to join for the sake of plunder, with the certainty of the Rohillas joining if he evinced strength and power without being opposed, that if he were not followed, and that by me, the Doab would have been in such a state, that if not lost for a time, it would have been totally unprofitable to your Lordship's government. The sequel has proved clearly to me that I acted perfectly right. . . . The people in all parts have assisted Holkar, and have been perfectly ready to rise (in some parts they did show themselves openly) had he not been so closely pressed in the rear. . . . Believe me, I have had

---

[47] See C. A. Bayly, *Indian Society and the Making of the British Empire* (Cambridge: Cambridge University Press, 1990), p. 80.

a most trying time: had we failed in any instance, what would have been the fate of India God only knows. I tremble at the thought of it.

Lake caught up with Holkar, launched a surprise attack on his soldiers, and won a major victory at Deig. He then, once again, launched a follow-up campaign against the enemy soldiers who had escaped. He emphasized the importance of the speed of his march in pursuit of Holkar, concluding that: "I am now quite clear that the country has been saved by this pursuit; every information I receive of the deep laid plan for destroying our government leaves me not a doubt that if I had remained on the other side of the Jumna nothing would have prevented the country from being up in arms, and the junction of Sumroo's Begum, Seiks, and Rohillas."[48]

Richard Wellesley wrote back, praising Lake and confirming that the object of the campaign was the demilitarization of the area. Wellesley noted that the local rajah, the Rajah of Bhurpore, had reneged on his agreement with the British and had aided Jeswunt Rao Holkar at Deig on 13 November. As a result, he was fair game, and Lake was ordered to pursue "the entire reduction of the power and resources of the Rajah." After seizing all his forts, land, and property, Lake was further ordered to set up the civil administration of justice and revenue. Wellesley was emphatic, however, that Lake should still "consider the pursuit of Holkar's personal army to be the principal object of the war;... you will constantly bear in mind my opinion that the entire destruction of whatever force may be attached to the person of this freebooter is indispensably required for the tranquillity of India." As for the rajah, "Your Excellency's proceedings against the Rajah of Bhurpore are calculated to serve as an example to other petty states," so Lake was ordered to circulate letters to other chiefs explaining what he was doing to the rajah and why. Any subordinates of the rajah and any subordinates of Holkar who did not immediately submit and surrender to Lake were to be executed just after being captured.[49] Any forts in hostile areas not garrisoned by the British were to be destroyed.

The process of the demilitarization also included the destruction of local military and quasi-military forces. Localized military clans led by chiefs called poligars and large nomadic groups of Hindu mendicants, the Sannyasi, who were armed and who extracted resources from the villages through which they passed, were also a threat to the British monopoly of force. The Sannyasi bands were observed in battle in the

[48] Martin, *Despatches*, vol. 4, Lt. Gen. Lake to R. Wellesley by private channel, 18 November 1804, pp. 241–242, and Lake to Wellesley, 19 November 1804, p. 245.
[49] Ibid., Wellesley to Lake, 20 December 1804, pp. 261–263.

sixteenth century by the emperor Akbar and by Europeans, who in the eighteenth century recorded the existence of multiple bands, each ranging in size from five to six thousand. These bands employed local informants who would tell them which villages were wealthy and ill-defended. They operated in Bengal and the areas of early interest to the EIC and were of particular concern to Warren Hastings.[50] To the problem of religious military bands had to be added the problem of large bands of thieves, the dacoits, who, in the view of British administrators at the end of the eighteenth century, posed as much of a threat to British political-military dominance as the overtly political groups. The EIC recorded fifteen hundred dacoit attacks per year in 1803–1807, and Governor General Lord Minto wrote of the dacoits that "they had established a terrorism as perfect as that which was the foundation of the French Republican power. . . . The sirdars, or captains of the bands, were esteemed and even called hakim or ruling power . . . , while the real government did not possess either authority or influence enough to obtain from the people the smallest aid towards their own protection."[51]

The task of dealing with locally based bands of raiders, religious or otherwise, was and is a problem of antiguerrilla or counterinsurgency warfare. In the eighteenth century as in the twentieth century, counterinsurgency was based on controlling territory to provide protection to the local population in conditions where the guerrillas outnumbered the regular friendly soldiers. Operating in the field, Arthur Wellesley laid out the objective of his strategy for denying the Indian guerrillas sanctuaries from which they could attack EIC areas with regard to one local military chieftain, Dhoondiah Waugh: "If we do not get him, we must expect a general insurrection of all the discontented and disaffected of these countries. I have information that letters have been received by most of them, either from him, or from others written in his name, calling upon them to take the opportunity to rebel against the Company's government, or that of their allies; and his invasion of our territory is looked to as a circumstance favorable to their views. The destruction of this man, therefore, is absolutely essential to our tranquillity." He also wrote that, "we ought not to quit the field as long as there is a discontented or unsubdued polygar in the country."[52]

[50] Rai Sahib Mohan Ghosh, *Sannyasi and Fakir Raiders in Bengal* (Calcutta: Bengal Secretariat Book Depot, 1930), pp. 9, 13–14, 18–19.

[51] P. J. Marshall, *Bengal: The British Bridgehead, Eastern India, 1740–1828* (Cambridge: Cambridge University Press, 1987), p. 98. See also Basudev Chatterji, "The Darogah and the Countryside: The Imposition of Police Control and Its Impact, 1793–1837," *Indian Economic and Social History Review* 18 (January–March 1981): 19–42.

[52] Brett-James, *Wellington at War*, Arthur Wellesley to Mornington, 29 May 1800, p. 39, and to Major Thomas Munro, 7 May 1800, pp. 37–38.

But how could this be done in a country where EIC forces had to control huge territories and were surrounded, as Arthur Wellesley wrote at the time, by "polygars, nairs, and moplas [all warlike subcastes of armed hill peoples] in arms on all sides of us?" In 1800 Arthur Wellesley laid out what, with some modifications, became the British strategy for the pacification of the countryside: "The result of my observations and considerations upon the mode of carrying on war in jungly countries is just this, that as long as the jungle is thick, the enemy can conceal himself in it, and from his concealment, attack the [friendly] troops, their followers, and their baggage, the operation must be unsuccessful on our side." Large British forces were vulnerable to guerrillas because they had to be accompanied by large numbers of unarmed support troops. Small British military or police forces could march without baggage through the countryside, but they would be attacked and defeated by the larger enemy forces that they would encounter sooner or later. If large forces and small forces could not operate because of their different vulnerabilities, what was the solution? Arthur Wellesley continued: "I know of no mode of doing this excepting to deprive the enemy of his concealment by cutting away the lower part of the jungle to a considerable distance from the road. . . . In order to be successful we must secure those who supply us with all we want, and the best mode of doing this is . . . to deprive the enemy of his concealment." The countryside had to be made safe enough that unarmed people could grow and transport food and small groups of police could keep the peace. In modern language, the countryside had to be pacified. How could this be done? Arthur Wellesley laid out his thoughts in his memorandum. The EIC had to pull its troops back to secure bases, then clear the countryside along rural roads immediately adjacent to those bases. Then the EIC would push forward its advanced posts and, under their military cover, send out working parties to clear jungle for two or three miles. They would then move the work camp forward a few miles and continue the process until the most advanced post was reached. With the roads secure, small cavalry detachments could move quickly if guerrilla forces raided caravans or camps: "After having thus got myself well forward in the country, my posts well established and supplied, and my communications with my rear well secured, as well as that between one post and another, I would begin to carry on the war on a more active plan, and I would send out light detachments in all directions in order to hunt out every Nair who should be in the country."[53]

The clearing of the Indian jungles that Arthur Wellesley sought for military purposes did occur, partly as a result of military policy, but

[53] Ibid., Arthur Wellesley to Lt. Colonel John Sartorius, 18 September 1800, pp. 45–46.

largely as a result of British agricultural policy. The British systematically encouraged the agricultural development of forest lands adjacent to villages to provide jobs for sepoys after retirement, to increase the agricultural revenue paid to the EIC, but also to deny that forest land to guerrilla bands, to which deforested land provided less sanctuary. The owners of useful, cleared land had an incentive to inform the EIC when armed, hostile groups were present on or transited their lands. In the mid–eighteenth century, as C. A. Bayly has noted, earlier Indian rulers had begun the process of the deforestation of the subcontinent, largely for the same military purposes as the EIC.

> But the British who could draw on their experience of "clearings" in Scotland and Ireland took ecological warfare to a new level. Arthur Wellesley drove roads through the forests of Malabar and cleared trees to a mile on either side in his campaign against the Pychee Raja (1800–1802). The territories of the poligars and even the Company's allies were also speedily cleared to deny them to Pindaris and tribesmen as hiding places. Sir Thomas Munro remarked to a young Rajaof Pudokottai in 1826 that the forest had been dense when he traveled this way as a young officer in the 1780s, but now "the woods had been almost cut down and cultivation was going on, some thin woods remaining in places."

The increasing commercialization of logging activities and agriculture also had the effect of taking more and more land out of the forest. Nomadic herdsmen were encouraged or forced to take up sedentary farming. Sedentary farming tended to facilitate stable, hierarchical social structures and so probably increased the strength of the caste system to areas where it was spread. The result at the social level was an India "of settled arable farming, of caste Hindus, and specialist agricultural produce. . . . The stranger, older India of forest and nomad . . . began to disappear."[54]

The question of the impact of the British Empire on Indian society has always been a highly political one, with imperial rulers arguing that their rule was of unambiguous value to the Indian population, and Indian nationalists arguing that the benefits of imperial rule had been exaggerated and the costs ignored. The impact of British rule on peasant standards of living, on caste practices, and on social conflict or cooperation among agrarian classes has been extensively debated.[55] But even the ac-

---

[54] Bayly, *Indian Society and the Making of the British Empire*, pp. 108, 138–139, 144.

[55] See, for example, Neil Charlesworth, *Peasants and Imperial Rule: Agriculture and Agrarian Society in the Bombay Presidency, 1850–1935* (Cambridge: Cambridge University Press, 1985), pp. 1–10, 159–161, 202; Richard G. Fox, *Lions of the Punjab: Culture in the Making* (Berkeley: University of California Press, 1985), pp. 32–33, 39, 44; and P. J. Marshall, *Bengal*, pp. 1, 9, 12, 13–14.

ademic writers most skeptical of British imperial claims of having brought internal peace to India agree that the British did achieve the demilitarization of India. P. J. Marshall, for example, threw doubt on the claim that Bengal was in internal chaos before the British Empire brought order: "It is not necessarily the case that a Pax Britannica had been established by the 1820s that was qualitatively superior to the pax of the Nawabs." What Marshall can agree on is that the British Empire "did in time reduce the use of overt violence within its provinces, and that it did this by establishing a near monopoly of the means of force under its own control. These achievements certainly had important social consequences."[56] Indian writers such as Basudev Chatterji echo the finding that the EIC achieved "what John McLane calls 'the demilitarization of the zamindars.' In every area the British brought under control, they forced the disbandment of local military forces and systematically destroyed the forts and fortified houses of local land controllers."[57] Bayly noted that the combination of counterinsurgency, deforestation, and the opening of professional military jobs to certain indigenous military groups all combined to give the EIC "a monopoly on physical force" with which it ruled "a peasantry now increasingly disarmed," a relationship that "set it apart even in its early days from all the regimes which had preceded it."[58]

What we are in a position to say is that the British Empire may have been acquired without a strategic plan issued from London, but it was not created in a fit of absentmindedness. It arose from the conscious act of a group of men who wished to bring about a different relationship between the military power of the state and the local society, something they achieved by separating the army from the influences of the indigenous social structures and then using that professionalized army to demilitarize Indian society. Those elements of the sepoy army that were most professional and separate from Indian society, the armies of the Bombay and Madras Presidencies, were sufficiently detached from their loyalties to local Indian social structures that they remained loyal to the EIC and fought to demilitarize Indian society once again at the time of the Great Mutiny.

THE DECLINE OF THE MILITARY EFFECTIVENESS OF THE EIC ARMY

The effectiveness of the EIC army, so dramatic when it was originally established, declined after the major wars of pacification had been fought and won. After internal peace was established in India, the EIC forces

---

[56] Marshall, *Bengal*, p. 138.
[57] Chatterji, "Darogah and the Countryside," pp. 22
[58] Bayly, *Indian Society and the Making of the British Empire*, p. 110.

were a peacetime army radically separated from society. It fell victim to the fate of other peacetime armies with strong organizational identities and weak ties to their own society, becoming more interested in its corporate self-interests than in its fighting power. It remained adequate for the purpose of suppressing local insurrections, but the weaknesses of the army were revealed in wars against external powers. This may help explain the anomaly of a relative lack of organized, violent Indian opposition to British rule, combined with a deep-seated fear in the minds of the British of a Russian military threat to India.

The decline of the military performance of the sepoy army was uneven geographically and over time. Certain units were worse than others, and efforts at reform periodically arrested or reversed the decline in military performance. The most important weakness in the Indian army that affected all portions of it was the result, paradoxically, of a program of reform. There had always been two British armies in India: European regiments commanded by the King's officers that represented the Royal Army in India, and the EIC sepoy army composed of European officers and Indian soldiers. Tension existed between those two armies, because Royal Army officers tended to be younger (promotion was faster in the Royal Army than in the Indian army), and from higher social classes (poor men like Clive enlisted as officers in the Indian army to make their fortunes, whereas Royal Army officers tended to be aristocratic). Before 1796 this tension was less because officers for the sepoy units were selected from among the junior officers in the Royal Army units already in India. This policy was based on the reasonable judgment that it was good for young officers to gain some experience of Indian languages and conditions before taking on the task of commanding Indian troops. In a misguided effort to create a distinct Indian army with its own officer corps, reforms instituted in 1796 ended the earlier practice in favor of sending military cadets direct from the army academy at Woolwich, England, to units of the Indian army, where they immediately took command of Indian soldiers. In plain language, this meant that fifteen-year-old boys with no knowledge of India were placed in positions of enormous power over Indian soldiers. The social results could have been predicted and had devastating consequences for the effectiveness of the EIC army.

The increasingly difficult relations between the British officers and the Indian soldiers in the two generations before the Great Mutiny has been noted—by Rudyard Kipling among many others. It has been argued that the development of Protestant missionary zeal in India affected the Indian army by increasing the moral contempt held by British officers for the "heathen" Indians and by reducing the frequency with which British officers made common-law marriages with Indian wives.[59] There is abun-

---

[59] See, for example, Mason, *Matter of Honour*, pp. 173–174.

dant testimony that the British military contempt for Indians grew after 1800, but the cause appears to have had more to do with the policies affecting the recruitment and training of British officers in India. By taking officers for the Indian army direct from Woolwich, the Indian government created a situation in which boys devoid of any real knowledge of the military or Indian languages were sent to command troops in isolated areas under conditions where they had much time, many Indian servants, few military responsibilities, and hundreds of Indian soldiers, far older than they, under their complete control. Amiya Barat commented succinctly, "It is not surprising, therefore, to find a gradual yet marked worsening in the relationship between European officers and their sepoys over the period 1796 to 1852 . . . which was to contribute so adversely to the later history of the sepoy army."[60] Less polite commentators have suggested that setting up boys as the more or less absolute commanders of groups of racially and linguistically distinct men was a situation likely to produce permanent adolescence in the boys.

The misguided policy of officer recruitment affected all EIC armies. The quality of the officers in the Indian army under the command of the Bengal Presidency was particularly bad, for reasons having to do with its proximity to Calcutta, center of EIC administration. Pay for officers was poor everywhere in India, but opportunities for making more money outside the army—legally—were best around Calcutta. Officers in the Bengal army had the best chance, because of their location, of obtaining appointments not in the field but with the Indian army staff or civil authorities. If officers were interested in making money illegally by trading in the local economy, again, the opportunities were greatest where EIC rule created illicit supplies and markets for goods, that is, in and around Calcutta. As a result, a particularly severe problem existed with Indian regiments in the Bengal army without their normal complement of officers, with officers who were present but not attentive, or with officers who were too dull to seek and achieve better jobs. This added to the language problem because the British officers best able to do useful staff, civilian, or black market work outside their regiment were those who had taken the trouble to learn an Indian language.[61]

This army did not face any significant organized military opposition after the defeat of the Maratha armies in the second Maratha War, but the impact of British agricultural policies, so successful in pacifying In-

---

[60] Barat, *Bengal Army*, pp. 73–77, 79, 114. See also the memoir, generally accepted as genuine, of a sepoy who noted the decline in the ability of his English officers to speak his language and the increase in their abuse of the Indian troops: Sita Ram, *From Sepoy to Subedar*, ed. James Lunt (London: Papermac, 1988), pp. 23, 25. For a hair-raising word picture of daily life among the officers of the Indian army before the Great Mutiny, see Christopher Hibbert, *The Great Mutiny* (London: Penguin, 1982), pp. 40–46.

[61] Barat, *Bengal Native Infantry*, pp. 105–111.

dia, created longer-term problems. Subcaste structures remained strong, and caste interests were often adversely affected by the transfers of land that were part of the British system. With respect to their original problem and objective, the British had succeeded. The problem of achieving internal tranquility against guerrillas aided by former regular soldiers was more or less solved by the campaigns waged by Warren Hastings against the Maratha remnants and their allies of convenience—the former soldiers living as raiders, the Pindaris—which ended in 1818.[62] After that, the Indian army largely occupied itself by suppressing peasant rebellions such as that of the Khurda people of Orissa in 1817; the Tapang Rebellion of 1827, also in Orissa; and dacoit attacks all over India, which often appear to have been difficult to distinguish from peasant rebellions against landlords and money lenders.

On the other hand, these persistent, low-level rebellions had their origins in the reaction against the British system of land revenues and agricultural policy, which pushed farmers toward a cash system and market competition and which led to changes in land tenure that were deeply resented.[63] These peasant rebellions represented a continuation of the struggle for control of land by subcastes under the new conditions created by British imperial rule that favored some subcastes more than others. The leader of one subcaste whose land had been bought by Pathans—outsiders—"spoke for all tribal insurgents of the nineteenth century when he explained why his people had taken to arms in 1832: 'The Pathans have taken our [land], and the Singh our sisters. . . . Our lives we considered of no value, and being of one caste and brethren, it was agreed upon that we should commence to cut, plunder, and murder, and eat.' "[64] For British rule, the ultimate consequences of this tension were played out in the period after the one examined in this chapter, but their origins lay clearly in the basic British program for the demilitarization of Indian society.

ASSESSING THE POWER OF THE EIC ARMY

Dealing with low-level peasant violence was well within the capacity of the Indian army. Because it involved using Indian soldiers to kill In-

[62]Cadell, *Bombay Army*, pp. 149–158.
[63]See, for example, P. K. Pattanaik, *A Forgotten Chapter of Orissan History, 1568–1828* (Calcutta: Punthis Pustak, 1979), pp. 146–148, 171, 178, 181, 229, 231; Ranajit Guha, *Elementary Aspects of Peasant Insurgency in Colonial India* (Delhi: Oxford University Press, 1983), pp. 7–9, 82, 87, 110–111.
[64]Guha, *Peasant Insurgency*, p. 281. For a discussion of how British agricultural and irrigation policy favored some subcastes in the Punjab and displaced many peasants who then became soldiers in the Indian army, see Fox, *Lions of the Punjab*, pp. 33–44.

dian civilians, this military task, more than any other, required the separation of the Indian military from its loyalties to indigenous Indian social structures. Earlier in this chapter I examined how this separation was achieved by building the Indian army out of a number of self-contained, inwardly looking military communities with their own languages and habits and divorced from society. But these self-contained units were also, by the same process, divorced from one another—linguistically, sociologically, and geographically. Conducting coordinated, integrated campaigns against external enemies with an army so fragmented presented a severe military problem. The capabilities of individual Indian army companies or regiments were impressive when one company or regiment dealt with the same kind of disorganized local troops as it had originally encountered in India itself. In Afghanistan, for example, the local social and tribal fissures could be manipulated by the British working with local allies, and the British army could defeat most any local army in the field.[65] But when many units of the Indian army had to be combined to fight a large war, these isolated military communities had to cooperate with one another. If they fought extended campaigns, these units took many casualties, and new soldiers had to be rapidly recruited from a society with which the army had only narrow and limited contacts. Recruits could not come from anywhere in India but only from the community that had provided men in the past. Extended campaigns, such as those fought in Nepal and Afghanistan, and protracted wars strained the army. In summary, the Indian army in the British period had major problems in conducting large-scale external wars.

As early as 1814, commentators noted that "incessant internal duties performed by scattered small units prevent the army from 'acting and manoeuvering in bodies . . . [which] is deemed indispensable to the proper organization of any regular army intended for the defense of great continental domains.' "[66] The logistics of an army that did not fight extended, intense wars was also strained by external deployment in large-scale wars. One analysis of the Indian army concluded that it was effective when used "for minor purposes, seldom involving actual warfare and never involving any significant portion of the Indian army." When called on to do more than that, as in World War I, the bravery of individual Indian soldiers was visible for all to see, but so were the lo-

[65]J. A. Norris, *The First Afghan War, 1838–1842* (Cambridge: Cambridge University Press, 1967), pp. 186–190, 261–262 on how the British supported rival claimants to the Afghan throne, 329–334, and 354 on the Battle of Bamiyan, after which the British governor-general Lord Auckland concludes that "5,000 of their insurgents can be beaten by 500 of our troops."

[66]John Pemble, *The Invasion of Nepal: John Company at War* (Oxford: Clarendon, 1971), p. 96, citing the commander in chief of the EIC armies, General George Nugent.

gistical inadequacies of the army, and "its recruiting practice, meant for a much smaller army, revealed their inadequacy to a major war effort." Moreover, the individual, isolated nature of Indian army military training meant that each unit fought its own way, which was disastrous for large-scale, coordinated military operations. "Each [battalion] depot enrolled and maintained its own recruits and maintained the records of its own battalion. . . . As each depot trained its own recruits through its own officers, uniformity in training could not be achieved. The standard of training and efficiency differed from depot to depot."[67]

In short, the British created an army in India that was significantly more powerful than the armies of the Mughal Empire because it was professional and as such not subject to the internal divisions always in operation in the Mughal army. Those armies were so effective that they could be used to defeat and then demilitarize large areas of India and so create domestic peace, unlike the Mughal armies, and were available for use outside India, again unlike the Mughals. This was not due to British moral superiority but to a form of military organization that increased the cohesion of the army by divorcing it from society. Those British armies in India that were more divorced from society, notably the Madras and Bombay armies, were also less affected by social unrest in the larger society and the lingering influence of Indian social structures on the men in the army at the time of the Great Mutiny. The possibility that other Indian rulers might also create such professional armies dictated the British strategy in India. But the divorce of the army from society had a price. It could not fight the same large-scale wars as those fought by an army that was organized on the assumption that it would be supported by a cohesive national-scale society. This was the military legacy of the Indian Empire inherited by India after independence.

[67] DeWitt C. Ellinwood and S. D. Pradhan, introduction to *India and World War I*, ed. Ellinwood and Pradham (New Delhi: Manohar, 1978), pp. 1–8, and Pradhan, "Indian Army and the First World War," in *India and World War I*, pp. 49–67. See also T. H. Heathcote, *The Indian Army: The Garrison of British Imperial Rule, 1822–1922* (London: David and Charles, 1974).

[6]

India and Its Army after Independence

How have Indian society and the Indian Army interacted in the period since independence? How have the internal military organization and military effectiveness of the Indian Army developed? In this chapter I will provide at least partial answers to these questions by using the model elaborated in Chapter 1. To recall, the two independent variables highlighted in Chapter 1 were the nature of Indian social structures and the degree of separation of the military from society. Following this approach, I will look at the dominant structures of modern Indian society and the way they have affected the internal structures of a number of nonmilitary organizations in modern India. The army of India will then be examined, to see whether and how it has separated itself from Indian society in ways not possible for nonmilitary organizations. The degree and character of this separation will be examined separately with regard to the rank-and-file soldiers and the officers of the Indian army. Then, some effort will be made to see how the pattern of relations between the army and Indian society differs from that found in other multi-lingual, multi-ethnic societies. Finally, I will assess the consequences of the relation between Indian society and the army with regard to the performance of the Indian Army in war.

What kind of military behavior should we expect to see from the postindependence Indian Army? If the structures of Indian society did not change overnight when India gained independence, the major difference between imperial and postindependence India would be the emergence of a new nationalist ruling political elite. Given the rise to power of a new civilian political class, the model on which this book is based would predict much greater tension between the military and civilian political society if the Indian Army retained the degree of separation it had from Indian civilian society under British rule, which it did. This prediction of increased tension between the military and civilian society differs from what might be the more conventional prediction of improved civil-military relations in a newly independent country. In many countries that fought for independence, the military emerged alongside the civilian nationalist leadership, and both reflected the social forces that generated them. The Indian Army did not fight for independence. Until 1947, it fought for the British Empire, sometimes against Indian nationalists. It was able to do so because of its separation from Indian society. That separation, maintained after independence, had serious consequences for the nature of the relations between the army and Indian society.

When we think in the abstract about Indian military development after independence, several possibilities are conceivable. First, the Indian Army after independence, unlike the imperial Indian Army, might have become a national army, somehow representative of Indian society as a whole. To be sure, there would be a period in which the imperial military legacy would continue to influence Indian military organization and civil-military relations. When British rule in India ended in 1947, the Indian military no longer served a foreign government, but it retained a British army officer, General Bucher, as the Chief of Army Staff (COAS) throughout its first war with Pakistan, until 15 January 1949, when he was replaced by the first Indian COAS, General Cariappa.[1] But this imperial inheritance might quickly fade away. If the Indian Army had become a national army representative of the Indian people and Indian society, the process of transformation could have taken two forms. First, the postindependence army of India could have ended the British practice of selective military recruitment from certain groups in India which was created to facilitate the use of the Indian Army as an internal instrument of control and which created an army that was not demographically representative of India. Second, it would have meant the end of the related practice of segregation of subcaste groups in the army so that rival, communally homogenous military units could be more easily used to check one another within the military and against rioting civilians from other communal groups. The stated goal of the new Indian government was to create a modern secular state that dealt with individuals as individuals, not as members of different communal groups. A military policy consistent with this would have been, over time, to recruit and assign soldiers to units on the basis of their individual characteristics

[1] Maj. K. C. Praval, *Indian Army after Independence*, ed. Maj. Shankar Bhaduri (New Delhi: Lancer International, 1990), pp. 85, 98.

and the functional needs of the military. This process of adjustment would have taken time, but the Indian military would less and less resemble its imperial ancestor and more and more resemble the armies of other modern democracies.

Alternatively, the Indian Army, liberated from British control, might have become more "Indian," in the sense that it recruited from all groups in India but kept them segregated by groups in the army. In this sense, the army would be reflective of the norms and social structures of Indian society as a whole. What it might mean for a former imperial institution to become more "Indian" could be determined by looking at what happened to other erstwhile imperial bureaucracies, such as the police and civil service, after independence. If the Indian Army became more representative of Indian society, it might be argued that Indian social structures in some sense determined that nature of the Indian military.

Finally, the Indian Army might have reflected Indian social structures but maintained or increased its isolation from society. Perhaps the need to sustain a professional military in the context of Indian society might lead Indian military leaders after independence to maintain the same patterns of military organization created by the British. Indian military leaders might do this out of organizational inertia but also because they would wish to maintain certain military capabilities and had to do so in the face of the same Indian social realities that faced the British. If that were the case, we might expect the Indian Army to converge not toward the pattern of other democracies or to other postindependence bureaucracies but toward the pattern displayed by other professional armies confronting similar internal communal divisions. The argument of this chapter will be that, in fact, such was the case, and that postindependence army, in its internal structure and its relation to Indian society, has more in common with the imperial army of Hapsburg Austria before World War I than any other. The Indian Army did not converge toward the pattern of other postcolonial armies, nor did it develop a unique "Hindu" character. It was shaped by the interaction between divisive social structures and political decisions about the separation of the army from society.

The task of collecting evidence to see precisely which kind of army emerged is difficult in the case of India. Senior Indian Army officers have noted in print that theirs "is . . . perhaps one of the most secretive armies among democratic nations."[2] Information about the equipment and lo-

---

[2] Brigadier S. C. Sardeshpande, "The Indian Army since Independence: Its Military Character," *Combat* [published by the Indian Army College of Combat at Mhow] (Decem-

cation of Indian army units is not officially available.[3] The army even forbids units competing against each other in sporting events from posting their unit designations on the scoreboards for fear of giving away state secrets.[4] In particular, information about the subcaste, "ethnic," or religious composition of the Indian military has been kept secret by the government. As one Indian analyst noted, "Despite its invaluable use as a guide to the attitudes and behavior of the officer corps, the particular corporate character of the Indian Army, especially in terms of its officers' specific ethnic or religious origins, has always been unavailable due to government security considerations."[5] Nonetheless, in a democratic society in which individuals have even circumscribed rights to publish and, more important, in which concerns about the internal well-being of the military are discussed in the pages of military journals, information about the composition of the military does become available to outside observers.

After information about the composition of the Indian military has been presented and discussed, we can consider whether the internal character of the Indian military, however it may or may not have been affected by social structures, has had any effect on the military performance of the Indian military in war. Once again, collecting information about this subject is far from simple because of the decision of the Indian government to withhold information commonly available in other democratic societies. To give only the most striking example, as of 1995 there were no official histories of any of India's major wars since independence.[6] Perhaps there will never be official histories of these wars based on official documents. D. K. Palit, a retired senior Indian military officer

---

ber 1980): 24–33. *Combat* and *Infantry Journal* use volume numbers intermittently and inconsistently, so generally only dates are noted.

[3]See Ravi Rikhye, "A New Armoured Force for India," *United Service Institution of India Journal* [henceforth *USII Journal*] no. 431 (April–June 1973): 137–145, in which was stated that "because of security, the author has been unable to obtain exact figures" about the number of tanks assigned to an Indian armored division; Lorne J. Kavic, *India's Quest for Security: Defence Policies, 1947–1965* (Berkeley: University of California Press, 1967), whose table of contents noted that maps giving the approximate location of Indian units stationed in India had to be withdrawn from the Indian editions of this book.

[4]Brigadier N. B. Grant (ret.), "The Eleventh Command—Thou Shalt Not Disclose," *USII Journal* no. 464 (April–June 1981): 178–183.

[5]Apurba Kundu, "The Indian Army's Continued Overdependence on 'Martial Races' Officers," in *Indian Defence Review*, ed. Matthew Thomas (New Delhi: Lancer, July 1991), pp. 69–84.

[6]Lt. Gen. Mohan Thapan, "India's Defence: Mid-1991," *Army Quarterly and Defence Journal* 121 [formerly *Journal of the Royal United Services Institution*] (Gulf War issue, 1991): 218–220: "The sad reality is that, to date, no official history has been published of the four wars in which the Indian Army has been engaged since 1947; or of the counterinsurgency operations it has undertaken."

who served on the army general staff during the 1962 war against China has written that he was approached by the official historian of the Indian Ministry of Defence, who asked for the help of the retired officer in reconstructing the operational history of that war. His help was necessary, the historian noted, because most Indian General Staff records for that period had been destroyed.[7] Until recently, only hagiographic and journalistic accounts of India's wars have been available. In the *Infantry Journal*, a professional journal published by the Infantry School at Mhow in India, there were only two brief articles critically reviewing the combat performance of the army in the 1965 war, none about the 1962 war, and one reviewing the 1971 war.[8] There are similar lacunae in the more specialized professional military journal *Combat* and the more general *United Service Institution of India Journal*. During the 1980s, however, military histories began to appear. These were written by senior officers who participated in the wars of 1962, 1965, and 1971, based on their campaign or operations diaries that they had taken with them after they retired. These accounts now provide scholars with something approaching objective historical records.[9] Although such histories may be incomplete and partisan, they are much more detailed and self-critical than anything that was available when Stephen Cohen published his pathbreaking book on the Indian Army in 1970.[10]

In the pages that follow, attention will be directed almost exclusively toward the Indian Army. The navy and air force are important and growing components of the Indian military and have internal arrangements and relations with Indian society that differ from those associated with the army. But they have yet to play a significant role in war, and they impinge only marginally on the relation between Indian society and its armed forces. One indication of the magnitude of the role played by the

[7] D. K. Palit, *War in High Himalaya: The Indian Army in Crisis in 1962* (New Delhi: Lancer, 1991), p. vii. Palit was the Director of Military Operations reporting to the Chief of the General Staff of the Indian Army during the 1962 war.

[8] Maj. Gen. D. K. Palit, "The Two Elements of Tactics," *Infantry Journal* [published by the Indian Army Infantry School at Mhow] (April 1966): 9–12; Brigadier Sheodan Singh, "Destruction of Enemy Armour," *Infantry Journal* (April 1966): 13–15; Brigadier A. K. Mehta, "Operation Nutcracker—The Battle of Akhura," *Infantry Journal* (March 1983): 63–68.

[9] Palit, *War in High Himalaya*; Harbakhsh Singh, *War Dispatches: The Indo-Pak Conflict 1965* (New Delhi: Lancer, 1991), p. 1. Harbakhsh Singh was general officer commanding in chief, Headquarters, Western Command, during the 1965 war; Sukhwant Singh, *The Liberation of Bangladesh* (New Delhi: Vikas, 1980), p. 1. Sukhwant Singh was the Deputy Director of Military Operations in the 1971 war.

[10] Stephen P. Cohen, *The Indian Army: Its Contribution to the Development of a Nation*, 2d ed., (New Delhi: Oxford University Press, 1990). The bibliographical essay added to the 1990 edition is invaluable, but it also appeared before the books by Palit and Harbakhsh Singh had been published.

navy and air force is provided by their casualty figures. The army has taken some forty thousand casualties in India's wars since independence. The navy and air force together have taken 625. This is only 1.5 percent of the Army's casualties, and far less than the seventy-three hundred casualties experienced by those two services in peacetime training and preparations.[11]

INDIAN SOCIETY AND INSTITUTIONS AFTER INDEPENDENCE

What do we know of the ways in which the structures of Indian society have affected other institutions in India that were inherited from the British? Studies of such organizations can provide some indication of how the Indian Army might have been affected by Indian society after independence. A number of works have addressed this subject. One of the first and most gloomy is the essay by Edward Shils on Indian intellectuals after independence. In that famous work, Shils argued, on the basis of approximately five hundred interviews in India, that Indian intellectuals, among whom he included the military leadership, have "so far not succeeded in finding a wholly hospitable soil in India" and were not yet capable of generating self-sustaining intellectual traditions that supported original research and critical analysis. He quoted one noted Indian scientist who, when told that Shils was studying the growth and transmission of a scientific tradition in India, replied: "Sir, your inquiry is an easy one and has been completed. There is no scientific tradition in India!" Shils stated that he repeatedly observed Indian scientists who studied abroad, displayed a great capacity for research, but who on their return to India would "fade away" in terms of their original research. The causes of this alleged phenomenon were several, in Shils' view, and institutional and social factors were intertwined. For example, the stimulus to do original research did not exist in India because "the national impersonal institutions for the exercise of severe standards of judgment do not yet exist . . . [and] cannot come into operation if they are not supported by face-to-face relationships."[12]

As he expanded his argument, Shils gave greater weight to the impact of social structures and beliefs. The extended family and traditional Hindu practices, which Shils found prevalent among even those intellectuals who had claimed to have rejected them, reduced the psy-

[11] Lt. Gen. M. L. Chibber (ret.), "Introduction of National Service in India for Defence and Development," in *Indian Defence Review*, ed. Matthew Thomas (New Delhi: Lancer, January 1986), pp. 35–44, Table 3.

[12] Edward Shils, *The Intellectual between Tradition and Modernity: The Indian Situation* (The Hague: Mouton, 1961), pp. 48, 50.

chological salience of the individual and the desire to strive for individual achievement. The survival of the caste system, "not just in its ... prohibitions but in its more profound penetration into the fundamental categories of sociality—cuts human beings off from each other," affecting not only the realm of intellectual discourse but behavior in bureaucratic settings. The one group of Indians among whom Shils claimed to have found the most deeply seated commitment to serious intellectual endeavors and the most productive and critical activity was the Indian Administrative Service (IAS), the successors to the British Imperial Civil Service. He did not find these men to be concerned about their possible psychological separation and alienation from Indian society (he quoted one as saying, "I don't feel out of touch with the people, they might feel out of touch with me but that is their concern, not mine"). But he did report considerable hostility among Indian politicians and intellectuals toward members of the IAS, who were characterized as "brown Englishmen." Many other Indian intellectuals, Shils found, were not so self-assured and commonly wondered to themselves and to Shils if it was legitimate for them to do their work in English and participate in a broader, English-speaking culture.[13]

On the basis of his survey, Shils made some rather broad claims about the impact of Indian social structures on Indian institutions after independence. Caste, he argued, remained a powerful force that permeated institutions, including the primarily intellectual institutions. The divisive effects of caste narrowed the social and intellectual horizons of Indian intellectuals in ways that made it difficult to sustain the activity of institutions created by the British. To the extent that Indian intellectuals associated themselves with a more universal culture of intellectuals, they were perceived as alienated from Indian society and, indeed, often saw themselves to be so alienated.

Are these findings supported by studies of other Indian institutions? The Congress Party, the political organization which helped to bring independence to India and which has governed India for the bulk of its postindependence political life, is one Indian institution that has been intensively studied to see whether and to what extent it has been affected by caste structures. As we saw in Chapter 2, there has been a scholarly debate about whether and the extent to which the internal structures of the Congress Party after independence mirrored the caste structures of the larger Indian society in which it resided. After reviewing this debate between Susan Rudolph and Lloyd Rudolph, on one hand, and Myron Weiner, on the other, Francine Frankel found that

---

[13] Ibid., pp. 12–13, 24, 62–64, 67, 69–70, 92–93. The quote concerning the survival of the caste system is on p. 70, quotes concerning the IAS are on pp. 67 and 93.

the weight of evidence clearly did not support the proposition that Western political ideas had transformed or eliminated caste structures. Turning then to Weiner's book, Frankel found considerable evidence that the internal structure of the Congress Party did reflect the ambient caste structures. In *Party Building in a New Nation,* which was based on a 1962 survey of five Indian political districts from widely separated regions, Weiner discussed the general pattern of organization displayed by the Congress Party: "In its efforts to win, Congress adapts itself to the local power structures. It recruits from among those who have local power and influence. It trains its cadres to perform political roles similar to those performed in the traditional society before there was party politics. . . . It utilizes traditional methods of dispute settlement to maintain cohesion within the party." As of 1962, Frankel wrote, modern party organization was the tool of the prosperous landholding castes to maintain or improve their social position. Although there were multicaste alliances, these alliances served interests defined by caste. Loyalty of the socially dominant landholders to the Congress Party was maintained by patronage, not through ideology, and was weak; faction fights were bitter, and alliances, short-lived. Frankel clearly believed that the data available in the early 1960s showed that modern Indian political institutions continued to be shaped in important ways by Indian social structures and norms.[14]

In searching for more recent studies of the impact of caste structures on political organizations in India, we saw in Chapter 2 how Atul Kohli established a correlation between the strength of caste practices across a range of Indian states, and the stability and effectiveness of state governments.[15] But bureaucracies in general—and military bureaucracies in particular—may be more isolated than mass political movements from prevailing social structures. Men and women often join a bureaucracy for life and conceivably could be recruited, trained, and rewarded in ways that lead them to adopt norms quite different from those of the larger society. Indian bureaucracies were and are to some degree meritocratic. In 1954, only 4.16 percent of those taking the examination for entry into the Indian senior civil service qualified, and the civil service was perceived by Indian academics as being more open to talent than were Indian private sector businesses.[16] In practice, however, Indian

---

[14] Francine Frankel, "Indian Political Development," *World Politics* 21 (April 1969): 448–468. I quote Myron Weiner, *Party Building in a New Nation,* as cited in Frankel's article.

[15] Atul Kohli, *Democracy and Discontent: India's Growing Crisis of Governability* (New York: Cambridge University Press, 1990), pp. 15–18, 184–188, 269, 271.

[16] V. M. Sinha, *The Superior Civil Services in India: A Study in Administrative Development, 1947–1957* (Jaipur, India: Institute for Research and Advanced Studies, 1985), p. 77: Private sector jobs were "a closed preserve for the friends and relatives of the managing

scholars have found that the dominant castes had controlled Indian government bureaucracies to suit their own interests, much as the Congress Party had been. Conducted in 1963–1965, a study of the Bihar Secretariat, headquarters of the Bihar state government, found that 83 percent of those interviewed belonged to upper-caste groups, with only 13 percent coming from Backward classes and 4 percent from Scheduled Castes or Tribes, who were given jobs by constitutional mandate. This caste dominance was not receding over time. Higher-caste representation in a newly created department of the secretariat was 90 percent. Bureaucratic institutions modeled on Western bureaucracies were transformed by pressures originating from the social structures of the host society. In the words of G. K. Prasad, author of the study:

> In a society characterised by caste, joint family and kinship, the bureaucratic model fails to attain the required degree of hierarchy and impersonality and thus the model in practice is more dysfunctional than functional.
> . . . The joint family of Indian society binds all its members in economic and kinship ties which are governed by a culturally determined norm with its set of obligations and expectations. The process of fulfilling these obligations and expectations fosters and perpetuates a sense of belonging and loyalty which is further strengthened by caste structure. . . . Intrusion of caste, communal and kinship consideration has become such a common phenomenon that even if these considerations may not influence a particular decision, suspicion remains.[17]

Other studies of large Indian state bureaucracies came to similar conclusions. One survey of 236 workers in a government shipyard and of 58 employees of government agencies found clusters of subcaste members within organizations—Anglo-Indians (people of mixed British and Indian ancestry) and Christians in railway and port jobs, untouchables working as janitors in hospitals, Brahmins in clerical cadres in banks and schools. "An important reason for the perpetuation of such ethnic [sic] clustering was the preference given to relatives of employees, even after independence, in these organizations." Until 1970, for example, it was the formal policy of the State Bank of India to give preference when hiring to family members of existing employees. Interviews confirmed that personal kinship links brought at least 65 percent of the port workers their jobs. Workers who came from the

---

agents and directors." See pp. 292–293 on rapid promotion and mobility offered by the civil service in this period, with the departure of British and Muslim civil servants.

[17] G. K. Prasad, *Bureaucracy in India: A Sociological Study* (New Delhi: Stirling, 1974), pp. 16, 115.

lower-status Scheduled Castes and Tribes reported that despite their qualifications for higher-skilled jobs and the nominal policy of reserving some jobs for them, they were given lower-skilled jobs and passed over for promotion. Members of higher-status castes complained about the privileges they believed were given to the Scheduled Castes and Tribes.[18]

The Indian police might be expected to be most like the military with regard to an emphasis on high levels of internal discipline and resistance to social pressures not consistent with its professional responsibilities. After independence, the police retained the forms and structures they inherited from the British. Centrally organized and trained as one national bureaucracy, with operational control devolved to the states of India, the bulk of the Indian police are controlled by the states of India. Beginning in the 1970s, this police force became increasingly affected by forces operating in Indian society. Specifically, it became politicized. Many Indian police officers carried out and supported the emergency measures enacted by Indira Gandhi and the Congress Party. When the opposition Janata Party won an electoral victory that ended Indira Gandhi's emergency rule, it censured many of these police. When the Congress Party regained power, the investigation of these officers was halted, and censured officers were rehabilitated, reinforcing their ties to the Congress Party. At the local level, local politicians "sat in police stations in order to serve as a buffer between their supporters and the police." Police station chiefs were courted by politicians. In the face of these challenges to their professional autonomy, the elite of the Indian police, the Indian Police Service (IPS) officers, might have protested. In the words of David Bayley, an American academic observer, "One might have thought that the IPS, with its proud tradition of national service, might draw together as a group to resist improper demands from the political realm and to defend officers who take a stand on principle. This has rarely happened, and certainly not consistently." Within the police force, the hierarchical nature of Indian social structures are replicated. Officers are stratified, with one class of senior officers and three levels of lower officers, with very little promotion from one level up to another. Violent job actions by the lower levels have increased in severity over time.[19] Unlike police forces in Europe or Japan, this stratification creates problems of internal control for the senior police officers: "The chasm socially between officers

[18]C. V. Raghavulu, *Organizational Conflict in Indian Government Organizations* (Delhi: Academic Publications, 1984), pp. 14, 45–51.

[19]David H. Bayley, "The Police and Political Order in India," *Asian Survey* 23 (April 1983): 484–496.

and rank-and-file is so great, trust so uninstinctive, that effective super-vision is severely compromised."[20]

In addition to the police, there are the armed paramilitary forces of India, including the Central Reserve Police (CRP), the Border Security Forces (BSF), the Central Industrial Security Force (CISF), and various local constabularies such as the Assam Rifles. They, too, have been in-fluenced by Indian social tensions. The numbers of soldiers in these forces are not published by the Indian government, but their estimated size has been increasing since the 1970s, as has their political role. Dur-ing the Emergency, the paramilitary forces controlled by New Delhi may have reached a level of over 500,000 men, and their combined strength was between 242,000 and 300,000 in the early 1980s. State-controlled constabularies grew by about 50 percent in the period 1969–1981. The use of these forces in political roles to suppress opposition political activity peaked during the period of the Emergency, when "they served as effective instruments of coercion without much regard to the liberal-democratic values which had been enshrined in the con-stitution by India's founding fathers." However, this practice began at least as early as 1970, when the paramilitary forces were used against political groups in West Bengal, and has continued after the Emer-gency.[21]

A pattern can be identified without too much difficulty. Political in-stitutions, both those inherited from the British and those created to resist British rule, have been subject in India after independence to influences from the ambient social structures. Institutional norms that initially ran counter to those of the host society, as in the case of the police and meritocratic civil service recruiting practices, were gradually bent to re-flect Indian social structures. What were the consequences? Indian bu-reaucracies after independence were not necessarily demographically representative of Indian society, given that certain clusters of communal groups came to dominate portions of bureaucracies in ways that did not reflect their numerical strength in Indian society as a whole. The com-position of nonmilitary bureaucracies did reflect the prevailing distri-bution of power and influence in society as was embodied in the social structures associated with caste. Indian nonmilitary bureaucracies did not, on the whole, appear to have based themselves on a set of norms and social practices radically different from those of the host society. In

---

[20] David H. Bayley, *Patterns of Policing: A Comparative International Analysis* (New Bruns-wick, N.J.: Rutgers University Press, 1985), pp. 174–175, 185.

[21] "Joe," "Paramilitary Forces—At What Cost?" *USII Journal* 466 (October–December 1981): 359–362; quotation regarding political uses of police from K. P. Misra, "Paramilitary Forces in India," *Armed Forces and Society* 6 (Spring 1980): 371–388, quote from p. 379.

that sense, they have not divorced themselves from Indian society but have been shaped in their internal organization by Indian social structures.

What has been the relationship of the Indian Army to Indian society since independence? Has it been influenced by Indian social structures as were the bureaucracies reviewed above, or has the special nature of the army allowed it to separate itself in varying ways from society? The answers to these questions are quite complicated, but to summarize the evidence quickly, the army has been separated from society in a number of ways to help it perform its military missions in the face of growing tensions in Indian society. The rank-and-file soldiers in the Indian infantry are not demographically representative of India as a whole and do contain deliberately constructed clusters of subcastes. The Indian officer corps is also recruited selectively, is not representative of the Indian population, and does display both the alienation and inability to sustain independent intellectual activity that Shils observed in Indian intellectuals more generally. The combination of the patterns of recruitment, training, and deployment in rank-and-file soldiers and in the officer corps, taken together, creates an army that is characterized by many small, inward-looking military communities, one which is not responsive to changes in the external environment and which is viewed with suspicion by the civilian leadership.

In what ways is the Indian Army isolated from society? Some of the most obvious physical indicators suggest that the army, the infantry in particular, has been kept separate from society. Officers describing typical tours of duty comment that they are routinely deployed in peacetime to army stations in the hills "for years with short breaks." The normal tour in a high-altitude station is said to be four years, followed by two years of duty at a peace station, during which the officer is on field exercises one hundred miles from his family perhaps half the time. On the whole, "half to two-thirds of his total service is in field areas." The result of this physical isolation is claimed to be psychological isolation. In the words of army officer K. P. Singh: "Despite thirty-one years of independence we are still reluctant to release ourselves from psychological subjection to the old British colonial way of life. Officers who served under the British are serious when they say our army is more British today than it used to be. The most unfortunate result has been an increased isolation of the army from the rest of national life."[22] Another retired officer noted that he spent twenty of thirty-two years in the army in operational areas away from his family, a separation from society that he thought beneficial to the army.[23] Yet another noted that as of the late 1970s, Indian troops were still deployed on the cease-fire lines with Pakistan where they were left at the end of the 1947–1948 war, which "tied down two-thirds of the Indian field force to holding the dominating heights in penny packets and this commitment continues to this day."[24]

Are these impressions of the Indian Army accurate? It is not uncommon for officers of any army to emphasize, favorably or unfavorably, the harshness of military life in the boondocks and the lack of understanding between themselves and their civilian counterparts. Is there systematic evidence that would help us better understand the relationship of the army to Indian society?

We may begin again with the simplest data about enlisted soldiers. The percentage of Indians in the Indian military in the 1980s was 0.18 percent, one-tenth the fraction in China and one-seventh of the figure in the United States. The rank-and-file soldiers are volunteers and are said by retired senior officers to come from the lower socioeconomic strata of society. Until 1977, soldiers enlisted for seven years, plus eight years in the reserves. After 1977, soldiers enlisted for a term of seventeen years.[25] Brigadier General N. K. Mayne, who was then serving in the Army and who had served in the Military Training Directorate, noted in 1984 the practices used to select recruits from among those who volunteered. Selection was based on a physical exam of the volunteer, stated Mayne. "And his pedigree [that is, his subcaste] determines the regiment he will belong to. Only a certain proportion of the recruits need to be literate. And that is all. There is no intelligence test, no aptitude test, no other test. Even a *Chowkidar* [watchman] is selected with better care."[26] Subsequently, intelligence testing was introduced to screen recruits, largely because of the massive oversubscription of vacancies in the infantry.[27]

Once in the army, the recruit goes through a period of basic training more lengthy than in Western armies, in large part because of the need

[22] Maj. K. P. Singh, "The Declining Popularity of the Infantry," *Infantry Journal* (September 1980): 16–28.
[23] Maj. Gen. O. S. Kalkat, "Art of Command," *Infantry Journal* (March 1978): 1–5.
[24] Maj. Gen. Sukhwant Singh, *India's Wars since Independence*, vol. 3, *General Trends* (Delhi: Vikas, 1982), pp. 5, 57.
[25] Chibber, "National Service in India."
[26] Brigadier N. K. Mayne, "Selection and Training of Infantry Soldiers," *Infantry Journal* (September 1984): 23–29.
[27] Interview by author with Indian Army officer formerly with the Military Education Corps, New Delhi, November 1992.

to bring the recruit up to some minimum standards of health and education. In the early 1980s, army Basic Training was extended from thirty-six to fifty-two weeks,, to include a sixteen-week Pre-Basic training that aimed "at enabling the recruit to qualify for up to third class certificate of education and map reading." Basic literacy and physical conditioning requirements also had to be met before the army could "introduce the recruit to soldiering."[28] Much of the need for Pre-Basic training was related to literacy. Before the 1970s, recruits would admit that they were illiterate and attend literacy classes in the army. After that time, many recruits came into the army with the equivalent of American high school diplomas. Half of those with diplomas were still illiterate, but they had their certificates and objected to being singled out for remedial training. To solve this problem, all recruits were put through Pre-Basic training.[29]

After Basic Training, soldiers were given additional training. In the 1950s, this training appears to have been composed primarily of close-order drill, and officers complained about this emphasis, noting that it led soldiers to place pebbles in the magazines of their rifles, which ruined the rifles but which produced a fine sound when the butt of the rifle was smashed to the ground in drill.[30] Army officers commenting on peacetime training of the troops thirty years later found little had changed. Lt. Col. S. S. Chandel wrote in 1980 that "the chief limitation in the training of infantry is an . . . undue emphasis on . . . things like cleanliness and neatness of the lines, demonstrations staged to score more for the purpose of showmanship than instructional value, extraordinary emphasis on games and competitions [that] consume such a disproportionate amount of time . . . that precious time is wasted." Soldiers spent thirty-five to forty-two days in individual training per year, and thirty days in field training with their units, training that was characterized by Brig. Gen. Gurdial Singh as nothing more than map exercises staged in the open air: "The training value of these exercises for the troops which close in with the enemy is insignificant. The system is not conducive to mutual understanding between the troops which would be operating together in battle." In particular, there was little training that would help soldiers in dissimilar units (for example, infantry and armor) understand how to

---

[28] Brigadier J. M. Singh, "A Fresh Look at Infantry Training," *Infantry Journal* (March 1982): 11–17.

[29] Interview by author with Indian Army officer formerly with the Military Education Corps, New Delhi, November 1992. On the role of the Education Corps in increasing literacy in the army, see Maj. Prakash Menon, "Military Role—Nation Building," *Combat* (April 1985): 6.

[30] Maj. J. Nazereth, "What Is the Importance of Drill in Training?" *USII Journal* 85 (July–September 1955): 241.

fight together in war.[31] Brigadier Mayne summed up the situation as he saw it in 1983 by writing, "Anyone who has spent some time in an infantry battalion will have noticed the soul-killing routine of training . . . the same lessons repeated ad nauseam from the day of their recruitment till their retirement."[32]

Although unfortunate, why should this be of interest to anyone other than students of military training practices? Step back and look at the treatment of recruits. The Indian Army takes a tiny, self-selected portion of the Indian population, puts it through a lengthy basic training that gradually teaches the recruits narrow military skills and habits of soldiering, and then keeps the soldiers occupied with routine tasks and mechanical drill with other soldiers in their unit for seventeen years, much of it in isolated army bases and stations. It is difficult to imagine a set of practices better suited to developing and maintaining in the recruits a mental separation from Indian society as well as a narrow concentration on day-to-day tasks. Indeed, the soldier is placed in an environment in which it is difficult for the soldier to empathize with army units other than his own, let alone with the army as a whole or with civilian society.

The narrowness of outlook of the rank-and-file soldier in the Indian Army is reinforced by what is perhaps its most distinctive feature: its segregation of soldiers in units by what is called class and what appears in fact to be subcaste, a practice retained from when the Indian army was under British rule. The Indian Army is organized essentially by regiments and battalions, which may be single-class, fixed-class, mixed-class or all-class. Infantry regiments identified by subcaste and kept from British times, such as the Sikh, Jat, Rajput, and Dogra regiments, continued after independence to recruit men into their battalions on the basis of caste and are single-class units. New infantry battalions created after independence were also, in the majority, created as single-class units. Fixed-class units may have more than one subcaste in them, but soldiers from different subcastes are kept segregated in smaller units within the battalion. Thus, a fixed-class battalion may include soldiers from different castes, but they are segregated at the company level. Mixed-class units are heterogeneous by subcaste, but all soldiers originate from one region in India, which reduces their effective heterogeneity. Only a few units in the infantry, such as the Brigade of Guards—formed after independence—the paratroop brigades, and the armor and artillery

---

[31] Lt. Col. S. S. Chandel, "Organizing Company Training," *Infantry Journal* (September 1980): 74–84; Brig. Gen. Gurdial Singh, "Combined Arms Concept and Training," *USII Journal* 113 (April–June 1983): 234.

[32] Mayne, "Selection and Training of Infantry Soldiers."

branches are all-class units, taking their recruits without regard to class or caste. The overall practice results in some striking anomalies. Sikhs compose 2 percent of India's population but have their own battalions, which compose 11 percent of the army, whereas no Bengali battalions or regiments exist, though there are some Bengali companies.[33]

This practice has generated intense debate within the military but has been changed very little from the time of independence. Efforts in 1947 and 1984 failed to abolish the single-class infantry units and to open recruitment into the army to all Indians without regard to subcaste, efforts that in both cases were blocked by senior Indian Army officers.[34] This practice carries along with it a quota system for promoting soldiers on the basis of their seniority and their communal identity. Captain Rajinder Singh wrote that "each regiment in the infantry is based on a region/caste. Even the infantry battalions have a set ratio for various groups of people. The promotion ratios are fixed class-wise notwithstanding the competency of individuals." Originally introduced to safeguard the promotions of Backward Castes, "this sordid practice has led to a deteriorating standard of NCOs [noncommissioned officers, such as sergeants] . . . in infantry battalions . . . [and] tends to retard the combat potential of our present day army. In such a system, there is no interplay of men from one regiment to another because of regional and caste barriers. Thus the 'very best' sometimes have to be 'discarded' for want of appropriate vacancies." Particularly ironic given the problem in the army with literacy, noted Brigadier V. K. Pasricha, was that the subcaste quota system limited the number of soldiers that could be taken from high-literacy areas of India, such as West Bengal and Kerala.[35] The quota system is alleged to affect the giving of military honors and awards. "India being a land of diverse communities and religions does put a strain on government during war. The minorities have to be shown that their contribution and sacrifice is being properly appreciated. . . . The practice [however] . . . becomes blatantly obvious and defeats its own

[33]Lt. Gen. S. K. Sinha, "Class Composition of the Army," in *Indian Defence Review*, ed. Matthew Thomas (New Delhi: Lancer, July 1986), pp. 82–83.

[34]Palit, *War in High Himalaya*, p. 12; Cohen, *Indian Army*, p. 211 n. 16.

[35]Capt. Rajindar Singh, "Restructuring Class Composition Infantry Battalions," *Infantry Journal* (March 1982): 43–48. On the regional imbalance in recruiting caused by this system see also Lt. Col. Sirdehpande, "Towards a National Army," *USII Journal* 104 (January–March 1974): 51 ff. on the overrepresentation in the army of soldiers from the Punjab, Haryana, Himachal Pradesh, Maharashtra, Rajasthan, and western and northern Uttar Pradesh and the underrepresentation of soldiers from Gujarat, Karnataka (Mysore), Orissa, Bengal, and Madhya Pradesh, from which recruitment is said to be "negligible." On the quota/seniority system for promoting soldiers to noncommissioned officer rank and its effects, such as the promotion of illiterates, see Brigadier V. K. Pasricha, "Hierarchical Contributions to Weakness in Our JCOs and NCOs," *Combat* (May 1980): 29–37.

purpose. Even a deserving winner is observed suspiciously. The respect for the award is reduced."[36]

Defenders of the system argue to varying degrees that Indian soldiers from different castes cannot be expected to fight well alongside one another. One officer rejected the idea of reform in 1973 on the grounds that "we have to accept the fact that lingual, racial, and regional considerations continue to be a bigger binding force than the far cry of nationalism which is beyond the comprehension of a simple, rustic villager who is our soldier."[37] Another argued that while the system was an anachronism from British times, there was no need to change it.[38] Still another acknowledged that "the present system encourages provincialism and regionalism at the expense of nationalism and secularism," but it has functioned well enough in war, because "it is well known that the simple soldier of rural background, even today, derives most of his motivation from his caste, community, religion, and the tradition of his unit." It is argued that the alternative to single- or fixed-class units would be more divisive for the army and India. If men from different regions and castes were in the same unit and competed for promotion on the basis of merit, there would be different levels of achievement among the groups because men from different groups would have different levels of education before they entered the army. For example, individuals from Kerala tended to be more literate than the average Indian and would therefore do better in a meritocratic army. "In a mixed group unit, due to this variation, it [sic] will result in unhealthy and uneven competition, besides making promotion system difficult [sic]."[39]

It is, in principle, possible to seek data to see whether the assumptions underlying the opposition to or support for the single-class army unit are valid. Soldiers could be asked if they fought well because of national patriotism, because of loyalty to the fellow caste members with whom they served, or because of other factors. Although such surveys may not provide completely accurate insights into the motivation of soldiers in combat, they do provide some indication of the sentiment of soldiers and have been used, for example, to show that American soldiers in World War II fought primarily "to get the job done" and end the task (39 percent); and to support the fellow members of their combat unit, their

[36] Maj. Randhir Singh, "Our Honor and Awards," *Infantry Journal* (September 1980): 29–36.

[37] Lt. Col. Bakshi, "Should We Do Away with Class Based Units in the Infantry?" *Infantry Journal* (October 1973): 62–69.

[38] Maj. B. S. Siohi, "Regimental Traditions and the National Cause," *Infantry Journal* (October 1975).

[39] Lt. Col. D. K. Madan, "Reorganizing Infantry Battalions," *Infantry Journal* (March 1982): 39–42.

"buddies" (15 percent); and less so for conventional forms of patriotism (5 percent).[40] The only such publicly available survey of the soldiers in the Indian Army was published in somewhat different forms in *Infantry Journal* and in *Combat* in August 1988. The author of the survey interpreted the results in the most favorable light in print, saying that the survey showed that "ours is a ticking, kicking, alert army with remarkable endurance and potential for endurance and self-reliance."[41] The survey polled soldiers, noncommissioned officers, and officers from twenty-three infantry, two rural constabulary-type units (Ladakh Scouts, Assam Rifles), and seventeen combat support or support units, for a total of forty-two units, which had served on the border with China in the Northeast Frontier Province and in Ladakh, in deserts, and in other field areas. Because twenty-five of the forty-two units polled were infantry or regional units, the sample includes many soldiers who served in single-, fixed-, or mixed-class units, whereas the other seventeen units are presumably all-class units. The survey results, however, are not broken down by unit or unit type but simply presented in the aggregate. There are some anomalies in the study. The soldiers were asked twenty questions, but it is not stated whether multiple responses were permitted. The number of answers given by soldiers added up to exactly 807 for sixteen of the questions, but in the case of the four questions most closely related to the motivation of soldiers in combat, the total number of answers was much less, 357. No explanation of this was provided. One question that asked what would make a soldier fight better drew 807 responses, so it is not clear that only combat units were asked combat-related questions.

With regard to the motivation of soldiers in dangerous situations, the survey asked, "What makes you face extreme danger resolutely and repeatedly?" Patriotism scored low among the soldiers, with only 80 of 357 replying yes, but higher than any other single response. The fact that the soldier's *sathis* (buddies) and platoon mates were equally in danger scored 73 out of 357, the soldier's *izzat* (honor/self-respect based on subcaste definitions of duty) scored 52, unit reputation scored 60, the teaching and tradition of the soldier scored 62, and leadership of the commander scored 30. None of the forty-two officers surveyed with fifteen years or more of service indicated that patriotism or leadership was a factor, with responses about evenly distributed among the other four responses. When the same question was asked in slightly different form

---

[40] Samuel A. Stouffer et al., *The American Soldier: Combat and Its Aftermath*, vol. 2 (Princeton: Princeton University Press, 1949), table 1, "Combat Incentives Named by Enlisted Infantrymen," p. 109.

[41] Maj. Gen. S. C. Sardeshpande, "Psychological and Motivational Factors Affecting Soldiers," *Combat* (August 1988): 17–28.

("What makes you brave and inspires you to sacrifice?"), patriotism again scored low (62 out of 357) while other responses included duty (72), the presence of buddies and fellow soldiers in the platoon and company (70), leadership (68), teaching and tradition (55), and anger and revenge (30).

These results are ambiguous. While patriotism scored low as a factor motivating Indian soldiers in combat, it also scored low in the American army in World War II. Loyalty to a soldier's buddies in the platoon and company or loyalty to the unit is not necessarily the same as loyalty to the soldier's subcaste or regional group, but in the Indian Army, because infantry units—particularly at the small-unit level, that is, platoon and company—are overwhelmingly homogenous by subcaste, loyalty to buddies, unit, and caste are all combined. Responses to the question, "What will make you fight better?" were similarly ambiguous, with "good and brave sathis " (283 of 807), "hard training and tough life of a soldier" (218), and "good commanders and understanding but tough leaders" (137) scoring highest and pay and entertainment-related factors scoring lowest (83 and 86). The one question that made explicit reference to caste was "What motivates you best?" Here religion and caste received 71 out of 807, while the unit's "reputation, deeds and achievements" received 312, with leaders (153), pay and promotion (115), and izzat (156) scoring lower.[42]

What may fairly be concluded from this evidence? The Indians who debate the merits and demerits of the single-class infantry units are most concerned with the question of whether the old system is necessary to sustain combat performance. The evidence is mixed. It must be remembered that the artillery, armor, paratroops, engineers, signal corps, and some infantry units, not to mention the air force and navy, are and have been mixed and have performed without notable failure in war, whereas some single-class units have had poor performance in war, as will be reviewed below. On the other hand, it is understandable if the Indian Army declined to reform itself radically to remove the single-class infantry unit as the result of one survey that suggested that military loyalties to units and buddies may be related to common communal affiliations— but may not.

The question central to this book, however, is whether the single-class infantry unit serves to increase the isolation of the soldier from the influences of Indian society. Here, the evidence and trends are more clear. There are two phenomena at work. The single-class unit, combined with the length of "time with the colors," habitual small-unit training, and

---

[42] Maj. Gen. S. C. Sardeshpande, "Psychological and Motivational Factors Affecting Soldiers," *Infantry Journal* (August 1988): 24–30, responses to questions 11, 12, 14, 20.

remote deployments, tends to generate intense loyalty to the small military units, which simultaneously restricts the horizons of the soldier to the very narrow sphere of men in his platoon, company, and perhaps battalion who speak his language and share his dietary habits and ways of life. The increase in the term of enlistment from seven to seventeen years and the raising of new single-class units demonstrates that the trend is toward practices that reinforce this attachment to the small unit. The isolation and promotion of men by communal affiliation in the army is clearly reflective of perceived social realities imported from the larger society. Like the Indian society, the Indian infantry is heterogeneous and divided into compartments. In that sense, the Indian Army infantry may be said to reflect Indian social structures. But the effect is to create hundreds of small cohesive communities in the infantry that have relatively little to do with each other and even less to do with the society from which they come. In that sense, the Indian rank-and-file soldier is clearly isolated from Indian society as a whole.

This military structure of small, insular units will tend to produce an army that can be expected to be cohesive at the platoon and company level, less so at the battalion level, and even less at higher levels of organization. Such an army will tend to have difficulty carrying out military operations that require cooperation of units above the battalion level, such as a combined arms war involving rapidly moving battles and infantry, armor, signals, and artillery units. Even infantry units will have difficulty working together when heterogeneous infantry units are hastily assembled in war. The second phenomenon will tend to produce an army that is isolated from tensions and influences from the larger Indian society. In particular, the political influences and tensions that have affected the rank-and-file Indian police officer will be less powerful in affecting the Indian soldier because of relation to unit and the isolation of that unit from society.

THE TREATMENT OF SUBGROUPS IN OTHER MULTIETHNIC ARMIES

Are there other caste-based or at least multinational, multilingual states with which we can compare India? If so, how do they handle the problem of recruitment and military organization? In the case of Pakistan, systematic, quantitative information about the composition of the military is less available than it is in India. In the words of one scholar, Clive Dewey: "The most basic information on the most elementary matters is completely unavailable. We know next to nothing—to cite an obvious example—about recruitment. . . . There are no data; only vapid generalizations. . . . Historians have a better idea of how the Bengal Infantry operated two hundred years ago."[43]

While difficult, obtaining at least partial information has not been impossible. In the aggregate, despite being Muslim, the dominant social structures of Pakistan do reflect caste divisions. The Pakistani Army after independence retained the British model and organized itself into single-class units. Pakistan is predominantly Punjabi, however, and more ethnically and religiously homogeneous than India. The Pakistani Army is also overwhelmingly Punjabi. The national security demands on Pakistan are large relative to its disposable resources, such that the military takes a larger share of the people and economic resources of Pakistan than is the case in India (1.1 percent of the population in the military versus 0.18 percent for India; the Pakistani military budget has been 45 to 65 percent of the total federal budget in the period 1949–1977 and 7 to 10 percent of GNP in 1971–1985). These aspects of Pakistani society and the relationship of the Pakistani to that society help explain why the army has penetrated and been penetrated by Punjabi society, which also dominates the civilian elite of Pakistan.[44] Despite common origins in the British imperial army and despite social structures that span the Indian-Pakistani border, the Pakistani Army has developed along a different path with regard to its isolation from society.

Immediately after independence, 60 percent of the soldiers in the Pakistani Army were Punjabi Muslims, as were their officers. The bulk of the remaining soldiers came from the Northwest Frontier Province. Only a small number of Bengalis from East Pakistan were organized in two single-class battalions that kept them separate from the rest of the army. The independence of Bangladesh removed these soldiers entirely in 1971. Surveys of former soldiers indicate that by the 1980s, 75 percent of them came from three districts in the Punjab and two districts of the Northwest Frontier Province that contain only 9 percent of the male population of Pakistan. Although the single-class regiments have been gradually eliminated in the Army in favor of integrated units, the highly selective recruitment into the Pakistani Army has maintained high levels of homogeneity in the units. Unlike in the Indian Army, soldiers are not kept separate from society. One estimate is that a soldier spends two hundred days per year away from his military unit, on annual or casual leave, national holiday, or weekends. While away from his unit, the soldier returns to civilian life. The amount of time a soldier spends in formal

[43]Clive Dewey, "The Rural Roots of Pakistani Militarism," in *Political Inheritance of Pakistan*, ed. D. A. Low (London: Macmillan, 1991), pp. 255–283.
[44]S. K. Sinha, "Class Composition of the Army," p. 80; Dewey, "Rural Roots of Pakistani Militarism," table 11.2, p. 258.

military training is therefore small, at most sixty-five days a year, and his contact with civilian life remains active and important. His physical and psychological separation from civilian society is weak. It is not surprising that the soldiers in the Pakistani Army have also come to reflect the interests of the Punjabi civilian social structures from which they have been overwhelmingly drawn, with which they maintain continuous contact.[45] The differences in civil-military relations between India and Pakistan—the penetration of civilian politics by the Pakistani Army and the penetration of the Army by civilian politics, phenomena usually absent in India—are relatively simple to explain, despite the real similarities between the two cases. Starting with similar social structures, the differences between the two countries' armies have to do with variations in their degree of isolation from the host civilian society. This variation explains why the resulting patterns of civil-military relations differ.

In searching for other relevant comparisons, some historical oddities emerge. There was a modern South Asian army that did not adopt the patterns of organization introduced by the British. The soldiers of the Indian National Army (INA), which was created by Subhas Chandra Bose—with help from the Germans and Japanese—from Indian Army POWS captured in North Africa and in Southeast Asia during World War II, were completely integrated in their units. Soldiers from different castes and religions ate in a common mess and served together in units. Some problems related to the ritual cleanliness of animals to be eaten by Sikhs and Muslims were settled by having Germans slaughter the animals. Never well equipped by their Axis patrons, they appear to have fought reasonably well as units, though their battles came at the war's end when the Japanese were not able to keep their own troops supplied, let alone their Indian clients.[46] The INA did inspire much national support from a wide range of Indians, especially when the postwar trial of INA leaders put a Hindu, a Muslim, and a Sikh officer in the dock.[47] But the INA was clearly a unique institution, with some of its soldiers trained by German officers and swearing allegiance to Adolf Hitler, not to mention being bound together in a fight against the British, which INA soldiers had to win or risk execution as traitors. Conclusions about military organizations and their relationship to their host society can not be easily drawn from a comparison between the INA and the Indian Army after independence.

Other Southeast Asian countries also had multiethnic populations but

---

[45] Stephen P. Cohen, *The Pakistani Army* (Karachi: Oxford University Press, 1992), pp. 42–44, 46, 52, 62, 113.

[46] Leonard Gordon, *Brothers against the Raj: A Biography of Indian Nationalists Sarat and Subhas Chandra Bose* (New York: Columbia University Press, 1990), pp. 456–459, 512–517.

[47] B. M. Kaul, *The Untold Story* (Bombay: Allied Publishers, 1967), pp. 72–73.

[218]

did not adopt military personnel practices resembling those of India. The Democratic Republic of Vietnam included men and women of Chinese origin and their own Montagnard population. From POW and émigré testimony we know that soldiers of the People's Army of Vietnam (PAVN) in 1970 received two months of basic training (compared with the twelve months for Indian soldiers) and that ethnic Chinese were formally excluded from conscription, although after 1968 heavy pressure was brought to bear on them to volunteer. Purges of the officer corps in 1976 and 1979 revealed that some senior officers were ethnically Chinese and Montagnard. Although some special units in the late 1950s were composed of troops from South Vietnam who had rallied to the north and had a semiethnic character, there is no indication of any other ethnically organized units in the PAVN.[48]

Outside South Asia, the United States was a clearly multiethnic nation that just as clearly rejected Indian patterns of military organization after World War II. The Soviet Union, also a multinational, multilingual empire, did recruit selectively from its population. After the Bolshevik movement and during the civil wars, when central control from Moscow was weak, the Workers' and Peasants' Army (RKKA, the Russian acronym) maintained ethnically organized military units. In 1923, the RKKA was reorganized into four separate armies: a small cadre army primarily of Russians; a territorially organized militia; national military divisions from larger union republics and autonomous national districts; and, within larger cadre units, ethnic companies, battalions, and regiments recruited from smaller nationalities. But in 1938, "the Soviet Army began dismantling both its territorial militia forces and its national-territorial formations," apparently in preparation for war with Japan or Germany. Even while they existed, the ethnically organized units of the Soviet army, according to 1982 Soviet military publications, were primarily used for training, not combat, functions. Ethnically organized divisions after recruitment were broken down into smaller and smaller units and mixed together with other Slavic units to form multinational divisions. The ethnic units were essentially political concessions meant to demonstrate the political equality of the republics in the USSR. In World War II, ethnic units were re-created in the first two years after the German invasion, as the Slavic manpower of western Russia, Byelorussia, and the Ukraine was lost to German control, forcing the creation of new units dominated

---

[48] Douglas Pike, *PAVN: People's Army of Vietnam* (Novato, Calif.: Presidio, 1986), pp. 157, 281–282 for discussion of basic training and Chinese and Montagnard officers. See David Chanoff and Doan Van Toai, *Portrait of the Enemy: The Other Side of the War in Vietnam Told through Interviews with North Vietnamese, Former Vietcong, and Southern Opposition Leaders* (New York: Random House, 1986), pp. 50–55, on the treatment of ethnic Chinese, and p. 149 on units formed from southerners.

by Kazakhs, Caucasians, and Central Asian troops. But when the Soviet army went on the offensive in 1943 and regained control of Slav-populated areas, the ethnically organized units were flooded with Slavic soldiers, thus their ethnic composition no longer differed from the "cadre" military units. Remaining ethnic units in World War II were used only reluctantly by Moscow outside their own territorial areas. In 1955, at the time of formation of the Warsaw Pact, the ethnic units of the Soviet army were dissolved.[49] After that, non-Slavic Central Asian conscripts into the army were segregated in noncombat transport and construction units. For combat units, the Soviet military used a system of military personnel "buyers." Each military unit would have buyers who were given a quota of conscripts to be taken from each of the many geographically dispersed military commissariats that registered the local men reaching military age. This prevented macroconcentrations of, for example, Estonians in the army, though microconcentrations could appear, since a buyer could go to Estonia and fill the quota for Estonians from one city or even neighborhood. In wartime, however, mobilization would be performed by military districts and conceivably could have produced regionally based, ethnically homogenous units.[50] Unlike modern India, the totalitarian Soviet system enabled the military to ignore the misery of soldiers who were forced to serve with others with whom they could not communicate and under officers who despised them. The Soviet peacetime military, as a result, did not resemble the Indian military.

None of these cases provide an ideal comparison with the Indian military. The United States is wealthy as well as multiethnic, whereas India is poor. The Soviet Union and Vietnam were totalitarian warfare states, whereas India is democratic and spends little on its military. What is striking, however, is the general pattern in major, modern multiethnic states toward integration of soldiers into military units as individuals and the rejection of ethnically based units except in extreme national emergencies. If social structures made no difference to military organi-

[49]Christopher D. Jones, "Historical Precedents: Ethnic Units and the Soviet Armed Forces,", in Teresa Rakowska-Harmstone, Christopher D. Jones, John Jaworsky, and Ivan Sylvain, *Warsaw Pact: The Question of Cohesion Phase 2*, vol. 1, *The Greater Socialist Army: Integration and Reliability, Operational Research and Analysis Establishment*, (ORAE) Paper no. 29 (Ottawa, Canada: ORAE, February 1984), pp. 84–146.

[50]See S. Enders Wimbush and Alex Alexiev, *The Ethnic Factor in the Soviet Armed Forces*, R-2787–NA (Santa Monica, Calif.: Rand Corporation, 1982), pp. 8, 14. For multiethnic problems in other Warsaw Pact armies, see Condoleeza P. Rice, "The Problem of Military Elite Cohesion in Eastern Europe," *Air University Review* 33 (January–February 1982): 64–76; A. Ross Johnson, Robert W. Dean, and Alex Alexiev, *East European Military Establishments: The Warsaw Pact Northern Tier* R-2417/1–AF/FF (Santa Monica, Calif.: Rand Corporation, 1980), pp. 161–162.

zations, the Indian military might be expected to converge in its recruitment patterns toward those of other modern militaries that draw from multiethnic populations, such that we would see the individual integration of soldiers into the Indian infantry. This has not happened.

INDIAN SOCIETY AND THE STRUCTURE OF THE INDIAN ARMY: THE OFFICER CORPS

An army has soldiers, but it also has officers. Are Indian Army officers recruited, trained, and employed in ways that tend to make them more or less removed from Indian society and more or less affected by Indian social structures and norms? To take the simplest question first, from where do Indian officers come? Although, as noted above, the specific ethnic or religious affiliation of army soldiers has never been officially released, during the 1990s, official and unofficial statistics about the regional origins of the forty thousand army officers began to emerge.

The main source of data is schools that educate the officer corps.[51] During the latter stages of the British rule in India, small numbers of Indians were admitted first to Sandhurst and then to the Indian Military Academy (IMA) at Dehra Dun. Because of the British preference for the so-called martial races, Indians admitted into Sandhurst in the period 1919–1925 and then into the IMA in the period 1932–1936 came overwhelmingly from the northwestern regions of India. During those periods, the Punjab contributed 41 to 42 percent of the cadets, and the Northwest Frontier Province, 6 to 12 percent, shares that exceeded their share of the entire Indian population by factors of six to eighteen times. In contrast, in 1932–1936, Bengali cadets were underrepresented by a factor of sixteen, that is, they sent roughly one-sixteenth the number they would have sent if their share of cadets were equal to their share of the Indian population. Overall, the northwest areas of India contributed 68 percent of the cadets in 1932–1936.

In the period 1978–1982, 57 percent of the cadets attending the IMA came from the same northwestern area. But the share of India's total population coming from the northwest had declined in the intervening fifty years, so the degree to which this region was overrepresented at the IMA declined hardly at all, going from 2.6:1 in 1932–1936 to 2.5:1 in 1978–

[51] Apurba Kundu, "Overdependence on 'Martial Races' Officers," tables 1, 2, 3; B. P. N. Sinha and Sunil Chandra, *Valour and Wisdom: Genesis and Growth of the Indian Military Academy* (New Delhi: Oxford and IBH Publishing, 1992), table 8, pp. 254–255; Daljit Singh, "Military Education in India: Changes from the British Tradition," *USII Journal* (July–September 1974): 227–237, stating that 75 percent of new recruits into the Indian Military Academy came from northern India.

1982, while the underrepresentation of the more populous but traditionally "nonmartial" areas decreased, from 0.2:1 in 1932–1936 to 0.6:1 in 1978–1982. During the interwar years, Sikhs composed about one-fourth of the Indian Army. The present-day areas of Punjab, Haryana, and Chandigarh have large Sikh populations and together contain 4.4 percent of the Indian population but contribute 21 percent of the cadets attending the IMA in 1978–1982.

From where do these officers come socially? Here the available evidence is somewhat contradictory. All sources, official and nonofficial, agree that the share of the officer corps coming from princely or aristocratic backgrounds has dropped sharply in comparison with preindependence times, from 22.5 percent in 1937 to 0 percent in 1985 and 1987. But are army officers increasingly or decreasingly coming from the sons of officers? That is, do the officers form a more or less self-perpetuating, separate class? The number of commissioned officers who were themselves sons of commissioned officers had to be small before independence because Indians were admitted into the officer corps only in small numbers. As a result, it is not surprising that the IMA's authorized history states that the number of commissioned officers' sons attending the IMA rose in the 1980s, from 16.5 percent to 23.4 percent, while the percent coming from the sons of noncommissioned officers or Junior Commissioned Officers (JCOs) fell from 1985 to 1987.[52] Indian officers writing in military journals, however, allege that the trend is in the opposite direction. It is claimed that declining pay and promotion opportunities, beginning with an absolute pay cut of 40 percent right after independence in 1947, and reductions in pay and promotion relative to the Indian Administrative Service (the senior civil service) have driven more and more officers' sons away from army careers. Captain Rajiv Kumar wrote that "a recent study revealed that a majority of officers joining the Army now hail from families of ex-ORs [other ranks, that is, rank-and-file soldiers] or JCOs. This has narrowed the gap between the soldier and the officer."[53]

Official data on the social origins of Indian Army officers were assembled in the mid-1970s for the purposes of a commission that was review-

[52]Sinha and Chandra, *Valour and Wisdom*, p. 256. Junior Commissioned Officer, formerly Viceroy Commissioned Officer, is a grade of officer including subadars and havildars, intermediate between noncommissioned officers such as sergeants, and commissioned officers, beginning with lieutenants. Created to act as a link between English-speaking British officers and Indian troops, JCOs have been much criticized as superfluous within the modern Indian Army but are still in existence.

[53]Brigadier B. K. Sinha, "Career Prospects for Officers in Armed Forces," *USII Journal* 412 (July–September 1968): 261–269; Capt. Rajiv Kumar, "Man Management: The Present Environ," *USII Journal* 471 (January–March 1983): 29–42.

ing the pay scale for officers. The findings, which were made available selectively through military journals, were not reassuring. For example, the commission determined that in 1974–1975, only 70 percent of the openings in the IMA were filled. Only 30 percent of the openings in the Officers Technical School were filled. The analysis of the five classes entering the IMA before the commission's study showed that 88 percent of the entering officer candidates were in *"the lowest acceptable grade."* At the National Defense Academy (NDA) at Pune, which has an undergraduate curriculum and which sends its graduates either to the IMA, in the case of future army officers, or to their equivalents for the navy and air force, 30 percent of the students were sons of JCOs and noncommissioned officers, and 20 percent the sons of civilians, who had sent them to *sainik* (soldier) preparatory schools for students who go on to serve in the military. Of those sons of civilians who applied to the NDA, 40 percent had been unable to gain entry into a civilian university. Only 10 percent of the students at the NDA were the sons of Indian military officers, almost all of whom (90 percent) had failed to gain entrance into civilian universities. For a period of several years, no son of an army general had entered the army.[54]

Just what do these figures signify? Clearly, they suggest that a career in the officer corps of the Indian Army has declined in social status. This could have happened as a result of political tension between the military and the larger society. In the United States, applications to the U.S. Military Academy at West Point fell in 1967 to the point where vacancies threatened to appear in the entering classes. Two years of the war in Vietnam had created political tensions that reduced the appeal of an officer's career.[55] More systematic U.S. Department of Defense surveys of U.S. Army first and second lieutenants serving in 1976 (and who would therefore have entered either a service academy or a college ROTC program six to eight years earlier, during the Vietnam War) showed that 30 percent of those then currently serving officers had fathers who had been commissioned officers, 51 percent had fathers who had served as enlisted men, and 19 percent had fathers who had not served in the military at all. These figures suggest that the Vietnam War may have led to an in-

---

[54]Brigadier N. B. Grant, "The Soldier and His Alienation from Society," *Combat* (November 1976). 46; Maj. Gen. D. Som Dutt, *Recruitment into the Officer Corps of the Armed Forces: Report on the United Services Institution of India Seminar of 14 February 1977,* (New Delhi: United Service Institution of India Special Seminar, 1976), p. 11, emphasis in original.

[55]Gen. Norman Schwarzkopf remembers that as an instructor at "West Point we weren't immune to the controversy over Vietnam. In 1967 . . . the admissions office barely found enough candidates to fill the entering class. . . . The admissions office began softpedalling the fact that West Point was a military institution." Norman H. Schwarzkopf, *The Autobiography: It Doesn't Take a Hero* (New York: Bantam, 1992), p. 137.

creased tendency for the U.S. Army to draw its officers from a more narrow and somewhat distinct segment of the American population, as was the case in India. However, the relevance of this survey was diminished by the fact that the high representation of officers with fathers with military experience (81 percent) was affected by the World War II generational phenomenon: in 1976, twenty-five-year-old males were very likely to have had fathers who served in World War II, which gave more military experience to more Americans than was or is typical.[56] Subsequent surveys showed that by 1986–1987, the recruitment of officers into the U.S. Army from high-quality sources—in particular ROTC scholarship students—had tripled relative to 1960, suggesting that more and better students were seeking careers as officers, despite good civilian economic conditions, and thus that the social stigma associated with a military career had disappeared.[57]

The patterns of officer recruitment in India could have changed because the relative material incentives to become an officer declined. In India, the pay of officers in the 1960s and 1970s did not keep pace with that of civil servants of comparable ages, let alone with inflation.[58] Specifically, a pay commission found that the total benefits of a company commander in the Indian Army with the rank of major, which included pay and in-kind concessions, such as subsidized housing, had *decreased* during the period 1947–1982 by almost 60 percent (1,060 rupees per month in 1947 versus 400 rupees in 1982, both in 1947 rupees). For a battalion commander with the rank of lieutenant colonel, the trend was worse, with a decline of almost 70 percent (1,365 rupees versus 419). This was in contrast to the pay of JCOs at the ranks of squad commander (*havildar*) and platoon commander (*subadar*), both of which had increased slightly in real terms (127 rupees up to 159, and 173 up to 189).[59] In part, this reflected the general reduction in military and civil service pay immediately after independence. Cash pay for starting civil servants was reduced from the 450 rupees a month paid by the British to entry-level Imperial Civil Servants, to 350 rupees for new IAS officers. At a time when the per capita annual income of India was about 280 rupees and the pay of a servant was about 10 rupees a month, the government of independent India decided that it could not maintain the level of pay for

[56] John H. Faris, "The All-Volunteer Force: Recruitment from Military Families," *Armed Forces and Society* 7 (Summer 1981): 545–559, table 7.

[57] William P. Snyder, "Officer Recruitment for the All-Volunteer Force: Trends and Prospects," *Armed Forces and Society* 10 (Spring 1984): 401–425, Table 4.

[58] Lt. Col. Bhimaya, "Some Thoughts on Improvement of Career Prospects of an Average Army Officer," *Infantry Journal* (September 1976): 78–90.

[59] Lt. Gen. M. L. Chibber, *United Service Institution of India Paper no. 8: Leadership in the Indian Army during the Eighties and Nineties* (New Delhi: Kashmir House, n.d.).

its military and civilian officers that had been established by the British for mostly British officers. But subsequently, top pay for IAS officers was allowed to rise to 3,000 rupees a month plus "dearness allowances" related to a cost-of-living index.[60] In consequence, by 1970, "while 16.6% of IAS officers drew salary of more than Rs 2,000/month . . . only 0.32% of the officers in the army did so."[61]

This situation was somewhat ameliorated by pay increases in 1987, which nearly doubled officer pay and gave officers and enlisted men free-food allowances.[62] The effects of this pay hike on officer recruitment are not yet clear, but it may explain the 1987 increase at the IMA of sons of army officers. However, the loss of status of officers relative to other professions—as reflected in such informal but powerful social status indicators as the standing of officers in the marriage market—that was first reported by scholars in the mid-1960s has persisted.[63] In 1985, for example, students at mainstream Indian high schools (ignoring convent schools and soldier schools) ranked the military profession eleventh out of fifteen listed professions, behind the senior civil services, medicine, science, and foreign businesses. Another study carried out for Indian Army Headquarters in the 1970s showed that a "steep fall" in the number of officer candidates coming from families that earned more than one thousand rupees a month.[64]

All soldiers in democracies complain about their pay and social status. The point of this review of Indian Army officer pay and recruitment is to suggest what the longer-term trends in the composition of the officer corps may be. Since independence, the officer corps has *not* been consistently filled by sons of higher-ranking military officers. Instead, what appears to be happening is that the officer corps has increasingly come from the lower middle classes—in particular, from the sons of JCOs and noncommissioned officers. This change has *reduced* one of the major sources of alienation between the officer corps and Indian society that was noticeable in the first twenty-five years after independence. Indians of that generation who entered the army officer corps while it served the British tended to have been upper middle class in origins, to have gone to English schools, and to have been more Anglicized than other Indians

[60] V. M. Sinha, *Superior Civil Services in India*, pp. 75–80, 85, 97.

[61] Brigadier B. N. Grant, *Report of United Service Institution of India Seminar no. 2: Retiring Age in the Armed Forces* (New Delhi: Kashmir House, n.d), p. 6.

[62] Cohen, *Indian Army*, "Epilogue to 1990 Edition," p. 217.

[63] Kavic, *India's Quest for Security*, pp 142–144.

[64] R. P. Gautam, "Status of Services vis-à-vis Other Services," *USII Journal* 480 (April–June 1985): 164. See also R. P. Gautam, "Causes of Higher Secondary Students' Preference for Military Career," *USII Journal* 458 (October–December 1979): 380–390; Lt. Col. Ram Narayan, "Crisis of Leadership," *Infantry Journal* (April 1976): 65–72.

of their social class. They were termed King's Commissioned Indian Officers (KCIOs). After independence, because of their early start in the officer corps, they rose in rank after the British and Muslim offers in the Indian Army were withdrawn. As a result, they tended to dominate the senior ranks of the army for many years thereafter.

This was noticed and bitterly resented not only by many younger officers who entered the army after independence and who had not served the British but also by the civilian political leadership of India who had begun their careers as nationalist enemies of the British government in India, of which the Indian Army was a part. This sense of separation between the older and younger officers and between the officer corps as a whole and the civilian nationalist leadership of India was accentuated by small measures. For example, reductions in pay after independence for the officer corps and the civil service were *not* applied to the KCIOs. Preindependence army officers lived, as a result, much better than the officers who were commissioned after independence, when the Indian Army was an authentic national army. The first non-British chief of army staff (COAS), General Cariappa, himself a KCIO, defended this exemption. A young Indian officer in the army at that time, Sukhwant Singh, wrote that "such disparities affected officers' morale to such an extent that some of our best talent . . . left the Army." When asked why he allowed such a state of affairs, Cariappa allegedly told the officer, " 'After all, KCIOs are only a handful. Why do you grudge their privileges?' " This tension fed intrigues within the senior officer corps, which after independence led to trumped-up charges and court martials over petty issues.[65]

Other factors contributed to the alienation of the older generals from much of Indian society. General Thimayya was COAS in 1960 and by caste a Coorg from Mysore. His grandfather was a large planter who drank whiskey, hunted, ate meat, and who, perhaps as a result, socialized more easily with the British planters of his area. Thimayya's biographer, Humphrey Evans, noted that he grew up in a house called "Sunnyside," attended British schools along with his brother before attending Sandhurst in 1924, and "although nominally . . . Hindu, they [Thimayya and his brothers] have been only lightly touched by Hindu customs"—for example, Thimayya went to weekend parties with teenage girls his own age. Evans also painted a word portrait of his first visit to Thimayya's home in 1954. He was greeted at the door, where Thimayya's wife, "Nina, wearing velvet toreador slacks and smoking through a long cigarette holder, was talking in French to a lady diplomat. Mireille, her teen-age daughter, wearing American jeans, was helping servants serve

[65]Sukhwant Singh, *India's Wars since Independence*, 3:5–6.

lemonade and beer." Nina, an Indian woman, was born in India but had spent much of her youth in Paris. Evans accompanied Thimayya on a tiger-hunting expedition, the purpose of which was to obtain tiger skins for ritual use in Thimayya's old British regiment, the Highland Light Infantry. Evans told Thimayya that it was an outrage that his former imperial masters should ask him, a four-star general of independent India, to take on this task, particularly since Thimayya was known to dislike hunting. No, Thimayya said, "the British pride of regiment is such that the major general [of the regiment] could make the request without embarrassment assuming Thimayya would be honored. 'And he is right. I'm not only honored, I'm delighted,' Timmy said. 'And that's what bothers me. I can't think of one reason why I should be.' "[66]

As this exchange indicates, Thimayya was a complex figure. He was a genuine hero and viewed as such within the Indian Army, and when Nehru forced his resignation, it was resented within the army. He had, like Jawaharlal Nehru, viewed with disgust many of the religious practices of the Hindus, such as the kidnapping of children into prostitution and the use of narcotics, both of which he observed to be sanctioned by Hindu priests.[67] Unlike Nehru, as an army officer serving in India, he had obligations to try and prevent such practices. In 1929, he also met Jawaharlal Nehru's father, Motilal Nehru, one of the leading nationalist figures of the time. Motilal Nehru approached him at a party and asked, " 'Does wearing a foreigner's uniform make you feel like a foreigner?' " To which he replied, " 'It's not the uniform. . . . We don't like foreigners. But our own people won't accept us as Indian.' " He asked Motilal Nehru if he should resign from the army and was told he should stay in, for independent India would need her own trained officers. He stayed in the army, witnessed the expulsion, on supposedly trumped-up charges, of other Indian officers who supported the nationalist movement and helped suppress, peacefully, anti-British mutinies of Indian army units during World War II and anti-British riots in Hyderabad in 1942. He was in a particularly painful position because his older brother, he knew, had joined the INA, which was fighting the British alongside the Japanese, and it was not clear to Thimayya whether it was he or his brother who was the traitor. He narrowly missed having to arrest his own brother when the city of Rangoon was captured from INA forces by Thimayya's brigade.[68]

In addition to creating individual officers who were internally divided,

[66] Humphrey Evans, *Thimayya of India: A Soldier's Life* (New York: Harcourt Brace, 1960), pp. 7–8, 25–27, 30, 34, 144.
[67] See the discussion of Nehru's memoirs in Chapter 2.
[68] Evans, *Thimayya of India*, pp. 112, 114–117, 124, 169, 179–181, 226.

the imperial past of Indian officers created divisions after independence between army officers who had been apolitical before 1947 and those who had openly supported independence. General B. M. Kaul, who rose to play a major but unsuccessful role in the 1962 war against China, was also a KCIO but one who had publicly supported Indian independence during World War II and who had been reported to the British internal security police, he wrote, by a fellow Indian officer in the army. He wrote that he had helped repair radios for clandestine nationalist groups and had obtained police documents that he supplied to nationalist leaders for the defense of INA officers put on trial for treason by the British after World War II. When he became chief of the general staff (CGS), he noted:

> Some of our senior officers were in the habit of making tendentious and indiscreet remarks openly against our national leaders and extolled the erstwhile British rulers of India. . . . I came to know of specific cases of anti-national and indiscreet utterances—some in the presence of foreigners—on the part of a few senior officers. I accordingly brought them to the notice of my Army Chief, General P. N. Thapar, in writing, who put this matter up to Defence Minister Menon. . . . Nehru passed strictures against one and a court of inquiry was held to investigate the allegations against the other. The court . . . exonerated this officer. Government, however, conveyed its displeasure, with the knowledge of Nehru, to this officer.

It has been alleged that the officer in question was General, later Field Marshall, S. Manekshaw. In general, Kaul felt that "these staunch supporters of the British Raj, when India became independent in 1947 felt greatly embarrassed but . . . they dexterously switched their loyalties. They had, all the same, an uneasy conscience due to their role in British times and felt unsafe in Free India. They, therefore, did not look without dismay upon the access given to me by many of our national leaders, especially Nehru, after they came into power. . . . I became anathema to these men."[69]

Kaul was promoted by Defense Minister Krishna Menon over the heads of many of his senior officers and was given special access to Nehru. He was the Chief of the General Staff and of an army corps during the 1962 war and was blamed for many of the defeats during that war. He may well have sought to explain his problems and the hostility of his fellow officers by claiming he was a true patriot, whereas they were not. But the hostility between Kaul and the older KCIO officers was real and was attested to by those who had little sympathy for either.

[69] Kaul, *Untold Story*, pp. x–xi, 60–62, 74, 317–318.

Matters were not helped by the reported charge that the KCIOs after independence were still "proudly displaying battle honours won fighting against their countrymen in the service of the British."[70] This tension was a factor present at least until the early 1970s, when the last of that generation of officers retired, though its memory yet influences the Indian Army. There were still in 1992 Indian officers who affected British military manners and other army officers who resented them.[71]

It is this form of alienation that the changing patterns of officer recruitment have affected. Drawn from neither the aristocratic nor markedly Anglicized segments of the upper middle classes, Indian officers in the 1980s and 1990s are close to the social origins of their troops and of Indian society as a whole. This has not, however, been an unmixed blessing. Officers drawn increasingly from the lower strata of Indian society are aware of the fact that they are the social equals of the men they command and are sensitive about it. One officer of the new generation gave his opinion of a typical younger officer: "It is unlikely that he is even a second grader [that is, not first or even second rate], and almost never the pick of society. . . . More often than not he is likely to be a reject or potential reject of all comparable or even some inferior civil services and has joined the service for a job and a settled life with creature comforts."[72] When the officer corps clearly came from a different social strata, relations between the officers and the men were hierarchical but well defined. Rank-and-file soldiers with long service in the army and from the same social origins as the officers are said to be more willing to challenge their officers and are more sensitive to perceived snobbery. One officer wrote that "even a few gestures in our present social environment can give rise to accusations of social disparity and social exploitation by the officer class. It has to be realised that the atmosphere is sensitive." Another study explicitly noted that between officers and men, relations have become worse because of the changes downward in the social origins of the officer corps. "Firstly, the social line having somewhat merged, the *jawan* [literally, youth, or a rank-and-file soldier] hasn't the same respect for his erstwhile colleague who now struts about as an officer, shoving him about. . . . The nearness of the socio-economic class has not brought togetherness, rather an aloofness has grown between the men and the officers. The latter being totally immersed in

---

[70]See Palit, *War in High Himalaya*, pp. 74, 88; Maj. Gen. Sukhwant Singh (ret.), *India's Wars since Independence*, vol. 2, *Defence of the Western Border* (New Delhi: Vikas, 1981), p. 255.

[71]Interview by author with a retired Indian Army general, New Delhi, November 1992.

[72]On the generational split in the officer corps between those commissioned before 1960 and those after, see Lt. Col. V. P. Sharma, "Cohesion among Officers," *Infantry Journal* (March 1983): 8–12.

self-advancement on all and many planes, which is not lost on the *jawans* [*sic*]."[73] Another officer wrote that the "majority of modern military leaders come from different walks of life. . . . Thus, the modern military leaders, while they are supposed to carry the social milieu, they, under the 'brand name' of 'being modern' adopt western style of living including the half baked ethos of the west. . . . This neo-western style from 'the sons of the soil' is not easily accepted by the troops. And as such they feel alienated from their leaders." And yet another discussed specific cases of bad relations between officers and men, commenting that relations between Indian officers and the men they commanded "has remained static over the past 30 years and we run the Army on British ideas as existing in the 1940s; there may have been a detraction but certainly no advance."[74]

What are the consequences of this changing pattern of officer recruitment? First, the historical pattern of recruitment from the Anglicized upper middle classes created a predicament after independence which lasted more than a generation and which contributed to a sense within the officer corps of a psychological separation from Indian society as a whole as well as to tensions between the officer corps and the civilian political leadership of India. This tension is the most likely explanation of the fact that the official status of the Indian officer corps was downgraded immediately after independence and its political role circumscribed. The position and title of "commander in chief" of the armed forces, which existed until 1947, was eliminated. In its place was put a set of chiefs of service staffs. Although the position of Chief of Defence Staff has been proposed by the army, it has been vetoed consistently. No military officers, even after their retirement, are permitted to serve in any capacity in the Indian Ministry of Defence, which is entirely staffed by civil servants. One study of the relationship between the Indian officer corps and the Indian civilian political decision-making structures concluded that in contrast to other newly independent countries, "in India . . . civilian authorities control the military and limit its role in the security policy-making process. Although there are military inputs into the formulation and conduct of external defense policy, basic doctrines and policies are developed by the elected civilian government."[75] D. K. Palit,

[73] Kumar, "Man Management"; Indira Awasthny, "Alienated Leadership," *USII Journal* 474 (October–December 1983): 325–328.

[74] Maj. Purushottam S. Bhatnagar, "Leadership Concern," *Infantry Journal* (August 1988): 31–35. Increasing problems between officers and soldiers because the officers felt the need to assert themselves more blatantly because they were of the same social status as their troops were expressed to this author in interviews with military families in New Delhi, November 1992. On the new problems between officers and men, see also Brigadier H. S. Sodhi, "Officer-Man Relationship of the Future," *Infantry Journal* (April 1974): 109–119.

[75] Raju G. C. Thomas, *Indian Security Policy* (Princeton: Princeton University Press, 1986),

retired senior Indian military officer writing in 1991, described the problem in these terms: the Indian government after independence in general, and Nehru in particular, had a low opinion of army officers "whom he regarded, with good reason, as shallow, westernised, British aping products of the raj, who had taken no part in the freedom movement." As a result, there was a "structured gap in communication between the government and the military [that] has never been brought out. . . . However efficient, professional and effective the Indian forces may be, within the Indian political system they exist largely in a vacuum. At the top, they have little contact with the government (either with political leaders or even the bureaucrats in the ministries) and underneath, they are kept out of contact with the people. The Indian armed forces contradict the cliché: they are not an expression of the society from which they issue; they never have been."[76]

Other factors affected the Indian pattern of officer-government relations, including the fear of a military coup d'état, and the initial commitment to nonviolence in Indian foreign policy. But those factors do not explain the unusually large role and power given to generals like B. M. Kaul who had established their nationalist credentials with Nehru, whereas the cultural alienation of the British-trained officers from the Indian nationalists explains both the systematic downgrading of the military after independence and the selective patronage extended to certain officers. This tension between the officers and civilian rulers could be expected to last as long as the senior levels of the Indian military were populated with officers with Anglicized social backgrounds who had been socialized into the army during the period of British rule. This alienation of the officer corps might be expected to diminish as the recruitment patterns shifted to draw officers from lower social strata. But the tension between officers and civilians may have been transmitted from Nehru to his daughter and was certainly institutionalized by her government. In Palit's judgment, "Neither Nehru's daughter nor his grandson were perceptive enough to close the gap between the politicians and the military. . . . The military continues to be kept at a distance. Consultation with the General Staff is not considered a prerequisite of political decision-making today any more than it was at independence."[77]

---

pp. 125–131, 160. See also Stephen Cohen, "The Military and Indian Democracy," in Atul Kohli, ed., *India's Democracy* (Princeton: Princeton University Press, 1988), p. 119, on the "divide and rule" tactics used by Indian civilian officials vis-à-vis the Indian military; Maj. Gen. A. M. Malik, "National Security Management Structures," *Trishul: Journal of the Defence Services Staff College* 1 (1989): 20–49, noting that "there is a clear lack of civil-military balance and the bureaucrat continues to retain too much control on the Defense apparatus."
[76] Palit, *War in High Himalaya*, pp. 2–3, 21.
[77] Ibid., p. 21.

[231]

What was once a set of personalized social conflicts has become part of the structure of Indian military politics.

The fact that recruitment from the sons of higher-ranking officers has in practice been replaced not by increased recruitment from civilians but with the sons of noncommissioned officers suggests that a slightly different phenomenon has been at work and will affect future civil-military relations. The new pattern of officer recruitment means the Indian officer corps continues to remain a self-sustaining and separate body of men, with few social links to senior civilian officials. To recall, the figures on the intake of student cadets into the IMA mentioned above show that sons of noncommissioned officers, plus sons who came from schools designed to place their graduates in military academies, plus sons of higher-ranking officers accounted for 60 percent of the incoming cadets.

EDUCATION AND INTELLECTUAL TRENDS IN THE INDIAN ARMY
OFFICER CORPS

The education and training of the army officer corps could in theory be part of a process in which the attitudes and habits of thought of Indian officers after independence might have been gradually altered such that the officers became more attuned to specifically Indian social and military realities, as opposed to the imperial social and military roles they inherited from the British. The consistent testimony of Indian Army officers is that, on the whole, this has not happened. To begin with, as one colonel in the army noted, an officer usually "remains with a unit for nearly 20 years. This not only limits his horizons, but impedes his development."[78] Another noted that an officer would typically command a platoon from the time of commissioning until about the age of thirty-five, and he would then command a company until the age of thirty-eight. Two-thirds of them would continue to hold that command until retiring. The officer noted that in World War II, by contrast, the average age for a company commander was between twenty and thirty years of age.[79] As a result, most officers simply were not exposed to advanced training outside small units of not more than a few hundred men.

Confinement to a small unit had the effect of perpetuating inherited concepts and habits of thought. One Indian officer, Sukhwant Singh, recalled that in the 1970s at the level of military operations, the dominant experience of Indian Army officers after independence was of serving in

---

[78] Col. R. M. Sewal, "Is the Army Over Officered?" *Combat* (April 1987): 14–19.
[79] Maj. Bhartendra Singh, "A Career in the Army," *USII Journal* 377 (October–December 1959): 347–350.

the Indian Army 4th Division under General Montgomery in North Africa. This was the school in which they first learned large-scale warfare. For better or for worse, Montgomery favored carefully preplanned battles with elaborate preparations during which material superiority over the enemy and defensive "killing zones" were established. If necessary, the British troops would withdraw, trading space for time, and would then launch a well-prepared counterattack. Indian Army officers emerged from this "school," in the view of Sukhwant Singh, badly "attuned to the requirements of a short war. The Army, trained over years according to the typical World War II step-by-step approach, found it hard to adjust to swift battle and mobile warfare," particularly in the Indian-Pakistani context in which trading space for time in the border area could have serious and permanent political consequences.[80]

The British lessons from World War II were kept alive in the Indian Army after independence not only in the memories of Indian officers who had served under Montgomery but also by the fact that British army officers continued to command Indian military training establishments well into the 1950s. British officers headed the Directorate of Military Training at least through 1954, also commanding the Staff College and the Infantry School after independence.[81] Indian Army officers continued to attend the British Staff College at Camberly through 1955, perhaps longer, where they, interestingly, found their British instructors to be more supportive, less intimidating, and more inclined to solicit the opinions of their students than the Indian students expected. They found far less formal social activity in the British army than in the Indian, noting that "it was heartening to note that the practice of constant 'sirring' is not very prevalent in the British Army."[82] Higher-ranking officers from the Indian Army also attended the Imperial Defence College Course in Great Britain, where only 3 of 122 lectures were devoted to the political problems of South Asia (India, Pakistan, and Ceylon) and where the bulk of the specifically military lectures were devoted to the British problems of conducting global war, including nuclear war, against the Soviet Union.[83] India established its own National Defence College in 1960 in New Delhi, explicitly on the model of the Imperial Defence College.[84]

The inertia in Indian professional military education seems to have been reflected in the dearth of critical military analyses published in In-

---

[80] Sukhwant Singh, *India's Wars since Independence*, 3:1–2, 29.

[81] Ibid., pp. 6, 11.

[82] Lt. Col. M. R. Rajwade, "Some Impressions of the Staff College at Camberly," *USII Journal* 360 (July–September 1955): 235–240.

[83] Brigadier C. R. Mangat-Rai, "The Imperial Defence College Course," *USII Journal* 360 (July–September 1955): 297–302.

[84] National Defence College brochure (New Delhi: 1989), p. 3.

dian military journals. During the 1960s and 1970s, as was noted at the beginning of this chapter, there was remarkably little discussion in these professional journals of the wars that India itself fought with China and Pakistan. The testimony of retired senior Indian Army officers is that no analytical or critical lessons of the 1965 war were developed or promulgated internally by the army.[85] In addition, the few articles in Indian military journals about wars fought by other countries tend to be dismissive. This suggests that the Indian Army has not been prompted either by its own wars or by the wars of others to engage in an effort to rethink its basic concepts in the light of military events after World War II. Army officers commenting in 1969 on the American war in Vietnam noted the introduction of sophisticated military technology but concluded that they had been ineffective in Vietnam and were of no relevance to India.[86] A seminar composed of retired senior officers met in September 1973 and decided that although military technology was changing, the doctrine, structure, and equipment of an Indian infantry battalion was sound and should not be altered.[87] Observations of the 1973 Arab-Israeli War did not lead most Indian Army officers to rethink the structure of their army or the concepts governing its use in battle. At another seminar in 1976, one Indian general concluded, "Basically our system of command and control is a sound one, from Corps Headquarters downwards." Another general reviewed the location of Indian Army bases and noted that the major supplies for the army were still where the British had left them, although the British had used those bases to supply the army when it deployed overseas. As a result, they were poorly placed to supply the postindependence army, which was stationed largely on India's land frontiers. He decided that thirty years after independence, there was a need for change, but that change would be difficult and was unlikely. General D. K. Palit commented that "so far, most of the battles fought by our army have been more or less on the pattern of World War II—both tactics-wise and weapons-wise. Hence, our organisational frame-work has remained more or less unchanged. That situation is about to change because of a new generation of weapons—the Precision Guided Munitions" (PGMs), the effectiveness of

[85] Sukhwant Singh, *India's Wars since Independence*, 2:276. Harbakhsh Singh did prepare a training memo in April 1966 based on his command experiences in 1965, but that training in the Indian Army remained "stereotyped" and "monotonous." See his *War Dispatches*, p. 201.

[86] Maj. Gen. D. Som Dutt, "The Military Implications of Advances in Technology on Strategy," *USII Journal* 415 (April–June 1969): 124–132. For a more neutral Indian evaluation of U.S. military technology in Vietnam, see Maj. M. S. Sekhon, "The Future Trends in Weapons and Tactics," *USII Journal* 444 (July–September 1976): 254–263.

[87] Maj. Gen. D. Som Dutt (ret.), *Re-organization of the Infantry Division* (New Delhi: United Service Institution of India Seminar no. 1, September 1973), pp. 1–10.

which had been demonstrated in the 1973 Middle East war. The Indian Army, he argued, would have to break itself up into smaller units if it wanted to survive against a Pakistani Army that could soon have PGMs, courtesy of some of its Middle Eastern friends, and command of Indian military units would have to become far more decentralized. "Such changes in weapons and tactics will demand a thorough re-think into the Organisation of the Army." Palit was promptly rebutted by Lt. Gen. Harbakhsh Singh, who had commanded the Indian Army against West Pakistan in 1965. He observed: "From my own experience, I am convinced that every sophisticated weapon can be met by a less sophisticated weapon, so long as we have a larger number of them. We should not go in for too much sophistication."[88]

Debates among younger Indian officers about tactical and operational issues tended to reflect a satisfaction with existing army military concepts. For example, in the 1920s and 1930s in Europe and the United States, there were extended discussions of whether tank units, used independently, had created the opportunity for rapid mobile warfare or whether the tank should be used to support the infantry, moving only as quickly as the infantry could march. In India in 1976, young army officers were not only rejecting the importance of PGMs but also the importance of the independent use of armored units on the battlefield: "There is unequivocal assent on the fact that the first priority in allocation of armour is provisioning of the armoured regiment of the infantry division."[89]

More recent Indian discussions of the U.S.-Iraq war of 1991 by army generals suggest that little has changed in the practice of that army. Contrasting the performance of coalition armored units with Indian armored performance in the 1965 and 1971 wars, the verdict was that "there is not much that can be said in favour of the handling of our armoured formations. Our armoured brigade commanders were readily willing [in the 1965 and 1971 wars] to allow their brigades to be treated as 'tank brigades' and their regiments parcelled out to infantry formations." The tactical "Bible" of the army was said still to be a British War Office manual reprinted in India. The officer concluded that what India needed was a professional debate on the future of its military doctrine, a debate that he had not yet observed.[90] Other Indian generals were less impressed

---

[88] Lt. Gen. M. L. Thapan (ret.), *Review of the Organizational Pattern of the Indian Army* (New Delhi: United Service Institution of India Seminar no. 7, March 1976), pp. 9–11, 27–28, 33–35. The quote is on p. 36.

[89] Lt. Col. J. K. Dutt, "Wanted: A Doctrine for Armour," *USII Journal* 449 (October–December 1977): 45–52.

[90] Brigadier R. D. Law, "The Gulf War—The Last Hundred Hours: Lessons for the Indian Mechanised Forces," *USII Journal* 505 (July–September 1991): 346–364.

with the 1991 war, arguing that since Iraq was so vastly overmatched in every political and military aspect, its rapid defeat was no surprise and contained no lessons for India.[91] Similarly, the commander of an Indian division in the operations in Sri Lanka asserted in print that "the army shows little signs of adjusting to war realities and strengthening its motivational repertoire based on war performance. It wallows in peace-time procedures, perceptions, and practices."[92]

A review of the overall content of the instruction at Indian military training and educational establishments was published by Brigadier S. S. Chandel in 1988. He described the hierarchy of schools for officers: the Defence Service Staff College attended by officers with a minimum of six years of service, the Higher Command Course at the College of Combat at Mhow, then the National Defence College for officers who had reached the rank of Brigadier. His evaluation of the curriculum stands on its own. At the Staff College, "the stress, despite the lip service to the superior intellectual matters, is primarily on the form, neatness, and presentation. ... This may be due to the reason that we simply inherited the current mode of instructional input from the British who on their part themselves had a vested interest in keeping their [Indian] Army leadership at a lower edge of sharpness. We ourselves do not feel like reviewing the validity of it in the context of accelerated pace of change in the strategic, technological and internal security environments." The defeat at the hands of China in 1962 and then the "stalemate" in 1965 did create the perception at the Indian officer schools that "our military planner need[ed] to be something more than an excellent calligrapher/neat paper binder/sketcher." As a result, the Higher Command Course was created. In this course, officers were led on tours of various Indian theaters of war which are accompanied by war gaming. This took the bulk of the forty-week course.

In the remainder period are crammed in such diverse subjects as counterinsurgency warfare, NBC [nuclear, biological, and chemical] warfare, automatic data processing and management capsule, a whiff of Air Force and Navy and discussions of the views of the great masters and theorists of war such as Clausewitz, Liddell Hart, Mahan, Makinder, etc. Having gone through this course, these officers are posted to administrative appointments while their logistically trained counterparts who have been attending Long Defence Management Course are posted to main operational jobs. This amusing travesty of reason aside, a few points need to be made. ... As to the intellectual preparation, our officers, as a general rule,

[91] Maj. Gen. Virender Uberoy, "The Incredible War," *Combat* (December 1991).
[92] Lt. Gen. S. C. Sardeshpande, "Internal Security," *Combat* (December 1991): 13–20.

tend to read very narrowly. The military classics and humanities hardly find a place in their general reading diet. Therefore, deep perception of military issues as related to the society and future perspective is beyond their ken.

Students at the Indian National Defence College take a forty-six-week course during which they discuss political-military issues, but after graduation or even later, they are "rarely posted to the Minister of Defence." and cannot expect to have access to any national forum discussing national security matters, except at a purely technical level.[93] At the level of political-military affairs, the instructional material distributed to the students attending the Indian National Defence College course in 1989 gives some indication of the political-military issues that were emphasized in the education of higher-ranking Indian officers. That material reviewed the global situation, region by region, and commented on the then superpower relationship between the United States and the Soviet Union, asserting that the superpowers had "probably contrived" the cold war "to secure the achievements of [World War II] and the victory." Now both superpowers were in retreat.[94]

But for our present purpose, what is perhaps most relevant is the instructional material at the National Defence College reviewing India's own internal situation. The picture presented to the students was bleak. "Our social structure has many inequalities and disparities. Communalism, regionalism, casteism, and linguism as also [*sic*] the existence of underprivileged sections and economic disparities. . . . Added to the cankers of communalism, casteism, and regionalism is the problem of the general erosion of standards in public life, in politics, in administration, and a general decline in moral and ethical values. As a result, it is said that an erosion in the core values of Indian society is taking place which poses a threat to the nation's stability and cohesion." The cohesion of the Indian bureaucracy that had held the country together had "allegedly been eroded."[95]

Articles in Indian military journals from the 1980s elaborate the same theme of Indian social disintegration. One article noted that "in the last

---

[93] Brigadier S. S. Chandel, "Training of Higher Commanders," *Infantry Journal* (August 1988): 17–23.

[94] J. Daulat Singh, *Super-Powers and Europe Study — 1989* (New Delhi: National Defence College, 1989), pp. 1–8. The quote is on p. 1.

[95] Air Vice Marshall Mohan, *Socio-Political Study of India*, (New Delhi: National Defence College, 1989), pp. 1–3. Brigadier S. K. Bahri, director of the faculty of studies at the College of Combat at Mhow also listed internal communal violence and poverty as serious national security problems. See his "India's National Security: Internal Threats to Security," *Combat* (August 1982): 31–36.

two or three decades, institutions and personalities which generated and trained selfless, honest, social and political workers have gradually disappeared from the scene. . . . The methods employed by various political parties and groups to capture power from village level to national level have generated violence, corruption, and insecurity."[96] A 1990 article in the Indian military operations research journal commented that violent crime, indiscipline, and insubordination were increasing in the Indian military.[97] Another article in 1991 argued that the use of the Indian military to control Indian civilian populations would increase along with "the increasing murkiness of politics, weakening of social and economic fabric, and proliferation of class-caste communal violence," and this had weakened the traditional apolitical stance of the officer corps.[98] A 1990 *Combat* article also noted the growing instability in Indian society and drew the logical conclusion: "The distinct life of the Army must remain as a safeguard against the disregard of their ethos."[99] Retired Lt. Gen. S. K. Sinha commented on the upward trends in Indian social violence, the perception that "there has been a collapse of the administrative system due to widespread corruption and politicization at all levels. Political interference has undermined the functioning of the police and its discipline and morale have suffered greatly." He then reached the same conclusion: "The Army has been an island of discipline in a rising sea of indiscipline in our country. The soldier living in his barracks can be kept better disciplined than a soldier constantly exposed to the indiscipline of society."[100]

What may we infer from these debates in Indian military professional journals and schools? First, there appears to be support, in the form of testimony from Indian military officers, for Edward Shils's 1961 observation that the intellectual classes in India have had difficulty in sustaining intellectually critical and creative debates. Having begun life after independence by and large as a culturally alien element in India, the army officer corps retained the habits of mind and the institutions that perpetuated those habits of mind inherited from the British. This tended to keep them a separate enclave in Indian society, distrusted by civilian

---

[96] D. D. Khanna, "India's National Security Problems," *Combat* (April 1982): 19–28.

[97] Maj. Ramdesh Halgali, "Military Tradition and the Present Day Officer," *Defence Management* 17 (October 1990): 8–13. Maj. Harinder Singh also noted that increase in disciplinary cases, poor quality and low number of recruits into officer corps, and declining morale in the Indian Army in the 1980s, in *Infantry Journal* (March 1984): 25–27.

[98] Lt. Gen. S. C. Sardeshpande, "The Indian Army and Internal Security," *Combat* 18 (December 1991): 13–20.

[99] Col. Israr Khan, "Influence of Changing Indian Society in the Army," *Combat* 17 (April 1990): 19–26.

[100] Lt. Gen. S. K. Sinha (ret.), "Aid to the Civil Authority," *Trishul: Journal of the Defence Services Staff College* 1 (1989): 79–93.

political leaders. But the reasons for this perpetuation of British patterns of military organization seems not to have been simply the dead hand of caste or inertia, as Shils suggested. Instead, on the part of the Indian military, it appears to have been, at least in part, the consciously adopted reaction to trends in Indian society. After observing several decades of independence, rising levels of corruption, violence, and political instability in Indian society as a whole, the army officer corps has come to value the separation of the army from Indian society and wishes to maintain it. A prolonged period of independence has reduced some of the British influence on the officer corps but has not created in the army the sense that it wishes to give up its separation from Indian society. In that sense, this period of independence does not seem to have reduced the feeling of "us" versus "them" when the army officer corps looks out at Indian society.

SOCIAL STRUCTURE, MILITARY ORGANIZATION,
AND MILITARY POWER

We now have some partial answers to the questions sketched out at the beginning of this chapter. The Indian Army did not end the selective recruitment and deployment practices that separated it from Indian society before independence. The relationship remained one of deliberate isolation from society. The rank-and-file soldiers of the army did not become more representative of the population of India by regions, remaining members of small, homogenous, inward-looking units which were kept physically and psychologically isolated from Indian society and which led organizational lives dominated by drill and routine inherited from the period when they served the British Empire. With regard to the Indian officer corps, they did become somewhat more "Indian" in their class origins, as they were drawn less from the upper middle classess over time. But they did not become more representative of the Indian population either regionally or by social origins, continuing instead to be drawn from military families from northwest India. They too tended to live professional lives that were focused on their own small units that were isolated from the rest of society. The nature of their education and training was not such as to expand their military or political horizons. Together, these phenomena created tensions within the military and between the military and society that are manifested in civil-military relations.

What have been the consequences of this pattern of military organization? Did it have any impact on the conduct of India's wars since independence? In reviewing the performance of the army in battle, care must be exercised not to attribute immediately whatever military failings that army may have had to its patterns of organization that affected its relationship to Indian society. Poor officers, training, and equipment are not unique to any pattern of civil-military relations. But it may be possible to identify cases in which the isolated, fragmented, and inward-looking character of the Indian Army may reasonably be associated with its military performance.

Indian officers commenting on the performance of their army in the 1962 war with China have asserted that organization of the army into single-class units affected combat performance. D. K. Palit, who commanded the Seventh Brigade of the Fourth Division that faced China in the Northeast Frontier Area (NEFA) in 1959 and 1960 and who was subsequently director of military operations during the 1962 war, found much to criticize in Indian military policy and performance that was not related to Indian social issues: poor intelligence preparation, poor military planning and equipment, and so on. Some of the civil-military problems he described—the ignorance of high-level civilian officials about military realities such as logistics—would sound familiar to any military person in almost any society.[101]

But certain problems, in his view, were directly related to the relationship of the army to Indian society. Indian civil-military relations, in his judgment, were far worse than in other democratic countries in wartime and were the result of the gulf between Indian military officers and civilians, a gulf created by Indian officers of a generation that had risen within an isolated military environment, had been shaped by the British, and was out of tune with the larger civilian society. Nehru had engineered the resignation of a popular but British-styled COAS, General Thimayya, and had made General Kaul the CGS, the position below the top spot of COAS. Nehru had done this because Kaul, atypical of Indian officers of that generation, had known Nehru and supported the nationalist movement before 1947 and because Nehru could not tolerate the other "British-aping" Indian generals. Nehru and Defense Minister Krishna Menon then used Kaul to circumvent the Indian military hierarchy, going so far as to keep Kaul in day-to-day command of Indian troops on the Chinese border when Kaul was ill and bedridden in New Delhi, but still able to meet with Menon.[102] For decades after this, the

---

[101] Palit, *War in High Himalaya*, pp. 94–95: "I had yet to become accustomed to the political culture that prevailed in South Block [New Delhi home of the civilian Ministry of Defence and the home secretary] in the aftermath of the border confrontation. There was a propensity to ignore military reality and adopt an emotional attitude that pandered to patriotic urges while shrugging away inter-related problems with optimistic assumptions."

[102] Ibid., pp. 74, 235.

Indian military would remember and resent this extreme form of civilian intervention in its affairs, which was the product of the gulf created by the reaction of the Indian military before and after independence to its social environment.

At the level of military operations, Palit also claimed that the organization of the Fourth Division and its policy-driven relationship to Indian society did affect its military performance in 1962. He asserted, for example, that no effort was made to mobilize local tribes in the border area to support the army or to construct local defenses: "It is no exaggeration to remark that the Indian Army in Assam behaved much in the matter of an imperial force operating in overseas territory. The army lived and worked in a self-constructed cocoon." Though Indian territory, the NEFA was off-limits to army families, "thereby adding to the feeling of alienation from which both officers and men suffered. In a tribal army such as ours, in which the various castes and regional sub-races are kept segregated in class-composed regiments . . . there is always the danger that in dire adversity men will lack the motivation to stand and fight for unfamiliar territory outside their home regions. I feel sure that this was partly the cause of 4th Division's ignominious abandonment of Se-la defences in 1962. . . . The colonial outlook of the Indian Army in NEFA was nowhere better exemplified than in its unwillingness to enlist the cooperation of friendly tribals, especially the Mompas of Towang," who had suffered under Tibetan rule and who, initially, were pro-Indian. As a result of Indian neglect, "when the crisis arose it was the Chinese who utilized the Mompas . . . as guides and informers and for providing safehouses."[103]

In addition, the fragmented and self-contained nature of the Indian Army led to serious problems when the rapid escalation of the crisis with China in 1962 forced it to deploy additional troops rapidly to the border areas and then to replace casualties inflicted by the Chinese. In armies in which combat units are more or less uniform in their composition and habits, the rapid integration of units that have not worked together before is difficult, but not impossible, in crisis situations. For example, the unexpected invasion of the Republic of Korea forced the United States Army to activate units from the United States rapidly. The Third Battalion of the Seventh Cavalry Regiment was hastily organized and activated at Fort Benning. Composed of all kinds of

---

[103] Ibid., pp. 56–59. B. N. Mullik, *My Years with Nehru: The Chinese Betrayal* (New Delhi: Allied, 1971), p. 423, confirms that no military training was given to the Indian citizens in NEFA because "any training to them on those lines would have been opposed by the army as posing a security danger." Mullik was the head of the Intelligence Bureau serving the home secretary from 1950 until 1966 and was, in effect, the senior intelligence official in the Indian government during this period.

troops—demonstration troops from the army school at Fort Benning, cooks and drivers reassigned as riflemen, as well as regulars—it was shipped directly to Pusan after its formation. Although this battalion was initially pushed back by Chinese troops, it held together and then pushed back the Chinese.[104] Task Force Smith from the Twenty-fourth Division in Japan was the first American force to encounter enemy troops in Korea. It too had been forced to integrate commissioned and noncommissioned officers into its units rapidly on the eve of combat. Although this caused initial problems, the judgment of historians is that this motley assembly performed as well as it could given that it was outnumbered and underequipped, holding back the enemy as long as possible and then withdrawing to safety.[105]

In November 1962, the Indians had five battalions deployed in the forward areas in the NEFA where the Indian Fourth Division was operating, while Palit estimated that the Chinese had the equivalent of six Indian infantry battalions in the area. The simple balance of forces, therefore, appears to have been roughly equal. Like the first American troops sent to Korea, the Indian units had been either rapidly pulled together, combining units from Calcutta with others from around India, or filled out with other units after having taken early casualties. The Fourth Division, specifically, had been "reconstructed" in the NEFA after a Chinese attack in October and after two of its brigades were pulled for use elsewhere. Colonel Palit and General Kaul (director of the general staff) agree that this attempt to combine rapidly units that had had separate and different military lives produced a composite unit that lacked military cohesion. Palit is most blunt: "The stark truth is that the [Indian] defences were never tested [at Se-la]: a battle for the pass was never fought. In the event, the men of the reconstructed 4th Division abandoned their positions and fled well before a Chinese offensive was launched."[106] The commander of the Fourth Division itself argues that among the higher Indian commanders, "private animosities, personal weaknesses and, in many cases, total lack of mutual confidence gave rise to farcical situations that led to disaster," while at the troop level, field

[104]Rick Megahan, "Battalion Command in Combat" (master's thesis, U.S. Army Staff College, Fort Leavenworth, Kans., 1990), p. 131.

[105]Roy K. Flint, "Task Force Smith and the 24th Division: Delay and Withdrawal, 5–19 July 1950," in *America's First Battles, 1776–1965,* ed. Charles E. Heller and William A. Stoft (Lawrence: University Press of Kansas, 1986), pp. 276, 296.

[106]Palit, *War in High Himalaya,* p. 257; on the Indian Army's capabilities relative to the Chinese, see also pp. 240–242, 264, 299; Kaul, *Untold Story,* op. cit, p. 438. Mullik confirms Palit's claim that the Chinese superiority in troop strength in NEFA was "marginal and the superiority of weapons was felt only in the case of mortars." See Mullik, *My Years with Nehru,* p. 421.

conditions prevented him from engaging in training that could have helped him pull his troops together.[107]

It would clearly be incorrect to attribute all the problems of cohesion in the Indian Army to the subcaste-based system that provided soldiers for Indian single-class infantry battalions or to attribute the relatively better American performance purely to the absence of such a system. Indian commanders had never been allowed by the British to learn how to plan and execute large-scale battles, and they were forced to fight in an area where the terrain and logistics situation favored the Chinese. The American army in Korea could draw on a rich pool of combat-tested officers at all levels. But Indian single-class units, each of which spoke different languages and each of whose officers trained and lived separately for decades, surely had more problems in rapidly learning to work together than did military units not so organized. The Henderson-Brooke Report, commissioned by the Indian government to inquire into the failures in the army in 1962 and written by a retired Indian Army officer of that name, has yet to be declassified, but retired officials have cited it in part. That inquiry alludes to the lack of understanding and confidence among army units, concluding that within the army there was a "need for realization of responsibilities at various levels which must work with trust and confidence in each other. Difficulties had arisen when there was departure from the accepted chain [of command]."[108]

That the Indian Army retained the practice of recruiting officers and men predominantly from the northwest areas of India created the belief in other countries that the Indians themselves believed that certain groups in India fought well, whereas other groups fought badly. This, in turn, reinforced existing prejudices or beliefs in the military strengths and weaknesses of India, and these beliefs affected strategic calculations. During the 1962 crisis, India greatly feared a Pakistani attack while China was also putting pressure on it. In his memoirs, B. N. Mullik, director of the Intelligence Bureau of the Home Ministry, claims to have had at the time accounts of private conversations between the Pakistani president Ayub Khan and his army and air force chiefs, during which Khan argued that "the only fighting material in India consisted of the Sikhs, the Gurkhas, and the Rajputs. He gave an analysis of how these three races would react to the fighting against Pakistan and against China." The Pakistani military, bolstered by Ayub Khan's belief in India's weakness, created a threat that led the Indian Army to keep most of its best forces on the Pakistani border. As a result, to reinforce the Chinese border areas

---

[107] Maj. Gen. Niranjan Prasad (ret.), *The Fall of Towang, 1962* (New Delhi : Palit and Palit, 1981), pp. 13, 20.
[108] Mullik, *My Years with Nehru*, p. 475.

the army was "forced to pull out units in battalion strength from the south and central areas to form new brigades and divisions, why [sic] there was want of cohesion amongst the various units."[109]

Even within a single-class unit, there were problems related to the nature of social structures in Indian society. When Chinese troops penetrated Indian lines to threaten headquarters units, rear-area support troops—for example, cooks and sweepers—could not help defend their positions because they had no weapons and had received no combat training, unlike the cooks and drivers mobilized by the Seventh Cavalry Regiment. Some years later, in the 1970s, General Sam Manekshaw as COAS tried to reverse this policy by giving combat training and weapons to the noncombatant soldiers in the army. He was met by resistance, and his policy was challenged by his successor, General Bewoor, whose reported comment appears to reflect the ancient caste-based antipathy to the outcastes who were and are given the job of sweeper: "Little does Sam know that brooms cannot be replaced by rifles."[110] Kaul reports that these internal caste divisions within Indian units were exploited by the Chinese. In POW camps, the Chinese "created misunderstandings between our officers and other ranks. . . . For instance, some of them [the Chinese officers] would pose to be officers and then sweep the floors and do other menial work."[111]

After the difficulties experienced during the 1962 border war with China, the Indian Army was enlarged and its funding was increased. Greater attention was paid to military affairs by Indian civilian officials. In most of the accounts of the 1965 war, Indian writers say that by then the army had reformed, that the territorial gains made by the army in 1965 "wiped out the shame" of the territorial losses in 1962, that the war had a "profoundly unifying effect on India," and that Pakistani efforts to raise the Muslims of Kashmir against the Indian government at the outset of the 1965 war failed completely.[112] The detailed military account of that war by the commander of the Indian forces opposite West Pakistan, General Harbakhsh Singh, indicates that General Sukhwant Singh was correct when he wrote that the "lavish praise for all the services [after the 1965 war was over] and image building by the propaganda media clouded an objective analysis of the war which would have taught

---

[109] Ibid., pp. 332–333.

[110] Sukhwant Singh, *India's Wars since Independence*, 3:94.

[111] Kaul, *Untold Story*, p. 439.

[112] See what until recently has been the standard account of the 1965 war, Russell Brines, *The Indo-Pakistani Conflict* (London: Curwen, 1968), pp. 349–351. Even Harbakhsh Singh's excellent and honest book has some of this obligatory mythology, which the rest of his book belies; see *War Dispatches*, p. 205.

many lessons for the future, and the Official Secrets Act hid many sins."[113]

There are two separate issues. First, were the internal divisions within Indian society a strategic factor in the war? All accounts agree that Pakistan tried by means of infiltrators to set off a rebellion in Jammu and Kashmir that would force the Indian Army in that area to disperse its forces to retain Indian control. Once that had been accomplished, the Pakistani Army would launch its Operation Grand Slam that would try to penetrate perhaps sixty miles into the area, cutting the main road. All accounts until now suggest that the effort to pin down the Indian Army by inspiring rebellion failed. Second, were there military weaknesses in the Indian Army in 1965 of the kind visible in 1962 which stemmed from the internal organization of the army and which divorced it from Indian society? In particular, did the single-class organization of the infantry have any effect?

With regard to the strategic implications of divisions within Indian society, the testimony of General Harbakhsh Singh is instructive. He and his staff had begun concrete planning in May 1965 for a Pakistani attack. His plans assumed substantial infiltration by guerrillas and irregular forces in Jammu and Kashmir. The actual infiltration began on 5 August 1965, and captured documents showed that the irregular forces planned to set up a "Revolutionary Council" in Jammu and Kashmir that would invite in Pakistani forces. Singh states that, in fact, infiltration into a major city in the area, Srinagar City, prompted the state government of Jammu and Kashmir to call for martial law and for the Indian Army to secure the state. Singh also states that he was telephoned by the Indian defense secretary, who stated that the Indian cabinet, meeting in emergency session, was prepared to declare martial law. Singh argued vigorously against this, saying that the infiltration was controllable and if the government dispersed the army to enforce martial law, it would be reacting in exactly the way that the enemy had planned. It was only Singh's last-minute opposition that prevented the successful development of the initial phase of the Pakistani plan. Singh's stance was particularly noteworthy because initially the infiltrators did have considerable success. By 21 August, they had secured local support in one of his division sectors (the Twenty-fifth Division area of operational responsibility). The infiltrators had created problems so severe that the commander of that division, in what Singh called a "flagrant violation of my orders," refused to obey Singh's order to advance on the grounds that the commander's troops were heavily committed in counterinfiltra-

[113]Sukhwant Singh, *India's Wars since Independence*, 3:29.

tion operations. After the war, Singh's assessment was that the Pakistani combination of infiltration by irregulars supported by conventional army attacks "enabled the enemy to hold large areas both in frontage and in depth." Pakistani infiltration also showed the Indian Army the need to give combat training to rear-area, noncombat troops, training that they still lacked.[114] A reasonable conclusion would be that the internal divisions in Indian society were not merely the product of wishful thinking in Pakistan but strategic realities.

With regard to the internal structure of the Indian Army, the evidence is ambiguous about the battlefield effects of the single-class organization of the Indian infantry. Failure in coordination between different units could provide one indication of the impact of the fragmentation of the army into inward-looking, caste-based military units. Reflecting on the lessons of the 1962 war, one might also try to assess the impact of single-class organization by looking at newly formed, large military units to see if they had significant problems integrating heterogeneous, subcaste-based battalions. Older established units could also be examined to provide a comparative baseline. Some of the units that fought in the war were older, well-established units. Others had been raised two to four years before 1965 or were rapidly assembled from units scattered all over India. There were three active sectors in the 1965 war: the XV Corps area in the Srinagar area in Jammu and Kashmir, the XI Corps area in the Khem Karan vicinity of the Punjab between Amritsar and Lahore, and the I Corps area around the city of Sialkot. Both XI Corps and I Corps were supposed to advance into Pakistan to help relieve the pressure caused by the Pakistani advance into Jammu and Kashmir. XI Corps had no newly formed infantry divisions, and I Corps had four of five infantry divisions formed from units dispersed over India. These units had not trained as divisions or with one another. In addition, Indian tank units, which were formed without regard to the origins of their soldiers, participated in both sectors. This comparison is hardly a controlled experiment, because differences in the performance displayed by these two corps on the offensive could reflect different levels of training as well as non-caste-related problems of rapidly integrating Indian units.

With regard to the infantry, Indian units in both sectors performed poorly, in the judgment of the Indian theater commander. In XI Corps area, the well-rehearsed offensive of the Fifteenth Division, an older, established division, achieved complete surprise on 6 September but then stalled before the day was half over. In Harbakhsh Singh's opinion, "There was nothing wrong with the machinery—the men manipulating it were found wanting." On the first day, one infantry battalion fell back

---

[114]Harbakhsh Singh, *War Dispatches*, pp. 11, 15, 29–30, 41–43, 199.

after a largely imaginary Pakistani counteroffensive. Another "gave way and broke line," was reformed, and then broke again. On the night of 6–7 September, the commander of another battalion withdrew from his defensive position without permission, "leaving the rest of the battalion to its fate." By the afternoon of 7 September, in the Fourth Mountain Division, two and a half battalions of six had abandoned their positions. On 10 September two battalions in another division "withdrew in the face of allegedly heavy enemy pressure." On 13 September, two more infantry battalions "broke . . . and abandoned their defences." The Indian armored brigade did successfully ambush a Pakistani armored division, destroying seventy-five Pakistani tanks. The Indian forces as a whole captured 140 square miles of territory, but in Singh's final judgment, XI Corps experienced "a sickening repetition of command failures."[115]

In the I Corps area of Sialkot, there was a similar shambles. The planned called for a combined infantry and armored force to advance rapidly into Pakistan. Instead, "the brisk outburst soon limped to a dead halt" on the morning of 8 September, the same morning the offensive began. Armored regiment commanders lost control of their units, truck units bogged down, and infantry and armor did not cooperate, which allowed Pakistani antitank fire to halt the Indian tanks. By 19 September in one brigade, "all control at battalion and brigade level was lost and the formation ceased to be a cohesive force." Indian tank gunners were better than Pakistani tank gunners, largely because the Pakistanis did not understand the sophisticated fire control equipment on their newly acquired, American-built Patton tanks. The Indian forces did at one point advance eleven miles in fifteen days, the most rapid advance any Indian force would achieve in the war, but this gain which Harbaksh Singh attributed to a "fluke of chance," since pervasive misunderstandings between Indian commanders "thwarted cohesive action" and Indian tank commanders "appeared to be ignorant" of the idea of striking rapidly to give the enemy no time to react.[116]

Singh attributed the shortcomings of his force to the conservatism of his officers but did not speculate on the source of that conservatism. Certainly, there does not seem to be any significant difference in the performance of newly formed versus old, established infantry units in the two corps area. The performance of Indian tank units, which were integrated units, was somewhat better than that of the infantry, but the cause of this difference is not readily apparent. Interview data suggest that Indian Army units that took casualties in that war and that needed replacements were normally given men from the same subcaste already

[115]Ibid., pp. 90–91, 94–96, 99–101, 108–109, 124.
[116]Ibid., pp. 129–130, 143, 149, 155, 159, 161–162.

in the unit. On one occasion when this was not possible, however, a unit commander polled his troops to see if they would accept men from a different caste, and the men voted to do so.[117] The only justifiable conclusion is that in 1965 the Indian Army displayed low levels of cohesion within infantry units, which led to their early collapse in battle; low levels of cohesion among infantry units, which affected their ability to cooperate on the battlefield; and perhaps even lower levels of cohesion between tank and infantry units, which had different social compositions. It is plausible, but not proven, that the organization of the infantry into separate, inward-looking units, plus tensions between officers and soldiers, contributed to this lack of cohesion.

The Indian victory in the 1971 war against Pakistan might have reflected changes in the army and its relationship to Indian civilian leaders and Indian society. Indira Gandhi did allow her military commanders far more operational discretion in that war and prevented the kind of civilian interference in the military encouraged by her father in 1962. The Indian advances into East Pakistan from the east, north, northwest, and southwest did lead to a quick Indian victory at a low cost to India. The Indian Army advance from the northwest, for example, took 18,000 Pakistani POWs and suffered only 371 Indians killed in action.[118] However, writing almost twenty years later, the COAS at the time of the war, Field Marshall Sam Manekshaw, reviewed all the functions of war that had to be integrated in India to produce successful military operations in wartime. He then wrote, "Now do not tell me that I did all this in 1971. I must tell you there was a difference then. The [military] operation in erstwhile East Pakistan was not worth talking about, China could not operate due to the time of operations [winter] that we had selected, and we had planned only on strategic defence for the Western theater of operations."[119] The conditions of 1971 were indeed unusual. India had the initiative and refrained from overt military actions until it had nine months to prepare for war. It used this time to assemble troops and equipment from all over India on the borders with East Pakistan and then to train them. India's military factories stopped production of weapons and produced nothing but spare parts for eight months to make Indian units ready for combat. Officers were surreptitiously called back from leave and were sent to their units. A mutual defense treaty was signed with the Soviet Union in August 1971 to secure India's strategic

[117] Interview conducted by the author, October 1993, Cambridge, Massachusetts, with the retired flag rank Indian officer who had commanded the unit needing replacements.
[118] Sukhwant Singh, *India's Wars since Independence*, vol. 1, *The Liberation of Bangladesh* (New Delhi: Vikas, 1980), p. 177.
[119] Field Marshall Sam Manekshaw, "Organization for National Security," *Trishul* (January 1990): 5–12.

flanks. The Indian military knew that one-third of the Pakistani infantry in East Pakistan were Bengali and considered unreliable by the Punjabi West Pakistani military commanders.[120] India was training and militarily supporting the Mukti Bahini guerrillas who were actively resisting the martial law government of East Pakistan. This guerrilla had forced the East Pakistani military to disperse and exhaust itself in police duties.[121] Brigadier S. C. Sardeshpande's comment after the war was succinct: under such circumstances, "the Indian Army really had no choice but to win. Prudence lies in viewing our success in Bangladesh in this light."[122] Even so, the Indian commander, then General Manekshaw, vetoed any plans that called for the rapid movement of Indian Army units from their bases to the front: "You should realize that my formations are not the German Panzer divisions. They take their own time to move."[123]

It is noteworthy that even the improved civil-military relations that prevailed during the 1971 war did not extend so far as to the regular inclusion of India's military service chiefs in the prime minister's Political Affairs Committee. They continued to be invited only occasionally, when the civilian officials required their presence. Decision making at the highest levels was said to be largely confined to Indira Gandhi's Kashmiri Brahmin "Mafia."[124]

At the operational level, in East Pakistan, the Indian Army did succeed in moving into the capital of Dacca in fourteen days (3–16 December) against very light resistance in a campaign that avoided attacks on any enemy strongpoints. In the west, the Indian plan was tied to a counterattack after Pakistan attacked. A large-scale Pakistani invasion never occurred, so fighting in this theater was limited to small border clashes. Even so, the Indian military record, as judged by an Indian general staff officer active during the war, Sukhwant Singh, was not impressive. A local Indian attack in the Kashmir border area failed when the Indian commander was killed and his troops then retreated. In the Battle of Daruchian in the Poonch area, Indian company-size attacks failed, and Indian troops broke and ran, while the battalion commander did not exercise effective control of his troops. At the Battle of the Chhamb salient, the biggest in the war, the Indian plan was to wait for a Pakistani attack and then to counterattack. However, Pakistani ar-

---

[120] Sukhwant Singh, *India's Wars since Independence* 1:2, 19, 27, 42–43.

[121] For the best discussion of the political events leading up to and during the 1971 war, see Richard Sisson and Leo E. Rose, *War and Secession: Pakistan, India, and the Creation of Bangladesh* (Berkeley: University of California Press, 1990), pp. 142–145, 155–156, 183, 211–213. See also Sukhwant Singh, *India's Wars since Independence* 1:137.

[122] Sardeshpande, "Indian Army since Independence."

[123] Sukhwant Singh, *India's Wars since Independence* 1:49.

[124] Sisson and Rose, *War and Secession*, pp. 139–140.

tillery shelling killed several key Indian commanders, and so the local Indian counterattack was never executed. The Pakistani incursion ended only when the Pakistani commander was killed and his forces pulled back. In the defensive battle of the Hussainiwalla enclave on the Ferozepur-Lahore highway, the Fifteenth Punjab Battalion, formerly the First Patalias, withdrew unnecessarily after taking only light casualties. This happened because its commander allowed himself to stay behind at his headquarters while his battalion became involved in combat on the other side of a major river. Then a colonel, Sukhwant Singh was sent by the army to investigate the causes of military failure at the Battle of Fazilka in the Punjab. There, the Indian Army was pushed back and then launched five unsuccessful frontal attacks along the exact same route against the same heavily defended enemy position, until the brigadier in charge of the area was, in effect, relieved of command. The most rapid Indian advance in this theater against light paramilitary opposition was fourteen miles in four days. Against opposition by regular Pakistani troops, the most rapid Indian advance was eight miles in fourteen days.[125]

All military operations, closely scrutinized, reveal failures of command and cohesion, and sweeping judgments concerning the Indian Army should not be passed too hastily. The judgment of senior Indian officers, however, seems to be that in the more favorable circumstances of 1971, the army displayed the same major characteristics in war that it did in 1965 and 1962, except insofar as lengthy and slow preparation could reduce the problems of integrating units drawn from all over the country. One effort by the army to survey the performance of its officers overall in 1971 found depressingly little evidence that lower-level commanders were willing to take initiatives in battle. Seven Indian battalions that engaged in combat in the 1971 war carried out a total of fifty-six patrols. Only one was led by a noncommissioned officer. This was said to reflect a general pattern of overly centralized command relations.[126] Civil-military relations were better, but a major gap still existed between the two camps.

Reviewing the evidence from three wars, it may be concluded that the internal organization of the Indian Army did have consequences for its battlefield performance, though other factors contributed to its military problems. At the political-military level, tensions between civilian political leaders, on the one hand, and the uniformed military, on the other,

---

[125] Sukhwant Singh, *India's Wars since Independence* 2:12–13, 30, 101, 107, 140–147, 149–165.

[126] Lt. Col. C. B. Gupta, "Training of Infantry Non-commissioned Officers," *Infantry Journal* (September 1978): 81.

which derived from the isolation of the army officer corps, also affected the conduct of military operations in three of India's wars.

This tension also appears to have affected the emerging nuclear weapons command and control arrangements in India. In a democratic state with a professional military that historically did not interfere in politics, one might expect civilian political leaders to trust military leaders with a significant role in the custody of and planning for use of nuclear weapons. This is the generalization that one scholar has made from the American, British, and Israeli cases.[127] Initially, civilians might play an unusually large role in military matters involving nuclear weapons, because of the small numbers of such weapons, their special status, and the special role of civilian scientists in their creation. In particular, civilians might play an important role in the custody and control of nuclear weapons, to the relative detriment of the uniformed military. After twenty years, however, military influence and control would be expected to grow in those cases where there was a stable democracy and a professional, apolitical officer corps. To the extent that one made predictions about Indian nuclear weapons custody and command and control without regard to the impact of Indian social structures and the patterns of military organization that they helped to shape, one would predict a gradually growing role for the Indian military in nuclear weapons–related areas.

Empirically, this appears not to have been the case. The following statements were made in interviews conducted in 1990 and 1993 with retired chief of staff of the Indian Army, General K. Sundarji; the then secretary of the Defence Research and Development Organization of the Indian Ministry of Defense and scientific adviser to the prime minister, Dr. V. S. Arunachalam; and the senior civilian defense analyst in India, K. Subramanyam.[128] Dr. Arunachalam, though formally denying that India had nuclear weapons, said that it would be reasonable for non-Indians to assume that since the 1974 Indian nuclear test shot, the government of India had worked very hard at resolving the command and control problems for nuclear weapons. In fact, he said, the civilian leadership had fought a long and difficult struggle with the Indian military to decide who would control nuclear weapons and how they would be used. This struggle was resolved in favor of the civilians. The outcome was that the Indian military would not be and has not been told how many nuclear weapons India might have, nor was it told in peacetime

---

[127] This is the deductive conclusion reached by Peter Feaver in his article "Command and Control in Emerging Nuclear States," *International Security* 17 (Winter 1992/1993): 160–187.
[128] Interviews conducted by author, Pune, India, December 1990, and Cambridge, Massachusetts, March 1993.

how nuclear weapons would be used in war. Though he did not say so, the inescapable implication is that the Indian military does not have custody of nuclear weapons components in peacetime. Since the military cannot plan for nuclear war, the problem of doctrine for nuclear weapons use has been handled by civilians by writing a set of detailed instructions on how to obtain access to nuclear weapons and how to employ them. These sealed instructions have been given to a certain theater commander with instructions to open them in the event that nuclear weapons have been used against India and have destroyed the Indian national command authority at New Delhi. To quote Arunachalam, "If New Delhi goes up in a mushroom cloud, a certain theater commander will go to a safe, open his book, and begin reading at page one, paragraph one, and will act step by step on the basis of what he reads." The technical means for command and control are rudimentary but adequate for Indian needs. No provision has been made to harden Indian communications against the effects of electromagnetic pulse (EMP), because it is thought that the number of nuclear weapons that would be used against India would sufficiently small and the campaign sufficiently short that EMP blackout would not be bad enough to interfere with the execution of Indian plans.

Much of what Arunachalam said was placed in broader context by the remarks of General Sundarji. He said that India has adopted a pure minimum deterrence posture. This was done for two reasons. First, India cannot afford to develop a nuclear force to destroy Pakistani nuclear weapons because the Pakistanis have dispersed and hidden their nuclear weapons, and India does not have enough resources to find and strike them. Second, India has sufficient nonnuclear forces to handle Pakistani nonnuclear attacks and thus does not need to threaten Pakistan with a nuclear first strike to deter war. When asked what India would do if the Pakistani Army achieved some limited initial territorial gains in an invasion of Kashmir, halted, and then threatened to use nuclear weapons if India tried to push it back, Sundarji said India would call the Pakistani nuclear bluff and simply proceed with its nonnuclear counterattack.

The alleged Indian posture has several advantages. It would make the Indian problems of obtaining warning and of executing its nuclear strike much simpler. There would be no need for India to retaliate quickly. Although the Indian retaliation after Pakistani nuclear weapons were used would not be delayed indefinitely, it was asserted that it would be acceptable for India to retaliate in something like twelve to forty-eight hours. Capabilities to execute a slow-motion nuclear war would be much cheaper and easier for India to build. Most important, this posture would deny the military custody of nuclear weapons or any control over nuclear weapons in peacetime. Twenty years after first exploding a nuclear

[252]

weapon, India has not moved toward greater confidence in its military with regard to nuclear weapons.

THE HAPSBURG EMPIRE OF ASIA

The argument of this chapter has been elaborated and evaluated at length but is essentially straightforward. After independence the Indian military retained British military practices that tended to isolate the army from Indian society by selective recruitment of officers and soldiers; by creating homogenous, inward-looking infantry units; by long-term enlistments and deployments in the field; and by repetitive and mindless training. This limited the levels of cooperation and cohesion possible in the Indian military, particularly when it was forced to respond rapidly to a military crisis or when it had to replace heavy combat casualties quickly. Efforts to change this military system were rejected, partly out of inertia, but partly out of a deliberate desire to prevent the social divisions of postindependence India from having a negative effect on the army, as they had on other Indian institutions. This had the positive effect of limiting the politicization and corruption of the army. But this isolation, combined with the fact that the preindependence army had also been isolated from Indian society and professionally obedient to the imperial government, created rifts between the Indian Army and Indian society, and between the army officer corps and the Indian civilian political leadership, as well as within the officer corps. Isolation and the inward-looking nature of the many small units in the army also tended to impede military adjustment to changing external realities. This aspect of the Indian military affected Indian military effectiveness by affecting command relations and military capabilities in the 1962, 1965, and 1971 wars. It also appears to have influenced the planning and preparation for nuclear weapons use.

But legitimate doubts about the causal relationship between Indian social structures and Indian military organization and performance remain. Were the problems of Indian military performance and strategy the result of the way the army chose to react to its social environment or simply of poverty or general incompetence? Comparisons were made at points between the Indian and the American armies. But were the relative problems in the Indian Army simply the result of the lack of military experience at various levels or other factors unrelated to Indian social structures? Was it simply military inertia rather than choices in the face of Indian social realities that led the Indian military after independence to retain British military practices? Clear-cut, controlled experiments are not available to provide conclusive answers, but one historical comparison does suggest that military organizations facing similar social environments can react in similar ways to produce problems like those the Indian military developed after independence.

The Pakistani Army, the other major South Asian army, was originally organized internally by subcaste and then by region but is more homogenous than the Indian Army and is much less isolated from Punjabi society than the Indian Army is from Indian society. On the whole, as judged by their Indian adversaries, the regular Pakistani military (as distinguished from the mixed regular and irregular forces that faced India in East Pakistan in 1971) has not performed all that differently from the Indian Army.[129] The Pakistani military has clearly played a much larger role in domestic politics than has the Indian Army in India. Whether that means that the Pakistani Army is seen as an institution that reflects the dominant social structures or only that the external threats have created a Pakistani Army that is more internally powerful than the Indian Army is difficult to determine. A clear confirmation or refutation of the arguments made with regard to the Indian military is hard to extract from the Pakistani case.

Curiously, a European army, that of the Hapsburg Austrian Empire, may provide the best comparison to test any conclusions about the consequences of separating an army from its social origins. The historian of the Hapsburg officer corps, Istvan Deak, wrote "Probably only one major army, that of the Indian republic, could be said truly to resemble the Hapsburg. It, too, is a multinational force, with no dominant ethnic group and a barely dominant religion; it uses a language, or rather, several languages of convenience; it suffers from the overrepresentation in its officer corps of certain confessional and ethnic groups, such as the Sikh, and it preaches a supranational all-Indian ideology designed to override all ethnic, religious, and local considerations." The Hapsburg Joint Army used German for command and service, just as the Indian Army used English and then Hindi, but none of these languages were the language of instruction or of communication with the rank-and-file, except in German-speaking units. Hapsburg and Indian Army officers had to learn the languages of their men. In the case of the Hapsburg monarchy, the men could speak any of ten major and scores of minor languages. The Hapsburg officers, like Indian officers, were "often themselves the sons of soldiers [not officers] and living a life of political isolation, constitut[ing] a solid caste," with officers coming from lower

---

[129] "It was observed [in the 1965 war] that the basic tactical concept of the Pak Army did not vary fundamentally from our own." Pakistani officer performance was a mixture of bravery and mediocrity, while their infantry was sensitive to being outflanked. See Harbakhsh Singh, *War Dispatches*, pp. 186–189.

social origins most grateful for the increased status that an army career could give them and most in need of membership in a castelike institution that would mark their departure from their low social origins. In both cases, narrowly focused, mechanical military educational curricula were used for many years to increase the psychological distance of the officers from their civilian social origins. In both cases, officers, increasingly from lower social classes, aggressively asserted their authority and kept their distance from the soldiers because the officers "of lower-middle class backgrounds had to create artificially the social prestige which came naturally to their Junker counterparts." In both cases, "the heart of the . . . army was the regiment." Regiments were distinguished by individual customs, distinctive uniform, and the self-contained life of their men and their officer corps. This isolation of the army from society into self-contained units produced an army that, despite its frequent use against civilian uprisings, on the whole remained cohesive, even in World War I, though "almost every unit, of whatever nationality, experienced a 'black day' " in which unit cohesion broke down and troops ran from their positions. In particular, there is general agreement that the soldiers and officers of the imperial army remained reliable, loyal, and cohesive, like the Indian Army before, during, and after the partition of India. But because the primary mission of the Hapsburg Imperial Army for decades was the preservation of internal order, it was less well suited to fighting external wars and lost such wars—to France and Sardinia in 1859 and to Prussia in 1866—and fared poorly on the battlefield in World War I. The Austrian military leadership's "greatest preoccupation" in 1914 "remained as it had been for a hundred years—the problems arising out of the multinational composition of the army." As a result, the Austrian senior officers "with sublime indifference continued to disregard the [tactical] lessons of the [1905 Russo-Japanese] Manchurian and Balkan wars." Though national units in the imperial army were generally loyal, the senior officer corps lived in constant fear of nationalist mutinies or derelictions of duty on the battlefield. The failure of one Czech regiment to fight Russian troops in 1915 brought military calls for more controls on Czech units and martial law in Bohemia. Yet the imperial army survived the death of the Emperor Francis Joseph in 1916 and the Brusilov offensive launched by Russia in 1916, and it did not collapse until November 1918, when the political disintegration of the empire was followed by incidents in which imperial units of different nationalities began shooting at each other.[130]

[130] On the social origins and composition of the Austrian officer corps, see Istvan Deak, *Beyond Nationalism: A Social and Political History of the Hapsburg Officer Corps* (New York: Oxford University Press, 1990). The long quote from Deak about the similarities between

The similarities in the social structures, the military institutions that evolved in response to them, and the military implications of those institutions between the Hapsburg Austrian Empire and postindependence India are striking. They suggest that the fragmented nature of both societies—not other cultural factors, such as the spiritual aspects of the Hindu religion, or other noncultural ingredients, such as the British imperial institutional legacy—were and are powerful factors in shaping the modern Indian military.

---

the Indian and Austrian armies is on p. 5. The quote concerning the "solid caste" of officers in the Austrian army is on p. 8. The quote concerning the aggressive behavior of lower-status officers is on pp. 102–103. On the way in which narrow military curricula were used and the way in which officer recruitment from lower social classes led to increases in the exclusiveness and castelike nature of the officer corps in the Hapsburg Empire, see the 1908 memorandum by General Moritz von Auffenberg, military adviser to the Archduke Francis Ferdinand, quoted in Robert A. Kann, "The Social Prestige of the Officer Corps in the Hapsburg Empire from the Eighteenth Century to 1918," in *War and Society in East Central Europe*, vol. 1, ed. Bela K. Kiraly and Gunther E. Rothenberg (New York: Brooklyn College Press, 1979), pp. 129–131. For the military preparations (or lack thereof) for and performance of the Austrian Imperial Army in World War I, see Gunther E. Rothenberg, *The Army of Francis Joseph* (West Lafayette, Ind.: Purdue University Press, 1976), pp. 174–175, 184–185, 196–197, 221. The quotes concerning the indifference and the preoccupations of the Austrian Army leaders are on pp. 174–175.

[7]

Conclusions

What is the evidence that Indian social structures affected the amount of military power Indian states could generate? Was it possible to assess, however imperfectly, the strength and character of dominant social structures and the levels of internal social conflict generated by them? Was it possible to disentangle all the sources of military power and vulnerabilities in order to identify the conditions under which armies were weakened by the transfer of the ambient social structures into the military in ways that reduced their internal cohesion? Was it possible to assess in a reliable way the degree to which a military had isolated itself from its host society? Did civil-military tension arise from that isolation, and did that tension reduce the military power usable by the state?

Put more broadly, did the examination of India and its armies in comparative perspective shed any light on how we should, in general, think about the relationship of societies to the military organizations which emerge from them but which may not be wholly reflective of them? The dominant perspective on this issue, as noted in Chapter 1, is that advanced by Samuel Huntington in *The Soldier and the State*. In a compelling fashion he argued that armies cannot and should not reflect the social and political divisions of their societies. Civilians should exert objective control and insist on the professionalization of the military, renouncing the attempt to achieve subjective control and giving up the effort to have the military mirror society, because that effort succeeds only in importing into the military the tensions present in the larger society. The examination of India was based on the perspective that the Huntingtonian separation of the military from society could be achieved, albeit with an inescapable level of military tension as a result, a tension that would affect the ability of the state to wield its military arm.[1]

Finally, on the basis of the study of India and its implications, can we speculate about future developments in military power? Can we pose any meaningful questions about how states and societies might generate military power in the future? Might we be led to ask certain questions about ourselves, that is, about American society and its military?

The Findings on India

In the case of India, at least, the empirical questions posed at the outset could be answered, to some degree, with uncertainties that increased the further back in history the study went. Inquiries into four periods in Indian history strongly suggested that social structures played a major role in explaining the variations in Indian military power and were more important than some factors commonly accepted as the causes of variations in military power, such as technology. Thus, social structures were not simply a way to explain "residual" variations in military power. The second independent variable, the degree of isolation of the military from its society, was also important in every historical period. Taken as a whole, Indian history did repeatedly display the impact of Indian social structures on its military power and the problems of separating Indian armies from their host society. Multiple independent observations established the dominance of caste structures in India during the four historical periods, although the character and strength of caste organizations did vary over time. Indian caste structures existed in the ancient period. But at the time of the Alexandrian invasions, those caste divisions did not appear, in the eyes of historians and in terms of the data presented in Chapter 3, to have been markedly stronger than internal social divisions found in noteworthy ancient non-Indian societies, such as Sparta. What mattered most in this period was the degree of separation that an army established from its own society by means, most usually, of continuous campaigns abroad which physically separated an army from its society and which made it dependent primarily on itself and the resources it could extract by conquest. This degree of separation produced strong Carthaginian and Macedonian armies from groups of soldiers divided by social structures of all kinds. The society of republican Rome was notably more cohesive than other ancient societies, and it produced a strong army. But the Roman legions separated themselves from Italian

---

[1] Samuel P. Huntington, *The Soldier and the State: The Theory and Politics of Civil-Military Relations* (New York: Vintage, 1957).

[258]

society by professional training as well as prolonged foreign campaigning so that even when Italian society became badly divided, the legions remained strong. The armies of India were not separated from Indian society, either by professional training or by foreign campaigning, and it was not difficult to find accounts of battlefield pathologies afflicting the Indian army in its battles against Alexander. These accounts have been accepted by Indian military historians as accurate, but they remain, by and large, accounts by the victors and, by themselves, are not conclusive.

A way to perform more quantitative assessments of the level of internal social conflicts emerged from the study of the ancient period, though it could not be applied to ancient India itself. Good data about the incidence of soldiers in ancient Rome were available, and it was striking to note that as Italian society dissolved into the Social War, the number of soldiers as a percent of the total population, in the absence of a foreign military threat, increased strikingly. The fraction of the total Italian population in arms during the Social War reached 9 percent, a level higher than during the invasion by Hannibal. Thus a useful if imperfect way to measure variations in the levels of internal social conflict associated with caste structures might be the incidence of soldiers in peacetime. Such a figure might be a more objective measure of levels of militarized conflict across social structures, one that could be used to make comparisons in this variable over time in India and across Indian and non-Indian cases. In the medieval period in India, reliable figures about the number of soldiers in India that could also be cross-checked were available.

For example, in the late sixteenth and early seventeenth centuries, at the height of the Mughal Empire under the emperor Akbar, when the external threats were at their lowest point and efforts by the medieval Indian state to institutionalize tolerance in Indian society reached their peak, there was, according to Mughal records that could be cross-checked, approximately 4 percent of the Indian population under Mughal rule serving as soldiers. What were the comparable figures in Europe at the beginning of the seventeenth century? Estimates of the percentage of the European population in arms at the time of the Thirty Years' War vary. The best estimate produced by my study was that 0.5 percent of the population of the warring societies was in the military at any given point during the Thirty Years' War. The highest estimates of the fraction of the population of any European state in the military in this period range around 5 percent. It is generally accepted on the basis of studies by Irfan Habib that the Indian military populations during this period were the product of conflicts among castes over control of land. The conclusion can hardly be avoided that the social structures of India produced militarized social conflicts at least as high as that present in Europe at the time of intense, simultaneous interstate and internal war.

This militarization of social conflict in India, moreover, declined by an order of magnitude under British rule, as the British demilitarized Indian civil society and established a monopoly of military power. The British East India Company did not immediately change the nature of Indian caste structures, though this did occur more slowly over time. The British did very rapidly demilitarize the conflicts across Indian social structures. I began by arguing that the social structures most relevant to the generation of military power would be those that played a military role. Any decline in militarized social conflict should have been relevant for the levels of military power that the British could generate from Indian society surplus to the military power needed to maintain control over Indian society. This decline in fact occurred, and the British began to export Indian military power out of South Asia as early as 1798, something the Mughal emperors had never been able to do, even for the purpose of regaining control over territories in Central Asia that were of great importance to the Mughal elites.

It was relatively easy to establish when and to what degree an Indian army was divorced from its host society. In ancient and Mughal India, the army and the society thoroughly interpenetrated each other, as they did in many, but not all, contemporary non-Indian cases. The Ottoman Army that was a contemporary of the Mughal Army was radically isolated from Ottoman society by recruitment and institutional arrangements. Did that isolation lead to cohesion in the military, and did that cohesion lead to enhanced military power relative to the armies of India? The Ottoman army was clearly more isolated from its society than the Mughal Army, but there were no direct Ottoman/Mughal military clashes to facilitate the comparison of the military power that was generated by the two societies.

The study of Mughal India showed that Indian society displayed important variations in the character of its social structures from north to south and east to west but also that there were significantly high levels of social division arising out of caste structures throughout Mughal India. Those divisions were clearly and obviously replicated in the Mughal Army. Some areas in India appeared to have been less divided by social structures—specifically, in the Marathi-speaking areas of the west—and more progress seems to have been made toward creating cohesive armies in that area. Overall, Mughal military power never exceeded that which was necessary to maintain internal order as Indian subcastes armed themselves against other Indians. The army of the Mughal state could never dominate Indian society. The army of contemporary Ottoman Turkey could and did militarily dominate and then destroy existing social structures, in ways that facilitated the generation of a surplus of military power. Europe in the medieval and early modern period displayed re-

[260]

peated and ultimately successful efforts not to eliminate all divisive social structures but to make them militarily unimportant by first disarming the peasantry and then the aristocracy. Such efforts were made in Mughal India but failed. The double failure to demilitarize Indian social conflicts in this period and to isolate the Mughal Army from Mughal society was unquestionably a major factor underlying the comparative military weakness of that empire. But can we conclude that the Mughal Empire was weaker than other contemporary empires because Indian social structures were more divisive than other contemporary social structures? We would need better independent measures of those social structures in India and elsewhere and of Indian military power in this period before we could argue conclusively for the power of social structures in determining the levels of military power that a society can generate.

Measuring the increase in military power that could be generated from a given society by shifting from an army that reflected society to one that was isolated from society was relatively straightforward in the case of British India. In striking contrast with the foreign Mughal rulers, the foreign French and then the British could and did build a cohesive military from the same Indian social material available to Indian rulers by isolating the military from Indian society. The increase in military power produced by that isolation, while all other factors affecting military power were held constant, was easy to measure because Indian armies created by the British fought other Indian armies from the same areas with the same weapons and were able to defeat armies ten times their own size. Some local Indian rulers then began to imitate the European model of military organization, with some success. As a result, the British developed an internal strategy for pacifying India to preempt possible efforts on the part of local Indian rulers to overmatch British military power by employing their methods of military organization. To hinder guerrilla warriors and to give land to Indian soldiers who could be persuaded to give up warfare as a profession, this strategy self-consciously combined military development to build decisive military power by isolating Indian armies from Indian society, military diplomacy in which the British offered military protection to Indian rulers who gave up their own armies, military campaigns to defeat local armies, and agrarian policies designed to increase arable land.

The crucial step in this strategy was the initial one to develop locally decisive, British-controlled military power, despite the fact that local Indian rulers had more troops and comparable military technology at their disposal. The fact that the British were able to do this demonstrates the power of professional military organization in building cohesive armies by separating soldiers from their fragmented societies. The British built an army composed of many small and inward-looking military communities that were isolated from one another and separated from the host society. The three armies of the British East India Company had varying levels of separation from their host societies, and those variations appear to explain their differences in reliability at the time of the Great Mutiny of 1857. The data do not allow us to say whether, given enough time, professional military organizations could have emerged spontaneously in India without the challenge and example of the European presence or whether the failures of the Mughal period would have been repeated.

After independence, the Indian Army remained a collection of small, isolated, and inward-looking military communities. The separation of the Indian military from Indian society preserved the coherence of the army but also led to a reduction in the effective military power of the Indian state. The British-built Indian Army no longer served the British after independence, but rather the Indian nationalist leaders who had been the target of British military power in India. This led to civil-military tensions that markedly affected the ability of the Indian state to use available Indian military power in war, most strikingly in the 1962 war. This tension also appears to have affected peacetime nuclear planning. In addition, the particular mechanisms relied upon for separating the Indian military from Indian society—the closely knit, small military units of the Indian Army—made that army after independence ill-suited for any intense, fluid war that required the cooperation of many units on the battlefield, despite soldiers being killed and needing to be replaced. But other factors limited the capacity of the Indian Army for intense warfare, and isolating the importance of single causes of military effectiveness in wartime is extremely difficult. Other militaries in poor Asian countries did not adopt Indian patterns of military organization when dealing with ethnically heterogeneous populations, such as the treatment of ethnic Chinese in the Democratic Republic of Vietnam, yet they produced strikingly successful military organizations. In addition, the Hapsburg Austrian Empire organized itself along lines that bore a remarkable similarity to the army of postindependence India, in response to analogous internal social divisions, and the Hapsburg army displayed pathologies that strongly resembled those of the modern Indian Army. While not conclusive, these additional cases tend to support the arguments I have advanced.

If we look to the future of the Indian Army, the prospects are mixed. There is clear evidence that the separation of the army from Indian society that preserved its strength and prevented its corruption is breaking down. The increased levels of internal violence in India in the 1980s have been handled primarily by the Indian police and Indian paramilitary forces. But the regular army has also been increasingly called on to handle domestic unrest, precisely because it was perceived as the one national institution which had not been captured by domestic social interests and which could therefore be expected to be impartial when confronted with local parties locked in conflict. But the repeated use of the regular army in local disputes inevitably involved it in the support of some groups against others. The more often the army is used, the harder it is to maintain its professional isolation. As one senior army officer noted with regard to the use of the army in Aid to the Civil Authority, as it was and is called under the British and Indian governments, "It is very ironical that in the last four years [1985–1989] the Army has been used much more for such duties than in the 200 years of British rule." Independent Indian scholars have confirmed that the Indian Army was used for internal security purposes 341 times in the period 1930–1939. It was so used 721 times in the period 1982–1989.[2] It is unclear whether the trends in domestic political violence and the involvement of the army in Indian politics will persist. Consistent with the argument of this book, the violence of the 1980s was fueled in part by the availability of weapons within India as a result to some extent of the war in Afghanistan, which greatly increased the number of automatic rifles for sale in South Asia. Indian society was, to some extent, remilitarized. I have argued that social structures are of particular importance for the military power of the state when those structures have military roles and power of their own. To the extent that the militarization of Indian social conflicts in the 1980s was the temporary result of the increased availability of weapons to hostile groups within India, the future may not resemble the recent past. Much of the recent Indian domestic conflict has not, however, depended on the availability of modern weapons. Whether such conflict will be moderated by or exacerbated by more rapid Indian economic growth is also unclear.

THE SOLDIER AND SOCIETY

Can the framework for the analysis of military organizations and the societies they serve laid out in this book be useful to scholars looking at other societies? Let us begin by noting the factors not accounted for here and the factors that would limit the general power of this analysis. The

[2]Lt. Gen. S. K. Sinha (ret.), "Aid to the Civil Authority," *Trishhul: Journal of the Defense Services Staff College* 1 (1989): 79–93. Namrata Namrain, "Co-option and Control: The Role of the Colonial Army in India, 1918–1947" (Ph.D. diss., Cambridge University, 1992), p. 79.

argument in this book did not take into account a number of factors that
have diminished the impact of social structures on military performance.
Specifically, religion and civic religions such as ideologies have led people to ignore or downplay the importance of existing social structures in
order to serve or defend their beliefs. The great Arab conquests were
possible not because Islam eliminated the social structures of the Arab
world but because it led Arabs to set aside the conflicts emerging from
those social structures. Other European nationalist ideologies have had
similar effects. In the case of India, the power of the nationalist ideology
originally set forth by the Congress Party did not appear to have had
that unifying effect, but in other cases, modern secular ideologies could
unify badly divided societies in ways that did not occur in modern India.
The argument in this book cannot explain the important cases in which
ideology was a force for unity, though it could help explain why movements that initially benefited from ideologically based unity weakened
when they subsequently fragmented along lines determined by preexisting social structures.

High levels of perceived military threat can, undoubtedly, play some
role in encouraging people to set aside the conflicts emerging from existing social structures. Historically, India has faced high levels of military threat in the unambiguous sense that it has been repeatedly
conquered by foreigners. This did not lead to the suppression of the
internal divisions in India related to its social structures. On the other
hand, it could plausibly be asserted that neither the Soviet Union during
World War II nor Israel during the period 1948–1994 were countries
based on homogenous societies, nor did they deploy armies that were
radically divorced from society. Nonetheless, those two societies produced effective armies, and this outcome was the result in part of the
fact that the citizens perceived a high level of shared danger. Some societies are unified by external threats and some are not, and a full understanding of the military effectiveness of societies would involve an
exploration of the ways in which threats do or do not come to be perceived as equally shared by all members of those societies.[3]

The argument set forth in this book also has some problems explaining
the military effectiveness of the United States in World War II. At that
time, the American army was a mass army, it took high casualties, and
it used citizen soldiers who had not been separated from society by long
service. According to the schema laid down in Chapter 1, the American
army should have been strongly affected by the divisions in American

[3] For a full discussion of the interaction between external military threats and levels of
tension within a society, see Michael Desch, "Soldiers, States, and Structure: Civil-Military
Relations in a Changing Environment," ms.

society, and its military effectiveness should have been influenced. The United States had serious class, ethnic, and racial divisions in 1941. The American people have always been well armed, though it would be difficult to say that in the middle of the twentieth century, internal social conflicts in the United States were militarized. Yet in terms of the military power it could generate, the United States has been judged to have been more militarily effective than most countries during that war. Some understanding of the unifying impact of American liberal ideology and the perceived threat posed by the Axis powers is probably necessary in coming to grips with this success of the United States. But if American society becomes more strongly divided and if the relationship between the American people and the American military becomes more problematic, there may well be consequences for American military effectiveness.

Yet the argument here does appear to have some aspects that make it relevant to other cases. In particular, the historical examination of India does clearly suggest that the model of the relationship between an army and its host society—the model set forth in Huntington's The *Soldier and the State*—may usefully be supplemented by the model underlying this book. In his book, Huntington posited that military officers should be thought of as members of a profession. They had the same character as members of other professions, having to master, in a standard and institutionalized way, a body of knowledge relevant to the performance of their jobs. They judged themselves by reference to objective standards of performance that were shared by other members of their profession. Their standing in their field was a matter of objective, professional criteria. The only way in which they differed from members of other professions was in the kind of job they performed: the management of violence for the purposes of the state.

This was and is a productive way of thinking about the behavior of military officers. It is not the only way, and it may not always be the most appropriate way. Other political scientists have argued with equal logic that it is most appropriate to think of military officers as bureaucrats, belonging to a hierarchical, functionally rational, self-interested organization. They would not behave like professionals but like bureaucrats. That is, they would respond to the incentives created by their location in the bureaucratic structure and not necessarily to the norms and standards of the same people who performed the same task as they did. This could and would lead to conflicts within the military, primarily about resource allocation, even if all the relevant players shared the same professional task of managing violence, even if they shared the same professional training. Officers might not even think about the management of violence as much as they thought about the advancement of the interests of their component of the bureaucracy. Un-

[265]

der many circumstances, particularly prolonged periods of peace, the bureaucratic approach is clearly a powerful way of thinking about the behavior of military officers.

One consequence of both the professional and the bureaucratic approaches to the study of the military is that they deliberately downplay the variations if the behavior of the military that may occur because of differences in the societies from which the military springs. If the military is a professional organization, what matters for its behavior is the nature of the profession, which is universal in its general character, with local variations that result from objective differences in the nature of the task and the means available for the pursuit of the task. There is no strong link between these local differences and the nature of the society from which the officer came. Differences in military behavior will be the result of differences in strategic geography, wealth, technology, and the enemy. If the military officer is a bureaucrat, his or her behavior will be universal to the extent that the bureaucracy conforms to the dictates of functional, Weberian rationality. If there are local differences, they will be created by the different incentives presented by different bureaucratic structures. Again, there would seem to be no strong link between the structure of a bureaucracy and the nature of the society in which it is located.

There is a third way of thinking about the behavior of military officers that leads to a closer examination of the relationship of the officer corps to its host society. In *Winning the Next War*, I suggested that an officer corps might be neither a professional organization nor a bureaucracy.

> Looking at the armed forces of the United States, for example, one notices that each service is far from monolithic and is not composed by sub-units simply pursuing their own organizational self-interests. U.S. Army officers may come from the infantry, artillery, armor, aviation, airborne, or special forces. Navy officers may be carrier pilots from the fighter or attack communities, antisubmarine warfare pilots, submariners, surface ship commanders, or from an amphibious force.. . . . There is no permanent norm defining what is or is not the dominant professional activity of the organization. Many theories concerning the relative priority of roles and missions compete. . . .
>
> If we start with this perspective, we will be inclined to regard military organizations as complex political communities in which the central concerns are those of any political community: who should rule, and how the "citizens" should live. . . . Military organizations have this political character to a greater degree than other bureaucratic organizations because military organizations are more divorced from the rest of society than other bureaucracies. An officer becomes an officer at an early age, in many cases as the product of a service academy. . . . Military organizations gov-

ern almost every aspect of the lives of the members of their community. They determine who will live and die, in wartime, and how; who will be honored and who will sit on the sidelines when war occurs.[4]

If this approach has some validity, it suggests that the military, as a political community resident within a larger political community, that is, its host society, will tend to be affected by the dominant patterns of behavior in the larger community, because both the host society and the military are concerned with the same questions: who should rule, and how men and women should live. They cannot escape a tense dialogue on these two questions. The military is not only a technical, professional group with an objectively based understanding of its professional tasks. It has guns and strong beliefs about how people should live with one another. The military can strengthen its divorce and isolation from society, but to do so would not end the dialogue. No political community will tolerate forever another political community within it which is massively armed and which has views on politics and society that are incompatible with those of the larger society. It was Huntington's argument that the military could permanently shut itself off from society by concentrating on the optimum performance of objectively defined, technical, and nonpolitical tasks. If the military is a political community, that is, by definition, impossible. The military and its host society will interact in different ways, but they can never go their own separate paths.

Looking at the United States, this perspective may shed light on some interesting historical problems and future possibilities. In the past, American military power required mass armies. Mass armies found it more difficult to isolate themselves from their host societies, and so, Barry Posen has argued, military development has contributed to the development of mass nationalism that suppresses the divisive impact of existing social structures.[5] The power of mass nationalism as a means of suppressing social divisions has varied. In the United States, Charles Moskos has argued that over the course of the war in Vietnam, noteworthy variations in the military power of the American army appeared that are best explained by the increases in the levels of social conflict in American society and the spread of those conflicts to the army despite the barriers of professionalization.[6]

But other ways of generating military power do not involve the con-

---

[4] Stephen Peter Rosen, *Winning the Next War* (Ithaca: Cornell University Press, 1991), p. 19.

[5] Barry Posen, "Nationalism, the Mass Army, and Military Power," *International Security* 18 (Fall 1993): 80–124.

[6] Charles C. Moskos, "The American Combat Soldier in Vietnam," *Journal of Social Issues* 31, no. 4 (1975): 25–37.

struction of mass armies along with their necessary links back to society. Nuclear weapons are one way. Developments in military technology that go under the name of the "Revolution in Military Affairs"[7] may be another way to build military power by relying not on mass armies but on information technologies. It may produce military power that is more politically useful than nuclear weapons. In addition, in the United States the trend is clearly toward a smaller, increasingly professional military, drawn from selected segments of that society, and engaged in technical or overseas activities that keep it separate from the influence of changes in American social structures. The American military is growing more isolated from society and no longer serves as a mass school for nationalism. At the same time, it is possible that American society as a whole will come to be more structured by divisions along ethnic, linguistic, or even gender lines. The increasing isolation of the American military and the changes in American society may lead to the emergence of the military as a coherent but alienated institution in a fragmented society, with consequences for American civil-military relations that deserve some thought.[8]

Externally, there are visible in some portions of the world increasingly high levels of internal social conflict, conflict that reduces the ability of those societies to generate military power. The argument in this book provides some interesting grounds for speculation if it is applied to these trends in the United States and abroad. Imagine that the United States succeeds in generating levels of military power much greater than current levels by means of a small military isolated from American society. Imagine also that certain foreign societies continue to be increasingly fragmented and unable to generate significant military power. The consequences of the intersection of these two sets of phenomena could be dramatic. In the past, the military juxtaposition of small, coherent, professional armies making use of superior technology, with weak links to their host society, on the one hand, with less sophisticated mass armies affected by social differences on the other, has occasionally produced bursts of military expansion: Alexander the Great, the Roman legions, and the growth of Rome in antiquity; the wave of European overseas imperialism fueled by the professionalization of European armies against the mass armies of Asia and Africa; the continental expansion of America, Germany, and Czarist Russia in the nineteenth century; the explosion of Nazi Germany in the middle of the twentieth century. Imperialism

[7] Andrew F. Krepinevich, "Cavalry to Computer," *National Interest* 37 (Fall 1994): 43–49.

[8] Charles J. Dunlap, "The Origins of the American Military Coup of 2012," *Parameters* 22, no. 4 (Winter 1992/1993): 2–20

can be thought of as the result in part of differences in social structures that affect military organizations plus differences in degrees of military professionalization. It may well be the case that obvious political factors will limit this tendency toward military expansion by the United States. But other large and increasingly wealthy and technologically advanced societies may take advantage of technological opportunities to create powerful military organizations with weak links back to their host societies. They may face disintegrating societies on their borders and may regard military expansion as historically and politically legitimate. It is important to remember that in this book I developed an understanding of the links between societies and their military organizations in order to explain cases of striking military strength, as well as weakness. The study of that link in the emerging global military environment may be a way to explore shifts in the global balance of power and their consequences.

Index